Arms and Men

WALTER MILLIS

Arms and Men

A STUDY IN AMERICAN
MILITARY HISTORY

RUTGERS UNIVERSITY PRESS
New Brunswick, New Jersey

First published in paperback by Rutgers University Press in 1981 by
arrangement with G. P. Putnam's Sons.

Third Printing, 1986

Library of Congress Cataloging in Publication Data

Millis, Walter, 1899–1968.
Arms and men.

Bibliography: p.
Includes index.
1. United States—History, Military. 2. United States—Armed Forces—
History. 3. United States—Military policy. I. Title.
E181.M699 1984   973   84-4711
ISBN 0-8135-0931-9 (pbk.)

Foreword

THIS BOOK was not designed and is not presented as a history of American military policy. It offers at most a commentary on that history. I have endeavored to observe the appropriate historical canons; I have not endeavored to review all the relevant literature—now enormous in its extent—or to explore original and unpublished sources. These tasks have been ably performed by others, to whom I am glad to acknowledge my debt. A great deal of excellent research in the field of military policy and on the social and political implications of military history has appeared in recent years; there is more constantly coming, and I have not sought to imitate labors which others are performing more skillfully and studiously than I could. It has occurred to me, however, that it might be useful to try to draw some of this material together into a single perspective which might put some of the familiar facts into new and suggestive relationships and elucidate something of the significance of the military factor in the gigantic social and political issues of our times.

Most writing on the military factor in American affairs has suffered under certain limitations. It has usually been concerned only with narrow segments of a field which deserves to be examined as a whole. Until recent years it was largely the product of military men—like Upton, or Mahan, or McAuley Palmer or Ganoe—who were arguing a military thesis of one kind or another with too little appreciation of the economic, social and political factors which affect all issues of military preparedness and war. Civilian historians were overwhelmingly concerned with battle tactics and strategy; when they enlarged their view to include the politics and economics surrounding the clash of arms, it was still only in relation to the specific struggle they were examining. The institution of war and its continuous peacetime concomitants of military policy and preparation seldom, as such, attracted their attention.

While doubtless not the first book of its kind, it seems to me that Harold and Margaret Sprout's *The Rise of American Naval Power,* which appeared in 1939, was something of a turning buoy to a new course. It marked the entry of the professional political and social historian, equipped with all the technical apparatus of his art, into the broad field of military plan and policy as a whole. Perhaps it was an unduly modest entry. If the soldiers were too little aware of the power of the social historian's techniques, the historians may have been overimpressed by the soldiers' technical authority in their specialized field. The historians have often appeared too readily to accept the established military dogmas, and to have been timid in bringing their own critical powers to bear on questionable platitudes sanctified by generations of military experts. Mahan was almost as sacred to the Sprouts as he still is to the U. S. Naval Institute. It is still fair to say, I think, that the Sprouts' study put the military problem into a new context so far, at least, as American audiences were concerned.

It helped to advance a generally dawning realization that war, war preparations, military tactics and strategy, military manpower questions, military economics, are not problems arising only suddenly and sporadically in moments of international "emergency"; they are continuous factors within the fabric of our society. Military institutions and their consequences are as essential elements of our social and political history as are our religious, economic, legal or partisan political institutions.

Much work has since been done by many minds along the lines of this general conception. There are today many books available on one or another facet of what might be called the sociology of war. The American participation in the Second World War has been recorded by highly-trained, professional historians—almost none of them primarily military men—with a voluminousness beyond anything produced after our earlier wars. Unfortunately, parallel with this newer attitude toward the history of war, there has come the contemporary transformation in the whole character of war itself. The advent of the nuclear arsenals has at least seemed to render most of the military history of the Second War as outdated and inapplicable as the history of the War with Mexico. It has certainly left all current military planning and policy in a state of lamentable confusion, uncertainty and obvious inconsistency.

The question which presented itself to me was this: Is it possible, by retraversing the history of American military institutions in the light of the newer attitudes, to shed any illumination upon the extraordinarily difficult, the seemingly insoluble, military problems which confront the nation today? The book which follows is an experimental attempt to answer that question. Its conclusions are, inescapably, inadequate. It is no more than a brief review of the now rather extensive military history of the United States in relation to its political, economic and social implications. But as such it may be of contemporary interest.

W. M.

Contents

Arms and Men

CHAPTER I

The Democratization of War

1.

THE military history of the United States can with some precision be said to have begun at Concord on April 19, 1775.

> By the rude bridge that arched the flood,
> Their flag to April's breeze unfurled,
> Here once the embattled farmers stood
> And fired the shot heard round the world.

The hackneyed lines state the situation with economy and exactness. It was a shot which was heard—neither a proclamation nor any other political act, but a raw appeal to force and bloodshed. And a world amply inured to bloodshed both heard and heeded it because it was fired by "embattled farmers," an armed peasantry making its revolutionary appearance upon the formalized stage of eighteenth-century war and international politics.

The United States was born in an act of violence. The political Declaration of Independence was not to come for another year and more; but it was the yokels at Concord Bridge who forced the issue, and if they had not applied their trigger fingers to their flintlock muskets on that April day it might never have come at all. In the light of that beginning, it is strange how little attention later generations were to give to the military factor in the origins and development of

13

our institutions. It is strange how few have recognized that the great period of world war and world upheaval which filled the forty years between 1775 and 1815 represented not only a political, social and economic revolution but a military revolution as well. It was to bring great changes in military means and institutions; these changes were closely interlinked with the changes in the other fields, and were perhaps fundamental to them. As a nation, we have seldom been accustomed to think in military terms and have seldom re-examined this aspect of the processes by which the nation was formed. Yet they were certainly of prime significance to subsequent national and international history.

The American Revolution was of course a shattering challenge to the political, social and economic structure of the eighteenth-century Hanoverian Empire. But first it was a challenge to the eighteenth-century military system, the cradle in which that empire had grown and the framework which held together its basic institutions. In the moment in which a hastily assembled horde of "embattled farmers"—militiamen who not only possessed guns but knew how to use them with effect—stood up against the disciplined ranks of George III's professional army, an age was coming to its end. A balanced military, political and social structure was confronted with an act of violence of a kind with which it was unprepared to cope and for which in the end it was to find no answer. Eight years later the British government was forced to admit that it could devise no military solution for the problem thus presented. And within a few more years the world was forced to recognize that the delicate complex of political and social stabilities which had been erected on the eighteenth-century system of warfare had become an anachronism.

The red-coated British infantry battalions holding Boston in the spring of 1775 were developed products of that system. Behind them at the time there lay over a century and a half of history and military tradition. Their organization and tactics are usually traced to the armies of Gustavus Adolphus, which had appeared in Europe contemporaneously with the earlier British settlements in North America. The leading features of the military system which they represented had been imported into England with the formation of Cromwell's New

Model army. The men-of-war which supported Gage in Boston belonged to a naval service which had taken on its basic characteristics (and discovered its world power) under the Commonwealth; while Gage's regulars were directly descended from the small standing army formed at the Restoration of 1660 out of elements drawn both from the New Model and the former royalist forces.[1] Both the British Army and the Royal Navy, as the colonists confronted them in 1775, were established institutions, hammered by frequent wars into experienced and well-organized military instruments, much more efficient and effective under the conditions of their times than later generations have realized.

The military system which they represented may be schematically described. Not the least of the triumphs of eighteenth-century rationalism was its success in isolating and specializing the military function in society. The statesmen of that day were generally willing to accept the ancient scourge of war as an inevitable concomitant of the international social order. They were ready to admit, perhaps more realistically than many of their successors, that behind all the moral and legal imperatives there has always remained an element of brute force; that violence was not only an ultimate but possibly an indispensable sanction in human affairs. Issues of pride, greed, ambition or interest were bound to arise among men, for which there could be no decision except by force, but which yet had to be decided in one sense or another if society was to continue to operate. The eighteenth century, as a rule, approached war in the spirit of Grotius, who sought to regularize and limit its savageries, not in the spirit of the nineteenth-century philosophical pacifists, who hoped to abolish it. Consciously or unconsciously, the genius of the age was directed toward confining its effects, reducing its devastations within the bounds of reason and law, and ensuring that it returned its necessary decisions with a minimum of disruption to the normal life of the community.

Many factors, from the political and economic structure of the age

[1] This army included five regiments, all of which remain on the British Army list today: Russell's Foot Guards (the Grenadiers) and the 1st and 2d Life Guards from the royalist veterans; Monk's Foot Guards (the Coldstream) and Lord Oxford's Horse Guards from the Commonwealth side.

down to the peculiar characteristics of its weapons, conspired to produce substantially this result. In theory, at least, the conduct of foreign policy and war was the prerogative of the king, not of the community. In practice, the king was no doubt prompted by those powerful national economic or political interests which have always governed chiefs of state, no less than by his personal and dynastic ambitions. But the theory that war was the king's rather than the community's business helped to confine its scope and destructiveness. "In England," Tom Paine scornfully declared, "a King hath little more to do than to make war and give away places; which in plain terms is to impoverish the nation and set it together by the ears." It reflects an attitude toward war under which the all-devouring total wars of today could scarcely have flourished.

It was the king's task to protect the national interest, the national honor and the national safety against invasion. To enable him to fulfill it he was allowed, very grudgingly as a rule, the funds necessary to procure his "king's ships" and the proprietary battalions of "his" army. Such forces, both because they were expensive and because of the ever-present danger that the king would use them to tyrannize over the great domestic interests, were only cautiously expanded in time of danger and were reduced as rapidly as possible upon the outbreak of peace.

At the same time, the general population was largely or wholly disarmed. The medieval militias fell into decay or disappeared throughout most of Europe. Their pikes and long bows were outmoded by firearms, which were too expensive to be easily acquired, for which the European peasant had no particular need and which the ruling groups had no desire to see in the hands of poachers, freebooters or potential mobs. With the loss of arms, the general population lost most of its sense of military responsibility and participation. Even as late as 1806, and in Prussia—where Frederick the Great's wars and brutal conscriptions had produced what was perhaps the nearest eighteenth-century approach to the modern "popular" mass army—the newspaper press, as Gordon Craig observes, could treat the "shattering" events of Napoleon's victory "as indifferently as if they were writing of a war between the Shah of Persia and the Emir of Kabul." The soldier's function had become specialized. His was but one trade among many others; not much more hazardous than eighteenth-century life in general, and imbued with not much more national significance than many civilian occupations. The small royal armies generally marched and fought across the open terrain of Western Europe in what was otherwise largely a military vacuum.

They were composed of a class apart: the professional, long-service soldiers and seamen who could be hired, cajoled or pressed into doing the nation's fighting for it, with a minimum of interference in the civilian's pursuit of profit or pleasure. By an admirable economy they were drawn, generally speaking, from the least productive elements at the two ends of the social scale. They were usually officered from the younger sons of the feudal nobility, those children of the rising bureaucracy who could find no better place, and sons of the new commercial and technical classes who found military service a convenient avenue to social betterment. "To pitchfork the knave or fool of the family into the Army was the whole duty of a thoughtful parent." [2] In the British Army the troops were theoretically volunteers; actually, they were the sweepings of jails, ginmills and poorhouses, oafs from the farm beguiled into "taking the King's shilling," adventurers and unfortunates who might find a home in the army or be pressed into long years of servitude within the wooden walls of the men-of-war. Enlistment was for life or, what frequently amounted to the same thing, for the "duration."

In the construction of the system there was, since this was still a predominantly mercantile age, a heavy reliance on the profit motive. It seems shocking by modern ideas; but it was a factor which further limited the impact of the system upon the community as a whole. The men, no less than the ships and weapons, were supplied on a kind of contract basis. When George III's ministers hired Hessians on the hoof at so much per head for the American war, the transaction was neither so unusual, nor so different from the manner in which they procured their British recruits, as is often supposed. It has even been suggested that the protests of the Whig nobles against the use of these foreign

[2] Henry Belcher, *The First American Civil War* (London, 1911), Vol. I, p. 269.

mercenaries in a domestic quarrel may have been colored by business motives: "Among men who for years had been accustomed to take toll of all the good things going when Government was spending money, the contemplation of any harvest being under the management of German operators aroused feelings of distress and resentment." [3]

Originally, the colonel of a regiment was as much a business entrepreneur as a tactical commander, and considerably more so in those cases in which he left the field command to a "lieutenant colonel," or professional director, while he confined himself to managing the business side of the enterprise. He was provided with the king's warrant to beat the highways and byways for recruits; he was paid by the head for each one brought in; he thereafter had the concession for feeding, clothing and equipping them, from which he was free to enrich himself to the extent his conscience might allow. Regiments, like modern armaments plants or electronics factories, were frequently as much a speculative enterprise as a response to the calls of patriotism.

Venal and callous as this system may seem, it obviously arose from the fact that in the absence of effective administrative techniques private enterprise was the only available recourse. It was considerably modified as the eighteenth century advanced and as a more and more competent governmental bureaucracy began to take over a more centralized control of military operations from the free play of individual initiative. The bureaucratic administrative achievement which in 1776 massed at New York Howe's force of some hundreds of ships, mounting 1,200 guns and carrying 32,000 troops, is surely entitled to the respect of modern staff officers and logisticians. But despite the demonstrated power of the new bureaucracy, in 1775 many elements of this system of war by the profit motive remained deeply embedded in the military structure, where they still exerted a significant effect upon military policies. The purchase of commissions—as doctors long purchased their practices and as stockbrokers today purchase their seats upon the exchanges—though frequently "abolished," lingered in the British service until far into the nineteenth century. Prize money, last vestige of privateering and another survival of war by the profit motive,

[3] Belcher, *op. cit.*, Vol. I, p. 265.

was not finally excluded from American practice until the Spanish War of 1898.

If the profit motive was already dwindling in the military administration of the late eighteenth century, its influence remained. As long as the soldier was thought of not as a member and devoted defender of the national community, but simply as one of the community's hired or purchased instruments of defense like its ships and artillery, the costs of hiring and maintaining him remained important; and war was subjected to severe limitations of cost accounting from which it seems almost wholly to have freed itself in our day.

Because eighteenth-century royal troops were expensive and because their highly-trained, long service personnel was difficult of replacement, they were ordinarily used with the greatest possible economy. The idea of throwing away a whole generation of young men—as happened at Verdun and on the Somme in 1916—would have appalled an eighteenth-century king or general. Their need for economy of manpower helped to produce the oft-noted eighteenth-century emphasis on long-drawn maneuver, on "position" and "geometric" warfare rather than on pitched battle. The pitched battles, when they did occur, produced frightful casualty rates, easily rising to half or more of those engaged. This encouraged their avoidance, as well as maneuver and diplomacy. It encouraged the many compromise peaces, in which the monarchs preserved the core of their military force and national power at the sacrifice of some outlying territorial positions or overseas colonies, without putting everything to a total test of power. The monetary, no less than the manpower, costs of war (together with all the physical difficulties of transport and supply) repeatedly crippled military operations which might otherwise have been pressed to extreme ends.

Even the weapons system tended to reinforce these tendencies toward moderation. The basic arm of eighteenth-century land warfare was the large calibre, smooth-bore, flintlock musket with socket bayonet. It was awkward, slow and unpredictable in performance. It was usually silenced by rain or snow, a fact which contributed to the leisurely eighteenth-century habit of taking warfare regularly into winter quarters. Its killing range was no more than about two hundred yards, while it was so wildly inaccurate that aimed fire against a man-sized target was of little use at even fifty yards. As a result, combat could not even begin until the troops were practically face to face. "Don't fire until you see the whites of their eyes." [4] Reloading was so slow that once the piece had been fired it could seldom be discharged again until the forces were in hand-to-hand combat with bayonet and butt. But when the smooth-bore musket did hit, with its soft-lead, half-inch ball, it had a frightful stopping and killing power.

Much in eighteenth-century warfare that seems quaint or irrational to modern eyes in fact directly followed from these characteristics of the principal weapon. Because of their short range and inaccuracy, the muskets had to be massed and fired in volleys to get the full advantage of their crushing firepower, but the decision usually lay with the shock action of the ensuing bayonet charge. The attacker could evade the worst effects of the defensive volley by dispersion or by taking cover, but this meant that his bayonet charge would start in a scattered condition to arrive piecemeal, and so be easily disposed of by the serried mass. Consequently, the attack as well as the defense usually adopted a close-packed formation, accepting the horrible slaughter which this invited in order to conserve its own weight of fire and impact with the bayonet.

Thus the eighteenth-century infantry battalion became a solid block of men and firepower, maneuvered as such in a manner not unlike that of a naval vessel. In European campaigns it was generally supported by cavalry, used as a massed weapon of shock action as well as for reconnaissance and pursuit. Artillery was also available, but it was not yet well developed and was mainly important in siege warfare or the defense of prepared positions. The heavier guns were too ponderous for maneuver; those light enough for use in the field were too weak and short-ranged to be of much effect. It was the massed infantry battalion which was the core of the battle. To maintain its cohesion and make it stand up to the murderous volleys called for

[4] It is instructive to test this famous rule by walking down any populous city street and noting the distance at which one can distinguish the whites of the eyes of the approaching throng. The result will be an impressive demonstration of the ranges at which eighteenth-century battles had to be fought.

a brutally iron discipline. To control its fire and render it readily maneuverable under stress required a rigid, deeply-instilled close-order drill. Neither the discipline nor the intricate parade-ground evolutions were manifestations merely of pomp and militaristic ritual; both were functional necessities dictated by the weapons and technologies of the times.

The eighteenth-century weapons system reinforced the eighteenth-century economy, political and social structure and philosophical bent to produce a system of limited, professionalized warfare waged by a generally small and specialized minority unlucky enough to be caught in its toils. In whatever army or navy a man served in those days or however he got into it (and any service might include nationals of many countries) he was simply a cog in a war machine. "Let officers," as Hamilton once wrote, "be men of sense; but the nearer soldiers approach to machines perhaps the better." [5] The soldier had few if any home ties. He was isolated from and usually despised by the community he served. But he was brutally trained and flogged into a sense of duty that was expected to make him face unflinchingly the appalling carnage of an eighteenth-century battlefield or the unspeakable horrors of the cockpit of a 74 in action. The wonder is that so often he did so.

Such was the system of limited war by "royal hirelings" which faced the Colonial leaders in 1775. They had themselves, of course, been brought up in it; their statesmen thought in its terms; the officers who were to command the Colonial armies had, many of them, been trained in its battles. For three-quarters of a century small royal armies of conventional pattern had been contending in the New World for the prizes of empire. Differences in terrain and conditions had, to be sure, enforced some modifications in their military methods, though these are sometimes exaggerated. The regular forces had made much greater use of local levies than was practicable in Europe, where the material for them seldom existed. Because of the wooded and roadless character of the interior, cavalry had scarcely appeared in America. The deep forests, the surprises and concealments of Indian warfare

[5] To John Jay March 14, 1779, urging the enlistment of Negro troops. Quoted in George Livermore, *An Historical Research* (Boston, 1862), pp. 130 f.

had taught some tactical lessons which did not go unnoticed by professional soldiers, especially after Braddock's famous defeat in 1755.

It was in the following year that the Government provided for the raising of the Royal Americans as a regular regiment of the British Army. They were to be recruited from the Swiss and German settlers of Pennsylvania and Maryland, perhaps with the idea that such material would be particularly useful in backwoods fighting. But they were commanded by European professionals and were uniformed and equipped in conventional fashion.[6] American experience contributed to the development of the "light infantry" companies which were added to many of the standard infantry battalions during this period. Made up of picked men with lightened equipment to serve as scouts, skirmishers and flank guards, they were particularly useful in wooded and broken country; but as long as warfare was limited by the characteristics of the short-range musket they could not shake the predominance of the massed battalion which they served. The warfare of woods and river lines tended in other ways to modify and discourage the rigid, full-dress battle tactics of Europe. But when it came to rendering a final decision, these were still the accepted means. Only four years after the destruction of Braddock, two small, professional armies drawn up in conventional close order on the Plains of Abraham above Quebec and using conventional mass tactics, decided the destiny of the vast empire of New France.

It was not the backwoods tactics or terrain which was to destroy the eighteenth-century military system; the Revolution was not, for the most part, a backwoods war. It was certainly not the backwoods rifle, a weapon virtually unknown in New England in 1775, and which was not for another three-quarters of a century to develop into a practicable military arm for general use. Primarily, it was the presence in America of an armed populace and of a militia system which,

---

[6] Two of their four battalions were disbanded with the peace in 1763; the other two were removed to the West Indies in 1775. It was not until the Napoleonic era that they were converted to a rifle regiment, and the powderhorn buttons and greenish uniform which they still wear (as the King's Royal Rifle Corps) have no connection with their American origin or the American backwoods rifle. See Frederick E. Ray, Jr., and Frederick P. Todd, in *The Military Collector and Historian,* Vol. V, No. 3 (1953), p. 73.

despite its decay in the older seaboard settlements, still represented a living tradition.

"The Colonists in America," as Sawyer puts it, "were the greatest weapon-using people of that epoch in the world." On the frontier the gun was essential for defense against the Indians; in the settled areas it was still a necessary utensil for getting food or protecting property. The militia had tended to survive with the weapons. In the early days every settlement had been virtually a military colony; long after the necessity had passed, the enrolled militia companies and regiments had continued to play a role in local politics and community affairs not unlike that of many volunteer fire companies in rural communities today. And the succession of French and Indian Wars had continued to lend reality to their military function. Then as since, the militia proper was never regarded as more than a strictly local force for emergency defense of hearth and home. Large contingents of volunteers were, however, raised from its ranks for war service. Such were the 4,000 Massachusetts Bay men who took Louisburg in 1745; such was Colonel Washington's regularly enlisted Virginia Regiment which tried to keep the Indians in check after Braddock's disaster (with only casual help from the militia proper); such were the provincial troops who supported George Howe's and Amherst's regulars in the Seven Years' War. The veterans of these campaigns, returning to the civil population and its militia obligation, kept alive a considerable general body of military knowledge and experience among a populace accustomed to the use of arms in its daily life. And although in the settled communities the militia "muster days" may have degenerated into the glorious drunks so often associated with them, the laws requiring these musters and obliging every male citizen to provide himself with musket, powder, shot and a "cartouche box," remained on the books and were available in 1775.

As the threat of hostilities approached and the provincial assemblies, the committees of safety and the first Continental Congress sought to put the patriot cause in a posture of defense, the militia organizations within the colonies offered much more than a negligible recourse. Local companies were revitalized and put to drilling in earnest. Stocks of powder, lead, muskets and what few artillery pieces there were in

the country were rounded up, often from the unmanned royal or provincial forts. And in Massachusetts the Provincial Congress, realizing
the difficulties of mobilizing a force theoretically composed of every
able-bodied male in the community, resorted to the famous expedient
of the Minute Men. The youngest and most active on the militia rolls
were to be told off into special companies, to be ready "at a minute's
notice"; the more sedentary warriors were consigned to "alarm companies," to be used only in the last extremity of alarm.

It was perhaps our first example of an attempt to combine selective
service with a universal military obligation. The system was never fully
organized and was discarded in a few months with the establishment
of the Continental Army.[7] Yet it remains of great interest, for the
problem of how justly to distribute a military obligation which is universal by definition but which can practically be imposed upon only
a few has plagued our own and most other military systems from that
day. It lies always at the core of any compulsory military structure; we
were still struggling with it in adopting the National Reserve Act of
1955, and still finding answers which to many must seem less than
satisfactory.

The explosion finally came on April 19, 1775. The Minute Men,
together, it would seem, with everyone else in the countryside possessing a weapon and fired by patriot ardor, poured out to defend the
munition stocks at Concord and to repel the invader. This they did,
largely by force of numbers, by shooting from cover and because the
British had no objective. They had nowhere to go save back to Boston;
they retired with heavy losses into the city, and as the angry and
excited militia companies closed around them, the American Revolution had begun.

The first steps on the patriot side were almost by reflex action. The
militia companies were soon bound to drift away, but the Massachusetts Provincial Congress addressed itself with energy to raising
from them a volunteer force on the pattern of earlier wars. With
appeals to the neighboring colonies of New Hampshire, Rhode Island
and Connecticut, an army aggregating 35,000 men was projected. With

[7] Christopher Ward, *The War of the Revolution* (New York, Macmillan,
1952), Vol. I, p. 30.

remarkable speed regiments were formed and filled in all four colonies and hurried to Boston; generals were found from the veterans of the Seven Years' War; a rudimentary organization of brigades and divisions was established, and by the latter part of May Boston was surrounded by possibly 15,000 provincials—citizen soldiers in all stages of training and equipment, but most of them armed with muskets.

By that time Howe had arrived, accompanied by Clinton and Burgoyne; so had reinforcements sufficient to raise the British force to about 6,000 regulars and Marines. Obviously the siege would have to be broken up as soon as possible, and the Battle of Bunker Hill on June 19 was the first test of the practicability of doing so. Perhaps out of contempt for the "raw militia" before them the British failed to exploit their opportunities for maneuver; the troops were repeatedly thrown in frontal assault against entrenched positions with shocking losses. In the end, the patriots began to run out of ammunition and departed; the field was won but there was no decision. The Colonial besiegers remained as formidable as before; the British, however, had taken losses too frightful for a small army 3,000 miles from its base to risk repeating. No serious attempt to break out of the Boston perimeter was thereafter made.

2.

All this had happened before the Continental Congress had been able to get a grip on the situation. It reassembled at Philadelphia on May 10, three weeks after Lexington-Concord. It moved promptly to appoint a commander-in-chief, to establish a Continental currency and to adopt the troops at Boston as the core of a Continental Army. But by the time Washington could take command at Cambridge on July 2, Bunker Hill was already a fortnight in the past. Congress and its new general were assuming responsibility for a situation which had largely been created.

The statesmen at Philadelphia were of course keenly aware of the importance of popular political forces to the success of the cause on which they had embarked. But it was no part of their purpose to organize a "people's war" in a military sense. They can have had no prevision of the tremendous and destructive military potentials inherent in the coming age of popular democratic nationalism; if they had they would probably, as eighteenth-century rationalists, have been horrified by the prospect. The "Liberty" for which they were prepared to embroil the country and risk their own necks and fortunes was essentially the liberty of the country's major social, economic and other vested interests to develop for the common good free of outside interference. In defense of that kind of liberty they knew they had to enlist popular support, but they had no intention of raising a great popular guerilla war or immolating men, women and children alike upon the altars of patriotism.

Their aim was confined to expelling the "ministerial armies" and protecting themselves against subsequent "invasion" by resort to the established military methods of the time. Basically, that meant hiring a professional fighting force which would do the job, as eighteenth-century armies were accustomed to doing it, with a maximum of economy and a minimum of interference in the normal life of the community. The statesmen at Philadelphia set out to model their Continental Army on the familiar British example. It was to be small—just sufficient in force to deal with the "invader." It was to be recruited by voluntary and (it was hoped) long-service enlistment, with the aid of substantial pay and bounties; its battalion and divisional organization imitated the British example; its commanders were found among graduates of the British professional service whenever (as in the case of Gates or Charles Lee) such men were available; Henry Knox modeled his embryonic artillery "regiment," even to the designation, upon the Royal Regiment of Artillery, which he considered the best service of the kind in the world. The Continental Congress issued no calls for a mass uprising of the people. The nearest thing to that which the Revolution was to produce had taken place just after Concord, and had already begun to evaporate by the time Washington reached Cambridge.

The statesmen of 1775 were aware that they were fighting a new kind of war, but seem not to have foreseen the extent to which it was bound to modify the old methods. Shortly after taking command, Washington was confronted with the case of an officer who wanted to

throw up his commission over a question of rank. "In the usual con-
tests of Empire and Ambition," the general told him, "the conscience
of a soldier has so little share that he may very properly insist upon
his claims of Rank, and extend his pretensions even to Punctilio; but
in such a cause as this, where the Object is neither Glory nor extent
of territory, but a defense of all that is dear and valuable in Life,
surely every post ought to be deemed honorable in which a Man can
serve his Country." [8] That one sentence foretells the end of the
eighteenth-century attitudes toward war and politics. If war was ceasing
to be a mere contest of professionals for empire, ambition and glory,
but was coming to affect all that "is dear and valuable to Life," then
the state's military claims upon its citizens were being greatly enhanced. More than that, the citizen who, as a citizen rather than a
mercenary, bore arms in the state's service was establishing new claims
upon the state and new power over its institutions.

Washington may not have realized the full implications of his own
principle. Through most of the war he was to excoriate the failings
of the popular militias, to demand a long-service regular army and to
recommend larger enlistment bonuses on the sound ground that only
"interest" and not "patriotism" could bring men to serve for the long
pull. In the later years of the war he could cynically observe that the
original passion for liberty had faded and that self-interest remained
as the only motive to which the state could appeal in securing the duty
of its citizens. But even from the beginning, the political and social
consequences of summoning men to fight for liberty, rather than
merely for the pay and allowances, obtruded themselves. Very early,
there arose the embarrassing question of the Negroes.

Negro slavery existed everywhere in the colonies, though in New
England and the middle provinces in only a minor and attenuated
form. Crispus Attucks, who died in the Boston Massacre of 1770 and
so became one of the first martyrs to liberty, was a Negro slave. There
were many Negroes, both slaves and freedmen, in the patriot army
before Boston. When in October 1775 Washington reviewed the

---

[8] To Brigadier General John Thomas, July 23, 1775. John C. Fitzpatrick, ed.,
The Writings of George Washington (Washington, Government Printing Office),
Vol. 3, p. 359.

matter of permanent military organization with a committee from the Continental Congress, they presented a delicate problem of social and economic policy. The first decision was that Negroes, free or slave, be "rejected altogether" and recruiting officers were forbidden to enlist them. But Washington was soon reporting that "the free Negroes who have served in this army are very much dissatisfied with being discarded. As it is to be apprehended that they may seek employment in the Ministerial Army, I have . . . given license for their being enlisted." Congress acquiesced in respect to the freedmen, but insisted that "no others" should be accepted.

Yet the question presented many complexities. Lord Dunmore, the Royal Governor of Virginia, had already sought to raise Negro levies (and strike a heavy economic blow at the patriots) by promising freedom to those slaves of rebel owners who would enter the British service. The Negroes were proving themselves to be brave and competent soldiers; both sides could bid for their services with offers of freedom and many slave-holders, especially in the North, were glad to send their Negroes to military duty as substitutes for themselves. It was embarrassing to the patriots to be fighting for liberty while maintaining the institution of slavery; it was almost equally embarrassing, on the other hand, to be accused of raising a servile army to fight liberty's battles for them. In the South, with its large slave population and already developed plantation system, it seemed extremely dangerous as well. As the war progressed most of the northern and middle states were to provide for the enlistment of slaves, the owners to be compensated in one way or another and the Negroes, in Hamilton's phrase, to be given "their freedom with their muskets." South Carolina and Georgia never dared to go so far. Despite their lamentable failure to produce enough white soldiers for the war, despite heavy pressure—some of it from their own leaders—to supply the deficiency with Negro troops, despite the argument that military service would draw off "the most vigorous and enterprising" of the slaves, at the same time pacifying the others by opening to them a possible door to freedom, the risks of putting arms in the hands of their chattels and the economic costs of surrendering their property proved forbidding. Even for the sake of freedom they would not imperil their "peculiar institution." [9]

The problem of the Negroes was by no means the only indication of how far the military, no less than the political, revolution reached into the structure of Colonial society. The leaders set out to fight an unconventional war by conventional means, but the war imposed its own conditions. The Continental Army refused to imitate the example of its long-service British model. The 15,000 New Englanders before Boston, whom Congress had "adopted," had not enlisted for the "duration" but only for the "campaign"—which meant the summer fighting season—and their terms would run out with the year's end. As the year waned, it was at first too hastily assumed that they would re-enlist. The Congressional committee which reviewed the situation in October concluded that, together with troops raised elsewhere, twenty-six regiments from the four New England colonies—20,370 rank and file—would suffice, and that these could be secured by re-enlisting the men around Boston. The men decided otherwise. As their terms ran out they went home, leaving it to Washington and the Congress to find replacements. And too often they took with them the muskets and equipment so desperately needed for the new forces.

Washington's excoriating letters on the "extraordinary and reprehensible conduct" of these men who "might incline to go home when the time of their enlistment should be up" have often been quoted. Yet much as one must sympathize with the appalling problem of the general, who found himself compelled to discharge one army and recruit another while in immediate contact with the enemy, one cannot help feeling that there is something to be said for the home-going warriors. The country was prosperous and full of able-bodied persons who had done nothing for the cause. The first contingent had volunteered and served a long and uncomfortable (if, after Bunker Hill, not very dangerous) term in the Boston positions; why should it be their reward to do the fighting for the rest of the war? Here were the elements of another issue which has troubled all mass military systems ever since. There is an obvious injustice in any system which

[9] George Livermore, *An Historical Research* (Boston, 1862), *passim*.

operates in such a way that once a man volunteers or is drafted he thereafter carries a heavier military obligation than the man who gets off scot-free. A century and three-quarters later many reserve officers who felt that they had done their duty in the Second World War resented being called back to service in Korea, when there were so many men who, as youths or essential war workers, had escaped all military duty entirely. Yet the trained World War II veterans were the only ones available, and justly or unjustly the country had to call upon them. It is hard to design a mass system which will not lead to this result. In 1775 the New Englanders defied it by going home; it is an option which today is seldom open to the soldier of even a democratic state.

The immediate crisis was surmounted by calling in Massachusetts and New Hampshire militia to hold the lines for the few weeks until the new army could be recruited. This was finally accomplished, but only at the heavy price of again limiting the enlistment period to a year. In November Washington warned his forces, a trifle piously, that if they made their terms too stiff the future might conclude that "it was not principle that saved them" but that "they were bribed into the preservation of their liberties." [10] But a nation which seeks to hire an army in its defense has to meet the terms. It was also in November that Congress resolved to raise two battalions of Marines, directly as a Federal and not provincial force; they were to be enlisted "to serve for and during the present war." Washington, after inquiry, advised Philadelphia that this provision would prove "an insuperable Obstruction" to getting the men, and the service term was reduced to one year.

The disaster suffered by Arnold and Montgomery at Quebec on the last day of 1775 was in large part due to the fact that they had been forced into a premature assault before their troops, with their time expired, should leave them. Taking this as a text, Washington wrote the Congress in February: "The disadvantages attending the limited Inlistment of Troops is too apparent to those who are eye-witnesses of them to render any animadversions necessary"; and he strongly

[10] William Addleman Ganoe, *The History of the United States Army* (New York, Appleton, 1924), p. 14.

urged that if Congress saw any likelihood of the war lasting beyond 1776, the men should be re-enlisted for the duration, even if it required a "bounty of twenty, thirty or more Dollars to engage" them. It would "never do," he argued, again to let matters drift until the new terms of service were again approaching expiration.[11]

But Congress was more or less helpless. It lacked the money to bid high enough in bounties; it lacked the power to draft men; and the colonies, jealous enough of a "standing army" as it was, were reluctant to do so. As the war dragged on the states did resort to compulsion to fill their own organizations. Gradually, by one enactment or another, the long term of service—three years or the duration—was introduced into the volunteer service of the Continental Lines. But not in 1776. At the end of the second year of the war as at the end of the first, Washington was once more compelled to discharge one army and rebuild another in face of the enemy, while relying on the militias to hold the gap.

Meanwhile, however, the character of the war had changed. The patriots' attempt on Canada—carried out by Montgomery's Connecticut and New York troops and by Arnold's amazing march up the Kennebec—had ended in catastrophe. On the other hand, the southern militia, at the Battle of Moore's Bridge in February 1776, had established the patriot ascendancy in the Carolinas; Virginia troops destroyed the royalist base at Norfolk and in March the British evacuated Boston. The Canadian dream may have been extinguished, but within the thirteen colonies the king's writ no longer ran; the "lobster backs" no longer remained upon Colonial soil; the patriots were in full command of all agencies of governance and law, and the formal Declaration of Independence had become more or less inevitable. The first War of the Revolution had been won; the second, an attempt by the king's ministers to retake what they had lost, was about to begin.

This second war was to drag on through some five years of more or less active fighting and a sixth devoted to the writing of the peace. It is often said that Great Britain failed because of the slothfulness and disunity of her commanders, the venality and incompetence of the

[11] To the President of Congress, February 9, 1776. Fitzgerald, *op. cit.,* Vol. 4, p. 315.

ministry and the complicated chaos of her military administration—
all well-justified charges by modern standards. Yet the patriot cause
suffered in about equal measure from similar weaknesses. While
Washington was a tower of moral strength he was not an outstanding
tactician, and American generalship on the whole was not much better
than the British; the Continental Congress included abler men than
George III's ministries, but its lack of power offset this advantage;
while its military administration—which could never amass enough
men, food or clothing, which was responsible for such horrors as
Valley Forge or the almost equally bitter miseries at Morristown in
the preceding year—seems scarcely efficient even beside the British
example.

There is likewise little to support the popular belief that the Americans won because of superior tactical skills. The Colonial levies preferred to shoot from cover when they could, but so did the British and
Hessian regulars. Neither side could escape the limitations of their
short-range muskets and if the Americans were, on the whole, more
often found behind breastworks it was mainly because the British were
more often on the offensive. The first troops which Congress voted to
raise directly on its own authority were the celebrated six companies
of riflemen (later raised to ten) from the Pennsylvania, Maryland and
Virginia back country. These picturesque characters were a nine-days'
wonder when they arrived before Boston in their hunting shirts and
with their remarkable weapons, with which they could hit a bull's-eye
at the staggering range of two hundred yards. But the muzzle-loading
rifle of that day, for which a tight-fitting ball had to be laboriously
rammed or pounded down the length of the grooved barrel, was far
too slow and awkward in reloading, even by comparison with the
musket, to be practicable as a general combat weapon. It does not
appear that there was ever any large proportion of riflemen in the
American forces; while the British, although they had issued rifles to
their officers as early as the Seven Years' War, made no effort to introduce them generally.

When Steuben arrived at Valley Forge to instruct the Continentals,
what he taught them were the rigid mass tactics and close-order drill
of the Prussian system, and the Americans were grateful for it. The

teaching lay behind one of the more spectacular of the later successes: Wayne's storming of Stony Point by close discipline and the use of the bayonet alone. The peculiar terrain in the South produced a specialized form of warfare, the extensive use of cavalry as mounted infantry, but both sides were equally skillful in this tactic. Cavalry was scarcely used in the northern and middle states, and in American practice it was never, indeed, to develop as in Europe into a major instrument of "shock action." But amid the thinly peopled live-oak swamps and pine barrens of the southern tidewater, both sides put their men on horses to achieve strategic mobility, although generally fighting them on foot. The fame of the British cavalry leader, Banastre Tarleton, suggests that the British were no less adept at this than the Americans under Marion or Light Horse Harry Lee.

The disparity in numbers, wealth and military equipment between Great Britain and her revolted colonies was great. Britain had strong Tory "fifth columns" in America throughout the struggle. If her failure is to be ascribed neither to administration, command nor tactics, one must look for broader explanations. The truth seems to be that the reconquest of America presented a problem which was simply insoluble with the military instrumentalities of the times. Only fifteen years before Britain's small, professional armies had taken the wilderness empire of New France by capturing and holding one or two key positions. Throughout this period Britain was acquiring and expanding another empire in the densely populated but militarily and politically neutral expanse of India, using similar methods. But in America in 1776 it was facing something new—an armed as well as politically active countryside, occupying an area too big and too loosely organized to offer any key positions or any decisive point of attack.

Britain's greatest advantage was the Royal Navy, conferring a normally complete command of the sea and with it complete freedom of maneuver against an adversary which (like modern Chile) was little more than one long coastal strip. Her greatest disadvantage was that nowhere in this strip was there any critical point to maneuver against. To recapture the colonies it was not enough to defeat an army or even to take a capital. Either the British must physically occupy and hold every important center of government, commerce and military supply along the whole thousand miles of coast; or else they must re-establish sufficient centers of strength from which to launch a counter-revolution with the aid of their own sympathizers. Throughout the war, considerable loyalist or potentially loyalist elements remained within the rebellious states; and just as the Americans had hoped to take Canada by arousing the Canadian French against their lately acquired British masters, so the British based much of their strategy on the hope of raising the loyalists against the dictatorial control of the patriot forces. It was becoming, on both sides, a "popular" war, whether the leaders so intended it or not.

For the physical occupation of the country the British never had anything like enough troops; they could, for example, only take New York at the expense of evacuating Boston, or invade the South at the expense of leaving the northern war pretty much in a state of suspension. Against the alternative—counter-revolution—it was the much-despised and frequently unwarlike patriot militias which provided perhaps the strongest single bulwark. It was, indeed, the hope of raising counter-revolution which dictated the first move in the attempted reconquest: Sir Peter Parker's expedition to the Carolinas to revive the loyalist forces which had been shattered at Moore's Bridge. It was the steadfastness of the hastily recruited Carolina regiments and militia companies (aided by the stoutness of Moultrie's slave-built palmetto breastworks and the exceptional difficulties of navigation amid the sands of Charleston Harbor) which defeated the enterprise. And repeatedly it was the militia which met the critical emergency or, in less formal operations, kept control of the country, cut off foragers, captured British agents, intimidated the war-weary and disaffected or tarred and feathered the notorious Tories. The patriots' success in infiltrating and capturing the old militia organizations, by expelling and replacing officers of Tory sympathies, was perhaps as important to the outcome as any of their purely political achievements. While the regular armies marched and fought more or less ineffectually, it was the militia which presented the greatest single impediment to Britain's only practicable weapon, that of counter-revolution. The militia were often much less than ideal combat troops and they have come in for many hard words ever since. But their true military and political significance may have been underrated.[12]

The attempt on Charleston was made, and defeated, on June 28, 1776. This, however, had been planned only as a promising side issue. It was the following day that General Howe, with the first of the great main expedition under his command, arrived off Sandy Hook. Through the next six weeks the convoys, under their enormous clouds of sail, came in bearing thousands of men, including Clinton's and Cornwallis' forces from Charleston and the first big Hessian contingents. When Howe was ready to move in the latter part of August he had assembled an army of 32,000 men, backed by 10,000 seamen in ships mounting 1,200 guns. Taking ships and soldiery together it was probably the most formidable force which Britain had ever organized for an overseas operation.

Unfortunately, there was really nothing to be done with it. Howe had little difficulty in flushing Washington out of Long Island and New York and then harrying him across the Delaware. Washington could readily be defeated, but he could not be destroyed. The American capital at Philadelphia could first be threatened and finally taken; all that happened was that the rebel government decamped to Baltimore

[12] The term "militia" has always been rather loosely employed. Henry Knox's post-war return (as Secretary of War) recognized three classes of patriot troops: the Continental Lines, who were regulars enlisted and paid by Congress though retaining their state designations; the regularly enlisted state forces, amounting to thirteen little "regular" armies with their own bounty, pay and promotion systems, and the militia proper, summoned from their farms or shops for brief service when opportunity offered or emergency demanded.

According to the Knox return, in the year 1776, which saw the largest American forces under arms, there were in service 46,901 Continentals, 26,000 state militia, and an estimated 16,700 short-service militia proper, for a total of 89,661 —perhaps 3 per cent of the population.

In 1780 barely half as many saw service. Congress in that year called on the states for 41,760 Continentals, but got only 21,015; the states provided 5,811 of their own organized militia troops and there were an estimated 16,250 short-service militiamen under arms at one time or another, for a total of 43,076. In 1780 we put about 1.5 per cent of the population in the field, while the regularly enlisted Continental and state troops together came to no more than about 0.8 per cent. In World War II we put about 10 per cent of the population in uniform, though this far exceeded the numbers who saw combat service. American State Papers, Military Affairs, Vol. I, p. 17.

or to York in Pennsylvania and continued as before. The British could rally loyalist support wherever they held command; New York City was loyalist throughout the war and there were many eminent Philadelphians to enjoy the brilliant pleasures of the British occupation. In the North as well as in the South numerous loyalist battalions were raised to assist the regulars. But the British could never get at the countryside through the screens of the patriot militias.

This inability to reach the country left them tied to their sea communications. Their one major effort at strategic operations in the great inland wilderness was Burgoyne's advance down the Champlain-Hudson waterway in the summer of 1777. That operation, in an area where the country offered little to live on, broke down primarily because of the communications difficulty. The Continental forces under Gates and Arnold, of course, had a great deal to do with the result. But it was the Vermont militia who, with their repulse of a Hessian foraging party at the Battle of Bennington, sounded the death knell of the Burgoyne expedition. Burgoyne was stopped by Gates; but he was forced into surrender by a supply problem which, as winter approached, began to seem insoluble.

In the settled North, the British were simply left at a loss after Burgoyne's surrender in October 1777. They had taken Philadelphia a month before, but it was of no use to them. Howe went home. Clinton, replacing him, evacuated the city in the early summer of 1778, in order to try something else. The movement gave rise to the Battle of Monmouth, a harrying, rear-guard action. Except for American blunders and Charles Lee's peculiar conduct, it might have resulted in a significant success; but the British completed their retirement without serious damage and the battle was of little strategic effect. Having withdrawn into New York, the British reconsidered their problem; and despite subsequent operations at Newport, along the Connecticut shore and on the Hudson, they made no real attempt thereafter to recover the northern colonies.

The North was virtually lost; it remained only for the British to see what they might do in the southern theater. Savannah was taken in December 1778, and through 1779 and 1780 the numerous operations of the southern war resulted in the British capture of Charleston and of Wilmington on the Cape Fear. But the British were still confronted with the want of any decisive objective. Their victories, as at Camden on August 16, 1780, did not greatly help; neither were their defeats, as at King's Mountain or Cowpens, final. Virginia was the rich, settled and only really decisive area in the southern theater. In April 1781 Cornwallis set out from the Cape Fear to march into Virginia, but in that enterprise he, rather like Burgoyne, had to leave his communications behind him. Unable to bring the country to his support, he was dependent upon the sea; but when he retired into Yorktown in order to replenish his force from the Royal Navy, De Grasse temporarily intervened. Washington, with energy and foresight, had started a force of some 16,000 American and French troops to concentrate upon him. Cornwallis realized that without naval support the resultant siege could not be withstood, and on October 19, 1781 he marched out his troops to lay down their arms.

The British military system—experienced, trained and generally effective as it was under the conditions of the time—had found no answer for its American problem. To reverse the verdict thus substantially rendered at Yorktown would mean starting all over again, with another tremendous effort of mobilization which the mother country, already deeply embroiled elsewhere, had no desire to make. The combination of an armed populace, a loose-knit and democratically organized administration offering few points of attack and a huge terrain was too much for British arms which through those same years were successfully conquering the subcontinent of India.

Technically, the war was to last nearly two more years, but the fighting was virtually over. The southern seaports were evacuated one after another. In the spring of 1783 the news arrived of the signing of the preliminary peace, and the evacuation of New York began. On September 3, 1783 the final peace was concluded, and the United States of America entered upon its independent existence as one of the sovereign powers of the world.

3.

For the patriot leaders it had been a triumph of improvisation. They had built everything—government, finances, army, navy, foreign policy and public opinion—as they went along, in accordance with whatever models were available and out of whatever materials were at hand. And as usually happens with improvisations, they had built more than they knew.

They had, for one thing, started with an overwhelmingly agricultural community; they had emerged with the beginnings of a metallurgical industry, fostered by the demands of war. The logistic requirements of eighteenth-century warfare were still relatively simple: mainly food, clothing, powder, lead and guns. There was always enough food and clothing in the country (the problems here were of finance, procurement and distribution rather than of basic supply); lead was usually available and gunpowder could be scraped together out of humble materials by home industry. The guns presented greater difficulty. The American armament came largely from three sources: the accumulated stock of weapons in the hands of the people; captures from royal stocks and arsenals and later from British supply ships, and French aid. Long before the formal French recognition, the clandestine operations of Beaumarchais, dramatist and arms entrepreneur, yielded some 23,000 French army muskets, the "Charleville muskets," which were successfully landed early in 1777. But despite these supplies, the war put a stimulating pressure upon the operations of local ironworks, foundries, forges and gunsmiths.

The colonies had been considerable producers of iron even before the war. While he was still before Boston, Washington was confidently ordering from "two Furnaces" some "thirteen Inch" mortars to be cast and was "encouraged to hope . . . that they will be able to do it." Rifles came from the back-country shops, to which the art of making them had doubtless been brought by the German settlers in Pennsylvania. The achievements in building men-of-war, outfitting privateers or building Arnold's flotilla on Lake Champlain—with all they implied as to the availability not only of ship carpenters, sails and cordage but of iron for guns, anchors, fastenings and chain-plates—indicate that the domestic industry was by no means negligible. The forging of the great chain boom laid across the Hudson at West Point was a big accomplishment, as anyone who examines the massive links preserved at the Military Academy can attest. War and blockade applied a forcing bellows to these industrial beginnings; and in Massachusetts an ingenious farm boy turned his father's tool shed into a profitable nail factory. His name was Eli Whitney, and his diminutive factory with its two-man working force was an early hint of that remarkable interaction between war and industry which was to grow into a striking feature of the nineteenth century.

The Revolutionary leaders had done more than this, however. In fighting for liberty they had, without quite intending it, democratized politics; without intending it at all, they had also democratized war. It was not for another decade that the results of this achievement were to appear, as the invincible popular armies of the French Revolution burst in their torrent of fire upon the Europe of the Ancien Régime. It was not, indeed, for another century and a half that Americans, swathed in their splendid isolation, would begin themselves to appreciate the full implications of the military revolution begun by their forebears at Concord. Yet the democratic mass wars of the French Revolution and Napoleon were no more than a logical consequence of the general system of ideas and principles by which the American War had been brought to success. As the indictment in the Declaration of Independence makes plain, the colonies had rebelled not only against the political "tyranny" of the king's ministers but also against the irresponsible military power represented by the royal "standing armies." "A standing army, however necessary it may be, is always dangerous to the liberties of the people." The sentiment was endlessly repeated. What was seldom recognized was the force of the admission that an army, or some source of military power, was necessary. If military power was transferred from the king it could fall only on the whole body of the people. If this freed them from the arrogance and exactions of the "royal hirelings," it laid upon them, whether they liked it or not, an obligation which they could not refuse.

The Continental Congress struck another fairly lethal blow at the eighteenth-century military system when it financed the war with the printing press. It was under no illusions as to the economic or even the political consequences. The experienced merchant traders in its membership doubtless knew more about the subtleties and pitfalls of credit instruments than do the routinized bankers of today. They decided to manufacture their own money primarily because that was the only way they had of getting any. They had no taxing power themselves and could not compel contributions from the states. But the Army had to be fed and paid—at least within reason. It was either the printing press or surrender, and without much hesitation they chose the printing press.

A national political goal had overridden the old limitations imposed by the monetary economy of the mercantile age. In the past, a monarch unable to acquire the funds with which to hire and maintain his troops might have to suspend operations. The "war chest," an actual chest filled with actual gold pieces or their equivalents, was as standard a piece of military equipment as the ammunition wagons, and its loss by enemy capture was a serious military reverse. Congress, unable to provide General Washington with one, did not abandon the war. Instead it gave him paper money, authorizations to pledge the national credit, requisitions on the states and similar instruments. It was hoped, of course, that the states would ultimately provide the funds to redeem the paper; but it was realized that the result would be a national debt and, very probably, a currency inflation. The first had great political advantages: it would create a creditor class with an active interest in redemption and therefore in victory; it provided "a new bond of Union." As the second, inflation, developed Congress seems not to have been unduly concerned. Inflation is a kind of universal confiscatory taxation and therefore justifiable, if at all, on the grounds of a paramount national interest to which all may be compelled to contribute whether they are willing to do so or not.

War had been democratized and "nationalized," as it were; finally it had been freed from its economic shackles, and primitive means had been discovered for circumventing the money system in the service of a national interest. By 1783 the principal seeds had been sown from which were to spring the modern "socialization" of war and its development to those heights of total effort and total savagery to which we are now accustomed. The way had been opened for the confiscation of property as well as the conscription of life in the name of the all-powerful modern deity—the state.

So far as the United States was concerned, however, such developments lay in a remote future, beyond envisaging by the men of the time. What they did see very clearly was that military policy must be a first preoccupation of the new nation. Having just brought that nation to birth by resort to military violence, they were unlikely to underestimate the importance of the military factor in its political and social organization. They knew very well that theirs was a fragile ship being launched upon a perilous world sea; they knew that it was a basic requirement both to "provide for the common defense" against external danger and to establish the form and locus of military power within their system.

After the surrender at Yorktown no significant foreign threats remained. What did arise immediately were the internal problems of military policy, presented by the two chief instruments through which victory had been achieved. One was the Continental Army, concentrated at Newburgh, N. Y., in a state of idleness and increasing dissatisfaction. The other was the creditor group: the holders of the paper money and other evidences of the national indebtedness. The one had fought the war, in part at least, for the promise of pay and bounties; the other had, in effect, financed it. One might shrug off the first as a now useless standing army, battening on the people and imperiling their liberties; one might shrug off the second as heartless speculators who had cheated the original recipients of the paper and were now hoping to recoup undeserved fortunes. Neither seemed a complete answer when in January 1783 a delegation bearing the grievances of the Newburgh officer corps appeared at Philadelphia.

Since 1781 Congress had been passing into the control of the "nationalist" politicians, the conservative magnates who had been most hesitant over the plunge into independence, but who were now most desirous that independence should produce a strong central government, capable of servicing the national debt and of keeping unduly divisive or democratic tendencies under control with a national standing army. In the early months of 1783 there appeared the out-

lines of an intrigue in which the Army would combine with the nationalists and the creditors to impose such a government by force in the
interests of all three. "To me," Hamilton had written months before,
"it is an axiom that in our constitution an army is essential to the
American union." The Army and the creditors together would provide
a "cement" for a centralized, national government. Now Gouverneur
Morris wrote to Knox: "After you [the Army] have carried the post,
the creditors will garrison it for you." Washington's common sense
exploded these fantasies. He thought the officers were being used as
"mere puppets to establish Continental funds"; he indicated his dis-
trust of the politicians, and with his moving address to the Newburgh
officer corps on March 15 he demonstrated that his confidence in the
Army's loyalty and patriotism was well justified.[13] Considering the
reality and acuteness of the Army's grievances, which were never adequately redressed, this is a little surprising. But the Army had never
really contemplated mutiny in its own interests; never again did an
American regular establishment come even as near as that to using
the power of its arms in domestic politics, and the tradition then established has survived unblemished to this day.

Nevertheless, Washington, although a nationalist himself and fully
aware of the value of a standing army, felt that it was "indispensable"
to settle the Army's accounts and send it home. A large proportion of
the troops were "war men," enlisted for the duration, and now the
war was at an end. News of the preliminary peace was leaking out,
and on April 11 Congress proclaimed hostilities to be at an end.
Before the month was over the troops were rioting and discipline had
collapsed. Congress told Washington to furlough the "war men" with
three months' pay; and by June what was left of the Continental Army
had evaporated, as have all our subsequent war armies with the outbreak of peace, though the Continentals were more prompt than most
of their descendants. The nationalist hopes for a large, centrally controlled standing army evaporated with them.

Yet the problem of a permanent military organization remained.
It was in the midst of these somewhat disturbing events, on May 2,

[13] Merrill Jensen, *The New Nation* (New York, Knopf, 1950), pp. 50, 70 and
passim.

1783, that Washington sat down to catch up with a bit of delayed business, which was to give Hamilton his thoughts on a permanent peace establishment. Starting with the principle which had now become axiomatic, he observed: "Altho' a *large* standing Army in time of Peace hath ever been considered dangerous to the liberties of a Country, yet a few Troops, under certain circumstances, are not only safe, but indispensably necessary. Fortunately for us, our relative situation requires but few." With a realistic appraisal of the actual strategic situation, he cut the requirement for regulars to the bone; they would be needed only to garrison West Point (which Washington considered the one key position in the whole country) and to police the remote new land frontiers. There, far removed from any possible involvement in domestic politics, their task would be "to awe the Indians, protect our [fur] Trade, prevent the encroachment of our Neighbors of Canada and the Florida's, and guard us at least from surprizes." Four regiments of infantry and one of artillery—2,631 men in all—would suffice.

At the time there was but negligible danger of a serious war; should such a threat ever arise, it could come only from Europe, and in that case our best defense would again lie, as during the Revolution, in our *"distance"* from the European bases. Washington suggested that if funds ever became available for protection against Europe, they should go into "building and equipping a Navy," possibly backed by the fortification of its yards and bases, in order to exploit this advantage. The maintenance of a standing army adequate to meet a European attack was not only unnecessary but economically out of the question at the time, and even if the nation grew rich and populous enough to do so, it could not be done "without great oppression of the people." The idea of fortifying the entire coastline the general dismissed as "impracticable; at any rate amazingly expensive." But if major peril should ever appear, there remained a powerful recourse. It could be found in a "well-organized" militia. "The militia of this country," as the general said elsewhere, "must be considered as the palladium of our security and the first effective resort in case of hostility."

After all of Washington's wartime strictures on the conduct of the militia, this willingness to put the ultimate burden of national defense upon the citizen soldiers was to puzzle later students. Only long afterward was it pointed out—by John McAuley Palmer, who in 1930 rediscovered and first published this letter to Hamilton—that the "well-organized" militia which Washington envisaged would have been something very different from the militia levies of the Revolution. What Washington proposed was something very close to the universal and compulsory, but part-time, military service of the "Swiss system," which the general mentioned in his letter and which survives to this day in Switzerland. Washington began this section of his letter with a sweeping reaffirmation of the radical new military principles which the war had helped to establish:

> It may be laid down as a primary position, and the basis of our system, that every Citizen who enjoys the protection of a free Government, owes not only a proportion of his property, but even of his personal services to the defense of it, and consequently that the Citizens of America (with a few legal and official exceptions) from 18 to 50 years of Age should be borne on the Militia Rolls, provided with uniform Arms, and [be] so far accustomed to the use of them, that the Total strength of the Country might be called forth at a Short Notice on any very interesting Emergency.

This was a long advance over the old militia obligation for purely short-time, local service. Here was the "totalization" of war, even to the word itself. Here was a claim on both the property and the persons of all in the community, who were to be "provided with" (not themselves to provide, as in the old system) the arms of mass warfare and to be subject to mass call by "the Country." And the claim was asserted, interestingly enough, in the name of "free Government."

Washington went on to sketch out in considerable detail what would today be recognized as a universal and compulsory "ready reserve" system. His militia would have been uniformly organized and equipped throughout all the states, would obey uniform codes of training and discipline and meet rigidly specified drill periods, all laid down by the national authority. The general recognized the central difficulty of all mass systems: that among "such a Multitude of people" there would be a great many unsuited to or ill-spared for military service. He met it by reverting to the Massachusetts Minute Men suggesting that, as in their case, those from 18 to 25 be segregated into a front-line corps "always to be held in readiness for service," to be given from a week's to a month's field training every year and perhaps even to be organized under the national rather than the states' control. The remainder would go into a last-ditch reserve; but the young men would become "the Van and flower of the American forces, ever ready for Action and zealous to be employed whenever it may be necessary in the service of their Country." [14]

In his recommendations as to the immediate requirements of a regular establishment Washington is precise, factual and hard-headed. One cannot help feeling that this sketch of a dream army of militiamen is at least tinged with romanticism. His picture of a citizen army "ever ready for Action and zealous to be employed" surely reflects his heightened memories of the glorious days before Boston in '75 rather than his experiences with the variegated militia soldiers of the later years. His proposed militia sytem would have been enormously expensive, onerous upon the individual and unjustifiable by any visible military necessity; it would also, as the problem of the Newburgh officers was doing, have raised difficult issues of the internal balances of power. Washington must have known that there was not the slightest chance of the state and national politicians of 1783 adopting anything of the kind. It is difficult to suspect that very sober statesman of irony; but the plan reads almost like an ironic *reductio ad absurdum* of those great principles of "free Government" upon which his fellow citizens had embarked.

At all events, Washington's army of trained and combat-ready militiamen remained the "army of a dream" only. His real army of Continentals dissolved; in the great wave of reaction which came with the peace, the Congress itself came near to dissolving in absenteeism and disinterest, and amid the disputes as to what should be done and the general want of means with which to do anything, it was impossible

[14] Fitzgerald, *op. cit.,* Vol. 26, p. 374.

to establish even the patently necessary national frontier police force. On June 2, 1784 Congress directed the discharge of all remaining troops in the service of the United States except for "twenty-five privates to guard the stores at Fort Pitt and fifty-five to guard the stores at West Point, with a proportionate number of officers," none to be above the rank of captain. "Standing armies in time of peace," it observed, "are inconsistent with the principles of republican governments." The privateers had, naturally, long since gone out of business and the little national navy had been sold off. It was the end of the first national military system; whatever military provisions were to be made would be left to the states and their militias. The politicians were aware that this could be only a temporary expedient and that some sort of national force would have to be re-created; but that was to take time and much argument.

4.

Time was available, since there remained no important threat from any quarter. But the frontier problem was pressing. On the day after its act disbanding almost the last of the national army, Congress called on Pennsylvania, New Jersey, New York and Connecticut to furnish seven hundred men in all as a stop-gap force to garrison the western posts. They were to be raised from the militias, but they were to be enlisted for twelve months, and they were to be organized into the 1st Regiment, under the control of Henry Knox, the burly bookseller who had become Washington's chief of artillery and, on the abolition of the Boards of War and Admiralty, the nation's first Secretary of War. In due course, the recruits were gathered and shipped westward across the mountains where they were largely forgotten. But in 1787 Congress reaffirmed the establishment of seven hundred men to police the frontier and decreed a three-year term of enlistment.[15]

That was the summer through which the Philadelphia Convention had been laboring upon the new Constitution of the United States. While the 1st Regiment, scattered through its little backwoods log

[15] James Ripley Jacobs, *The Beginning of the U. S. Army, 1783–1812* (Princeton, Princeton University Press, 1947), p. 16.

forts, struggled with the only actual problems of defense then before us, the statesmen pondered the larger issues of permanent military policy. Though the point has not often been noticed, the Constitution was as much a military as a political and economic charter. Shays' Rebellion in Massachusetts (December 1786), led by debt-ridden ex-Continentals, had been an ugly shock and was a significant factor in the calling of the Philadelphia Convention. It had enforced the lesson that "national defense," as John Adams, recalling it, was afterward to write, "is one of the cardinal duties of a statesman." The foreign menaces might be negligible, but after Shays' Rebellion it was clearly necessary to resolve the issue between the "nationalist" and the "federalist" (states' rights) groups as to where the military power of the community was to reside.

The result, like nearly everything else in the Constitution, was to be a compromise. That the Founders were keenly interested in the problem it is impossible to doubt. In the third of the *Federalist Papers* (the first two were of a general and introductory character) Jay laid down the dictum that "among the many objects to which a wise and free people find it necessary to direct their attention, that of providing for their *safety* seems to be the first"; and this with the next six numbers were devoted to questions of external defense and protection against internal violence. Numbers 23 to 29 inclusive and Number 41 return to these subjects, and there are numerous other references to them throughout the papers. In his summary and final plea for ratification in the concluding Number 85, Hamilton's last word to the opposition is a warning against the hazards of "anarchy, civil war, a perpetual alienation of the States from each other, and perhaps the military despotism of a successful demagogue."

The problem was to provide for an effective defense against both foreign war and domestic upheaval without trenching too far upon the jealous sovereignty of the states or rousing the universal fear and loathing of irresponsible standing armies. The solution, as embodied in the Constitution, was balanced as nicely as were the political and economic clauses of that document. The national government was given power to maintain standing armies, but only under certain restrictions; the states were confirmed in their control of their militias which were considered the ultimate backbone of defense; and the people (under the Second Amendment) were confirmed in their right to bear arms, which preserved their final power over both national and state governing authorities.

A politically responsible President replaced the hereditary monarch as commander-in-chief. The first power (and duty) of Congress was: "To lay and collect Taxes, Duties, Imposts and Excises, to pay the Debts and provide for the common Defense and general Welfare of the United States." Defense, it is to be noted, came before general welfare. To provide for the common defense, Congress was empowered to declare war and issue letters of marque; to raise and support armies; to provide and maintain a navy; to provide for the calling out of the militia to execute the laws, suppress insurrections and repel invasions; to provide for "organizing, arming, and disciplining, the Militia, and for governing such Part of them as may be employed in the Service of the United States." This would have been a fairly sweeping grant of military power except for two provisos. Borrowing from the British Mutiny Acts, the Constitution limited Army appropriations to no more than two years (interestingly enough, there was no similar limitation on naval appropriations); while there was reserved to the states the right of appointing the militia officers and "the Authority of training the Militia according to the discipline prescribed by Congress." Militarily, no less than politically, it was to be a dual system. In effect, it was to be made into a triple system by the Second Amendment: "A well regulated Militia, being necessary to the security of a free state, the right of the people to keep and bear Arms, shall not be infringed" —a provision which in the military sphere had an effect not unlike that of the Tenth Amendment in the political when it reserved all powers, not delegated, to the states "or to the people."

The intended results seem obvious. The warmaking power and its concomitants would remain with the national government; in peace it would have power to provide such regular troops as were necessary for guard and police duty, but the two-year clause would prevent the creation of a great, vested military interest and make it possible to destroy a regular establishment which seemed to threaten "the liberties of the people." In times of serious emergency the state troops would be the principal reliance and the states would thus retain their control over national policy. This arrangement, as Hamilton pointed out in *The Federalist,* "will not only lessen the call for military establishments, but if circumstances should at any time oblige the government to form an army [that is, a national, regular army] of any magnitude, that army can never be formidable to the liberties of the people while there is a large body of citizens, little if at all inferior to them in discipline and the use of arms, who stand ready to defend their own rights." This curious intimation that the trained militia might find its function not in assisting in the national defense but in defending the people from the defenders whom the national government might have to raise, suggests how far the underlying dilemmas had been left unresolved. Nor did the Second Amendment, with its seeming *non sequitur*—guaranteeing the right to bear arms to the people because a "well-regulated Militia," in which the people took little interest, was necessary—really clarify matters. The Founders sought to balance military, as they did political, power between people, states and nation; but in the military as in the political field they wisely left the outcome of the shifts and power struggles which might ensue to be decided by the future.

They could more easily do so since any question of a major war was at the time academic; while it was plain, as Washington had pointed out, that if a serious war danger should materialize the nation's first and best defense would be on the sea. The authors of the Constitution were as familiar with the concepts and significance of sea power as if they had all sat for Captain Mahan's lectures at the Naval War College a century later. And the apparatus of sea warfare carried few of the political implications surrounding land armaments. Where Congress was empowered to "raise and support Armies" (under the two-year limit on Army appropriations), it was empowered "to provide and maintain a Navy," with no limitation. A navy was a semi-permanent institution; it took time to "provide" ships, and once built they remained in existence whether in active commission or laid up. The withholding of appropriations could not have as definitive an effect as in the case of army units. But above all, a navy by its nature could not usually intervene in domestic politics or be used for the suppression of liberty ashore. It was, as Madison observed in *The Federalist,* a fortunate circumstance that "maritime strength" would be our principal "source of security against danger from abroad." For it followed that "the batteries most capable of repelling foreign enterprises on our safety are happily such as can never be turned by a perfidious government against our liberties." The naval clause, he noted, had awakened no such opposition as was directed against nearly every other part of the Constitution; and it was finally accepted with comparatively little argument.

The result was a military policy which in its fundamentals was to rule in the United States for well over a century. The primary defense against major war would be on the sea, to be supported (a measure soon added) by the fortification of the principal ports and the naval bases and dockyards which they contained. A national, regular Army, professionally led and raised by voluntary enlistment but kept to the lowest possible limits, would provide for policing the frontiers and meeting such minor emergencies as were to be apprehended from the Indians or from our Canadian and Spanish neighbors. The states would maintain their universal and theoretically trained militias; these would provide local contingents to reinforce the regulars on the frontier when necessary. They would also maintain internal order and supply a reserve from which large national armies could, should the need ever arise, be recruited. A populace guaranteed in its right to bear arms (though not, interestingly enough, in its right to vote) would stand as a kind of balance behind the whole system. It seems a rational answer, under all the circumstances, to the actual military problems of the day. But it left a great deal unsettled.

Most obviously, it left unsettled the question of what constituted a "well-regulated" militia. The new Federal government tackled this matter with promptness. In 1790 Henry Knox, continued in his old post as Secretary of War in Washington's new Cabinet, produced his plan for a tightly-controlled national militia system, based on the ideas Washington had laid down seven years before and strikingly prophetic of modern military reserve systems. It would have enrolled all males from 18 to 60, but it would have segregated those from 18 through 20 into an "advance corps" (the old Minute Men) which was to be formed into light infantry companies, get thirty days' camp training every year and provide an immediately available reserve. They would then pass into a "main corps," subject to only four muster days a year, until at 45 they would retire among the gaffers, callable only in extreme local emergency. But the state politicians "execrated" this proposal for what would have amounted to a Federal reserve; it was immediately involved in the rising political struggle between the Federalists and the Jeffersonians. When a bill embodying it was finally brought up in March 1792 it was promptly eviscerated; the result, adopted on May 6, was "the notorious Militia Act of 1792."

This laid down—except for slaves, other colored men and Indians —the universal principle: "Every free, able-bodied, white, male citizen of the respective States" between 18 and 45 should, with certain minor exemptions, "be enrolled in the militia by the captain of the company within whose bounds such citizen shall reside." Having thus evoked a colossal mass of soldiery, the act went on to organize and equip it, with the most meticulous detail, into another "army of a dream" more visionary than Washington's. It was to be armed by the simple expedient of requiring every man to provide his own weapons. The act was specific on this, even down to the "two spare flints" and the rounds of ammunition (twenty-four in the case of the musketmen and twenty for the riflemen) with which each should equip himself. But it said nothing as to how this program was to be financed or enforced. It was specific again on the tables of organization up through brigades and divisions and on the number of general and staff officers to be appointed, but under the Constitution it had to leave the actual appointments to the state governors. The act was silent as to how this force was to be mobilized; but the point was met three years later (after the excitement of the Whiskey Rebellion) by an act providing for "the calling out of the militia" by the President. It stipulated that no one called by the national authority should be compelled to serve more than three months after reaching "the place of rendezvous" in any one year "nor more than in due rotation with every other able-bodied man of the same rank." Like selective service, of which the Minute Men were an early example, rotation is another device for spreading equitably a military obligation which rests upon all but which can in practice be exacted only from a few. It is interesting to note the appearance of the principle in 1795, a century and a half before it reappeared under the same name in the Korean War. But its significance in 1795 is simply as an indication of how far the militia was regarded as purely a local or stop-gap force for minor fracases. Washington's and Knox's concept of a national militia, trained and organized as a mobilizable reserve for major war, was inacceptable under the conditions and politics of the period.

Within fifteen years the Militia Act of 1792 had produced, as Palmer noted, an army greater than the largest ever massed against Napoleon himself. The state of Maryland, with a white population of less than 240,000 (equivalent to about three present-day Congressional districts) carried three major generals and fifty regiments of infantry on its rolls; the total for all the states included no less than 306 general officers, 1,033 infantry regiments and an aggregate strength of 647,827. That it was an army largely of paper and politics goes without saying.

For better or worse, the Militia Act of 1792 completed the theoretical structure of military policy. The practical problems—represented chiefly by the Indians of the Ohio country—had meanwhile been growing more and more urgent and unpleasant. The tiny 1st Regiment of regulars, numbering hardly a quarter of what Washington in 1783 had considered a minimum, was wholly insufficient; and the device of reinforcing it with the frontier militias was leading to lamentable results. The militia, when it turned up, proved to be a scratch lot of boys, invalids and substitutes, rather than the experienced woodsmen who had been expected; while their large want of discipline added to their unreliability as soldiers. As a result of one disaster after another, the regulars were repeatedly reorganized and grudgingly enlarged. In 1791 a 2nd Regiment was added, while a new idea was embodied in the same act. In addition to calling out the state militias, the President was authorized to raise six-month, volunteer "levies" directly by national authority. Upton considered this the beginning (though there was surely much precedent in the Continentals and earlier volunteer forces) of the system of volunteering directly for national service by which we were to meet all our major war crises down to 1917. The act also vested in the President the appointment of all commissioned officers in the "levies," a principle which, if it had been maintained, would have had an important effect on later military history. But this was too much for the state interests to accept; and an act of a few years later (1803) returned the appointive power, even for these national levies, to the governors. It was a power and a patronage to which the governors thereafter firmly clung.

In August 1794 "Mad Anthony" Wayne, the competent hero of Stony Point, with an adequate force of regulars as well as of militia, disposed of the Indian menace at the Battle of Fallen Timbers on the Maumee; this soon spelled the end for the small British garrisons which had remained in the fur trading posts, and peace descended on the Northwest. But by that time events much greater than the Indian raids were shaking the earth, at the same time bringing the problems of American defense into new and more ominous perspective.

5.

On a hot and violent July day in 1789 a Paris mob had stormed the Bastille. Already the winds of new doctrine and new methods sown by the American Revolution were being reaped in the whirlwinds of revolutionary France. Already the new spirit of popular, fanatic nationalism was overturning the ancient political systems; already the new energies of popular, democratic warfare were not only sweeping away the old, professional royal armies; they were also giving the first grim hints of that totalitarian military dictatorship in which—from the days of Napoleon to those of Hitler, Stalin, or Mao Tse-tung—"people's democracy" seems fated to end.

War came in Europe, in a desultory way, in 1792; by the spring of 1793 it had brought to France a colossal draft of 300,000 men and a Committee of Public Safety exercising dictatorial powers. By August it had brought the driving Carnot to the Ministry of War and the famous *levée en masse,* making its total claim over the lives, the property and even the thoughts of every Frenchman in the service of the unitary state.

The young men shall fight; the married men shall forge weapons
and transport supplies; the women will make tents and clothes
and will serve in the hospitals; the children will make up old linen
into lint; the old men will have themselves carried into the public
squares to rouse the courage of the fighting men, to preach hatred
of kings and the unity of the Republic.[16]

This was conscription, as universal and all-devouring as the administrative mechanisms and economic foundations of the time could make
it. It was a far cry from the efforts of the Continental Congress to raise
its free-born troops by high pay and bounties, or from Washington's
gentlemanly vision of a universally enrolled militia. Today it seems
something very ugly indeed; and there have been many to echo Nickerson's bitterness when he speaks of the way "in which men dedicated
to 'Liberty' perpetrated this greatest possible assault upon the liberties
of mankind." Yet one cannot so easily escape either the logic or the
responsibilities of history. It was the Americans who had cracked the
shell, the shell of the eighteenth-century military system, out of which
this monster sprang.

As early as December 1789 a committee report to the Assembly had
laid it down "as an axiom, that in France every citizen must be a
soldier and every soldier a citizen, or we shall never have a constitution." But what else had the American statesmen, with their rejection
of standing armies and their emphasis on the militia, been saying? The
military system proposed in this report—calling for a regular army to
guard the frontiers, a reserve of trained militia and a home guard and
general backstop of "armed citizens ready to defend their homes and
freedom"—bears an obviously close resemblance to the military system which the Federalist politicians in America were at that time trying to work out. In Revolutionary France a trained militia was "the
palladium of the Constitution" just as to Washington it had been the
"palladium of our security." In America, every able-bodied male was
theoretically required to provide himself with arms; in France, it was
argued that a man should be "recognized as an active citizen only to

---

[16] Hoffman Nickerson, *The Armed Horde, 1793–1939* (New York, Putnam's,
1940), p. 64.

the extent that he has procured weapons." The ideas out of which the *levée en masse* arose were replicas of those which had shaped Washington's proposals for a permanent establishment of ten years before; and the conscription of 1793, ugly as its visage was and is, serves to show where in any time of great national crisis those ideas were bound to lead.

The Federalists of Washington's and Adams' administrations did not like what it showed; they liked even less the demonstrations soon to follow of the tremendous military potential latent in democratic nationalism. At Hondschoote, near Dunkerque, in the fall of 1793, the raw French levies beat back the allied professionals in an action not unlike that of Lexington-Concord, but on a far greater scale. The French Revolution became an ominous military fact. It presented no immediate threat to the new nation beyond the Atlantic; but the United States was still very much a part of the Atlantic world, and that world might be less stable a system than it had seemed. The new American government looked more seriously than before to its military responsibilities, and in the spring of 1794 there was a sudden spate of military legislation.

The most celebrated of the 1794 acts was that authorizing the construction of six frigates, four of forty-four guns and two of thirty-six, which represents the real beginning of the United States Navy. Ostensibly, it had nothing to do with the war in Europe; according to the preamble, the ships were to protect our commerce from "the depredations committed by the Algerine corsairs" in the Mediterranean. The actual reasons were more complex. The frigate bill was accompanied by acts to fortify the principal harbors; to create a corps of regular "artillerists and engineers," with a strength of nearly 1,000, to man these defenses; and to establish four government arsenals in which to accumulate a stock of weapons. No doubt the great Federalist shipping interests desired protection against the Algerines, but those pirate galleys were scarcely likely to descend on Boston, New York or the Chesapeake.

It was not the Barbary pirates who provided the impetus for these martial measures; immediately it was the British and behind them the whole problem of how, amid the impending tramplings of the European giants, we were to protect our interests and stay out of the war. "Citizen" Genet had already tried to make the United States a base for French operations; he was dismissed and Congress adopted our first neutrality act in June 1794. With the British there still remained the unsettled issues over the northwestern frontier; while as they turned, according to their custom, to apply their sea power to the strangulation of the continental enemy, a new crop of difficulties arose. They were soon engaged upon the suppression of our lucrative war trade with France, upon the capture and condemnation of our ships and cargoes and upon the impressment of American seamen. In 1794 the Algerines were little more than a convenient pretext for the Federalist answer to these much greater issues—which was to get a little military strength in hand both to appease domestic clamor and make some weight on the international stage, but meanwhile to send John Jay to London to negotiate a treaty settlement.

Reasonable as this may seem, it raised most of the problems of foreign and military policy over which we have passionately argued ever since. To the Federalists, revolutionary France was the real enemy, but it was the British who were interfering with our interests— a situation like that which was to face Wilson as he struggled with the British blockade in 1915 and 1916. The frigate bill, like Franklin Roosevelt's gestures of "hemisphere defense" in 1940, had nothing to do, ostensibly, with the European war; but it was violently assailed by the "isolationists" of the late eighteenth century as tending to involve us in the struggle. History may never exactly repeat herself, but she is surely repetitious. The six-frigate bill led to a bitter debate. A national navy would be in some sense a substitute for the national, standing army which the Federalists had thought necessary as a "cement" for their centralized government. The bill was backed by the New Englanders and the seaport towns to the southward, not only because it would put some protection behind their commerce, but because it would help their shipbuilding, shipfitting and iron-founding interests. It would be a source of government contracts for what was then our principal industrial complex. It was opposed in the South and the back country not only because it implied a "standing navy" that might drag us into war, but because it meant the imposition of taxes to subsidize the seaboard and the industrialists.[17]

No one imagined that six frigates could challenge the great fleets of line-of-battle ships maintained in Europe. But they could be a make-weight in the power struggle. With even a small naval force in the Western Atlantic, as Hamilton had put it, "a price would be set not only on our friendship but on our neutrality." Hamilton, a native of the West Indies, no doubt saw what hostages those rich colonies offered to the United States whenever Europe should be deeply embroiled. His concept was not unlike that with which the Kaiser's Grand Admiral, von Tirpitz, over a century later, developed the German High Seas Fleet as a make-weight or "blackmail" force. But the back country was not interested in such subtleties of high politics; the frigate bill barely survived its first test in the House, and was enacted only after being amended to provide that the program would be suspended if peace were achieved with the Algerines. Two years later peace of a sort was achieved with the Algerines; but the Federalists after a bitter struggle managed to save three of the six ships. "To secure respect to a Neutral Flag," Washington observed in his message of December 1796, "requires a Naval force.... This may even prevent the necessity of going to War, by discouraging belligerent Powers from committing such violations of the rights of the Neutral party, as may first or last, leave no other option."

The belligerent powers were not easily discouraged, however. If the British were arrogant, the French social revolutionaries were insulting, and the spring of 1798 brought the quasi-war with the French Directory. John Adams managed by skill and good sense (not unaided by the threat of a new, rising "republican" party opposition) to keep it within the bounds of a kind of guerila conflict on the sea lanes. Nevertheless, it provided a further stimulus for our nascent military system. The first three frigates—*United States, Constitution,* and *Constellation*—were launched in 1797, while work was resumed and pressed on the remaining three (*Congress,* one of the 44's, was redesigned as a 38). The fortification program was enlarged and

[17] Harold and Margaret Sprout, *The Rise of American Naval Power* (Princeton, Princeton University Press, 1939), pp. 28 f.

carried forward by the seaboard communities with an enthusiasm (since these were defenses against the Jacobin subversives) which had not been manifest four years before, when it had been a question of possible war with Britain.

There was a host of other military measures: to raise a temporary army of 10,000 men with the Ex-President at their head; to enlarge the regular Army, to create a separate Navy Department, to supply weapons for the militia, to build 74-gun line-of-battle ships and so on. By 1800, with Bonaparte, who at least was no Jacobin, in command in France, the crisis passed; recruiting was suspended and most of these programs evaporated. But they left a certain residue. The masonry of the forts remained. So did the separate Navy Department and all six of the frigates. The regular Army was initially set at four infantry regiments and other troops; it was still a tiny force, but it was beginning to develop from a backwoods frontier police into a professional military service.

There were no less permanent results of a different kind. The appropriations for artillery and muskets had accelerated the development of the munitions and metallurgical industries. As a result of contracts dating from 1794, Brown and Francis, "owners of the Hope Furnace in Rhode Island," had been casting and boring 24-pounder and 32-pounder cannon for the fortresses as well as 24-pounders for the frigates; Samuel Hughes, owner of a Maryland "furnace," was producing numbers of these and smaller sizes. The Springfield Armory, established in 1794 for the government manufacture of muskets, had been slow in getting into its stride (what is now called "lead time" is no new phenomenon) but by the latter part of 1799 it had worked up to a capacity of over 5,000 muskets a year. This achievement was ascribed, significantly, to the fact that the "labor saving machines" which had been installed were working "to great advantage." [18]

The machine was coming to the support of war, and war was helping to subsidize the beginnings of the machine age. It was the government's demand for muskets at the time of the quasi-war which led Eli Whitney, the farm boy who had run a two-man nail factory during the

[18] Reports of the Secretary of War (McHenry), American State Papers, Vol. I, pp. 123 and 131.

Revolution, to apply for the contract which is usually considered to mark the birth of assembly-line mass production in the United States. Whitney was, of course, no more a militarist or "merchant of death" than, say, Henry Ford. At the time he was facing financial collapse as a result of the very success of his famous invention of a practicable cotton gin. In searching for a means to recover, he had conceived the whole system of ideas underlying the development of modern machine industry. He saw that technology had reached a point at which it might be possible to substitute accurately-made power tools for the skilled handcraftsmen who were so scarce in America. He also saw that to do this would require a division of operations; interchangeability of parts; final manufacture by assembly rather than hand finishing; and a volume market to sustain the high initial investment. Only one thing was needed to translate these conclusions into a successful industrial operation—a suitable product.

The government's demand for weapons was the perfect answer. In that day, only government could provide both the financing and the volume market. Whitney would have contracted to make almost any article which the government required in quantity, but muskets were the principal need. At a time when contracts were being let to other gunmakers for lots of a few hundred at the most, Whitney calmly offered to produce 10,000 stand of arms within two years. He was to have his own troubles with "lead time" and it was actually to take him nearer ten years than two to complete the contract. But finally he did so, thereby laying the foundations not only of modern war industry but of the modern industrial system as a whole.[19]

[19] No drawings or useful descriptions of Whitney's gun-making machines survive; only a letter by a ten-year old nephew who reported that "there is a drilling machine and a boureing machine to bour berels and a screw machine and too great large buildings, one nother shop and a stocking shop to stocking guns in, a blacksmith shop and a trip hammer shop and five hundred guns done." Jeannette Mirsky and Allan Nevins, *The World of Eli Whitney* (New York, Macmillan, 1952), *passim*.

There was, however, another early application of mass-production techniques, also in response to a military demand. This was the elder Brunel's system for the mass manufacture of pulley blocks for the Royal Navy. Models of Brunel's machines are in the Royal Naval Museum at Greenwich. Though carelessly preserved and (in 1953) relegated to a dark corner, they are perhaps as significant as any other exhibit in the collection.

Whitney also helped to preserve the function of the private entrepreneur in the great coming development of the war supply business. In the actual raising and fighting of troops, private enterprise had
long since given way to the government officer and administrative
bureaucracy. To that extent, war had been effectively nationalized or
"socialized." The appearance of a machine-powered war industry,
with its large capital requirements which only government was in a
position to meet and with government as its major if not its sole cus-
tomer, was an obvious invitation to extend this process of nationalization to the production of weapons as well as the provision of the
soldiery. The Springfield Armory was government owned and operated; so were the Navy yards; so was the second musket factory soon
set up at Harpers Ferry. These were also efficient establishments; also
installing labor-saving machinery and achieving unexpected results in
production totals. It seems not impossible that a government monopoly
might have been asserted over the whole area of war production.
Whitney himself was to have his serious troubles with officials who
wished to retain control over weapons manufacture in the government arsenals and thereby in their own hands. Had a government arms
monopoly been established, it would, to say the least, have had a
considerable effect upon our later industrial development.

When Jefferson took office in 1801, he found the government
already in possession, not only of the musket factories but of a large
number of iron mines and foundries acquired to supply the raw
materials. Jefferson, the agrarian, was perhaps the last man who
would have intentionally turned back a potentially vast industrial
development to the urban capitalists; but he also belonged to the
eighteenth century and this situation alarmed him. "Whether," he
advised the Congress, "this method of supplying what may be wanted
will be most advisable, or that of purchasing at market, where competition brings everything to its proper level of price and quality, is for
the Legislature to decide." [20] From that time on, the Legislature's
decision has, in general, been overwhelmingly in favor of the private
entrepreneur; but without Whitney's demonstration of the ability of

[20] ASP, Vol. I, p. 156.

private enterprise to meet large-scale demands, and of "the market's" capacity to produce cheaply at adequate standards of quality, the result might have been different.

It might also have been different if war production had bulked as large in the development of our own economy as it was to do in that of most of the other major powers throughout the Industrial Revolution of the nineteenth century. Except for the brief forcing period during the Civil War, the munitions, military supply and military shipbuilding industry was never more than a small part of our total industrial development. We were to maintain no great armies or navies; not until the late '80's were we even to begin to establish what might properly be called a munitions industry, and we did not have to struggle with problems of state-industry relationships like those presented by the Krupps in Germany, the Armstrongs in Britain, the Schneiders in France or the Mitsuis in Japan. The other powers were to find these problems difficult. We were scarcely aware of their existence. We certainly were not in 1800 when Federalism fell; when Jefferson, the Democratic-Republicans and the hinterlands came into power with a new century, and coincidentally with the brief interval of peace in Europe between the wars of the Revolution and those of Napoleon.

Again there was a new military policy—one which has received the scorn of many later critics, but which was not so illogical as it often seemed. It may be summarized as a policy of cutting all forms of military expenditure to the bone, of retiring into a continental position which was in fact impregnable as long as the great European quarrel preoccupied our only potential enemies, but in the meanwhile revitalizing and reorganizing the underlying military potential so that it would be available should need again arise. It is sometimes forgotten that Jefferson, who cut the already small regular Army in half, also founded the United States Military Academy and was the true father of our whole system of military education. It is forgotten that, while he planned to lay up the sea-going Navy, he kept the gun foundries and musket factories at full blast, and at least tried to reorganize the militia.

Jefferson, like his predecessors and successors, could not reorganize the militia. But in pursuing his basic aim, which was "to keep the country out of war" as well as to save money, he did considerably strengthen the underlying military base; when war finally came in 1812 the nation was at least capable of an effort (however bunglingly mobilized) much greater than it could have dreamed of making in 1800. It is an ironic reflection that the Jeffersonian policy failed less because of its military weakness than because of its military strength. The one factor it had failed to provide against was the bellicosity of the Jeffersonians. When the Westeners, in their desire to take Canada while Britain was otherwise occupied, forced the issue, it was the existence of the defensive forts, the accumulated stocks of cannon, muskets and ammunition in the arsenals, even the celebrated defensive coastal gunboats, which led to the mistaken belief that (as Henry Clay put it) "the militia of Kentucky are alone competent to place Montreal and Upper Canada at your feet."

It is ironic that Jefferson, believing in a passive foreign policy, should have begun his administration with an act of military power that was not without effect in promoting subsequent martial ardors. This time it was not the Algerines but the Tripolitanians who provided the incitation; and Jefferson strained his constitutional authority to order the Navy into the Mediterranean to repel their insults. The affair was to find a strangely exact echo over a century later when Woodrow Wilson—a pacifically-inclined Democratic President, just elected to replace the Republican heirs of federalism—acted with possibly extra-constitutional vigor against Mexico by ordering the occupation of Vera Cruz. In 1914 Mexico mattered no more than did the Barbary States in 1801 under the gathering shadows of European general war. But each episode helped to promote the martial enthusiasms and the military establishments which were to contribute to the nation's involvement in the approaching tragedy. The naval war with Tripoli forged the young American Navy into a combat service and gave it the leaders, discipline and tradition which were to make it our most effective arm in 1812. Mexico, in the 1914 and 1916 operations, performed a somewhat similar service for our armed forces.

The great war in Europe was resumed in 1803. Jefferson had profited miraculously in the meanwhile by playing the European empires against each other to achieve the Louisiana Purchase, the greatest territorial acquisition ever made without war, and one with the deepest impact on the internal politics and economics of the beneficiary state. While the Northeast fumed at this potential threat to its own power and influence, Jefferson could use the officer corps of the tiny regular Army as a source of competent, responsible and thoroughly loyal Federal agents not only to take over but to explore the new domain. In a world crawling with land speculators, local politicians and adventurers grinding every conceivable kind of ax, it was a help to be able to call on Army officers like Merriweather Lewis and William Clark, like Zebulon M. Pike (the younger Zebulon, who had come up as a company officer in the elder Zebulon's frontier regiment) and others, as well as on the enlisted regulars who made up the backbones of their exploration parties. Minuscule as it was and long before the effects of the military engineering courses at West Point could appear, the Army was beginning to provide that supply of trained administrators and technicians, capable and disinterested, to which the nation was to owe so much through all its later years.

But in face of the European War, Jeffersonian policy remained strictly isolationist and defensive. With Louisiana, including of course New Orleans and the assured navigation of the Mississippi, in American hands, this was the obvious course. The Army had been reduced to rather less than a minimum. The sea-going Navy should be put out of commission; it was useless as well as dangerous to attempt to enforce the neutral rights of our commerce against the great European naval powers. The defense of our commercial and naval ports could properly be left to seacoast fortifications and to the celebrated gunboats.

These were small, single-masted craft, the earlier ones only forty-five feet in length, armed with a single gun in the bow and manned by no more than eighteen or twenty men. Beside the towering three-deckers of the time they were patently absurd. The Jefferson administration ordered over 160 of them; they were never of any practical utility and have been objects of ridicule ever since. Yet they were not quite so ridiculous as they have seemed, if one accepts the Jeffersonian policy of avoiding any entanglement in the European War and simply providing a coastal defense against possible European incursions. The gunboats were actually a product of experience—our own experience off Algeria and Tripoli, where we had been waging a coastal war in which such types had proved valuable. The heavy ships, designed for fighting pelagic battles to establish the "command of the sea," were too deep of draft to work inshore. In Tripoli, light craft were a necessity and actually did much of the fighting. And in nearly every war since then, while the "battlewagons" might determine the broad question of "control," it has always been discovered (and usually belatedly) that light craft of shallow draft, able to work close in, were an essential requirement.

The gunboats really represented a naval equivalent of the militia. It was intended that normally they would be laid up, rather like the coastal fortifications, but would be available for instant manning in the case of coastal emergency. In any event, they were to accomplish little or nothing toward hindering the British incursions into the Chesapeake in 1813 and 1814. But neither were the ocean-going frigates, the Army nor the militia system. The gunboat idea may have been militarily unsound. It was not illogical under a policy which was willing to abandon the sea and its trade in order to concentrate on the development and expansion of the boundless West, leaving only a rear guard of citizen soldiery as a protection against any possible invasion from Europe.

Jeffersonian isolationism even considered the possibility of laying up the entire ocean-going Navy in dead storage, as it were, under the roof of one vast covered dock to be built on the shores of the Potomac. But all the while the great war in Europe was spreading in its scope and destructiveness; and the maintenance of American neutrality was becoming more and more dubious. In the summer of 1807 H.M.S. *Leopard* coolly attacked the new American frigate *Chesapeake* off the Virginia Capes, forced her to strike with a few lethal broadsides and took off several of her people as subject to British impressment. There was more passionate enthusiasm for war with Britain that summer than there was to be in 1812; and Jefferson called for a cautious increase in the Army as well as for other measures designed to provide some semblance of combat force. At the same time he sought to establish a strict neutrality by calling, in December, for the famous embargo act, intended not only to "keep us out of war" but to force the British and the French into such modifications of their trade restrictions as would enable us to stay out of it. The crisis passed. But it left behind it the act of April 1808, appropriating $200,000 annually for arming and equipping "the whole body of the militia of the United States . . . by and on account of the United States."

The armament of the militia, as well as its organization, thus became a Federal responsibility. But neither the constitutional nor the military consequences of this seemed important at the time. Jefferson, accepting the failure of the embargo, replaced it with the more moderate Non-Intercourse Act, signed just before he left office. Madison became President in March 1809. It was the year of Friedland, when Napoleon was to rise to his apogee of power and menace, and when the later Lord Wellington was to form Britain's desperate "peripheral" defense in Portugal. None of this need greatly have concerned the isolated new power beyond the Atlantic, which had already largely surrendered the maritime rights of commerce—the one factor which seemed directly to involve us in the struggle. The danger came, not from the tramplings of the belligerents upon our rights, but from the desires of our own expansionists and imperialists to profit by the embarrassment of the great contestants. The emotional and propagandist pressures behind the War of 1812 were generated by the British impressment of our seamen and the British interference with our commerce; the more material pressures were generated by the lust of the Western communities for Canada and the lust of the Southern communities for Spanish Florida. Thus we slid down into what was essentially a land war for territorial expansion under the impression that we were defending our maritime interests—an impression which the major maritime interests themselves never shared.

The declaration of war, long foreseen, was finally voted on June 18, 1812—just as Napoleon was setting in motion across the Niemen an army of some 600,000 men, by far the greatest armed force assembled under a single command since the statistically clouded times of the ancients. Neither Madison nor the War Hawks in Congress, of course, had any idea of getting involved in operations on such a scale as that. There were no more than four or five thousand British troops in the whole of Canada, and there was virtually nothing except a few Indian tribes in the Spanish Floridas. The underlying object of the war was quickly to snaffle up some unguarded real estate while the opportunity offered, meanwhile humbling the British pretensions upon the seas and causing enough loss and annoyance to British maritime commerce to exact a more respectful treatment from the Royal Navy.

With the forts and gunboats to defend our coasts, with the stocks of cannon and muskets which had been piling up in the arsenals, with the huge militia organization available on paper, the task looked easy. A report of December 1811 on our war potential was enthusiastic: "Upon the best authority, we state the [number of] furnaces, forges and bloomeries in the United States to be 530. The art of boring cannon . . . is so well understood" that an inspector had reported he had never had to reject a gun because of faulty bore. "We may have lead from mines in our country to any amount." There was ample sulphur in store and the resources of saltpeter were "inexhaustible." There were powder mills in every state. Springfield and Harpers Ferry were turning out 20,000 stand of small arms a year and private manufacture nearly 12,000 more. In addition to the weapons then in the hands of troops or on shipboard, there were some thousands of iron and brass pieces in store, including (in the Navy return) "two 26-pound brass cannon, trophies taken from the Tripolitans and intended as a present to the Bashaw of Tripoli." [21]

The organization to utilize these military resources was another matter. On the day war was declared the Navy numbered seventeen men-of-war. There were the three 44-gun frigates—*Constitution, President* and *United States*—and the three 36's, *Constellation, Congress* and *Chesapeake*. Two of the latter were out of commission and were not to be made ready until the end of the year. There was a miscellaneous group of smaller sloops, brigs and schooners, down to *Viper,* of only twelve guns. Small as it was, however, the Navy was a regular and professional service which, in commerce raiding, diversion and the two decisive actions on Lake Erie and Lake Champlain was to earn most of the glory which the war was to afford. The Army was in

[21] ASP, Vol. I, p. 303.

worse case, which was unfortunate, since what was contemplated was in fact a local land war. A return of 1805 had shown a total regular force of 2,732 men, scattered through no less than forty-three posts from Fort Sumner, Maine, to New Orleans and from Michilimackinack to Fort Wilkinson, Georgia. The largest single aggregate were the 375 men at New Orleans; the next largest, the 220 at Fort Detroit, while the smallest consisted of three men (one staff officer, one infantry lieutenant and one artillery private) at Fredericktown, Maryland. In the spring of 1808, after the excitement of the *Leopard* affair and the embargo, Congress authorized a sizeable increase of 6,000 men, and the War Hawks secured in January 1812 an authorization for ten more regiments. This brought the authorized strength to nearly 36,000. But in July 1812, when war had been declared, the actual strength stood at only 6,744, no better concentrated than before. For serious operations, there remained the militia.

The returns in the year 1813, covering mainly the years 1811 and 1812, show the magnificent total of 719,449 men and officers comprising the militia. But the condition of this imposing force is indicated by the fact that New York, for example, reporting fourteen major generals and nearly 76,000 infantry rank and file, also reported that she had on hand only 39,000 muskets. Virginia reported 60,000 infantry, excluding officers, and 14,000 muskets. The Legislature of Kentucky (which even in that day rejoiced in nine major generals and twenty brigadiers, the number of colonels being unstated) succinctly put the basic problem of the militia when it memorialized Congress in February 1812. The mobilization of this force, it observed, "would certainly present the spectacle of a perfect militia of the whole, which no age or country ever witnessed, and, most probably in a country or government like ours, never will be seen. And if a general draught were made, to be equal it must be impartial; and how many who would have neither arms, accoutrements or discipline, would thus be designated?" [22] It was a question which the Pentagon in 1955 was still struggling to answer.

But there was no time in the summer of 1812 to deal with such

[22] ASP, Vol. I, p. 318; the returns are from ASP I, pp. 176, 303, 320, 530.

subtleties. The Congress endeavored to meet the crisis of its own creation by enlisting an enormously expanded "regular" (though temporary) army, meanwhile relying on militia calls and volunteering to fill the gaps. The results were not good. Despite big bounties and land grants, the establishment of some fifty "regular" regiments where there had been but five or ten before did not produce either the trained officers or disciplined rank and file associated with the regular service. Led by superannuated and generally incompetent veterans of the Revolution (the only command material available) mixed detachments of the old regulars, volunteers, the newly enlisted "regular" forces and scratch levies of the militia, set out to conquer Canada. The British professionals opposing them were few in number; they did, however, have the powerful aid of their Indian allies, and in the end the Americans got nowhere. Only Oliver Hazard Perry's naval victory on Lake Erie in 1813 saved Detroit and prevented the British from putting the shoe of invasion on the other foot; only Macdonough's similar victory on Lake Champlain in 1814 stopped the British counterattack down the Champlain-Hudson waterway.

Time and training were to make the new regulars and their militia allies into an effective force, which could stand and fight a battle like Lundy's Lane to a draw, if not to a victory. A new leadership began to appear in the persons of younger men like Jacob Brown and Winfield Scott. In the South a lanky man already of middle age, his red hair turning to a grey mane—a planter, horse-trader, lawyer and politician who combined the offices of judge of the Superior Court of Tennessee and major general of the state's militia—was to arise suddenly as one of the born military captains of our history. Even his tough backwoods militia was to reveal many of the weaknesses of faintheartedness, indiscipline and premature war weariness which were manifested by their counterparts elsewhere. But under the driving hand and fiercely martial energy of Andrew Jackson they were to perform some remarkable feats in the war against the Creeks in 1812 and 1813; while New Orleans was to give a shattering demonstration of what could be done by raw troops under resolute as well as intelligent command.

But the war produced few Jacksons and very little of the fanatic nationalist spirit which alone can make an undisciplined popular army formidable. Despite the fortifications and the gunboats, a small British naval force roamed the Chesapeake at will during the summer of 1813, finding that not a few of the shore towns preferred to be counted out of the struggle rather than face the costs and pains of repelling the invader. New England was in a state approaching rebellion against the whole enterprise, a situation which revealed the weaknesses in the compromises of 1789 on which our military system had been founded. Massachusetts attempted to refuse the nation's call upon her militia on the ground that her troops could be summoned only to "repel invasion," not to invade another territory. The New Englanders, bitter over the destruction of their commerce first by the embargo and then by the war, took a certain revenge by means of their clandestine commerce with Canada, whereby they helped supply the enemy. Many of the Western militiamen were happy, as they approached the border, to discover in the Constitution a sound legal reason why they should avoid the perils and ardors of going any farther.

Then 1814 dawned, bringing the unexpected collapse of Napoleon and freeing Britain for a real military effort in America—something on which the War Hawks had never calculated. Pakenham's expedition of Peninsula veterans was readied for New Orleans. This was the main thrust; for the British in 1814 had no intention of trying to recapture the lost colonies. If they could take New Orleans, with its throttling control over the whole huge Mississippi Valley hinterland, they would secure a grip upon the young Republic which would be sufficient. To make matters sure, however, they organized another strong force to advance down the Champlain waterway; while to help this out they prepared a raiding expedition, much more powerful than that of the previous year, to operate in the Chesapeake.

It was only the Navy and Macdonough who saved us from the attack from the North. When the British were already at Plattsburg, the Governor of Vermont sought to withdraw his state forces from the battle, again on the ground that they were constitutionally required only to "repel invasion" and that an invasion of New York, across the lake, was none of Vermont's business. The Vermont troops were

obliged to disobey orders in order to remain in the fight. The raiding
force in the Chesapeake experienced no difficulty in scattering both
the scratch lot of militia and the distracted high command which
sought to defend Washington; they burned the White House, the
unfinished Capitol and other public buildings and drove James and
Dolly Madison to cover in Georgetown. But it was not significant.
Everybody on both sides knew that this was just a raid; while the very
formlessness and chaos of our military administration meant that the
capture of the capital was of little consequence. A week or two later
the British attempted to repeat their performance against Baltimore,
which as a shipping, communications and manufacturing center was
of considerably greater importance. But there the entrenched positions
at Fort McHenry made up for the deficiencies of the militia, and the
attack was broken off. Both sides by that time were trying to write
the peace; in December 1814 it was signed.

Basically, what had happened was that the American expansionists
of 1812 had tried to complete the Revolution by taking Canada and
the Floridas while the European powers were otherwise occupied.
They had failed in this rather modest (if somewhat felonious) aim for
a variety of reasons. The military system they had inherited from the
compromises of 1789—with its dual national and state control, with
its dichotomy of a mass popular base (the militia) and a volunteer,
professional service which actually carried the military burden—
proved unequal to fighting even a small war. The War Hawks had
raised no great sense of *national* unity and resolve with which to
energize a people's war; the professional regulars, on the other hand,
had been cut down to such tiny limits that they lacked the force to
conduct the affair in the manner of the many professional "colonial"
wars of the coming decades. A reasonably effective solution was hammered out under the pressure of experience; but by that time the great
war in Europe had ended and the opportunity had passed. Under the
circumstances, both sides were willing to call it quits. From the American point of view it had been much less than a glorious business; and
it might conceivably have led to some re-examination of the fissures
in the American military structure.

But then there came the famous denouement at New Orleans. The peace had been signed when Pakenham, on January 8, 1815, dressed his ranks and advanced in parade order against Jackson's cotton bales, artillery, entrenched pirates and militiamen and handful of regular troops. As the billowing smoke of the black powder rolled lethally along the lines, it wrote a queer and bloody end to the story which had begun forty years before at Concord and Bunker Hill. Once more a British professional, if not underestimating the "raw militia" before him, then certainly underestimating the strength of the breastworks behind which they lay, was marching up a massed line of battle to the slaughter. Unlike Howe, Pakenham had had many lessons from many fields to teach him better; again unlike Howe, he was to pay for it with his own life, as well as with the lives of one-third of his force, uselessly expended on what by that time had become an impossible military task. Jackson had but seven men killed out of his whole force, but some 2,000 British dead and wounded were laid in terrible windrows before his lines. It was a famous victory. Jackson himself had difficulty in controlling his militia after the battle; and New Orleans was not, perhaps, an unqualified recommendation for the American military system. But it seemed so at the time; and our nation passed into the new peace, the new age, a whole new world, more or less convinced that its military institutions were fundamentally sound. In relation to the actual problems of the day, the temper of the times and the situations confronting us, perhaps they were.

CHAPTER II

The Industrial Revolution

1.

THE Great War was over. Forty years of social, political and military upheaval had at last reached their agonizing end in the tortured dusk and wreck of Waterloo.

In the Atlantic world—and the young United States was still far more intimately a part of that world than it was to be through the ensuing century—peace had been re-established and was to reign substantially for many years. At the same time, the whole shape, impact and significance of war in Western society had been transformed. War, energized and fed by the flames of popular-democratic nationalism, had for a time assumed its ultimate or "ideal" form; it had become total, all-demanding, all-devouring. Pondering this strange fact, Clausewitz, the thoughtful German staff officer, was to produce his theory of "tensions" to explain how war, which had in general been limited and formalized during the eighteenth century, had developed into the appalling juggernaut which it had become under Napoleon. Yet to the question of why political tensions should arise to such extremes, Clausewitz had no very clear answer. Only today do students tend to find it in the fact that war had become nationalized and popularized; it had been converted from a struggle of governments, generally using a paid soldiery, into a struggle of peoples, more and more using government as the agent of their fears, passions and economic interests.

This could not have been apparent in the aftermath of 1815. The tensions of the Napoleonic period sank sharply away into a series of minor, peripheral or colonial conflicts which seldom tapped more than a fraction of the resources of the powers involved. The Napoleonic era left most of the European great powers committed to universal, conscript military systems, but these tended to decay in exemptions and deferments, and the long-service, professional and volunteer force to become the reliance for such military operations as might seem necessary. Britain and the United States reverted almost wholly to the volunteer and professional system; we maintained our swollen militia enrollments, but all reality was rapidly to drain out of them. As always after an exhausting struggle, the old ways, ideas and methods tended to reassert themselves. The military tended, in Vagt's phrase, to become less military and more "militaristic." What was left of the feudal classes resumed their ancient military prerogatives. The Prussian junker houses had looked with disfavor on the army reforms of Scharnhorst and Gneisenau, precisely because the creation of a popular, national army was so likely to end in popular control over national political and economic affairs. The British landed aristocracy reasserted its right to buy Army commissions for its younger sons and so to retain its command of the national armed forces—a claim which was to have lamentable consequences in the Crimea. The code of the "officer and the gentleman" not only preserved paying careers for the sons of the Prussian nobility or the British landed gentry; it operated much farther afield, leading to pistol duels in the American backwoods or enshrining the concepts of chivalric honor, class prejudice and privilege among the young gentlemen pursuing their military studies on the banks of the Hudson above West Point. Despite the mass conscriptions of the Napoleonic era and the achievements of the many brilliant amateur leaders they had produced, there was a general return to the aristocratic and professional concept. The colonial wars of the nineteenth century were to be waged largely by sons of the aristocracy, a few career technicians required to handle the new weapons and methods, and long-service rankers not very different from the men who fought at Minden, Rossbach, Quebec or Saints Passage.

The armies which went to Mexico in 1846 or to the Crimea in 1854 were in some respects closer to those of 1775 than they were to the great hosts mobilized in 1814 and 1815. But nothing is ever quite the same. If the democratic revolution in warfare had been muted and to some extent forgotten, the effects of another revolution were beginning to appear. This was the Industrial Revolution.

It was to find its base in the steam engine, and a crude form of steam engine had been pumping water out of British mine pits since the earlier years of the eighteenth century. Ten years before the outbreak of the American Revolution, James Watt had converted the device into a potentially practicable source of general power. Principles of more immediate military application were being worked out. As early as 1743 the remarkable British mathematician, Benjamin Robins, a Quaker, unraveled and expounded the ballistic mysteries which explained the accuracy of the rifled gun. The difficulty of muzzle-loading a rifle was, as has been said, the greatest bar to its introduction as a general combat weapon; but as early as 1776 the Scottish Major Patrick Ferguson, who was killed at King's Mountain in 1780, had demonstrated a primitive form of breech-loader.

Brunel's machines were making naval pulley blocks and Whitney was mass-producing muskets before the Napoleonic Wars were well under way. The wars were to see many other applications of the new science, the new source of power and the new techniques. Less than two years after Trafalgar, the greatest and climactic battle ot the sail-driven wooden warship, the world's first commercially successful steamboat was running on the Hudson. There were other portents of what science and steam-powered industry might do to war. H.M.S. *Shannon*, which captured Lawrence's *Chesapeake* in a famous action of the War of 1812, was a "scientific" gunnery ship. Her captain, Broke, had equipped her with such novelties as gunsights, range-quadrants and azimuth scales for the accurate laying of her guns, and he had drilled her people intensively in the use of these instruments. In land warfare there had been many developments, springing from the improving technology. The hollow explosive shell was replacing the solid round shot as an artillery projectile. Colonel Congreve had developed his lethal rockets. Their "red glare" over Fort McHenry was to give a line to our national anthem; and to be remembered a century later when the same principle was to produce some of the deadliest weapons of World War II.

Both the world's first operable submarine (Bushnell's *Turtle*, which was used ineffectively against the British in New York Harbor during the Revolution) and its first steam-driven man-of-war (Fulton's *Demologos*, a floating battery built during the War of 1812, which never saw service) had appeared before Waterloo. But these things were for the most part but rudimentary beginnings, primarily because the underlying industrial plant had not yet progressed to a point at which it could develop the inventions or supply the new devices in quantity. The Admiralty took only a tepid interest in Captain Broke's ingenious improvements in gun-laying; this was not unreasonable, because the standard naval guns of the period were so various and erratic that there was little point in aiming them more accurately.

By 1815 the Industrial Revolution was well under way, yet it had made no great impress upon the ancient arts of war and slaughter. In 1815 as in 1775 the basic arm on land was still the smooth-bore flint-lock musket. At sea, it was still the cast-iron truck gun, manhandled with spikes and tackles and discharged at pistol range for its shattering and splintering effect. The principal innovation was the carronade, developed by the Carron iron works in Scotland; it was pivot-mounted, had a larger bore, a greater smashing effect and an even shorter range. It did not materially alter the terms of conventional naval battle. H.M.S. *Victory,* Nelson's flagship at Trafalgar, had been laid down in 1759, nearly a half century before; untroubled by obsolescence, she was both relatively and absolutely as powerful a weapon in 1805 as at the time of her designing.

There had been changes in tactics, some the results of technical progress, some enforced by the masses of untrained levies which swelled the new popular armies. Napoleon was celebrated as an artillerist; and his gun founders had given him relatively light and maneuverable field pieces on efficient carriages, transforming the artillery from an instrument mainly of siege warfare into an important arm of field combat. In the mid-eighteenth century, when artillery took the field at all, the guns were normally dragged by locally-acquired teams under civilian drivers, while the cannoneers trudged beside them on foot. By 1815 the horses were integral to the unit; the drivers were soldiers; the cannoneers rode the limbers and ammunition wagons when speed was called for or, in the highly mobile "horse" artillery, were individually mounted. The guns had become a part of the battle line, whether in cavalry reconnaissance or the set battle piece, with a mobility equivalent to that of the arms they supported.

Cavalry had likewise developed as a weapon of shock action for breaking up and riding down the massed infantry battalion. The steel breastplated heavy cavalry was given its weight and protection, as in the case of the modern armored division, in order to crush the infantry against which it was hurled. The lance, a lightened version of the medieval knight's spear, was revived as a cavalry weapon; it was an idea introduced from Poland, as is attested by the fact that lancer regiments in most of the major armies continued to wear the Polish *schupska* headgear. This awkward and seemingly anachronistic weapon proved successful not only in cavalry combat but as a means of over-reaching the deadly hedge of infantry bayonets, on which the charging horses of other types of cavalry were too often impaled before the riders could bring their sabers into action.[1]

The infantry had also developed. It had learned to make much greater use of cover and entrenchment, to throw out skirmishers ahead of the main battle line—light infantry employed in greater numbers than before to develop an enemy position, deliver harassing fire and supply an advance screen. Rifle regiments were introduced as specialized troops—an interesting solution for one of the perennial problems of war, one around which more technical military argument has doubtless raged than around any other and one which was to be enormously aggravated by the march of military invention. The appearance of new weapons of specialized utility has always presented a problem: should they be distributed through the standard organization, with a few men from each unit selected and trained to wield them in situations in which they are useful, or should they be massed in the hands of specialist units which can deliver them in quantity in crises on any

---

[1] The lance long survived the technical conditions which made it practicable. It was as late as 1889, with rapid-firing, long-range rifled small arms well developed, that Germany converted all her cavalry into lancers. In 1914 the Uhlans solemnly carried their long shafts—useful only as a means of adding a foot or two to their "range"—into a war dominated by the machine gun and long-range artillery!

part of the battlefield where they may particularly be demanded?

When the hand grenade appeared in the latter part of the seventeenth century, it was customary to tell off three or four of the most powerful men in the battalion to be trained in lobbing grenades. By the eighteenth century each battalion had its grenadier company, composed of its tallest and strongest men, as well as its light infantry company, the two being the "flank companies" of the battalion mass. By Napoleonic times it had become common practice to detach the flank companies for formation into independent battalions—indeed, at Concord in 1775 it was only the flank companies of the Boston battalions which were used for the famous march—but by that time the grenadiers' special weapon was losing its utility, and the grenadier company or battalion was distinguished from others mainly by its morale and physique. In the mid-nineteenth century when the British formally recognized the designation by transforming their 1st Foot into the Grenadier Guards, the grenade itself was obsolete. By the time of its revival in World War I as the "Mills bomb" it was no longer a special weapon, but just another piece of lethal hardware which every harassed infantryman had to carry and learn how to use.

Again and again this issue has arisen. In the Civil War the problem was whether to distribute the artillery as accompanying guns to the infantry regiments, or mass it for independent maneuver and effect. We entered World War I with our machine guns concentrated in machine-gun battalions attached to the infantry regiments; we ended it with the machine guns distributed throughout the line. There is still bitter argument over the question of whether "tactical" aviation should remain the province of the Air Force, or whether the ground army should have its own air support or its own command over Air Force tactical units allotted to assist the ground forces. Many other arguments of the kind might be cited. In the Napoleonic era the rifle, which had originally been distributed only to officers or a few picked men, was given to specialist rifle regiments, which retained their morale and special function until the general introduction of rifled shoulder arms left them no different from anyone else.

Many other modern notes may be detected in Napoleonic warfare. An account of the British landing before Baltimore in 1814, by an anonymous British subaltern of infantry, reads curiously like an account of amphibious operations in the Pacific in World War II. It describes the fire-support ships standing by in the stream, the men leaping from the boats, rushing across the open beach and flinging themselves down in the dune grass at the crest to be ready for the opposition. Much had been learned about tactics. But the short-range flintlock musket still dominated the battle; the close-ordered, disciplined infantry battalion remained the backbone of Napoleonic as of eighteenth-century warfare. Wellington's "lines of Torres Vedras" were famous, and the power of entrenchment had been repeatedly demonstrated. But for decision you still had to come out and grapple with an enemy whom you could not reach at more than fifty or a hundred yards. And that still meant the massed infantry battalion, in line or column for attack, in line or (later) the hollow square for defense. The ships were "wooden walls." The armies, in the last analysis, were walls of human flesh and fighting madness.

Waterloo, the last great Armageddon in which all that tale of passion, agony, folly and brutality was to end, was a kind of epitome of the whole process of Napoleonic war. It mingled the new and the old, the portents of the future and the remnants of the past. It was, for one thing, a single and decisive battle—almost the last of its kind— with everything put at stake upon the events between one dawn and sunset; and with everything decided, when that red and terrible sunset fell, beyond repair or revocation. No one day's battle since has had a similar finality of effect. Though shedding rivers of blood, neither an Antietam nor a Gettysburg nor a Cold Harbor could bring the Civil War to an end; neither Verdun nor the Somme were more than intensified moments of nightmare in a nightmare process that dragged on and on thereafter; neither Stalingrad nor Alamein nor the Normandy beaches could do more than point toward a probable end which would still cost vast sacrifices to attain. Each of the several episodes of the Napoleonic wars had usually reached decision in a single great battle. Waterloo was the final and most decisive of these grim dramas. It was not often to be repeated. War was beginning to lose its one virtue—its power of decision.

The entire field of action was hardly more than three or four miles long and a couple of miles across. Within this narrow arena there was concentrated the whole art and practice of warfare as it had developed up to 1815. The armies mingled troops of half a dozen nations and of every kind: the long-service professionals, the officer aristocrats, the peasant conscripts, the enthusiastic volunteers and reluctant levies. The Duchess of Richmond's famous ball lay behind them, a brilliant mirror of the past; behind them, too, were the popular politicians and newly powerful journalists, portents of the propagandistic and populistic future.

Napoleon waited for the ground to dry so that he could mass and maneuver his modern artillery concentrations. There were clouds of skirmishers; there was the bitter, bloody fighting from cover around the farms of Hougomont and La Haye Sainte. The great charges of the heavy cavalry were alike reminiscent of the knightly past and prophetic of the future armored division; but under the conditions of the time they were for the most part ghastly failures. The ultimate decision went to the locked ranks of Wellington's red-coated infantry, drawn up in line or hollow square in the open; unprotected, largely unmaneuvered, but also unbroken under the fierce, sweaty surge of half-crazed men and horses flung against them. Theirs was a last great triumph of eighteenth-century drill and discipline, waiting under deadly shellfire to discharge their volleys at fifty yards and take the shock upon their hedge of bayonets. The artillery could not shake them; the armored cavalry was shattered; and when the Old Guard at last went up the slope on foot against them it, too, was torn to shreds. The close order infantry battalion won the field. But it was not often to happen that way again.

So an enormous past, in which political and economic difference had always resolved itself ultimately into the hand-to-hand combat of organized, suffering and cursing men, drifted away upon the battle smoke of Waterloo. The political processes which would make battle action only a part of the struggles of whole peoples were already well advanced. The technical developments of the Industrial Revolution, which were to increase enormously the size of armies, at the same time opening out the battlefield and gradually reducing the hand-to-hand fighter into a lonely and usually frightened machine-tender, were already on the horizon. For all its modern developments, Waterloo still belonged essentially with the wars of Alexander or Caesar, just as Trafalgar belonged essentially with those of the Roman trireme or the Spanish Armada.

Of course, this was not apparent to the statesmen of the time, especially not to those who walked the unpaved streets of the somewhat battered little capital of Washington in 1815. Our small war was over; so were the great wars out of which it had grown. Again we were faced with the question of a peacetime military policy, and the reaction was like that which has followed all our other conflicts. Obviously, the troops had to be demobilized; and the men were promptly paid off while the ships were sold or laid up. But we could not return to our previous defenseless state. In the spring of 1815, the permanent establishment of the regular Army, which had been raised to some fifty regiments and had attained an actual strength of over 38,000 in 1814, was reduced to a maximum of 10,000 men. This, however, was nearly four times the establishment which had been considered sufficient prior to the *Chesapeake-Leopard* affair in 1807. And in 1816, with no further danger of a renewal of maritime war, the first real naval building program—providing ultimately for nine 74-gun line-of-battle ships, twelve 44-gun frigates and three coast-defense steam batteries—was enacted. At the same time, a board of engineers was appointed to plan an extensive permanent system of seacoast fortifications.

These were proposals to provide a national, standing military establishment of at least respectable weight. But, just as has happened after subsequent wars, the bright beginnings of 1815 and 1816 were almost immediately to fade, as the post-war boom which had generated them passed duly into a post-war recession. As the enthusiasms of war and prosperity dwindled into the dullness of peace and deficits, it turned out that all these plans cost too much. The appropriations for the naval building program were cut in half. The heavier ships which had been completed were laid up; what money was available for new construction was put into assembling the timbers only, deferring actual building until such a time as there might seem to be some need for it. The fortification program was slow in starting and even more leisurely in prosecution. Fortress Monroe, the massive work at Old Point Comfort, was undertaken in 1817, the year in which the President for whom it was named took office, but it was to be years before most of the other products of the program were even begun. There had been little real analysis of either the naval or the coast-defense problems; both programs thus went largely by default. But when in the spring of 1820 Congress ordered the Secretary of War to bring in a plan for cutting the regular Army to 6,000 men, it compelled some serious restudy of the whole Army problem.

Monroe's Secretary of War was the gaunt and brilliant Mr. John C. Calhoun of South Carolina, who had been one of the fieriest of the War Hawks in 1812. Other events beside the Congressional resolution were forcing a reconsideration of military policy. In his final annual message (December 1816) President Madison had again urged, "as a subject of the highest importance to the national welfare," a reorganization of the militia. The remarkable exploits of Andrew Jackson, now one of the two major generals of the regular Army, in Florida during 1818, had raised some of the familiar issues of the militia. In authorizing Jackson's incursion, the administration had wanted it carried out with regular troops in a regular way. But despite the enlarged peacetime establishment there were still only a handful of regulars—mostly detachments of the 4th and 7th Infantry and 4th Artillery—available in the area. Jackson started with a force of Tennessee militia and was provided with troops which included Georgia militia as well as the few regulars. With his accustomed energy, Jackson not only proceeded to fight his own war—to annex Florida from the Spaniards as well as to punish the escaped slaves and hostile Creeks and Seminoles who were the supposed objects of the campaign —but also to raise his own volunteer army. He enrolled militiamen and friendly Indians; he freely handed out United States commissions to their officers (he made a brigadier general of the United States Army out of one Indian leader) without the War Department or the President even knowing their names. He also extirpated the escaped slaves and hostile Seminoles, hanged a couple of wandering British officers he discovered in the area, took Pensacola from the Spaniards and created the situation which soon led to the cession of the Floridas.

But a Senate investigating committee was severe. It observed that Jackson had not only arrogated to himself the power of Congress to raise armies and the power of the President and Senate to appoint national officers, but also "the power which had been expressly reserved to the states in the appointment of the officers of the militia." This last power, the committee significantly added, was "the more valuable to the states because, as they had surrendered to the general government the revenue and physical force of the nation, they could only look to the officers of the militia as a security against the possible abuse of the delegated power." [2] In 1818 this may have seemed no more than legalistic ammunition in the battle of politics and patronage. But in 1861 it was to appear that the reservation of this military power to the states had grim meaning.

At any rate, something had to be done about the underlying theory of our military establishment. To practiced soldiers like Winfield Scott or Jacob Brown, the militia system, the supposed backbone of the structure, was militarily useless; yet the Seminole War rather clearly indicated that a regular Army of even 10,000 men was too small for the normal requirements of Indian warfare and border police. And Secretary Calhoun was required to reduce it to 6,000. The result was Calhoun's "expansible army" plan. It was not, perhaps, wholly original—some have found previsions of it in Washington and Knox— but at least it came to grips with the inconsistencies of the dual system. In effect, it rejected the militia and the universal obligation altogether, except possibly as a source of general military training. Calhoun's "expansible army" was a national army, which would rely wholly on volunteers. It had, as he saw it, two tasks: to garrison the forts and posts and "keep in check our savage neighbors"; and to prepare against a war. The first could be accomplished by a comparatively few men. The second could be met by maintaining in peace a regular organization capable of swift "augmentation" in emergency to whatever strengths might be required. "At the commencement of hostilities," the Secretary observed, "there should be nothing either to newmodel or create. The only difference . . . between the peace and war

[2] Emory Upton, *The Military Policy of the United States* (Washington, 1904), p. 148.

formation of the Army ought to be in the increased magnitude of the latter."

This would be achieved by what would today be called "skeleton-izing." Each infantry company would have a peacetime strength of thirty-seven men, to be reinforced to seventy-seven in time of need. For a greater emergency, each battalion would divide itself, by a kind of biologic fission, into two, each of the same strength as the one. Thus, a regular establishment of a little over 6,000 men would rise in a first emergency to 11,000 and in a major crisis to over 19,000. Volunteers would supply the increments; the national officer cadre would largely exist; the discipline and training of the regulars would stiffen the recruits and soon be imparted to them. The result would be a powerful national force, unhampered by the state governors or the constitutional limitations on the use of the militia. Calhoun, who was to become our greatest theorist of minority and states' rights, may not in 1820 have seen clearly where such a plan must lead.

Logical as it may seem under the conditions of 1820, it was also open to criticism on military as well as constitutional grounds. The effectiveness of regular troops subjected to such extreme dilution by untrained recruits may be questioned. Given a still generally armed populace, with at least some militia training, this difficulty might have been overcome. The plan nevertheless called for large reserve stocks of weapons and a swollen (and expensive) peacetime officer cadre to make the "expansion" possible. In retrospect, the worst difficulty would seem to lie in the rigid upper limit of expansibility. What would be done if more than the 19,000 men to be produced in the second stage were required? So long as war was to remain through the nine-teenth, as it had been through much of the eighteenth, century a prob-lem which could be met by relatively small volunteer forces, repre-senting only a fraction of the total energies of the state, the Calhoun plan had merits of precision and efficiency. It was bound to collapse as soon as a great national effort was demanded, leaving the nation enmeshed again in all the problems of the universal obligation, the militia, and state and popular power. But all such issues proved at the time to be somewhat academic. In the new aura of peace and economy, Congress adopted the 6,000 man Army establishment, and forgot both the reorganization of the militia and the "expansible" provision for the regulars.

Calhoun's ideas were never put into effect, although their underlying assumptions were to remain at the foundation of our military policy down to the adoption of conscription in 1917. As late as Elihu Root's day, when the whole question had again to be re-examined after the Spanish-American War, the broad solution was still an expansible regular or national army, with the militia serving primarily as simply a training school for those who might volunteer for the national service. But there was no need in the 1820's to face the dilemmas inherited from 1789 and 1775. The militia remained as before. In 1821 the regular Army was fixed at seven regiments of infantry and four of artillery.[3]

The cavalry was abolished. So was the one rifle regiment. The Corps of Engineers was retained; and the cadets, who had been distributed to the various regiments, were assembled at the Military Academy, in an authorized strength of 250, where the Engineers would train them. The Ordnance Department was also abolished, its duties being transferred to the artillery, although a rudimentary staff organization was retained. The total authorized strength, men and officers, was 6,183. And this remained, substantially, the United States Army through many years to come, except as its number dwindled through the customary failure to fill the authorized total.

---

[3] The latter consisted of eight "foot" or garrison companies and one "light" company each. In the United States, there had never been anything like the development of field artillery under Napoleon. In the early post-Revolutionary formations, the artillerists had been integral with the infantry units, specialists handling the guns of the frontier log forts. The construction of coastal fortifications in the Quasi-War and the War of 1812 required artillery troops to man them; these were, however, also trained as infantry, and most of the missions which they actually discharged were (as in Florida in 1818) infantry missions. The "light" companies of the artillery regiments were supposed to supply the field artillery, but as they were given neither field guns nor horses until the 1830's they also served as infantry. "Heavy artillery" units were still being used as infantry in the Civil War; and it was not until the reorganization after 1898 that the old "artillery" regiments ceased to be primarily infantry troops.

A report of November 1823 shows no less than twelve line-of-battle ships and eight 44-gun frigates on the Navy list. But of the battleships only one was in commission, six were laid up and the other five were "building." Only one of the 44's was in commission; two were laid up and five were "building." The active fleet included, in addition to the two larger ships, one 36-gun frigate, twelve sloops of 30 guns or less and fifteen minor types. Like the Army ashore, the Navy at sea had begun its long career as a scattered police and patrol force, maintained to suppress occasional piracies, to keep a protective eye upon our far-ranging whaleships and commercial traders, to "show the flag" and lend a hand in minor diplomatic imbroglios in distant seas, but neither designed nor intended for the waging of major maritime war.

Peace had returned to the world. The great Napoleonic armies and fleets had for the most part been disbanded. Despite its humiliations, the War of 1812 had, indeed, completed the American Revolution; it had established the United States as the one dominant power in the whole of the western Atlantic and the Western world. The Spanish empire in the Americas was in the process of dissolution. When in 1817 the Rush-Bagot Agreement in effect demilitarized the Canadian border, it meant that all serious threat of invasion or interference by the great European military states was at an end. The Boundary Treaty of 1818, which carried the northern border along the 49th Parallel to the Rockies, and the acquisition of Florida and the delimitation of "Louisiana" by the treaty of the following year, stabilized the American position. Monroe's announcement of the famous "Doctrine," in 1823, tacitly enlisted the Royal Navy in support of the position thus established. It was virtually unassailable. We possessed a vast western empire, open for exploitation; we had free access for our shipping to the untrammeled empire of the sea. Within the confines of the first there was nothing to fear save a few Indians; within the great levels of the second there was, until some new political constellation should arise, no danger that a few scattered patrols could not adequately meet.

In 1815, immediately on the conclusion of the war with Britain, we had dispatched a naval force to the Mediterranean to conclude matters with the Barbary States; there was little further fighting, but for decades we were to keep ships regularly on cruise in that sea. It

was the first of the "distant stations" [4] which were to be established—
in the West Indies, on the Pacific Coast of the Americas, in the Far
East, off Brazil and off the African slave ports—where we were normally to keep small cruisers, usually operating as single ships rather
than in squadrons, with little concern for the naval defense of the
home territory. Neither on the sea nor on the western plains (so like
the sea, in their boundless expanses) was defense a serious concern.

It was still possible to argue the old theories. "The militia," as William H. Sumner, adjutant general of Massachusetts, wrote to former
President John Adams in 1823, "is intended for defense only; standing armies for aggression as well as defense. The history of all ages
proves that large armies are dangerous to civil liberty. Militia, however, can never be; for it is composed of citizens only, armed for the
preservation of their own liberties." Sumner's analysis of the militia—
as a strictly local but still readily mobilizable force for meeting local
invasion—made much sense in 1823; it also contained some oddities,
as in his plea that the four annual muster days afforded the working
classes a useful and desirable holiday from the routines of the factory
civilization which was even then beginning to overwhelm them.[5] But
such discussions were theoretical. Calhoun's expansible army had been
laid aside, on the one hand, and nothing was done about the militia
on the other. For years the practical issues were to go undecided; and
for years American military institutions were to remain small and
static. The little regular Army of eleven regiments—6,000 men in all
—met the requirements, and nothing further was undertaken.

                                        2.

If the services remained both small and static through this period,
however, changes were nevertheless taking place which were seriously
to affect them. By the late '30's and early '40's the railway nets were
beginning to creep out from the more important urban centers, while

[4] Robert Greenhalgh Albion in U. S. Naval Institute *Proceedings*, Vol. 80,
No. 3, p. 265.

[5] William H. Sumner, *An Inquiry into the Importance of the Militia in a Free
Commonwealth* (Boston, 1823), p. 7 and *passim*.

steam transportation on the waterways and on the ocean was rapidly developing. The consequences of the introduction of steam transport into land warfare would be long in appearing, but its rapid development on the rivers and the sea offered an early and patent challenge to naval design everywhere. Nothing had been done about the authorization of three coast-defense steam batteries in the naval bill of 1816. But by 1835 there were some seven hundred steam vessels (most of them river and lake boats) owned in the United States; more importantly, forges and ironworks capable of building engines for them were growing up, while active experimentation with steam men-of-war had begun abroad. In 1835 Mahlon Dickerson, Jackson's Secretary of the Navy, revived the 1816 authorization, and in the following year laid down U.S.S. *Fulton,* the second steam warship to be carried on the American Navy list. She was usually referred to as *Fulton II,* Fulton's own *Demologos* having been commonly called the *Fulton,* or, after the appearance of the new ship, *Fulton the First. Fulton II* was low-powered, mechanically inefficient and weakly armed. But under the initial command of Captain Matthew C. Perry (who with steam warships was later to open Japan to the world) she laid the foundations of the steam navy of the United States.

If subsequent progress seems today to have been rather slow, this was not solely due to the conservatism of the shellbacks. The problem of domesticating this still crude yet revolutionary invention in naval war was by no means easy. The side-wheel power plants gave little speed and, with their huge fuel consumption, very little cruising radius. At the same time, their paddles damaged or ruined the vessel's performance as a sailing ship. To a Navy whose principal mission was the patrol of remote oceans they offered little of apparent value.

The paddle wheels were, moreover, obviously and fatally vulnerable to gunfire; while the huge paddle boxes took up so much space along the side as to leave little room for the standard broadside battery of the time. After allowing for the weight of engines, boilers, fuel and boiler water, the ship's military force had to be drastically reduced. These were high prices to pay for what at the time amounted to little more than an ability to maneuver briefly in calms and light airs. In 1837, after reviving the experimental steamers, we laid down *Pennsylvania,* 120 guns, our greatest sail battleship.

The whole steam business was at best highly experimental, even abroad. But in 1839 Congress authorized three more ocean-going war steamers. The first two of these, U.S.S. *Mississippi* and *Missouri,* were laid down in the same year. They were handsome, bark-rigged paddle "frigates," though actually bearing little resemblance to the 44's and 36's of 1812. With them, the ranked, checker-painted gun tiers of Nelsonian days disappeared. They were armed with two 10-inch and eight 8-inch shell guns.[6]

The introduction of steam had coincided roughly with another almost equally revolutionary technical development. In 1822 a French artillery officer, Henri Joseph Paixhans, published a treatise in which he recommended, among other things, the rearmament of the French Navy with shell guns, at the same time offering his own design for an improved form of such weapon. The standard naval armament of the time was still the cast-iron long gun and the more recent short carronade, both firing solid round shot at short range for their battering effect on an enemy ship. The shell of that day was also a spherical projectile, but hollow and filled with a fused bursting charge. It had proved deadly against troops on land, but was too light to have much direct effect on a ship's structure. Once lodged in an enemy's timbers, however, the burst could produce terrific results in mowing down the enemy crew, while the incendiary consequences could be terrible to wooden warships carrying masses of tarred hemp rigging and inflammable canvas.

Nouvelle Arme was the title of Colonel Paixhans' treatise, and his purpose was to provide France with a "new weapon" which would at a stroke destroy the great numerical superiority of the Royal Navy and so sweep Britain from her mastery of the seas. It was an early appearance of an idea which was often to recur during the heady

---

[6] *Missouri* was accidentally destroyed by fire in the year after her completion. *Mississippi* survived to serve on blockade in the Mexican War and with Perry in the expedition to Japan. She was Perry's "favorite ship" and was highly regarded in the old Navy. She perished in action at Port Hudson in 1863 on the great river whose name she bore.

advance of nineteenth century technology, the idea that it would be possible to find in invention an "absolute" or "dominant" or "decisive" weapon which would once and for all turn the great balances of war and so decide the power struggle. Colonel Paixhans' hopes were doomed to the disappointment which has met all his successors, down to the creators of the atomic bomb. Then, as later, the only result was that the potential enemy promptly appropriated the idea, while simultaneously setting himself to discover the counter or antidote for it. Paixhans' proposals failed to sweep Britain from the seas. They did, however, turn the attention of naval designers everywhere to the importance of the shell gun, to the vulnerability of the wooden warship when exposed to it, and to the only possible answer: armor plate and iron construction.[7]

Mississippi and *Missouri* were wooden, paddle steamers, but were armed with shell guns. Each would have been almost helpless against the other. The answer for the problem of the vulnerable paddle wheels soon appeared in the shape of the screw propeller. The 1839 act had authorized three ships; only two had been undertaken. In 1841 the energetic Captain Robert F. Stockton, USN, who had met John Ericsson, the Swedish engineer and inventor, in England and had been impressed by his experiments with the "Archimedes screw," got authority to go ahead with the third ship. Stockton brought Ericsson to the United States to assist in her design. The result was U.S.S. *Princeton,* the world's first propeller-driven man-of-war; also the naturalization of Ericsson in the United States, where much was later to be heard from him.

The screw propeller solved the worst of the problems presented by the paddle wheels. Itself protected under water, the engines which drove it could also be kept low in the hull, protected beneath the water line. It freed the broadside for the mounting of guns; while it was not difficult to design the screw so that it could be disconnected, or even unshipped and brought on board, when the vessel was under sail. This restored the sailing characteristics of the ship, allowing her to cruise as before to the great distances then unattainable by steam while

[7] F. L. Robertson, *The Evolution of Naval Armament* (London, 1921), pp. 160 f.

keeping her steam plant as an auxiliary power source, then its principal military utility. So progressive and scientifically-minded an officer as John Dahlgren thought this combination of auxiliary steam and full sail power not a retrogression but a happy solution for the technical problem. After the appearance of *Princeton,* the United States built only two more large paddle war steamers.[8]

The broadside was again unencumbered, but the gun-studded wooden walls were not to return. The engine weight remained to cut down the weight of armament which could be carried, while Colonel Paixhans' ideas were increasing the weight of individual pieces. The hollow shell, being lighter than a solid round shot of the same size, could be used in larger calibers. But that meant bigger guns. The days of the time-honored truck gun, on its elmwood carriage with lignum vitae rollers, manhandled with spikes and tackles and hemp breachings, were coming to an end. The new ordnance was too heavy to be trained in that way. Even the solid-shot long guns had grown from the 32-pounders which armed the lower deck of H.M.S. *Victory* up to 68-pounders. *Princeton's* main armament consisted of two shell guns of the then enormous caliber of twelve inches, "pivot" mounted on the spar deck so that they were capable of being trained on either broadside. (She also carried twelve 42-pounder carronades.) Mechanical devices for training and controlling the recoil were becoming necessary, while the reduction in the number of pieces put a premium on securing for each a maximum arc of fire. From this it was to be only a step to the revolving, armored gun turret, which since about 1860 has characterized all the world's major warships.

But that had not come in the '40's. Neither had ballistics and metallurgy been keeping up with the designers. One of *Princeton's* monster

---

[8] The Ericsson screw was not in fact a sound design (it was shortly replaced by a more efficient wheel) while the engines he gave *Princeton* have, it is believed, never been duplicated. Their "pistons" were rectangular plates, which swung to and fro in horizontal, semi-cylindrical casings like "a barn door on its hinges." They nevertheless worked very well, taking *Princeton* through the Mexican War and continuing to perform reliably even after the original *Princeton* had been broken up and they had been reinstalled in a second ship of the same name. Frank M. Bennett, *The Steam Navy of the United States* (Pittsburgh, 1896), pp. 62 f.

guns had been designed by Ericsson; the other was a "copy" by Captain Stockton. On a celebrated trial trip and junket on the Potomac in 1844 the Stockton gun—it was being fired for a last time "just for fun"—blew up, killing the Secretary of State, the Secretary of the Navy and others, including Mr. David Gardiner. The last was the owner of Gardiner's Island (the baronial fief off the east end of Long Island, which remains to this day in the hands of the family to whom Charles I granted it in 1640) and the father of the young lady who, as a direct result of this tragic occurrence, became the second wife of President Tyler. On no other occasion in our history has a single explosion either wrought such havoc among the national high command or led to such romantic consequences.

Better technology was the answer to such disasters, and many minds were at work to supply it. But it was apparent (long before the grim practical demonstrations came in the Crimea and at Hampton Roads) that the only real reply to the incendiary shell gun would be iron armor. Initially, designers turned their attention to sheathing the wooden hulls with wrought-iron armor plate. But in 1842 Congress authorized a contract with Robert L. Stevens of Hoboken for an all-iron, armored, twin-screw war steamer, "shot and shell proof," with full mechanical power. Had this ship, which never received any other name than "the Stevens Battery," been completed, she would have provided the first true prototype of the modern steam-and-steel navy. However, after various changes and enlargements of design (the engines when they were completed in 1856 had a horsepower equal to that installed in Brunel's prodigious *Great Eastern*) the money ran out; the ship never left the yard, and hull and engines were finally broken up for old iron in 1875.[9]

The quarter-century after Waterloo was a period of tremendous technical development, but it saw few major wars in which the military applications of the new ideas could be tested. It is not surprising that

[9] Bennett, *op. cit.,* p. 59. U.S.S. *Michigan,* a small sidewheeler laid down at Erie in 1842 to meet the requirements of patrol on the Great Lakes under the provisions of the Rush-Bagot agreement, was also of all-iron construction, though unarmored. Her military importance was slight, but her durability was astonishing, and was to provide powerful support for iron ship construction. She remained in service until far into the twentieth century and is still afloat.

these applications remained crude and uncertain for as long as they did. But some inventions were so striking that they hardly needed test. Early in the period the appearance of the fulminate of mercury cap or exploder spelled the end of the long reign of the flintlock; it made available for the first time a military shoulder arm which could be fired with confidence in rain or snow. The United States government arsenals manufactured their last flintlock musket in 1842, four years before the Mexican War, and in addition to turning out the new percussion weapons began converting the accumulated stores of flintlocks to take the mercury caps. Many flintlocks were to survive to be fired on many battlefields thereafter, but only as anachronisms used for want of anything better.

The cap added greatly to the reliability of the smooth-bore. But before 1830 the problem of a serviceable military rifle was already on its way to solution. Another French Army officer, Delvigne, had established two basic principles: that a rifle bullet should be of elongated, ogival shape rather than a spherical ball; and that the difficulty of muzzle loading could be overcome by making such a bullet small enough to slip easily down the bore, but providing a means whereby its base would be expanded under the hammer blow of the powder charge so as to grip the spiral "lands" of the rifling on its way out. Many troubles were encountered in applying the second principle, and a really practical solution was not achieved until the late '40's with the famous "minnie ball," the contribution of another French officer, Colonel Minié, which in one modification or another was to slay so many tens of thousands of young Americans during the Civil War.[10] It was in the mid-'50's that, in American arsenals, the smooth-bore shoulder arms went the way the flintlocks had gone a decade before.

All the while the industrial and technological base to sustain such ideas and developments was building up in the United States as elsewhere. In this country, military requirements were never of primary importance—our industry grew on the civilian demand for rails, locomotives, steamboat and factory power plants, textile machinery—but

[10] Robertson, *op. cit.*, p. 195.

military requirements (to say nothing of civilian requirements for weapons on the frontier) provided a powerful added stimulus. And there was a strong interaction between civilian and military needs and between the engineers, inventors and factory managers who responded to both.

It is strikingly indicated by the fact that for many years the United States Military Academy at West Point was virtually our only higher technical and scientific school; and that its graduates were so often found among the leaders of our scientific, engineering and industrial development. Jefferson had found the Army officers useful as explorers and observers; the Navy was later on to use its officers in the same way—as in Charles Wilkes' explorations in the Pacific in the early '40's or Matthew Maury's pioneer work in oceanography—while the Army's Corps of Engineers was early to assume the responsibility for harbor development and civilian internal improvements which it has since retained. Many other officers resigned the service to take posts in civilian industry. George B. McClellan, of the West Point class of 1846, is an example. After service as an engineer under Scott in Mexico, he spent some years in the Army's civil engineering and exploratory duties, then resigning to become a railway executive. He was president of the Ohio & Mississippi Railroad when called back to arms in 1861.

In 1824 a New England youth, Robert P. Parrott, graduated from the Military Academy; he was commissioned in the 3rd Artillery, and within a few years found himself engaged mainly in ordnance work. In 1835 he resigned to become an executive in the West Point Foundry at Cold Spring, N. Y., the firm which the following year received the contract for the engines for *Fulton II*. Fulton's paddle wheels were independently driven, because neither the West Point firm nor any other in the country had the facilities to forge a crankshaft large enough to pass all the way across the ship. By the time the same firm received the contract for *Missouri's* engines in 1840 such deficiencies had been overcome. Parrott not only maintained the foundry, which he soon came to head, as one of the country's leading ironworks, but continued his interest in ordnance. By the eve of the Civil War he had developed the famous Parrott reinforced rifled gun. This was to become the major rifled weapon of the field artillery in that conflict, being produced by the hundreds in many calibers, and was again to slay its thousands of young Americans.

There are other illustrative figures. Two years after Parrott graduated from the Military Academy, John A. B. Dahlgren, the son of an American mother and a Swedish father, accepted appointment as midshipman in the Navy. With a strongly scientific and mathematical bent of mind, he early found himself on Coast Survey duty, where he helped lay out the basic triangulation for the coastal charts of the United States. From that he gravitated into naval ordnance. As the *Princeton* tragedy had shown, the problems of casting the new big guns were imperfectly understood. Dahlgren worked scientifically with studies of strains and powder pressures, finally modifying the Paixhans gun into a form which permitted it to be made safely in calibers up to eleven inches.

Two classmates, Josiah Gorgas from the Pennsylvania backwoods and T. J. Rodman from Indiana, graduated from West Point in 1841. Both made their careers as ordnance officers. Gorgas, after serving in Mexico and in various Federal arsenals, became Chief of Ordnance for the Confederacy and was largely responsible for the remarkable development of Confederate war industry. He was also the father of William C. Gorgas, the Army surgeon who was to become famous as the conqueror of yellow and malarial fever during the construction of the Panama Canal.

Rodman devoted himself to the metallurgy of his specialty. By the '50's it had become apparent that beyond a certain point an increase in the thickness of metal in a heavy gun yielded no corresponding increase in strength. The answer to the puzzle was hidden in the molecular structure of the metal itself. If the inner part of the gun tube failed under the force of the explosion, the outer parts would fail progressively no matter how much added thickness was provided. It was necessary to set up countervailing stresses in the metal. Rodman did it by casting his big guns hollow and then chilling them from the inside, thus forming a stressed inner layer which the outer thickness would support. The Rodman guns did not appear until the eve of the Civil

War, but when they did it became possible to cast 15-inch and even 20-inch smooth-bore shell guns which could be safely fired. The Rodman guns were to be the principal heavy weapons, ashore and afloat, during the Civil War; and until the appearance a few years later of the "built up" and wire-wound heavy gun, they put the United States in the forefront of the world's ordnance development. At the same time, Rodman's, like Dahlgren's, work added materially to the understanding of heavy metallurgy.

The process, of course, operated in both directions. While the military services were producing engineers to assist in industrial development, industry was also producing engineers and technicians who would lend the military indispensable assistance when war came again, in the meanwhile providing inventions which were to affect the Army's operations more deeply than military men could foresee. It was in 1844, for example, that Morse demonstrated his "magnetic telegraph," based on the work of Joseph Henry. Fifteen years later this device was to have far-reaching consequences for military operations.

But in the days of Jackson and Van Buren most of these developments still lay in a distant future. What Navy we maintained was scattered as single ships on cruise upon their "distant stations"; what Army we had was scattered in single companies or even smaller detachments all along the vast frontier, and for some years the Indians gave little trouble. The brief Black Hawk "War," in 1832, in which Abraham Lincoln served as a captain of militia, led to the restoration of a cavalry arm. The Indian fighting, which had continued intermittently for two centuries, had been predominantly woods warfare, in which the horse was of little use; now, however, the always-advancing frontier was breaking out of the great forests into the western plains country, and it was soon to meet the superb mounted warriors of the western tribes, utilizing the horses which the Conquistadores had brought them. For the Black Hawk War Congress authorized a battalion of "mounted rangers," which in 1833 became the 1st Regiment of Dragoons. Originally, the dragoon was a mounted infantryman, transported on horseback but normally fighting on foot. During the Napoleonic wars he had tended to lose this specialized character and

to merge with the cavalry proper, but the designation was still significant. And the United States Cavalry, thus reborn in 1832, was to
retain throughout its history a large element of the mounted infantryman in its composition. Even in the Civil War it was seldom used as
a shock weapon, and thereafter such use was to become virtually
impossible.

In 1838 a small beginning was made toward providing the United
States Army with a field artillery comparable to the arm which
Napoleon had brought to so high a state. The variegated militia corps
had included both cavalry and artillery units, and the reorganization
of 1821 had provided one "light" company for each of the four regular artillery regiments. But it was not until 1838 that it occurred to
Joel R. Poinsett, Van Buren's Secretary of War, that it might be well
to provide at least one light company with horses, field guns and
ammunition wagons. Poinsett was a South Carolina planter-politician
of wide interests; he not only developed the flamboyant poinsettia
blossom which preserves his name but also had a passion for war and
military history, which he sought to impart to our then somewhat
somnolent military establishment.

Brevet Major Samuel Ringgold of the 3rd Artillery—"a cavalier
and a gentleman who understands men as well as he does guns and
horses," according to a contemporary newspaper account—was chosen
to lead the new battery; in late 1838 he completed the conversion of
his regiment's C Company into a full six-gun battery of horse artillery.
It was to make a fine show at the "camp of instruction" which Poinsett
established near Trenton in the following summer—an early experiment both in combined maneuvers and in advertising the Army, two
objects toward which military training exercises have often been simultaneously directed ever since. One six-gun field battery, a hundred
dragoons and an infantry component supplied by a few foot companies
of "artillery," can have afforded no very effective training in the tactics
of combined arms. But the publicity seems to have been all that even
a modern PIO could desire. In addition to increases in the other arms
(necessitated by the Seminole War), Poinsett secured the conversion
of the light companies of the other three regiments to "mounted," or

what would now be called field, artillery.[11] These four batteries were to remain until the Mexican War the sole field artillery component of the United States Army. They possessed twenty-four guns in all, of which eight were later retired to storage.

When in the early '40's Manifest Destiny again began to dawn—over the far Oregon country and the vast plains of Texas, as it had dawned over Canada in 1812—all these beginnings were being made; none carried a hint, however, of the blood-soaked future to which they were to lead. The American military system, with its tiny regular land and sea forces and its heterogeneous militia, was hardly more than a confused and retrogressive survival from the Napoleonic age of giant wars. But the Industrial Revolution, which was to preside over its enormous later development and make possible its deployment upon the terrible stages of world power, was already far along its path.

3.

In 1835 the population of the United States was about 17,000,000. The twelve-regiment regular Army of that time had an authorized strength of 7,198 officers and men (5/100 of 1 per cent of the population), and an actual strength "present for duty" of little more than 4,000.

It included in all 116 companies of infantry, "artillery" and dragoons, averaging less than thirty men each, and scattered all around the enormous perimeter—Canada, the Northwest, beyond the Mississippi, the Gulf Coast and Florida. Eleven of these companies (536 men and officers) were in central Florida, where the Seminoles in their resentment of white encroachments were threatening trouble. In December 1835 this force was tragically reduced when Major Dade, setting out from Tampa for an interior post with 110 men, was ambushed and destroyed by the Indians, only three of the command escaping. There followed a prolonged and messy "war" in Florida, including a side

---

[11] William E. Birkhimer, *Historical Sketch of the Organization, Administration, Materiel and Tactics of the Artillery* (Washington, 1884), pp. 50 f. *Military Collector and Historian,* Vol. VI, No. 3, p. 52.

campaign against hostile Creeks in Georgia, which was to occupy a fair part of the regular Army over the next six years.

It was accompanied by most of the now familiar phenomena. There were not enough regulars, so calls and drafts had to be made on the militia of the neighboring states. The state troops turned up without arms and there were difficulties in finding weapons for them in the arsenals; they were called for only three months and, as usual, took this term seriously. Congress authorized Federal volunteers for six-months or one-year service. Militia and volunteers alike were, as usual, untrained, unreliable and disinclined to the heavy logistic jobs of building roads through the swamps and getting up supplies and rations; Winfield Scott got into trouble for indiscreetly intimating as much. Congress added a second regiment of dragoons and an eighth infantry regiment to the regular establishment, but resisted large-scale expansion of the Army. After the campaign of 1836 there were few pitched battles. The Indians broke up into small parties which easily lost themselves in the appalling swamps; and the problem resolved itself, as in the Philippines three-quarters of a century later, mainly into one of small patrol and bush-fighting actions. It was still gruelling, steaming, disease-infested work; and by 1837 it had absorbed no less than nine of the fourteen regular regiments. It leaves one, as military history so often does, with a sense of wonder at the stamina of the men—even the militiamen—who could go through such operations under the primitive ideas concerning rations, hygiene and medical care which prevailed in that day.

In the meantime, times were changing. The stabilized international situation so happily organized after 1815 was tending to break up. Texas declared her independence of Mexico in 1836, amid such horrors as the massacres at the Alamo and Goliad; when the outgoing Jackson administration recognized the new republic in March 1837 the shadow of a Mexican war was already upon the horizon. In the same year the Papineau rebellion in Canada fired some of our citizenry in the northern states with renewed dreams of Canadian conquest. General Scott himself was dispatched to the border to maintain peace and "neutrality"—but with no troops whatever, since they were all in Florida or the West.

The great tides of emigration and expansion were flowing again, from Louisiana into Texas and from the northern reaches of the Mississippi valley toward Oregon. At the end of both roads stood the old enemy, Great Britain. Yet since 1815 the American international position—with its freedom to exploit both the western riches and the commercial empire of the seas without having to trouble over the pains and costs of defending either—had really rested upon the acquiescence, if not the benevolent neutrality, of the Royal Navy. So long as Britain maintained her great preponderance in European waters there was not much to fear from France or the lesser maritime powers; and it was only a strong sea power which could possibly attack us. But if we came into collision with Great Britain we would be at once exposed everywhere to disasters like those which overtook us in the War of 1812.

Despite "incidents" there was never any real danger of war along the Canadian border, as it had been defined by the Ashburton Treaty of 1818. But that frontier, running west on the 49th Parallel, ended at the Rockies. The Oregon settlers had outrun it and were now in the area of joint occupation, where possession was disputed by the powerful Canadian fur interests. The Texas settlers at the same time were making good their hold on one empire which was clearly only an avenue to another: California and the Pacific ports south of the Columbia. The United States was threatening to grow from a peripheral member of the Atlantic complex into a continental power of ominous proportions and resources. Great Britain was ready enough to recognize the Republic of Texas as a vigorous small state which could feed Lancashire's cotton mills without undue interference from Washington, and which would offer potential bases from which a friendly European sea power might keep an eye upon the lucrative mouths of the Mississippi. But Britain was much less interested in seeing Texas pass under the Stars and Stripes; and her diplomacy at this time was directed toward preventing that consummation. It was a situation which piled fuel on the flames of American expansionism, even while it further compromised the military basis on which expansion rested.

In 1840 there was another "incident," over a British subject,

McLeod, arrested in New York on a murder charge because he boasted of having shot an American in the Papineau affair. The mighty Palmerston did not hesitate to growl threats of war; and one is struck by the freedom with which men were again beginning to think and talk of war. By that time, the Napoleonic era was a quarter of a century behind and the memories of its blood and agony were beginning to fade. The idea that "we can lick 'em easy" was again prevalent. Within a few years the cry "Fifty-four Forty or Fight!" was to seem a reasonable election slogan to a people which had not done much serious fighting for a long while.

While there was no war with Britain, there was in the early '40's a notable renewal of interest in matters of national defense. In 1840 the martial Poinsett brought in another sweeping plan to reorganize the militia—to create a trained "active" force of 100,000 men, to be raised by volunteering if possible and by state draft if not, with "reserve" and "mass" organizations behind it—a "radical reform, that stretched the Constitutional powers of the general government to such extent as to cause opposition." Needless to say, the opposition was successful. "This," in the words of a Congressional committee which reviewed the problem many years later, "appears to have been the last decided attempt to save the decaying system from dissolution. . . . The militia system by this time was virtually dead." But it was tending to be replaced in part by the organized, brilliantly uniformed, usually well-equipped and socially elite volunteer units which had survived, or were again growing up, within it. These were organizations like the Louisiana Artillery, the Richmond Light Infantry Blues, or New York's 7th Regiment of "National Guards," a designation which honored Lafayette's visit to America in 1824 and was to become ultimately a common name for all troops of this kind.

Poinsett failed, like so many before and after him, to reform the militia. But as the nation began to recover from the Panic of 1837, more money began to become available for the newly interesting subject of defense. In March 1841 "Tippecanoe and Tyler too" took office; Fate soon removed the first from the scene, but as Tyler's administration got under way there were a number of gestures looking toward improvement in the nation's military posture.

In 1841 the perennial seacoast fortification program took on a new burst of energy; the repair and rebuilding of a number of the old 1812 works (Castle Williams on Governor's Island in New York is an example) were pushed forward; while the completion of the more imposing brick and masonry structures planned after 1816 as elements in a "permanent" coast-defense system was taken energetically in hand. The names of not a few of these—Fort Morgan at Mobile, Pulaski on Cockspur Island at the mouth of the Savannah, Sumter in Charleston Harbor and others—were to be stamped upon our history in a way never dreamed of by their designers. Many of them, with their frowning gun galleries and vaulted casemates, their scarps and ditches and curtain-walls, survive today as handsome and interesting monuments to a military architecture which, barely a century old, is now as obsolete as a medieval castle.

The same year saw the introduction of the Model 1841 caplock musket as the standard military arm; it also saw the first introduction of shell guns into American naval armament. The two war steamers, *Mississippi* and *Missouri,* were approaching completion; Captain Stockton got authorization to begin his propeller ship, *Princeton.* And for the first time since 1815 we re-established, in addition to the cruisers hunting slavers and pirates on the "distant stations," a Home Squadron ostensibly for the protection of the Atlantic Coast. The dangers which it was presumably to meet could not have been taken very seriously, as the Home Squadron was only a tiny handful of ships; and many regarded it, with some reason, as pure "humbug." But at the end of 1841 the new Whig administration brought in a big new naval program.

It "precipitated one of the most enlightening parliamentary struggles in the history of American naval legislation." [12] In presenting it, the new Secretary of the Navy, William P. Upshur (who, after his promotion to Secretary of State, was to perish in the *Princeton* disaster), advanced two interesting ideas. One was that the United States should adopt, as a norm for its naval power, a strength at least one-half that of the strongest foreign nation—an early appearance in

[12] Harold and Margaret Sprout, *The Rise of American Naval Power* (Princeton, Princeton University Press, 1939), p. 121.

our naval debates of the relative or "ratio" system for determining naval building programs. The other idea was that the new ships should be of iron, in order to "foster the domestic iron industry," an explicit recognition of the importance of military orders in upbuilding a private heavy industry, as well as the importance of private industry in upbuilding a military posture. Both ideas were to play a considerable role in later history.

The debate was vigorous and all the arguments, old even then but to be repeated many times in many later naval debates, were thoroughly hashed over. The seaboard and the proprietors of the new foundries and ironworks were interested in the contracts; the interior and the farmers objected to the cost and had no interest in promoting a navalism for which no need was apparent and which might only invite foreign war and adventure. Armaments, which had been so feared in the eighteenth century as potential instruments of domestic oppression, were already assuming a new guise, as themselves probable causes of the international wars they were supposed to avert.

The first American peace societies had been founded in New York, New England and Ohio as early as 1815; through them earnest divines, merchants and publicists were soon concerting an organized popular peace movement which by 1828 had coalesced under the standard of the American Peace Society. It reflected a movement already spreading widely through the Atlantic world and in 1843 the first international peace congress was called at London. Charles Sumner was to provide the pacifists with a sensational weapon when, in a Fourth of July oration in 1845, delivered in the teeth of the approaching Oregon and Texas crises, he asked: "Can there be in our age any peace that is not honorable, any war that is not dishonorable?" and went on to imply that total disarmament was the only rational course. [13] The pacifists were already speaking with a voice which the authors of military policies and building programs would increasingly have to heed.

At all events, the Tyler administration failed in 1842 to get even as much money for the Navy as in the previous year. Whether be-

[13] Merle E. Curti, *The American Peace Crusade* (Durham, N. C., Duke University Press, 1919), pp. 5, 119.

cause of the pacifists, the economizers, the isolationists or the log-rollers and contract-grabbers, there was no big expansion program. The processes by which this decision was arrived at may have been intellectually disreputable, but perhaps it was just as well. Nothing proposed in 1841 could have equipped us for a war with Britain; and for a war with Mexico, which did impend, naval power was virtually useless. One might add that any big program adopted in 1842 would simply have loaded the Navy list with experimental or obsolete craft for which there would have been no future. The fortification program, enlarged during this period, has left its enduring monuments to the uncertainty of military prophecy in a time of rapid political and tech-nological change. The naval program, had it been adopted, would almost certainly have done the same.

Yet the air remained charged with heady emotions; an interest in military matters had revived, and while nobody made any genuine effort to prepare for war, the pressures were visibly rising. The egre-gious Mexican soldier-politician, Santa Anna, renewed his war on Texas, interfering with its trade and issuing proclamations breathing fire and slaughter. In 1844 Tyler submitted an annexation treaty to the Senate; by that time, unfortunately, the whole issue had become in-volved in the slavery cancer and the treaty failed. But in the autumn the humorless, unexciting and very practical Polk captured the Presi-dency for the Democrats with the blazing slogan of "Fifty-Four Forty or Fight"; and as the outgoing Tyler signed the annexation resolution which had been substituted for the treaty, the new President took office virtually committed to a two-front war against Britain and Mexico both.

Apparently, Polk knew what he was doing. That he never expected to fight a British war is, perhaps, attested by the fact that he never made the slightest preparation for one; while the marked patience and caution of his Mexican policy suggest that he hoped to complete the acquisition of Texas without resort to arms. To be sure, for Polk as for his countrymen war had lost the terrible connotations which the Napoleonic era had given it, and which were to be restored to it in the twentieth century. To Polk it was no more than an "instrument of policy," limited in scale and cost and not difficult to employ if necessary. To the modern reader there is something breath-taking about the casualness of Polk's attitude in the critical months. When in December 1845 his Secretary of State, Buchanan, argued that war might come with Britain in the "next two weeks" and urged him to begin "vigorous preparations for defense," the President coolly expressed his "concurrence," remarking that "if peace continued the expenditure would not be lost, and if war came such preparation would be indispensable." [14] But he did nothing about it. The truth is that with the slow communications of those days there was really no great hurry about preparing for a war which the enemy, no more than oneself, could mount except after lengthy preparation.

When in July 1845 Texas accepted the annexation statute, Zachary Taylor was in Louisiana with the larger part of three regular regiments, amounting to about 1,500 men in all. With this "army" Taylor advanced to Corpus Christi. The government rounded up for him as many more regular companies of infantry and dragoons as it could find; it sent him Major Ringgold's celebrated battery of horse artillery and he got a second field battery from the Louisiana volunteer militia of New Orleans; he also had help from the Texas Rangers.

"The multitude," as the New York *Herald* granted in August 1845, "cry aloud for war"; and the New York *Morning News* observed that "nine tenths of our people would rather have a little fighting than not." [15] By the end of the year Taylor still had less than 4,000 men and only twelve 6-pounder field guns. With this force he was ordered forward to the Rio Grande, while Polk and the Congress were still taking a strong and stubborn stand on Oregon. The belligerent Oregon Resolution passed on April 27. Though the facts were not learned in Washington until two weeks later, on the day before the Mexicans had crossed the Rio Grande and destroyed an outpost command of Taylor's force. The Mexican War had begun. Only then did Polk move to provide an army with which to fight it.

To Emory Upton, writing in the '80's, the Mexican War brought a "revolution in our military policy," because it marked the effective

[14] Allan Nevins, ed., *Polk: The Diary of a President, 1845–1849* (New York, Longmans, 1952), p. 36.
[15] Justin H. Smith, *The War with Mexico* (New York, 1919), Vol. I, p. 124.

end of the militia system as a serious reliance, even in theory, for major war, and the substitution of the volunteer principle that was thereafter generally to rule. Immediately on the outbreak, Taylor, acting under prior authorization, called up 5,000 militia from Texas and Louisiana. He got almost twice the numbers he called for, but it was a useless gesture; they arrived too late for the opening "battles" of Palo Alto and Resaca de la Palma and left, with their three-month term expired, too soon for the subsequent operations in Mexico. The militia as such played little further part in the war; with their three-month term and their constitutional protection against foreign service they were of small help in a war of this character, while the great distances over which operations had to be conducted ruled out the large armies and mass mobilizations which the militia system was supposed to produce. Since volunteers poured out with adventurous enthusiasm in quite adequate numbers, the war could safely be left to them. From first to last it was found necessary to put into uniform only a little over 100,000 men (one-half of 1 per cent of the population) as against the nearly half-million scratch troops who had seen some kind of service, long or short, in the War of 1812.

Upton's "revolution" was, perhaps, one more of theory than of fact. The volunteers who eagerly took ship for the "halls of Montezuma" and that marvelous Mexican land where "the girls are sweeter than candy" were not, after all, so very different from those who had gone to Louisburg in 1745, who had enlisted with the Continentals of the Revolution or had composed the temporary "regular" regiments in 1812. Nor were they so different from what the militia system would have produced, and the critics were to find in them many of the familiar faults. Though summoned under Federal authority, they were raised by the states; they retained their state designations and their officers, when not elected by the men, were appointed by the governors. Congress decreed that they were to serve for "twelve months or until the end of the war." Polk construed this ambiguous language as meaning that they might sign up for not more than twelve months, rather than that they had to serve (as the wording would seem to have allowed) for not less than the duration. As a result, General Scott was to find himself in 1847 in the position which had been so painfully familiar to General Washington. Just as he had climbed to the plateau of Mexico and was poised for the final stroke, his volunteer units evaporated with their time expired, and he had to suspend the war, at the cost of great subsequent loss of life, until they could be replaced.

In addition to calling the volunteers, Congress had authorized the President to fill the regular establishment to a company strength of one hundred men each. But with the attractive twelve-month option and the other amenities of volunteer life, the recruits naturally flocked to the volunteer units. To counter this, Congress in the second year of the war created a large number of temporary "regular" regiments; but they were locally recruited and officered and did not differ greatly from the volunteer forces. It must have been apparent at the time that the wholly makeshift system had its defects as a foundation for the national defense in a major war. But in Mexico it succeeded brilliantly. It was "a splendid little war," as John Hay was long afterward to describe the Spanish-American conflict; and Mexico perhaps merits the phrase even more than the war of 1898. Every battle was a victory; neither the money costs nor the casualties were unduly excessive; the rewards were tremendous. Because of its relation to the slavery issue it was often bitterly resented in the North and New England, yet it responded to a national mood of self-confident expansion and romanticism which made it generally "popular."

To be sure, it once more brought home the realization—always so shocking after prolonged periods of peace—that in war men get killed in agonizing and gruesome ways. The death of Major Ringgold at Palo Alto, the first action of the war, where his battery did so well, was a sensation, duly recorded along with many other gory episodes by Currier and Ives. The news dispatches, brought by steamer or expedited over those stretches where the "magnetic telegraph" now operated, included atrocity stories of a familiar kind. While over-all losses were not too heavy, there were some bloody and bitter conflicts—like Buena Vista, the worst action of the war, where Taylor's volunteer regiments were cut to pieces by Santa Anna and were only saved by the diminutive artillery standing to fire grape and canister point-blank into the massed infantry attack, with no infantry support of their own.

But it was the custom of that age to dwell upon the glory, rather than upon the stench and gore. There were as yet few war correspondents to enlighten home firesides upon the real misery and suffering—topics which would not have been considered suitable for the fireside anyway—and the handsome young officers coming home afterward with their honors and brevets were, most of them, professionals, trained to a professional disregard of suffering and weakness. Mexico is significant in that it was our first really professional war. Scott had learned his trade in the War of 1812 and had remained with it. Wool, Worth and Twiggs were all 1812 veterans who had stayed in the Army. Taylor and others had benefited by a postgraduate course in the Florida swamps. And the juniors, the company and battalion commanders and brilliant young staff officers, were the first crop from the United States Military Academy, magnificently justifying Washington, who had recommended, and Jefferson, who had established, that institution. "But for our graduated cadets," in Scott's oft-quoted verdict, "the War between the United States and Mexico might, and probably would, have lasted some four or five years, with, in its first half, more defeats than victories falling to our share."

One may wonder how much they really learned about war from old Dennis Mahan (father of the later famous admiral, and for years professor of military engineering) who, though steeped in Napoleonic military lore, never saw a battle and never ventured outdoors without an umbrella. They obviously had nothing approaching the technical training in half a dozen complex fields which must be at the fingertips of a modern platoon or battery commander. But somewhere along the line, at the Point or in the little detached garrisons or in their surveying and engineering work, they had acquired the military fundamentals: honor, initiative, physical courage, the abilty to obey orders, to take care of one's men and to get up the ammunition and the rations. These are the supreme virtues of the professional soldier, and Scott's and Taylor's young men proved that they possessed them. They with their well-drilled regulars made the numerous bloody little victories; the volunteers helped, of course, often behaving with credit, but they were well-leavened. Even the uniforms—the round, visored fatigue cap; the short jacket, not unlike the "Eisenhower jacket" of later fame; the loose trousers; or the even more informal gear, like Taylor's straw hat—showed a new professional practicality. And it was these young professionals, schooled in Mexico, who were to produce the high command on both sides in the Civil War. Lee and Grant, T. J. Jackson and Sherman, McClellan and Beauregard, Thomas and Joe Johnston and Bragg and a host of others now ranking among the military great were all graduates of West Point who learned their business in Mexico.

For those who suffered its toils and fevers, its deaths and horrible mutilations (not yet assuageable by the blessing of anesthetics) Mexico was probably no more fun than are most wars. But it was a success. Except in its domestic political implications, it had scarcely touched the great and comfortable public. It had been fought by the trained soldiers and the romantic youth, whose lives in those days were chancy enough at best and who had probably suffered no more ardors, in the main, than were considered good for them. The military system had on the whole worked well. With a larger regular establishment at the beginning the job could no doubt have been done sooner and at less cost; but there were no disasters, no important scandals, no instances of glaring incompetence—or none, at least, which came strongly to public notice. There was no cry for reform and none to parade the casualty lists, as happened after Korea, to prove the soulless incapacity of the administration which had waged the conflict. Instead, we elected Taylor to the Presidency and relapsed into the unfounded conviction that there were no great issues of military policy and organization remaining to be met.

4.

Thirteen years elapsed between the signing of the Treaty of Guadeloupe Hidalgo and the bombardment of Fort Sumter, a period oddly close to that which divides the Spanish-American from the First World War. But in the late '40's and '50's military policy was far more static than in the first decade of the twentieth century. The nation was bursting with new energies, new hopes, the responses to new challenges. But few of these seemed to have any serious military connotations.

The opening of the Southwest and the Pacific, the gold rush to California, the expansion of the rail and telegraph nets, the development of the new machine industry in iron-working, power plants and textiles, the opening of Japan in 1854, the expansion of the whale fishery and the development of the California and the China trade in the great era of the clipper ship, the development of steam navigation on the western rivers—all these were enough to consume men's minds and efforts, and none seemed to raise significant issues of war or defense. In 1854 the Europeans were to involve themselves in an obscurely motivated struggle in the Crimea; it meant little to the young Republic, and further removed any likelihood of European interference in our rushing affairs. The one great shadow was cast by the dark and sour cloud of sectional conflict; this involved impassioned and embittered politics, but it was domestic politics, and there were few in the mid-'50's to foresee that it would end in the greatest and ghastliest war since the Napoleonic era. The slavery issue did give rise to some promptings toward military adventure in the Caribbean, but no prevision of the internecine war is detectable in the still very casual military policies of the period.

With the end in Mexico, our first really "foreign" war, the "boys were brought home." The volunteers disbanded and the regular establishment was cut back to 10,000 men—more than pre-war, but not much more. Some evidences of combat experience remained. The field artillery, which had proved so brilliantly successful, was at first required to turn in its horses; ultimately, after various chops and changes, each of the four regular artillery regiments was allowed to retain two "mounted" batteries. But, as the Secretary of War severely observed in 1851, "this description of troops, although extremely effective in regular war, are utterly useless in the kind of service in which the Army is now employed" (border police and Indian fighting) and the artillery did not prosper. [16] On the other hand, the regular regiment of mounted riflemen, which had been authorized in 1846 for Oregon but had been diverted to Mexico, was retained. The plains Indians

[16] Birkhimer, *op. cit.,* p. 50.

were making cavalry more and more necessary, and in 1855 Congress added to the mounted riflemen and the two dragoon regiments the 1st and 2nd Regiments of "Cavalry," plainly so designated.

The Navy, which with no opposition at sea had found comparatively little to do in the war, returned to its old tasks of chasing slavers and pirates and "showing the flag" on the distant stations. It was not the war but its aftermath which gave rise to a resumption of naval building in the '50's. In the second year of the war, Congress had authorized the two big paddle frigates, *Powhatan* and *Susquehanna,* launched in 1850.[17] Both Polk and the Whigs who replaced him in 1849 were content to rest there. But the nationalist emotions and the visions of "Manifest Destiny" generated by the war rode strongly on the banners of Pierce and the Democrats, who took office in 1853. So, incidentally, did the renewed interest of the slave states in national expansion. The new chairman of the Senate Naval Affairs Committee was Stephen B. Mallory of Florida. The new Secretary of the Navy, who bore the disarming name of Dobbin, had produced by December not only a program of naval administrative reform but also one for the construction of six "first-class propeller frigates."

The Navy List at this time is not without interest. It showed no less than ten line-of-battle ships, from the mighty *Pennsylvania* (120 guns) built in 1837, down to *Columbus* (80), built in 1819. Four of these were still "on the stocks"; three were laid up and the three listed as "in commission," including both *Pennsylvania* and the old *Ohio,* were being used as "receiving ships" for recruits. There were thirteen 50-gun sailing frigates, of which most were laid up, a few cruising on distant stations. There were six "steam frigates," of which one, *Franklin,* was a former 50-gun frigate which the Navy was trying to

---

[17] These were the only big paddle ships built after Stockton's success with *Princeton.* They were never tested in action, but were otherwise successful. *Powhatan* particularly was a much-loved ship in the old Navy, comfortable, easy-going, reliable and highly seaworthy, as she proved by riding out a severe hurricane after the Civil War. Large classes of small paddle vessels of one sort or another were built or acquired during the Civil War to meet the demand for cheap and quickly available shoal-draft vessels; but it seems hardly just to accuse the old Navy of clinging stupidly to the paddle after *Princeton* had demonstrated the feasibility of the propeller.

convert to steam; the others were the paddle steamers *Mississippi,*
Powhatan and *Susquehanna* and a couple of minor craft. *Princeton,*
then "rebuilding," the ancient *Fulton* and the weak but durable Great
Lakes iron steamer *Michigan* were listed as "first-class steamers." In
addition, there were twenty-four sailing sloops and brigs and one
schooner on the list.

Secretary Dobbin's program for six "propeller frigates" went through
the Senate without debate and was adopted by the House (despite some
opposition from the interior) by the overwhelming vote of 112 to 43.
The reasons behind this enthusiasm seem to have been as confused and
short-sighted as those from which most peacetime military programs
spring. The new commitments on the Pacific Coast no doubt lent
logic to some measure of naval expansion. The new mood of aggressive nationalism reinforced the traditional support of New England
and the Atlantic coastal cities for any naval building. The developing
coal and iron industry in the Pennsylvania hinterlands was awakening
an interest in naval contracts in areas which had hitherto been hostile.
The Southern slave-holders, debarred from California by the Compromise of 1850, were thirsting for compensatory adventure in Cuba
of a kind which might well bring a clash with Spain and with British
sea power. The Crimean crisis in Europe supplied an argument, distinctly far-fetched, for more naval strength with which to protect our
neutral commerce from possible belligerent interference. Only from
the depths of the West did there come a protest, voiced by the old
Jacksonian, Thomas Hart Benton, against these plans for "aggression"
and "conquest." [18] Clearly, the sectional issue had not yet got into the
naval debate. Britain supplied the potential enemy—that necessity of
all military expansion programs—and Pierce probably hoped that by
promoting foreign excitements he could damp the sectional conflict.
The Southerners were in fact fond of stressing their devotion to the
Union in face of the "British threat."

Yet the six wooden steam frigates of the *Wabash* class were hardly
a sufficient answer to British sea power; it was soon realized that they
would not even be an answer to the problems of a naval war in the

[18] Sprouts, *op. cit.*, p. 143.

Caribbean, for they were too deep of draft for the Southern and Gulf Coast harbors on which they would have to base.[19] In December 1854 Secretary Dobbin produced a second program calling for smaller, lighter draft screw sloops. But the enthusiasm was now dwindling; the debate went on in a rather desultory fashion, sparked only now and then by renewed threats of "crisis" with Great Britain; and it was not until an end-of-session "log-jam" in March 1857, that Dobbin finally got through a bill for five such vessels. The Southerners who urged them could not have foreseen the uses to which they would be put. One of these five was *Hartford,* to become famous as Farragut's flagship, and all proved valuable weapons against the Confederacy. Buchanan's administration brought in a program for ten more, which was debated in the summer of 1858. The Panic of 1857 had in the meanwhile provided its own discouragements to naval expenditure, but seven—the *Iroquois* and *Pawnee* classes—were authorized. The rather curious result was that in the half-dozen years before the Civil War the Federal Navy was provided with eighteen reasonably modern and effective ships (six *Wabashes,* five *Hartfords* and seven *Iroquois*) largely by the efforts of the Southerners, against whom they were to be used. It was not until the frenetic early weeks of 1861 that the situation became clear. It was then the Northerners who, in February, demanded seven more screw sloops; the Southern Congressmen were now fiercely opposed, but with their ranks already decimated by secession it was too late. The bill passed the House by 113 to 38, and marked the beginning of the great Federal war Navy.

In the interval between 1848 and 1861 there was, in fact, no real revision of our military system or want of system. The Army was given its two new cavalry regiments [20] and dispatched into the now vaster

[19] Of these six fine and costly ships, only *Wabash* was to see much service when war did come along the southern coasts. *Merrimac* was captured by the Confederates and converted into the famous ironclad. *Roanoke* was razeed by the North and rebuilt as an armored turret ship, which proved a failure. *Minnesota, Colorado* and *Niagara* spent most of the war laid up or on "distant station."

[20] Joe Johnston was lieutenant colonel of the 1st Cavalry, and James E. B. Stuart, who had been too young for Mexico, was a captain. McClellan transferred from the Engineers to take a captain's commission, but did not serve. The 2nd Cavalry was known as "Jeff Davis's Own," after the then Secretary of

regions of the West to discharge its accustomed functions in police, exploration and Indian fighting. The naval building was more a matter of misguided domestic politics and log-rolling than anything else. Nothing much was done about the militia. There was a certain amount of popular interest in military affairs in the early 50's. New volunteer units appeared in some of the state forces—the later celebrated 71st New York was formed in 1851—and some of the states bestirred themselves to improve the training and equipment of the existing volunteer corps. But the impulse tended to evaporate as the decade wore on.

The regular services endeavored to keep up with modern developments. Lieutenant George B. McClellan of the Engineers was sent to Europe to examine the European military systems and got in on the last phases of the Crimean War, which he reported in careful detail and with admirable sketches from his own pencil. The Navy adopted the shell gun as its standard weapon, and Rodman developed his method for casting heavy ordnance. In the mid-'50's the Army adopted the rifled musket, on the Minié principle, as its shoulder arm, and ceased to manufacture smooth-bores. On the eve of the Civil War an Army board was considering the general introduction of rifled pieces into the field artillery (which then consisted of seven batteries, or about forty guns in all) and the Navy was studying the conversion of its wooden sailing fleet to steam. The vulnerability of wooden ships to shellfire as demonstrated in the Crimean War, and the success of the iron-plated French floating batteries at Kinburn in 1854, had not escaped the professionals. Military men were not unaware of the problems of the future. But they were a small and isolated group in our tumultuous community; while neither they nor anybody else had brought any fundamental criticism to bear upon the basic military

---

War, who was to become President of the Confederacy. Its colonel was Albert Sidney Johnston; its lieutenant colonel, Robert E. Lee, but its junior officers included men who were to become famous on both sides. Both George Stoneman, the Federal cavalry leader, and George Thomas, the Virginian who cast his lot with the North to become the "Rock of Chickamauga," held commissions in the 2nd Cavalry. John H. Herr and Edward S. Wallace, *The Story of the U. S. Cavalry* (Boston, Little, Brown, 1953), p. 75.

foundations of our society. We would manage again, if we ever had to, as we had managed in the past. The nation was not preparing for war; least of all was it preparing for the civil war which was so soon to engulf it.

If Polk's attitude on the eve of the Mexican War seems casual, the attitudes of the politicians and publicists of both sides who precipitated the Civil War must seem almost criminally reckless in the light of after-knowledge. Almost no one considered the available military means or attempted to estimate the possible costs. This was, and for years had been, a political quarrel; political issues had always been resolved at the polls or in Congressional votes, and few even thought of what they might mean if translated into military terms. To the South, secession was a political and legal, not a military, act; to some, at least, it was no more than a means of forcing a better political settlement within a restored Union. Until the guns actually opened on Fort Sumter, few in the North believed that the Southern challenge would be made good. The war was precipitated in a process of bluff and miscalculation; neither side had made any serious preparation to fight it (though the South had done something), and neither guessed at the power and ferocity with which the other would arise to the struggle. Both were to emerge in the end to confront a toll of death and suffering, devastation and bitterness so disproportionate to the original issues that even today there is little agreement as to just what the "causes" were or how they engendered a catastrophe of such appalling magnitude.

A part of the answer must surely lie in the Revolutionary and Napoleonic democratization of war. The war was hardly made by "the people" on either side; certainly, the secession majorities in the Southern conventions carried some dubious mandates, while the North never clearly faced the issue until it had been in effect decided at Fort Sumter. But it was made by the processes of popular democracy, by the politicians and the press and the propagandists operating in the framework of popular pressures and democratic mass politics. And the tremendous response to the first calls for volunteers on both sides would have been impossible except in the relatively new atmospheres of popular nationalism. Later on, as the strain and bloodshed grew, war-weariness and defeatism were to appear on both sides. But the Moloch had by that time been established and institutionalized; its votaries could no longer escape from it.

Another part of the answer must doubtless be found in the technological background. The Industrial Revolution was now coming fully of age; it provided the machines and methods which made possible both the suddenness with which the war came and the ferocity with which it was waged. The swift, disastrous course of events in late 1860 and the first months of 1861 could hardly have occurred without the railroad and the telegraph. Without these devices the South could not so quickly have assembled its conventions, formed its government, raised and concentrated its armies and issued the orders which precipitated the conflict. In retrospect, the decisive crisis at Sumter has the aspects of a trap sprung upon both sides more by the speed of telegraphic communications than by anyone's design.

Obviously, the war might well have come even had there been more time for moderation and compromise. Once joined, however, technology was to intensify the scope, deadliness and universality of the struggle with a speed that would previously have been impossible. The railroad and river steamboat enabled both sides to mobilize, supply and deploy armies of unprecedented size with an unprecedented promptness. Barely fifteen years before the United States had called to the colors no more than 104,000 men over the whole course of the Mexican War, while Scott's climactic campaign against Mexico City, late in the second year of the war, was carried out with only some 5,000 combat troops. In 1861 the Confederate Congress began by voting, two days after Lincoln's inauguration, an army of 100,000 volunteers. It is said to have had a third of them organized and under arms in a little over a month; and as early as mid-July it actually deployed about 18,000 men on the single battlefield of Bull Run. Lincoln, who had started by calling for 75,000 militia in mid-April, is said to have had something like 250,000 men under arms by July; and at Bull Run the North deployed a few more men than did the South. When in the immediately following days both sides took serious measure of the struggle lying before them, the Northern Congress voted an army of 500,000 men and the Southerners one of 400,000.

Forces of such size had not been heard of since Napoleon had scoured most of Western Europe for the Russian campaign of 1812.

Begun on this scale, the war was to be waged with a mounting intensity for which, again, the new steam-powered technology was in large part responsible. It is estimated that from first to last about 900,000 individuals served in the Confederate armies and about 1,500,000 in those of the North.[21] In providing these hosts with weapons, ammunition, accoutrements and clothing, as well as with transportation and supply, industry on both sides was to perform remarkable feats. Perhaps the most striking demonstration of the strength of the new technological base lay, not in its production from the already established plants, but in its ability to create new ones, especially in the South where virtually a whole war industry had to be, and was, evoked out of almost nothing.

The tempo of the struggle was never seriously slowed by want on either side of guns, ammunition or even transport. The American Revolution (also in large part a civil war) had dragged on through seven years in a series of small engagements widely separated in time and place, the forces growing smaller and their impact on the community less as the years went by. The Civil War rose in a steady and terrible crescendo of violence, of shocking casualty lists, of complete commitment of life and fortune; it took but four years to beat the weaker side into an exhaustion and defeat more nearly "total" than even France had suffered in 1814 and 1815. The grim novelty of this aspect of war in the age of steam was somewhat concealed at the time by the fact that it was a civil war, in which total triumph and complete restoration of the national authority was the natural outcome, indeed, the only alternative to a dissolution of the state. But the same technological factors were to operate in international as in internecine conflict; "limited" war between states was becoming less and less practicable and "total" solutions, gruesome and undesirable as they might be, less and less avoidable.

[21] The peak strength of the Southern army was 261,000 men, in June 1863. The Federal armies continued to grow, reaching a peak of 622,000 in April 1865. Clement Eaton, *A History of the Southern Confederacy* (New York, Macmillan, 1954), p. 89.

At all events, with the bombardment of Fort Sumter the South had managed to create an issue irresolvable by any means save force. Since there must always be some method of decision if human affairs are not to end in chaos, and since war had always served the necessary social purpose of returning decision when all resources of legal theory or political compromise had failed, war became "inevitable" and the "irrepressible conflict" was upon us. At the outset, it did not seem that the costs of the arbitrament would be unduly high. The North, with the obviously decisive preponderance of long-term strength, could bring the South to its senses in one effective blow; the South, which for the short run was actually not so far from equality of force as is sometimes supposed, could as easily convince the North that the task of reconquest was too grim to be worthwhile. Both were of course mistaken; and it has been argued ever since that had the nation been maintaining a powerful military system such mistakes would not have arisen and the tragedy would have been averted.

Upton's dictum that "20,000 regular troops at Bull Run would have routed the insurgents, settled the question of military resistance and relieved us from the pain and expense of four years of war" has been reiterated as endlessly and unquestioningly as many similar utterances about the origins of other wars. Yet it suffers from the defect of all such theses; it assumes that it would have been possible to alter one factor in a complex military-political equation while leaving all others unchanged. Twenty thousand trained and well-led national troops could no doubt have swept the 18,000 very green Confederates from the field of Manassas, and so probably have ended the war. But such a Federal force could not have existed. To deploy 20,000 regulars on the banks of Bull Run would have necessitated a much larger Federal standing army; there could have been no reason for creating such a force except to coerce the South, and Southern political power in the decade before the Civil War would naturally have vetoed any such proposal. The large standing army had been rejected from the beginning precisely in order to ensure that it could not be used by any one group, interest or section to coerce the rest of the community; the states had clung to their control over the militia as "security against the possible abuse of the delegated [war] power," and to maintain the independent state sovereignty which the slave states were now asserting. Implicit in Upton's military argument is almost the whole political and constitutional issue over which the Civil War was fought. Had that issue already been decided the war, naturally, would not and could not have taken place. After it had been concluded and the national power had been established, it was easy to dream of a national army which would have averted the bloodshed; but Upton's "20,000 regulars" were again an army of a dream only. Military power is never created and never exists in a political vacuum; war, as Clausewitz observed, is "an instrument of policy."

5.

The American people had to fight out their bitter differences within the framework of the military institutions and resources which they shared in common at the beginning of 1861. Hostilities in fact began in the competitive scramble to divide up what was available; indeed, it was Lincoln's call upon the militia which forced the border states to take sides. In this division, the South's share was not inconsiderable. The fact that virtually all the enlisted men of the regular Army remained loyal to the North (where most of them had been recruited) did not matter greatly, since they numbered only about 16,000 in all. The South's failure to secure any of the Navy (except *Merrimac,* captured at Norfolk, and the aged and useless *Fulton* which was at Pensacola) was more serious, especially as it had few shipyards and was devoid of a single engine works capable of turning out marine power plants. But the South had its own volunteer militia units, often fairly well equipped and trained; while the discrepancy in untrained military manpower was not as great as it has often seemed.

The South had only 1,140,000 white males between the ages of 15 and 40, as against over 4,000,000 for the North. But the South's slave population (3,500,000) released a larger proportion of her white men for military service than the North could spare. And, after due discount for romantic Southern legend, it still seems probable that at least in the early stages the Southern recruits provided the better military material. The agrarian South presented a combination of a slave-holding aristocracy with a population of small farmers, still living in many areas close to frontier conditions. In both groups there doubtless survived a wider general familiarity with firearms, with outdoor living and the kind of hardships imposed by campaign life than was to be found among the more settled and more heavily urbanized people of the North. Such aptitudes counted in a war in which there was seldom time for anything approaching adequate combat training. And the aristocratic South, which had contributed far more to the professional officer corps than it had to the rank and file of the small regular services, got much more than its share of the country's slim stock of experienced military brains and leadership.

If there were comparatively few trained men and officers, there was a considerable supply of weapons. Ever since the act of 1808 the Federal government had been manufacturing arms and equipment and distributing them to the states in the sum of $200,000 a year, allotted in proportion to the state returns of enrolled militia. Much of this material was wasted or lost; much of it became obsolete, but many useable arms remained under state control. These had been supplemented by the states' own purchases, or by the acquisitions of the volunteer corps at their private expense. The Federal government had at the same time gone on accumulating a surplus of weapons in its own arsenals against a time of need; it had armed its new seacoast forts with heavy artillery and built up reserves of naval guns and ammunition in the shipyards. There is a double irony in the fact that while the South had been instrumental in building the navy that was to be used against it, the North had provided the fortifications and artillery with which the South was to repel their attack.

The South occupied or soon captured all the seacoast fortifications (with the single important exception of Fort Taylor at Key West) and acquired the four hundred-odd heavy guns they contained. It seized the great Norfolk Navy Yard, with large stores of artillery and material. Out of the national stock of about 530,000 small arms in the Federal arsenals (of all degrees of modernity) the South secured about 135,-000 rifled and smooth-bore muskets. It raided the Federal arms factory at Harpers Ferry and managed to bring away not only some thousands of stand of rifles but much of the gun-making machinery, which was reinstalled at Richmond and at Fayetteville, N. C. There seems no way of comparing the munitions reserves in the hands of the states and private owners. Louisiana's Washington Artillery armed itself from the seizure of the Federal arsenal at Baton Rouge; Virginia, on the other hand (which possessed the South's one great industrial asset, the Tredegar Iron Works at Richmond), had by mid-June of 1861 organized and armed twenty field batteries of her own and provided 115 field pieces for these units and for those of other states.[22] The South initially had or seized quite enough to start with, and was to apply itself more energetically than the North to making up the deficiencies through purchase, importation and the organization of its war industry.

The South had both men and munitions enough to withstand any siege which the North could initially bring against it. For the later stages it could, while building its own war industry, draw upon the tremendous productivity of Britain and France, for the ocean-going steamship had now made European resources available much more freely than before. The South had its purchasing agents in London and Paris (and in New York as well!) before hostilities began. The obvious difficulty was that the North had the Navy; the South had none, and as soon as the North could get its ships back home from the far corners of the earth it would institute a blockade with a sea power which the South could not match.

It was out of this dilemma that there sprang the one most famous, if scarcely the most significant, military innovation associated with the Civil War—the steam-driven, ironclad warship. There was nothing new in the idea. The French had used ironclad floating batteries in the Crimea; in 1858 they had brought out the ironclad, sea-going frigate *Gloire* and the British had responded with the all-iron *Warrior*. Since 1854 the all-iron "Stevens battery" had been on the stocks at Hoboken. Progress with armored ships had not been rapid, however, partly out of conservatism, partly because difficult design problems remained unsolved. But Stephen Mallory, now the Confederate Secretary of the Navy, saw that he was faced with a situation which did not permit him

[22] Jennings Cropper Wise, *The Long Arm of Lee* (Lynchburg, 1915), pp. 34, 70. O. E. Hunt, in *The Photographic History of the Civil War,* Vol. V, p. 124.

to wait upon perfection. Ironclad floating batteries could be improvised; and however awkward, slow and unseaworthy they might be they could sally from the Southern ports to destroy or drive off the wooden blockaders. In his report of May 8, 1861, he established his celebrated ironclad policy, and by early July he had approved the plans for the conversion of the captured *Merrimac*. Throughout the war, the Confederates were to prove indefatigable and ingenious in their efforts to use armor as an answer to Federal command of the sea, and if they had possessed more rolling mills and ironworks they might have succeeded.[23]

The North awoke almost too late. Engaged upon a furious program of buying and building seakeeping wooden ships, it did not even appoint its ironclad board until August. In its report of September 16 it adopted three experimental designs; one of them was Ericsson's extraordinary little *Monitor,* which struggled into Hampton Roads on the disastrous evening of March 8, 1862 in the nick of time to halt *Virginia's* (or *Merrimac's*) murderous career. The still blazing wreck of *Congress* was providing its fiery tribute to the shell gun and the helplessness of the sail-driven wooden warship.

The battles in Hampton Roads on March 8 and 9, 1862 clearly wrote the doom both of sail power and unarmored wood construction. Yet it was to be a long time before sail power could finally be dispensed with, while it was the wooden warship which in fact did most of the naval work throughout the rest of the war. Armor was important on the Western rivers, and the North was to produce some thirty more vessels of the monitor type (as well as several high-freeboard armored ships) which were sufficient to bottle up or destroy all the other makeshift armored batteries which the South could improvise. But the sea-keeping wooden ships still had to bear the burden of blockade, transport and amphibious war as well as the far-ranging missions of commerce protection or destruction. The Civil War monitors, essentially coastal craft, were obsolete within a few years; and it was not until the '80's, when the design problems presented by an

[23] Joseph T. Durkin, *Stephen R. Mallory: Confederate Navy Chief* (Chapel Hill, N. C., University of North Carolina Press, 1954), *passim*.

oceangoing armored ship had been got in hand, that the revolution in naval architecture was effected.

The Civil War has often been considered the "first modern war" because of the number of "firsts" associated, not always accurately, with it—the first use of armored warships without sails, of steam-powered logistics by rail and river, of telegraphy, of photography, of aerial (balloon) observation. The war saw the first general use of rifled weapons and the appearance of breech-loading and magazine arms like the Colt revolver, the Hall carbine, the Sharps and Winchester rifles and several systems of early machine guns, like those of Gatling and Williamson. It saw the first extensive introduction of rifled field artillery, sometimes breech-loading. It saw the first considerable development of the marine mine or "torpedo" and a rudimentary form of submarine warfare; it also developed the land mine. It was to see the first mass disappearance into the ground, into trenches or behind breastworks. It improved the sanitary services and saw the first widespread introduction of anesthesia to mitigate the horrors of military medicine. It witnessed the first appearance in the United States of general conscription; it is also probably correct to say that it saw the first extensive application of mass-production and assembly-line techniques in several areas of American industrial production. It was out of the Civil War demand for uniforms, for example, and the mass methods adopted to meet it, that there developed the mass-produced, ready-made men's clothing industry.

But in spite of all such innovations, the great struggle was less "modern" than transitional. Much of the bloody past still clung to its operations and to the concepts which energized them; and it was not until the later years of the war that the new weapons and logistics began to draw the outlines of a different, if no less bloody, future. The enthusiastic volunteering of the young, still fired by the romantic nineteenth-century ideas of glory and honor, made it unnecessary to face until well on in the war the hard problems of conscription and of the military obligation in a democracy. There were similar unresolved issues in the technical field. One reason why the breech-loading and magazine rifles (which now existed in practicable form, together with the machine industry to produce them) were not more extensively introduced lay in the heavy demands they would make on the ammunition supply. Ordnance officers realized with alarm that a soldier so equipped would quickly fire away all the ammunition he could carry. And in spite of the railroads, the armies were still dependent on horse-drawn transport (over abominable roads) for resupply in the field. The logistic problem of feeding the new quick-loading and quick-firing weapons was a serious one. It was not unreasonable or obscurantist to conclude that the soldier should be made to stand and fight it out himself with whatever ball cartridge he could carry in his pouch. Powerful though it was, technology was then not equal in either production or supply to the concept of "substituting firepower for men"—a concept which in Korea a century later was to give rise to peaks of ammunition expenditure unheard of even in the Second World War.

Perhaps there was also conservatism of a kind involved. In 1861 (if not in 1865) war was still personal; it was a "fight" between men, individuals, whose individual prowess, courage and devotion counted, not a contest between machines. The fight obviously had to be organized, directed and nourished by leadership, as in such great and ghastly dramas as Antietam or Gettysburg, but it was still a personal and usually hand-to-hand encounter—a few sweating, desperately angered and terrified men engaged against their counterparts. The weapons were the tools of this personal struggle, like the broadsword or the battle ax of the Middle Ages; but the idea that the rifled musket or the breech-loading repeater of 1861 could itself impose new terms upon the fight was not readily acceptable. In 1861 war was not yet an engineering operation. The concept of firepower as a substitute or alternative for manpower, had not yet been invented, because it was the man who still did the fighting. Battle was still, in the last analysis, "we-uns agin they-uns," a struggle over a time period of no more than a day or two for a specific piece of ground, the possession of which would in its turn affect the course of the war and the ability of one side physically to gain occupancy and control of the other's territory and government. The veterans of those struggles were in after years to boast "I fit with Grant"—or Lee or Jackson, as the case might be. It is a phrase rarely heard from present-day veterans, who usually say that they "served" with this or that division or air force or headquar-

ters, and not often that they "fought" with it. The atmosphere at the
opening of the Civil War was not too propitious to the development of
"scientific" and "secret" weapons that would remove the whole issue
from the struggle of men. It was this sort of conservatism which may
have militated against the more extensive introduction of the machines
which were then already available. If so, it confirms the contention that
the War Between the States was a "transition" war.

The Civil War began at Bull Run with what was already, no doubt,
the anachronism of men standing up in ordered ranks in the open to
fight each other with ball, bayonet and butt; not until it was reaching
its end in the trenches before Petersburg was the killing being brought
down to the engineering operation which it was increasingly to become.
Some 200,000 battle dead separated that beginning from that end.
Many of the more romantic concepts of war—of its glory, its honor,
its respect for the weak, its rewards for the valorous, its obedience to
international law and etiquette—died with them. When it was over
the war of the "fight" was already deeply overlaid by the beginnings
of the war of organization and the machine, the war against civilians
and resources as well as against the uniformed soldiery of the enemy,
the war of conscripted peoples rather than of volunteer armies.

To ascribe the transition solely to material causes would be to take
a foolishly narrow view; but that material causes were of major importance it is scarcely possible to deny. And of them, the two most
significant were probably the caplock rifled musket and steam-powered
transport. It was the railroad and the river steamboat which robbed
the great battlefield victories of finality. It was these devices, managed
by telegraphic communications, which made it possible promptly
to repair the terrible casualties of the major battles, to resupply and
re-equip, to draw reinforcements from another theater to plug the gaps
which the enemy opened up, to maneuver not only armies but groups
of armies so as to prevent defeat from turning into destruction. Gettysburg may have represented "the high-water mark of the rebellion," but
it came only about halfway through a war which was to exact many
more lives afterward than before. In the Civil War there were no
"decisive" battles; there were no Austerlitzes or Waterloos. The battle
was still a single brief moment of supreme commitment, of maximum

savagery and sacrifice.[24] But when it was decided, the defeated side could always crawl away into the support of its bases and technological resources and make ready to fight again. In the end, the war was never exactly "won"; it ran down rather in the exhaustion of the weaker side.

The railroads endowed the armies with mobility and the power of prompt reinforcement and resupply; but in so doing they exacted (as Liddell Hart points out) the paradoxical price which has always been the cost of mechanical advance in war. In freeing the armies they also enslaved them—to their rail lines. The airplane is without doubt the most completely mobile weapon in the history of war, yet is bound remorselessly to its immovable bases and landing fields. A modern tank column can range enemy territory with a speed and invulnerability hitherto unknown in ground war, but it is tied to its gasoline supply. Mobility in war has two parts; speed is only one of them, freedom is the other. The steam warship could range the oceans with a speed and certainty unknown to sail, but was a slave to its coaling ports. The sail-driven battle line was slow and subject to the unpredictable vagaries of weather, but it was also free: a Nelsonian fleet could cruise for months, even years, at a time without once having to return to base.

The Civil War armies paid for their mobility and their ready resupply by being bound to their rail and river lines. The rail lines were still few, and so permitted of less flexibility than had been possible with the slower-paced but more numerous road nets of Napoleon's time, or than would be possible again when the railway and the hard road systems became much more extensive. Strategy in the Civil War tended more and more to center upon the protection of one's own and

[24] Upton, the Civil War veteran, commenting severely upon the behavior of the volunteers in Mexico, remarks that a unit which lost no more than 10 per cent of its strength in any major action of the Civil War would have been regarded as having been hardly seriously engaged. In the big Civil War battles casualties of 50 per cent for units were not unusual and of 80 or 90 per cent were not unheard of. While comparisons are very difficult, it is probably correct to say that in World War II a casualty rate of 10 per cent in any single action, or over any comparatively limited period of operations, would have been considered unacceptably high. When the capture of Tarawa atoll in April 1944 cost 17 per cent in casualties (about 6 per cent in deaths) it was considered something of a scandal.

the destruction of the enemy's rail lines. The importance of the rail-roads, moreover, further emphasized the importance of what went over them. Earlier wars had concentrated upon the capture or destruction of enemy armies in the field. The Civil War was one of the first in which "strategic warfare," as the Air Force has taught us to call it, assumed a dominant role.

The wholly strategic weapon of naval blockade was applied to the South from the beginning; it was comparatively ineffective in the earlier years, but was telling rather heavily toward the end. The North's success in securing complete command of the Ohio-Mississippi system was primarily a strategic victory, cutting off the South's access to the material and manpower resources of Louisiana and Texas, and opening the way to the capture of other important Southern resources. A crisis was caused in the South when the North took the Tennessee copper mines, which were vital even in that pre-electronic age for the supply of copper caps for the muskets. It was met by appropriating the many copper whiskey stills to be found in the country. The supply problems became worse when the North overran the coal-and-iron complex which had been painfully brought to birth in Alabama. One east-west rail line was lost at Chattanooga; and with the fall of Atlanta in the autumn of 1864, the South lost the heart of her internal rail net. Sherman's subsequent march to the sea gutted a great area of food and cotton production, as well as taking such significant war industry centers as Macon, where the South had developed much of her manufacture of small arms ammunition and military equipment. Sheridan's devastation of the beautiful Valley of Virginia in late 1864, in order to deny its abundance to the Confederacy, was another grim example of what "strategic" warfare against enemy resources had already come to imply, long before the era of airborne "fire-storms" and "population bombing." And the intense bitterness with which Sherman's and Sheridan's "war on women and children" was to be remembered in the South is its own indication of what violence it did to the established conventions of war; and of how novel—to Amer-icans, at least—were these rough lessons in what modern warfare was really coming to mean.

If steam transportation was one determining factor in shaping these new faces of war, the caplock rifled musket was another. This weapon not only had a faster and more dependable rate of fire than the smooth-bore flintlock; it also raised the killing range from some fifty to some five hundred yards. That alone spelled the end of the old-fashioned massed bayonet charge in dressed ranks, even more of the use of heavy cavalry as a shock weapon against infantry. There were, of course, many bayonet charges throughout the Civil War; but many were ghastly failures, while even the successes were ghastly enough— as Brady's dreadful photographs of such fields as Antietam or Gettysburg still show—to compel some other solution for the problem of achieving victory in battle.

The accurate range of the rifled musket was so great that it could be loaded and fired not once but several times as an enemy line approached. The attacker, on the other hand, could not easily stop to take accurate aim in reply, and he could do so even less if the defenders were behind a wall or in entrenchments. Something could be done by opening out and loosening up the attack formation and by throwing out skirmishers (when there was cover for them) to keep down the defender's fire. Yet battles could not be won with skirmishers or long-range sharpshooting. To win a field one had to arrive upon the enemy's position with weight and shock power enough to drive him; and there seemed no way of doing that save by ordering the devoted masses forward. As late as January 1863 Burnside at Fredericksburg, because he could think of nothing better, sent his battalions up an exposed slope against Barksdale's Mississippians lying behind the famous stone wall at the top of the rise. What the troops thought about such tactics by that time is suggested by the story that many lettered their names, next of kin and home addresses on their handkerchiefs and sewed these to the backs of their tunics before the advance. The "dog tag" was unheard of then. But when an infantry spontaneously provides its own, the time has come for the generals to exercise greater ingenuity.

Artillery offered a possible answer, and the Civil War witnessed a considerable development of that arm. The results, however, were not wholly satisfactory. When the war began, the standard field artillery pieces were the 6-pounder bronze gun and the 12-pounder bronze howitzer, both smooth-bores. The howitzer could be fired over the heads of the infantry front line and the gun, placed with the infantry, could rake an advancing battle line with grape and canister to terrible effect. Neither, however, had the range to deal with the rifled musket. Rifled artillery—the Model 1861 3-inch cast-iron rifle, the Parrott rifles, the similar Brooke rifles in the South and various other inventions—promptly appeared in quantity. The rifled gun had the range and accuracy to face the rifled musket, but its destructive power was small, especially against an enemy behind entrenchments. Although large numbers of rifled pieces were produced and used on both sides, the smooth-bores, like the bayonet charges against which they were principally useful, survived throughout the war. A return for Rosecrans' army in 1863 shows that about a half of his artillery were smooth-bores;[25] they were retained, not only because of the difficulty of replacing them, but because their shotgun discharge of grape at close quarters performed the same function as that of the machine gun in the First World War.

What was desired from the artillery was a means of searching out and softening up an enemy position before it was necessary to send home the infantry attack. The guns became of greater and greater importance. Both armies learned by experience to mass their artillery, as Napoleon had done. Where both had started by assigning a single 4-gun battery to an infantry brigade, both ended with artillery "brigades" assigned to divisions and with large reserve artillery formations assigned to corps and army. But the artillery was still unable to reduce the infantry casualties to endurable limits. According to a German student of the time, the "enormous losses" which continued to be sustained even under the massed batteries led to a "third period, where we find rifle pits, entrenchments, obstacles and cover of every description brought into requisition to such an extent that the axe and the spade appear to play almost as important a part as the firearms themselves.[26] According to Jac Weller, the proportion of field guns to infantry soldiers was about the same in the Napoleonic, the Civil and

[25] Birkhimer, *op. cit.,* p. 285.
[26] *United Service,* Vol. I, p. 530 (Oct. 1879).

the First World Wars. But in the Civil War the artillery was insufficiently developed to solve the problems it faced.

As the defense went increasingly behind earthworks, the attacker's artillery was unable to follow it with sufficient effect. It was not until a few years later that the development of the shrapnel shell [27] was to provide a means for searching out and destroying men beyond rifle range and behind defenses. While the preliminary artillery bombardment was used frequently throughout the Civil War, it was not very effective. At Gettysburg the batteries fired a strong preparation for Pickett's charge against Union infantry which was not even entrenched, but the preparation failed to prepare, as the bloody and decisive repulse was to demonstrate. The smooth-bores lacked range and the rifled field guns lacked killing power.

The armies had begun to dig in almost from the beginning; as the war progressed they dug with increasing fervor. Against artillery and the long-range rifled musket they used felled logs, hay bales, stone walls, railway cuts, road embankments and the shovel. "It was one of Professor Mahan's maxims," Uncle Billy Sherman remembered, "that the spade was as useful in war as the musket, and to this I will add the axe." [28] It is said that even Lee, the engineer, was neglectful of field fortification as late as Antietam, but by the time of the climactic campaign from Cold Harbor to Petersburg the armies were digging in at every momentary pause; until, before Petersburg, they arrived at a

---

[27] This gruesome device preserves the name of Lieutenant Henry Shrapnel of the Royal Artillery, who as early as 1784 had conceived the idea of partly filling the spherical shell of the time with musket balls to increase the deadliness of the burst. The expedient could not, however, achieve full effectiveness until the appearance of the rifled field gun, with its elongated projectile which retained its directional orientation throughout its flight. The modern shrapnel, first used effectively in the Franco-Prussian War, carries its explosive charge in the base. Timed to burst in the air just before reaching its target, it spews out a "pattern" of pellets, like that from a shotgun, with an effect on personnel much like that of the old smooth-bore grapeshot, but at a distance of 3,000 yards or more from the gun. The shrapnel shell was, indeed, said to be itself a smooth-bore gun, but one flung by the parent gun into close range before its discharge. Enormous quantities of shrapnel were fired in the First World War; then, as with most other weapons, technological change in both offense and defense overtook it, and it was little used in the Second World War.

[28] W. T. Sherman, *Memoirs* (New York, 1879), Vol. II, p. 396.

form of siege and trench warfare not outdone either by the trenches
of northern France during the First World War or the bunkers of
Korea. Naked flesh could no longer be asked or forced to stand up to
the sheets of lead which the new weapons were pouring out. The
armies went into the ground completely at the end. But perhaps the
most significant thing about this war was the fact that it was not really
decided by the armies. There was no "decisive" battle even at Petersburg. The South simply ran out of manpower—rather as Hitler's Germany did in 1945. It was at the same time, of course, running out of
much else. It had been cut to pieces by the campaign on the Mississippi
and the march through Georgia. Its war industry in Georgia and Alabama had been captured. The blockade had finally become effective;
the fall of Fort Fisher on the Cape Fear in 1865 had closed the last
outlet to the world. The last firm center of resistance in Virginia had
nothing more to stand on. Lee, a Virginia aristocrat, recognized the
situation as Hitler, the paranoiac, was never able to do. There was no
other possible outcome. But the Army of Northern Virginia had not
been defeated; it was surrendered.

War had changed. Where, in Napoleonic times, the great set battle
piece had usually decided the political issue, it was no longer capable
of doing so. The major struggle of armies had come down to a kind of
siege warfare in which now the whole people were involved—a struggle of fortification and concealment, of mines and countermines, on the
fighting fronts; and a struggle over communications and resources,
blockade, the capture of rail lines, the devastation of the productive
farm areas, the terrorization of civilians, the women and children
behind the lines. A new age of violence had dawned.

CHAPTER III

The Managerial Revolution

1.

IT COULD have been said on the morrow of the Civil War that some other way than this would have to be found for deciding those basic issues in human affairs which are irresolvable by the processes of law, politics or negotiation. It was irrational to defend an established order, established ideas and interests, by means so destructive as certainly to transform that order beyond recognition, whoever won or lost. The costs had been enormously disproportionate to the issues; while even the decision was to prove less decisive than it had appeared, as the politicians of Reconstruction struggled with problems they had not foreseen and as a "Solid South" arose to nullify in part the fruits of the great emancipation and to regain in our politics something of the power of which it had been deprived by arms. It was already evident, in the aftermath of 1865, that the arbitrament of war was no longer a final, a satisfactory or even an acceptable means of settling the political differences which had been so lightly confided to it.

Except, perhaps, within the rather narrow confines of the peace societies, such doubts about the functions of war itself had never been raised in the United States. But this struggle had been too gruesome; too many had longed for the day when "this cruel war is over." In the last bitter year there had been too many on both sides to ask whether it was worth while to continue; and had the Northern election of 1864 gone otherwise there might have been a "compromise" peace. In the dawn of victory there were few in the North to remember these doubts.

Yet there was a popular revulsion against war as such—as there has been after each of our subsequent conflicts, not excluding the brief and exhilarating adventure into colonial empire in 1898. In 1865 the revulsion ran deep. If it was not particularly vocal, it was eloquently manifested in events.

The Grand Army of the Republic, the finest military machine in existence at that time, made its three-day march down Pennsylvania Avenue—and dissolved. An Army and Navy of some power were maintained just long enough to see Napoleon III safely out of Mexico and his puppet Maximilian reduced to an untenable position. With the passage of this one threat of foreign embroilment, the Civil War military structure collapsed. The ships were sold; the guns were stored; the officers faded quickly back into law, politics, business or engineering; the troops returned to farm or factory or, many of them, to such new industrial ventures as the building of the transcontinental railroads. Within a few years the Navy as a combat force was virtually nonexistent, and the regular Army had been cut back to a minimum.

Enough was enough. North and South alike had "had it"; and when President Grant manifested some bizarre tendencies toward military adventure in the Caribbean he was easily dissuaded. In 1873 there was a queer crisis when the inept Spaniards captured the American-flag filibustering ship *Virginius,* took her into Santiago de Cuba and began shooting her crew and "passengers" in platoons. The United States attempted a naval mobilization, only to find that some of the mightiest of the 15-inch gun monitors, which had seemed so formidable in 1865, could barely navigate; and the crisis passed. In the disputed election of 1876 the idea of renewing the sectional war may have flared in some minds, but there was no reality behind it.

With the war's end it was, of course, once more necessary to devise a permanent military system; but no one even dreamed of devising a system which would be capable of refighting such another giant struggle as that which had just passed. Congress had enlarged the regular establishment at the opening of the war. The disappearance of the volunteers (in the year after Appomattox over a million men were mustered out of the Federal service) left an authorized regular Army of six regiments of cavalry, five of artillery and nineteen of infantry.

In mid-summer of 1866 Congress, faced with the policing of the conquered South and a growing Indian problem, added four more cavalry regiments and twenty-six additional regiments of infantry; but even this rather modest expansion could not withstand the inevitable postwar waves of economy. In 1869 the Army appropriations cut the infantry back to twenty-five small regiments.

The demands of the Indian wars forbade a cutback in the cavalry. It was the ten regular cavalry regiments which bore the brunt of the fighting on the Western plains; these are the troops so often celebrated since in celluloid and story. The 1866 act provided that two of the regiments should be composed of Negro soldiers; this gave rise to the 9th and the famous 10th Cavalry, whose dark-skinned troopers showed Theodore Roosevelt the way up Kettle Hill at San Juan in 1898. The 24th and 25th Infantry were also colored—though all, of course, were commanded by white officers. The five regiments of artillery preserved the illogical but traditional combination of field and fortress troops, each with two batteries of field artillery and ten "heavy" fortress companies. The regiments were purely administrative, since the battery and the company were the tactical units. (There was little use for field artillery in the West, although the mountain howitzer, packed by mules, and the Gatling gun were to prove valuable.) The 1869 act not only reduced the number of infantry regiments to twenty-five, but reduced the peacetime company strength to yield an aggregate for the whole Army of about 25,000 men. Such remained the structure, and the approximate strength, of the United States Army down to the Spanish-American War.

The Navy went back to sail. The end of the Civil War put a period to further naval building and experiment. Some of the best of the armor-clads were sold abroad. U.S.S. *Wampanoag,* a splendid, fast light cruiser with a tremendous power plant and an armament powerful enough to overcome Confederate commerce destroyers, was not completed until 1868. On her trials she achieved the then remarkable speed of 17¾ knots. But with no more Confederate cruisers at sea there was no further reason for maintaining a speed machine of this kind. The board which condemned her a year after the trials may have been swayed by jealousy and obscurantism; yet it is a fact that there was no use for her at the time, and when naval rivalry again became important in our affairs, *Wampanoag* would have been as great an anachronism as Ericsson's monitors. The Navy went back to distant patrol, which mainly meant cruising radius. It restored full sail power to the ships; it redesigned the propellers to allow for maximum efficiency under sail rather than maximum speed under power; it made it virtually a court-martial offense for a captain to burn coal. All this was patently "retrogressive." But it may also be said that it was what both the international and domestic situation indicated at the time. For those who look upon the development of military means as all-important, our failure to expand the Civil War beginnings in naval technology must seem lamentable; for those concerned with the ends which the military means are supposed to serve, the post-1865 naval policy will seem to have been rather strikingly successful. The Navy, to be sure, was left for the next fifteen years to disintegrate in obsolescence; yet no vital national interest was even remotely imperiled, the taxpayers probably saved a good deal of money, and such naval "incidents" as occurred—like the clash at Samoa in 1889—lacked the deadliness with which they would have been charged had the United States been engaged upon a challenge for command of the sea.

Thus the regular Army and Navy went back to their old duties. But, as always, it was not the regular establishments which presented the central problem of permanent military policy; it was the militia. "Another most decided effort was made, both in the Senate and House, to reorganize the militia, or rather to create a new militia system, and several bills for that purpose were introduced into the Thirty-ninth Congress [1867-'69]." [1] If the Mexican War had overthrown the militia system, the Civil War had destroyed it. Even the volunteer corps were in a somewhat ambiguous position. No one had thought it remarkable when these units, which had responded to Lincoln's first call for 75,000 militia, went home again after their three months' service was up. Great numbers of their people volunteered for service—New York's 7th Regiment, which departed the scene after Bull Run, claimed three major generals and 606 officers of all grades as graduates from

[1] House Report 763, 46th Cong., 2nd Sess.

its ranks—and many of its enlisted men must have served with honor. But the regiment itself went home to replenish its ranks from those of lesser ardor or with greater domestic commitments. It thus fulfilled its duty to provide the state with armed power for keeping order or suppressing tumult, while the state's young men were providing the nation with the means of waging major war. But the whole system was anomalous. The militia concept, with its theoretically universal obligation, its theoretically universal training and its traditional limitation to no more than three months' service in the field, was impractical. It seemed logical to scrap it altogether in favor of a frankly volunteer force of spare-time state troops. Such a force, which would have demonstrated its interest and willingness, could be given an effective organization and some real training; it would provide something like a true reserve for the tiny regular establishment.

Unhappily, the Thirty-ninth Congress found the militia problem as resistant as had all earlier statesmen; the reform bills did not pass, and it was not until after the Spanish-American War that the Militia Act of 1792 was finally to be repealed. But though it remained upon the books, the life had gone out of it. The states, partly by neglect of their mass systems and partly by encouragement of their volunteer units, in effect replaced the militia of the old concept with the National Guard, which was to remain through many modifications and vicissitudes as the nation's major reliance for a combat reserve.

It may seem odd that this complete acceptance of the volunteer principle, for reserve as well as for standing or regular forces, should have followed upon a war which saw the first introduction of general conscription into American military practice. But the Civil War was really fought by the young volunteers who poured out in their romantic thousands at the beginning. Both in the South and the North, conscription acted more as a support for and encouragement to volunteering than as a substitute for it. On neither side did conscription work very well, whereas the volunteers carried the terrible burdens of the great battles. Sherman summed it up in his memoirs: "We tried almost every system . . . —volunteer enlistments, the draft and bought substitutes—and I think that all officers of experience will confirm my assertion that the men who voluntarily enlisted at the outbreak of the war were the best, better than the conscript and far better than the bought substitute." [2] Sherman's rather simple solution was to rely on volunteers in a future emergency, to keep the combat units filled up with volunteer replacements, and if a prolonged war should make it difficult to get recruits to raise the pay "instead of tempting new men by exaggerated bounties." But how much pay would make a man face the Bloody Angle at Chancellorsville; what bounty would be "exaggerated" for those who could drive home a Pickett's charge? In giving his advice, Sherman could scarcely have been envisaging another total mobilization and all-out war. In those years, no one was.

Through the late '60's and the '70's even the volunteer state armies remained little more than paper organizations save in a few wealthy states—New York and Massachusetts are examples—and even there the military efficiency was not high. The "old Army" (there has always been an "old Army," presumably always will be) returned to the plains, as the Navy had returned to sail, and for years little more was heard of either, except for occasional colorful articles in the sedately romantic monthly magazines of the period. For a decade and a half after the Civil War we remained virtually without a military policy and without an effective military organization through which such a policy could have been expressed.

But if the great civilian public, with its energies engrossed in the creation of the industrial empire, was content with this situation, the professional soldiers and sailors were forced to take stock. By the mid-'70's it was apparent to any thoughtful soldier that his art was on the threshold of tremendous technical changes of unpredictable effect. The European conflicts of the '60's culminating in the Franco-Prussian War of 1870-71 had brought to battlefield application many of the devices which had appeared in only rudimentary form during the Civil War. The "needle-gun" (the Prussian breech-loading rifle which was introduced in the '40's), the mitrailleuse (the French multi-barreled machine gun, resembling the Gatling), the shrapnel shell in its modern form, breech-loading as well as rifled field artillery, more powerful and flexible rail nets and improved telegraphic communica-

[2] W. T. Sherman, *Memoirs* (New York, 1875), Vol. II, p. 386.

tions, were all much in evidence. As the decade advanced, Krupp in Germany, Creusot in France, Armstrong and Whitworth in Britain, were peddling their new armor plate, heavy ordnance and small arms through the world. The democratic and the industrial revolutions between them had provided war with enormously increased potentials of violence and devastation. The underlying problem confronting all the great powers was how to organize and apply these potentials to a genuine furtherance of the national interest.

The problem, though the fact was only dimly realized at the time, had become complicated in that the national was now also a popular interest—partly, indeed, as a result of the development of the great popular armies. As late as the Schleswig-Holstein crisis in 1864 Lord John Russell could severely observe that "the Great Powers had not the habit of consulting populations when questions affecting the Balance of Power had to be settled." Yet the Civil War was a people's struggle; and in France in the crisis of 1870 "for the first time foreign policy did not merely play up to public opinion; it was dictated by public opinion." [3] The military were coming into new and still obscure relationships, not merely to the governments but to the peoples whom they existed to serve. The war potentials were growing very great. How were sound policies to be established for controlling their development, command systems to be created capable of directing them in action or planning staffs to be brought into being which could direct their peacetime growth and prepare them for war? The basic problem was one of management; and the '70's stood on the threshold of what might be called the managerial revolution in war—a third great movement which was to reach its unexpected and terrible climax in the First World War.

It was natural, in that age, to find an immediate answer in "science"; and the scientific and methodical Germans led the way. It was the Germans who developed the general staff system, subsequently imitated by every significant military power; it was the Germans' brilliant series of "little" wars—Denmark in 1864, Austria in 1866 and France in 1870—which gave the Prussian Great General Staff its

[3] A. J. P. Taylor, *The Struggle for Mastery in Europe* (Oxford, 1954), p. 177.

enormous prestige. These wars had been highly efficient, as tidy as possible and victorious. The results had all been wrapped up neatly at the end in the Hall of Mirrors at Versailles, leaving everyone free to go home and get to work with a minimum of suffering or dislocation. Or so it seemed. With scientific study and careful advance planning war would become, like surgery, an almost clinical instrument—an unpleasant and drastic yet necessary tool in serving the needs of men and the state.

The Great General Staff was as much a school for the scientific study of war and the training of top commanders as it was an administrative organization through which command might be exercised. Military men everywhere, inextricably involved in the new problems of metallurgy, ballistics, electrical equipment, military and marine engineering (to say nothing of what would now be called "public relations"), were being forced into theoretical studies of many kinds, before which a Napoleonic general of division would have blanched. It is no accident that in 1880 W. S. Gilbert was lampooning the "modern major gineral" as the master of all things "animal, vegetable or mineral" except possibly the art of war itself. And it is perhaps symbolic that the United States Army, which like the Confederates had worn the French kepi when it was available throughout the Civil War, in 1872 adopted a variant of the German spiked helmet as its dress headgear.

The United States lay on the far periphery of European military development, and its small services afforded American officers neither the men, the ships nor the money for practical experiment in the new fields which were opening abroad. But the more thoughtful took a strong interest in what was going on and did what they could to keep the Army and Navy abreast of things. In 1873 the Army brought itself to abandon the slow-loading rifled musket in favor of a single-shot breech-loader (the .45 caliber Model 1873 Springfield)[4] and at about the same time decided that its mighty Rodman smooth-bores had seen

[4] The manual issued with the new rifle was signed by Colonel S. V. Benét, acting Chief of Ordnance and father of the famous poet. The gun was no doubt already outmoded by the magazine rifles, such as the Winchester, which were much used on the Western plains.

their day as seacoast artillery. After prolonged argument between partisans of muzzle-loading and breech-loading heavy guns, it was agreed that the breech-loaders, even in the largest calibers, had come to stay. The Navy was slower to read the future, and in 1872 it secured authority to build (and "rebuild") wooden screw sloops of large sail power. Such types were by that time admittedly useless for naval war. They were, however, still well adapted for the purposes of distant patrol, which was then the Navy's only apparent function. And one of them did carry a modern note. U.S.S. *Trenton* was the first naval vessel to be fitted with an electrical lighting system.

American military thought was stirring in other ways. The United States Naval Institute, our first center for the study of technical naval problems, was founded in 1873; in 1879 a new military journal, *The United Service,* published its first issue. In 1875 a naval officer, Chief Engineer J. W. King, was dispatched to Europe to study and report upon the striking new developments in naval architecture. And in the same year the brilliant and tragic Emory Upton set off westward around the world to examine the organization, and especially the schooling, of all the major armies.

Upton came from a farm in upstate New York and had graduated from West Point in the May class of 1861. Thus catapulted into the war as a second lieutenant of artillery he emerged from it, at the age of twenty-six, as a brevet major general, twice badly wounded and with a superb record of combat experience. Returning as an instructor to West Point he had developed a new system of infantry tactics and had established himself as a thoughtful soldier. On his way westward he stopped at St. Louis—where the Commanding General, disgusted with the Washington bureaucracy, had established his headquarters— to receive his letter of instructions. "The Armies of Europe," General Sherman told him, "seem to me to have been studied by American officers . . . until we know all that seems applicable to our system . . ., but Asia remains to us in America almost a sealed book." The "Asia" of which "Uncle Billy" was thinking was the Asia in which the British Raj with its Indian armies was facing the Czarist Russian imperialism in the north. Upton was instructed to spend "as much time as possible in Calcutta" in order to study "the systems of military government by which these nations utilize the peoples and resources of internal Asia." [5]

In the end, Upton covered Europe as well as Asia with great thoroughness. He returned to publish, in 1878, his *Armies of Asia and of Europe,* and to begin his *Military Policy of the United States from 1775,* the first serious contribution to that subject in our literature. The book was not quite complete when Upton killed himself in 1881; it was not formally published until Elihu Root rescued it from the archives in 1904. But it was read in manuscript by Sherman, Hancock and other high officers; Upton had made his ideas influential before his death and they were to become more so thereafter.

His thesis was that the United States had never had a military policy worthy of the name; that from want of forethought and preparation we had blundered through all our wars at enormous and unnecessary cost in life and money, [6] and that each struggle had repeated the mistakes demonstrated by the preceding one. It is a view which has been so completely accepted by almost all later commentators as now to seem almost axiomatic. Yet it is questionable whether earlier soldiers and statesmen—Polk and the Mexican War generals or Jackson after the War of 1812, for example—would have agreed with it. Nor was everyone in the late '70's prepared to accept its implications. It pointed directly toward the large, professional standing army. Upton was plainly impressed by the scientific Germans; he admired their reserve system, even though (as Palmer notes) neither he nor those who agreed with him ever dared to advocate its essential element, which was universal peacetime conscription.

In 1878 Congress set up a joint committee of House and Senate, the Burnside Committee, to consider the reorganization of the regular Army. Retrenchment appears to have been the chief interest of the committee and its report, recommending drastic reductions, retirements and consolidations, spread dismay through the small officer

[5] Emory Upton, *The Armies of Asia and Europe* (Washington, D. Appleton & Co., 1878), p. iv.

[6] True to his age, Upton was always careful to tabulate the dollars-and-cents expenditures, unaware of how dubious a validity subsequent generations would accord to this form of cost accounting.

corps. Little came of these proposals; but the report, with its papers from Sherman, Hancock, Upton and others, is illuminating as an indication of how the military problem appeared to some of our ablest minds at that period. Upton went back for his solution to Calhoun's "expansible army," and Sherman followed him. Hancock, on the other hand, objected to the idea that "our Army in peace should be a skeleton to be filled out for war. This theory, false in principle, has always failed in practice." The skeletonized peacetime companies would be too small for proper training and would be inundated by the volunteers in war. "Our standing Army should be a small, complete . . . healthy body . . . serving as a model for the national forces and not preserved as a skeleton . . . into which it is expected to infuse vitality . . . at the moment an emergency arises." All such issues were theoretical at the time; there was no peril to give them urgency, and Congress had no intention of doing anything about the Army anyway. As usual, there was no decision. But Upton had implanted the seed of a powerful idea, that of "adequate" preparedness beforehand to meet all the imponderables and unpredictables of war and policy.

Upton's work led to no concrete results in his lifetime. But it was he, perhaps more than Mahan, who really raised the banners of the new age. Science was entering even the backward military system of the United States. It was only a few weeks after Upton's death, as it happened, that Sherman got under way at Fort Leavenworth the School of Application for Infantry and Cavalry, the foundation of the Army's now elaborate higher educational system. By 1884 Stephen B. Luce was to have his infant (naval) War College established on Coasters' Harbor Island at Newport. In 1877 Chief Engineer King published his report *The Navies of the World,* a prototype for Upton's report on the armies. Even in the United States, the managerial revolution was beginning.

2.

On a rainy August day in 1880 a big crowd turned out at Columbus, Ohio, to hear an election address by President Hayes. In his entourage they had seen the much loved and respected figure of the Command-

ing General, and as the President reached his damp conclusion they
set up a roar for Uncle Billy Sherman. He spoke off the cuff:

> It delights my soul to look on you and see so many of the good
> old boys left yet. They are not afraid of rain; we have stood it
> many a time. . . . The war now is away back in the past and you
> [the veterans in the throng] can tell what books cannot. . . . There
> is many a boy here who looks on war as all glory, but, boys, it is
> all hell. You can bear this warning voice to generations yet to
> come. I look upon war with horror, but if it has to come I am
> here.

The audience cheered his statement that in need he would be
"here"; it saw nothing remarkable in the declaration that war is "all
hell," and Sherman himself even forgot that he had said it. Yet the
phrase gathered a slow momentum; it was repeated and repeated; it
went around the world, until today it is the one thing about W. T.
Sherman which everyone remembers.[7] It is a small incident, yet
symptomatic. The United States had reached the dividing line between
the generations—between Sherman's "boys," who knew so well what
kind of hell war was that they hardly noticed the phrase, and the
youngsters, who had only the books to go by and for whom war was
again seeming to be "all glory." Sherman's warning was repeated, not
because it was a warning, but because it was something surprisingly,
a bit shockingly, at variance with the new climate of romantic ideas
again growing up around the grim visage of war. It was about 1880
that there occurred a small sort of military revival in the United States.

It is usually remembered today, when it is remembered at all,
because of the early steps taken toward the rebuilding of the Navy.
But it concerned more than the Navy, and the causes were not simple.
The fading of the Civil War memories and the growth of the Civil
War legend had something to do with it. In August 1876 the annihila-
tion of Custer and his battalion of the 7th Cavalry at the Battle of
Little Big Horn had produced an enormous and lasting sensation. Ten
or twenty times as many lives might have been lost in even a secondary

---

[7] Lloyd Lewis, *Sherman: Fighting Prophet* (New York, Harcourt, Brace,
1932), pp. 635 f.

engagement of the Civil War, but those tragedies were fading from the popular consciousness. The "Custer Massacre" assumed a commanding place in the newspapers, the lithographic arts and popular history; it made war again exciting and raised some questionings, at least, as to the adequacy of our military institutions in face even of the Indians.

The following year there was a different object lesson. In the summer of 1877 the nation was swept by the terrible wave of railroad strikes, spreading riot, arson, murder and the startlingly novel specter of proletarian revolution through the land. In Baltimore, Pittsburgh, Chicago and San Francisco millions of dollars' worth of property was destroyed and scores of lives were lost. The great rail centers shrieked for military protection, only to discover that there was very little available. The state troops were called out, but were frequently found to be so sunk in patronage and politics as to be of doubtful value. There were appeals to the Federal government. When one company of regular troops got into Chicago it was received "like the relief of Lucknow." The Navy landed sailors and Marines at Philadelphia. There were demands for quadrupling the regular Army and establishing garrisoned posts in the industrial East. The strikes were soon broken and the panic passed (Congress was more interested at the time in economizing on the Army than in expanding it), but the states were led to take a new look at their volunteer militia organizations.

"The time has come," as one commentator declared, "when the people must decide whether they will support a regular Army of 75,000 men on a peace footing ... or encourage in each state the organization of a well-selected, clothed, instructed, disciplined, armed and equipped body of volunteer militia." [8] There was admittedly "a great variety of opinion as to the kind of military force best adapted for the suppression of domestic turbulence." But in the next couple of years Pennsylvania (where the worst troubles had occurred) revamped her militia units, and other states took steps in the same direction. And in 1879 delegates from some nineteen states met in New York to establish the National Guard Association; it was to begin the rebirth of the National Guard as the nation's primary military reserve.

[8] Thomas F. Rodenbaugh, in *The United Service* (1879), Vol. 1, pp. 283 f.

We were obviously a long way from the Militia Act of 1792, confronting military-social issues of a kind which its authors had only partially envisaged. It is not, perhaps, inconceivable that the Guard might have trended toward becoming a kind of elite corps for the protection of "the rich and well born." How different the military problem looked in 1880 from the way it has appeared both before and since is well exemplified in an article in *Harper's Magazine* of that year. While most of the state units, the author observed, had sunk to a parlous condition, there were exceptions to show what might be done with these organizations:

> Especially the 7th Regiment of New York, with unusual resources for the selection of strong, patriotic and wealthy young men of military tastes . . . and supported by a rich and appreciative community has been able, . . . in the perfection of its equipment and accomplishments, the importance of its services and lately in the completion of its magnificent armory at a cost of over $500,000 at private expense, to show what the citizen soldier may do for his country.

What the citizen soldiers of Antietam or Cold Harbor would have thought of this suggestion for a distinctly upper-class army of "strong, patriotic and wealthy young men," able to raise half a million in private funds for one regiment's armory, may be surmised. That there were difficulties about this concept did not go unnoticed; there were some to question whether a volunteer militia of this kind might not prove unreliable because of their possible "social or business connections" with the "mob." It is apparent that the real problems of military force as a social instrument, whether in international war or domestic turmoil, were still confused. Fortunately, in our rich, amorphous and varied national life there was no real chance of the Guard turning into a serious instrument of the class war. "Strike duty" was frequently thereafter to constitute one of its less attractive missions. Even today it has not wholly forgotten (nor is it too comfortable in the memory) that the primary reason for its revival was to provide the states with a means whereby their "laws may be enforced, social order maintained and [protection afforded] against the sudden violence of popular faction."

In the '80's, indeed, it was good for little else; it was certainly not a reserve army. While the state returns showed no less than seventeen divisions, including fifty-four brigades, some of the states reported more divisions or brigades than they did regiments. Only seven even provided for annual "encampments"; the reported fifty batteries of artillery were armed (when they were armed at all) almost entirely with the old muzzle-loading brass Napoleons. Even with these, mounted drill was "unheard of," and almost no attempt was made to instruct the gunners in firing their pieces with anything more than blank ammunition.[9] Except as a force to repress "popular faction" the Guard had little reality. But it was the renewed interest in the National Guard, generated by the strikes of 1877, which set it on the path to assuming what it now proudly considers its real function, that of providing a war reserve.

The Navy presented a rather different problem. It is not merely facetious to suggest that the naval revival of the '80's sprang less from any new strategic requirements—in fact there were none—than from the fact that the old Navy was falling so completely apart in rottenness of wood, the corruption of contractors and the obsolescence induced by the new technology that some action was becoming inescapable. Chief Engineer King returned from Europe to report, early in 1877, that "all the navies of Europe have been recently undergoing reconstruction; and there has never been a time during peace when such large expenditures for naval purposes were made as at present and such radical changes effected" in ship design, machinery, gunnery, tactics and torpedo warfare. Yet there was logic in the final report of Robeson, Grant's Secretary of the Navy, who thought our wooden ships sufficient for the "defensive purposes of a peaceful people, without colonies, with a dangerous coast and shallow harbors" and separated by a wide ocean from the "warlike naval powers" of Europe. The "expensive" new battleship types being developed in Britain and France were still unproven, and they were too deep of draft and too

<hr />

[9] Anon., *Harper's Magazine* (May 1880), Vol. LX, pp. 915-23.

limited in cruising radius to be any great threat to our ports.[10] There might seem, indeed, to have been no very good reason to imitate them. Unfortunately, however, we could not very well go on building and rebuilding wooden ships armed with smooth-bore guns when everyone knew that they could not stand up for five minutes against the more modern types now appearing abroad.

President Grant suffered during his last two years in office (1875-77) under a Democratic majority in the House, and in 1876 the Representatives began a series of investigations into the muddle of strategic concepts, politics and design difficulties which was resulting in an expenditure of some $15 million a year on the Navy without producing any effective combat strength whatever. The argument continued during the Hayes administration, and by the time Garfield arrived upon the scene in 1881 the leaders of both parties were more or less committed to the rehabilitation of the Navy. But how was it to be done? The real problem over the next few years was less one of devising a new weapons system to support our policies than of designing policies to fit the new weapons systems which were so embarrassingly proliferating in the world.

Garfield's Secretary of the Navy, William H. Hunt of Louisiana (he had been a pro-Union man during the war), appointed a board of officers to advise him on this rather difficult problem. Congress in 1882 added a statutory Advisory Board. The new policy, as finally worked out by these boards, by the Secretary and by the Congressional committees, was an essentially modest one. It amounted to forbidding the further repair of the wooden cruising fleet, diverting the money instead into a gradual replacement of that fleet with modern steel cruisers. At the same time, the five big monitors which had been saved after the Civil War and had been "rebuilding" ever since, would be completed to provide whatever might be needed in the way

[10] Some naval opinion agreed with the technical argument. Captain W. T. Truxtun, writing in the July 1879 issue of *United Service,* argued with typographical emphasis that "no vessel for *our* navy should be built that draws over ten feet at her load line.... We have no use for heavy and expensive frigates, while we do want vessels which can enter all our own ports.... Let us build some new *American* vessels, *but no heavy iron-plated cruisers." United Service,* Vol. I, p. 379.

of battleship strength. No important increase in expenditure was contemplated, and no change in strategic concept. The unarmored steel cruisers would have virtually the same strategic function as the wooden sloops, but they would at least have the speed, maneuverability and modern rifled armament with which to discharge it. The policy was embodied in various enactments, but it was brought to completion by the Naval Appropriations Act of 1883, under which three small steel cruisers—*Chicago, Boston* and *Atlanta*—and the "dispatch boat" *Dolphin* were laid down. They were our first modern ships; and all still carried full sail rig.

The strategic concept was unchanged; but there remained a certain doubt as to what the strategic concept was. The naval boards were aware that distant patrol of the few remaining wild corners of the oceans was ceasing to be a valid reason for expensive naval armament; and though there was much talk about "showing the flag" and "protecting our commerce," it was taking on, in the increasingly law-abiding atmosphere of the later nineteenth century, a somewhat hollow sound. There was too much force in the testy demand of an anti-Navy Representative from Indiana: "When in time of peace has our Navy been engaged in protecting commerce? . . . Ships of war no longer convoy merchant ships. . . . No government of Europe keeps up a navy for such a purpose." The proponents of naval rehabilitation had to justify the Navy as a necessary preparation for war. This was not easy, since no even distant threat of war was visible on the horizon of the time. Their answer was that in war the Navy's functions would be two: to protect our coastal cities against invasion or blockade, for which the monitors and the coastal forts would serve; and to strike "aggressively" with the cruising fleet against enemy commerce.

Later disciples of Mahan have poured out much scorn on this approach. It is true that it did not rise to envisage a "command of the sea" which would protect our own commerce from enemy cruisers (something which single-ship raiders could not do) and might also keep blockaders and invasion fleets away from our coasts entirely. It is true that it was a purely defensive policy; it is perhaps true (though more arguable) that by that time a "linear" coast defense, resting on forts and floating batteries, was a more costly and less effective defensive system than could have been provided by a sea-keeping battle fleet "in being." The fact is that American policy *was* profoundly defensive in inspiration, and that the sea-keeping battle fleet would not only have entailed expenditures beyond anything which the public was then prepared to accept but was also still of dubious practicality from a purely technical standpoint. Given both the financial and technological limitations and the actual political context of the times, the solution of 1883 was by no means so backward or so illogical as it has been represented.

No one in the '80's was thinking of war in terms of a major intercontinental struggle, which was technically much less possible at that time than it had been in 1775, or was to be again. Europe was none of our business, and the worst that was to be feared from Europe was, it was imagined, the kind of limited warfare of raids, of the capture of strong points, of the looting or ransom of coastal cities, which had pretty generally characterized war in the western Atlantic through the preceding two centuries. And the naval policy of the early '80's reflected a considerable practical experience. We had learned, both from the depredations of the Confederate raiders and also from the success of our privateers against Britain in 1812, that commerce destruction, if not a decisive weapon, could deal very discouraging blows against an opponent in a limited war. The commerce-destroyers were an important influence in bringing Britain to the Peace of Ghent. We had also learned from Secretary Mallory's crude ironclads that even coastal ships, if heavily armed and armored, could be a deadly threat to a blockade or amphibious landing.

The monitors which were to supply the heavy armored elements in the program were not the Civil War ships whose names they bore. The process of "rebuilding" had actually consisted in breaking them up, saving the names and what material was of value, and constructing around these memorabilia five low-freeboard coastal battleships with strong armor, breech-loading steel rifles of heavy caliber, even such innovations as electric searchlights. While these ships were unsuited to forming a sea-going battle line, they were quite capable of going to sea; and in their military characteristics they compared favorably with the battleship types then being developed in Britain and France.

They could not have disputed "command" of our waters with Britain's score of heavy armor-clads—assuming that these would ever have been able to reach or operate in the western Atlantic—but they might well have rendered blockade impossible and presented a very real embarrassment to any expeditionary force dispatched against us.

President Arthur put the position rather clearly in his annual message of December 1883:

> It is no part of our policy to create and maintain a Navy able to cope with that [sic] of the other great powers of the world.
>
> We have no wish for foreign conquest, and the peace which we have long enjoyed is in no seeming danger of interruption.
>
> But that our naval strength should be made adequate for the defense of our harbors, the protection of our commercial interests and the maintenance of our national honor is a proposition from which no patriotic citizen can withhold his assent.

When, little more than a decade later, it was to appear that we might have a "wish for foreign conquest" after all, the naval policy of the '80's was to undergo revision. But for the time it appeared to suffice very well for meeting the particular complex of military, political and financial considerations which had evoked it.

Modest as the new policy was, it raised further problems. In emphasizing coastal defense, it called attention to the fact that the Army's seacoast fortifications were as obsolete as the Navy's wooden sloops of war. From their vertical (and vulnerable) brick or stone walls, monuments to the fort building program of the '40's, there still frowned the smooth-bore Rodmans and now antiquated Parrott rifles which had only with difficulty withstood the attacks of the Civil War, and which would be helpless against the new high-powered ordnance. Worse than that, there was nowhere in the United States a source of supply for the new weapons, either for forts or ships, or for the armor plate which the ships were sure sooner or later to demand. Inquiry produced the fact that of the seven ironworks which had supplied artillery to the North during the Civil War, one was out of business and none of the remaining six was equipped to produce modern weapons or even knew what such manufacture might require. Some naval opinion had, indeed, advised against the use of steel rather than iron in the new cruisers, on the ground that the country lacked the facilities to produce the material.

The Naval Appropriations Act of 1883, recognizing this problem, had set up the Gun-Foundry Board, composed of Navy and Army officers, to deal with it. The Board found that it had to tour the growing heavy armament industries of Europe in order to secure the data for its report. It also realized that it had more than a purely technical problem on its hands; appointed to establish a new industry in the United States, it had to consider whether the industry should be retained in the socialistic hands of government or bestowed upon private enterprise. As in Eli Whitney's time, this was still a somewhat delicate issue between the bureaucrats and the entrepreneurs. In the '80's the private contractor was not quite yet the unsullied hero which he has since become. In 1883 a Representative could sarcastically exclaim that "it is an exceedingly refreshing idea that the Government of the United States cannot perform work of a given quality as cheaply as a contractor can." Few Representatives would today commit themselves to so heretical a view. The aura of scandal surrounding the "rebuilding" contracts which John Roach, the Pennsylvania shipbuilder, had secured, lent difficulty to the Gun-Foundry Board's problem. Its solution was statesmanlike. After pointing to the advantages and disadvantages of each of the various combinations of government, private and "partnership" arms manufacture which it had found in Europe, it decided for a mixed system. It recommended that government should induce private industry, with the offer of sufficiently generous contracts, to equip itself to supply the basic steels and forgings for guns and armor, while the government should assemble these materials into the finished guns in its own factories. Thus, government would never be wholly at the mercy of private monopoly in respect to designs and prices (as was the case with Germany vis-à-vis the Krupps), neither (as had been the case in France) would it be at the mercy of a secretive and probably backward technical bureaucracy of military men. The Board's recommendations were adopted. The Bethlehem, and later the Carnegie, steel companies began to equip themselves to provide the forgings; while for many years the Watervliet Arsenal in upper New York and the Naval Gun Factory in Washington were to fabricate and finish most of our supply of heavy ordnance, ashore and afloat.[11]

Naval building, having been revived, almost inevitably had to continue. In March 1885 Cleveland and the Democrats replaced Arthur and the Republicans. Under the able and somewhat controversial Wall Street financier, William C. Whitney, as Secretary of the Navy, they drove ahead with the reform of naval administration and with the construction of further small lots of unarmored steel cruising ships. In 1885 Congress established a board, under the new Secretary of War, William C. Endicott, to draw up a methodical plan for revamping the coast defenses. The Endicott Board's studies were thorough; its conclusions were somewhat breath-taking. It felt that it would be necessary to stud the coasts (including, interestingly enough, those of the Great Lakes) with no less than 1,305 medium and heavy guns, supported by mines, torpedo boat flotillas and floating batteries.[12] Their estimated total cost was over $127 million (a very large sum at that time) and the response of the Congress and the country was tepid. Amid numerous unresolved technical as well as fiscal difficulties it was to take time before much was actually accomplished. Nevertheless, still a third major period of fortification-building had been launched, and over the next fifteen years Congress was actually to spend some $60 million on modernizing and rearming the coastal works. The Great Lakes were not fortified, and the program never reached the heights envisaged by the Endicott Board. But the smooth-bores disappeared and the 1840 masonry was abandoned in favor of a new type of military architecture—concrete gun pits sunk below earth level, within which were mounted either the stubby, powerful 12-inch rifled mortars or the 10-inch and 12-inch "disappearing" rifled guns, all with underground magazines and protected, scientific fire-control systems. They were fitted with searchlights; they were supported by mine and torpedo defenses and light-caliber batteries to deal with beach attacks. They were never to "fire a shot in anger"; all

[11] Report of the Gun-Foundry Board, Ho. Exec., Doc. 97. 48th Cong., 1st Sess.
[12] Report of the Endicott Board, Ho. Exec. Docs., 49th Cong., 1st Sess., Vol. 28.

have long since been disarmed and dismantled, but in their time they represented defensive works of considerable power.

Aside from minor technical improvements in small-arms, tactics and equipment, the little field army was left to fight and ultimately win its Indian wars in much the condition in which it had emerged from the Civil War. Congress continued to produce reports and bills, and Presidents to make urgent recommendations in their messages (but usually far down on the list) for the reform of the militia. But no one, except perhaps the new National Guard Association, took much interest. The Cleveland administration believed in a reasonable modernization of the Navy, but it had no visions of an extravagant naval expansion. The conclusions of the Endicott Board well illustrate the still profoundly defensive (and curiously mercantilist) spirit in which military issues were then approached:

> Our richest ports, from their greater depth of water . . . are of all the most defenceless. The property at stake exposed to easy capture and destruction would amount to billions of dollars and the contributions which could be levied by a hostile fleet upon our seaports should be reckoned at hundreds of millions. . . . The plunder of one of our seaports might abundantly reimburse an enemy for the expenses of a war conducted against us.

The objects of the fortification program, in the Board's view, were to protect these ports, both for their intrinsic wealth and as centers of communication and naval bases, and to protect our coastal trade against the "crowd of fast cruisers and privateers" which would be loosed against it. We lacked the sea-going heavy ships to prevent such a descent, while the new cruisers which we were beginning to build should be employed in "depredating upon the enemy's property and commerce" rather than in trying to cover our own coastal communications.[13]

[13] The fortifications on Corregidor, built after the Spanish-American War and used by MacArthur as his base during the Bataan campaign, were improved versions of this type of harbor defense. The more important of our harbors still exhibit a kind of résumé of American military architecture. Thus, in New York, Castle Williams on Governor's Island represents the 1812 period; Fort Schuyler on Throg's Neck or Fort Wadsworth on Staten Island preserve the romantic

But the advance of technology began to press upon the essentially simple naval policy adopted in 1883. With the introduction of new processes armor was growing lighter as well as stronger; cruising ships as well as heavy vessels could carry it. The old conception of the "ironclad," ponderous and almost immobile under her weight of protection, was subject to revision. On the other hand, steel construction seemed to have removed much of the fire hazard which had been the basic impetus behind the introduction of armor. Perhaps the distinction between the cruiser (mainly useful against commerce) and the battleship (mainly useful against an enemy's armed ships) was growing indistinct. Then, as for long thereafter, the proper balance between speed, firepower and armor protection was not easily discernible. John Rodgers in 1881 thought the time approaching when "ships of war will throw off their armor and fight in the lightest rig"; and while this may seem a short-sighted prediction, it was curiously justified by the many later destroyer and cruiser types which were to do just that. In the '80's the whole problem was obscure, but it was apparent that the wholly unarmored small steel ships of the 1883 program were being outmoded. The Cleveland administration began to add "protective decks"—horizontal armor over the machinery spaces—to its cruiser designs, and as early as 1886 it was recommending a pair of odd vessels, variously described as "armored cruisers" or "second-class battleships."

One was to become U.S.S. *Texas;* the other, U.S.S. *Maine,* of famous and tragic memory. By the later '80's naval technology had

---

splendor of the masonry period of the '40's, while air travelers going into La Guardia Field can look down upon the empty emplacements of Fort Hamilton on the Shore Drive in Brooklyn, an early product of the Endicott Board's recommendations. By the time the new style was under development, however, it was realized that the defenses had to be pushed outward, and to find the empty remains of the metropolitan defenses dating from the '90's one would have to go to Sandy Hook or Plum Island, at the eastern entrance to Long Island Sound. Somewhere near Montauk Point there are the emplacements where 16-inch coast defense rifles were installed as late as the Second World War, the final effort at this type of defense. Today, it is all radar, rockets and aviation; and the old Coast Artillery has been swallowed by the Anti-Aircraft Artillery, just as the Cavalry has become Armor.

assumed quite a different look from that of even ten years before. Steam power had both demonstrated its reliability and achieved large cruising ranges; the full sail power carried by all our earlier steel ships was no longer necessary. Both armor and artillery had greatly improved. Arthur Whitehead's invention of the "automobile fish torpedo" —the familiar and deadly "tin fish" of later wars—had produced the torpedo boat and the "torpedo boat destroyer" as important naval types. It was also largely responsible for ending the obsession of the '80's with "ramming tactics." Both Civil War experience and the naval battle of Lissa in 1866 (when the Italian flagship was rammed and sunk by its Austrian counterpart) had created great confidence in the head-on charge of naval vessels. Ships were provided with huge, projecting ram bows, reminiscent of the Roman trireme, and much ingenuity was expended in giving them a maximum of fire ahead. *Maine* and *Texas,* with their staggered main battery turrets, permitting delivery of their full force directly ahead (or astern) and directly abeam, but with only one turret available for quartering fire, exemplified this school. They were never repeated in our Navy. The Whitehead torpedo meant that it would no longer be possible to close to ramming distance, and consequently called the concept of a head-on naval "charge" in question. By the late '80's the British were going back to the old parallel tactics of the line of battle, which had served their wooden walls so well; they restored their main battery turrets to the center line, one forward, one aft, whence they could deliver their full force over a wide arc on either broadside, without worrying unduly about ahead or astern fire, for which they were likely to have little use. In the American Navy, the tactics of the "charge" survived until the Santiago campaign (where they formed the basis of Admiral Sampson's standing orders) but the "charge" had long since disappeared from our naval design. Sampson's ships may still have carried ram bows, but their main battery turrets were back on the center line, as in the Royal Navy; they were designed primarily to "lie in the line" of broadside battle.

By the late '80's, the problem of the sea-keeping, sea-fighting, heavy armored ship was well on the way to solution. The later American Civil War monitors had been, for their day, ships of great power and invulnerability. They could go to sea, as several of them proved by long ocean voyages after the war, but they could not fight on it. In any kind of seaway their gun ports and the bases of their revolving turrets had to be so tightly caulked as to render them incapable of action. Now, however, the designers were coming up with seaworthy, heavily armed and armored ships which offered practicable replacements for Nelson's far-ranging 74's and 110's as the backbone of a pelagic naval power. Much of the confusion of the '70's and '80's may be ascribed to the want of such a type. But the reappearance of a practicable battleship, of great strength and force, which could both keep the sea and fight on it, which could form a battle line as Nelson's "liners" had done and serve as an expression of sea power by its very existence, both clarified the problem of naval strategy and tended to outmode the solution of 1883.

Maine and *Texas* represented no real departure from the 1883 concept, but were indications that technological advance was outrunning it. When they were authorized, neither the national policy nor the strategic position had changed. But the weapons were again changing; and we had to have weapons at least comparable with those appearing elsewhere. And at this point a new factor entered the equation. Captain Alfred Thayer Mahan appeared upon the scene.

In 1884 Rear Admiral Stephen B. Luce, a devoted exponent of the scientific and managerial revolution, finally won authorization to establish his naval War College and started looking about for a faculty. A likely possibility was the son of "old Dennis," who had given half the leaders of the Civil War their schoolbook training in military engineering and tactics. The naval son was at the time commanding one of the more debilitated screw sloops, *Wachusett,* off the West Coast of South America. But he had done a workmanlike history of the Gulf Coast blockade during the Civil War; and when Luce wrote to ask if he would accept appointment as lecturer on naval history and tactics, Mahan replied that he would like to very much, but would need time for preparation. He plunged at once into thought and reading, beginning with Mommsen's *History of Rome;* nearly a year passed before he was ordered to bring *Wachusett* home to the boneyard at San Francisco and was himself detached to the War College. Through most of the next year Mahan immersed himself in the Astor Place branch of the New York Public Library, but when he emerged he had his lecture course—which was to become *The Influence of Sea Power on History*—virtually complete. By the time he reached Newport in August 1886, Luce had been ordered to sea and Mahan found himself not only the lecturer on history and tactics but also the president of the infant War College.[14]

The lectures were well received and Mahan developed them, meanwhile fighting a left-handed battle to keep the War College alive against the scorn of the old salts and the distinctly unhelpful attitude of Secretary Whitney. Young Mr. Theodore Roosevelt, not yet an Assistant Secretary but with his *The Naval War of 1812* already a naval historian of repute, graced the college's platform. Mahan's contacts were widening and his ideas were spreading through the service and among the influential politicians. And then Benjamin Harrison was returned in the elections of 1888, and in the following March the Republicans took office with command of the Executive and both Houses of Congress for the first time since 1875.

3.

Foreign adventure was no more a part of Harrison's policy than it had been of Cleveland's or of Arthur's. But the Republicans were by tradition the nationalist party, and they were pro-Navy by both tradition and association. They drew much of their strength from the eastern seaboard and more of it from the new heavy industries. The Democrats had launched Bethlehem Steel into the gun-forging and armor-plate business; it was now getting its massive steam hammers set up and ready for orders. The Democrats had, as well, refused to concentrate naval building in the government yards, and considerable private ship- and engine-building interests were interested in naval contracts. The actual political and strategic situation remained unaltered, but new ship designs were appearing abroad. Could we do less than imitate them? Benjamin F. Tracy of New York, Harrison's Secre-

---

[14] W. D. Puleston, *Mahan* (New Haven, Yale University Press, 1939), *passim.*

tary of the Navy, was an energetic and forward-looking type. He began at once to lay about him in the antiquated naval bureaus; he acquainted himself with the latest in naval thought and, as he prepared his first annual report which would embody his program, it seems probable that he had much advice from Captain Mahan. Indeed, some of its phrases (such as: "abandon all claim to influence and control upon the sea") suggest that the captain helped to write it. When it appeared in November 1889 it was something of a shocker.

It began bluntly with one of those tabular comparisons of our own modest establishment with the great European navies which were to become standard features of later naval debates. This demonstrated, according to Mr. Tracy, that "the United States cannot take rank as a naval power. . . . Any one of the powers named could without serious difficulty . . . secure in a single raid upon our coast an amount of money sufficient to meet the expenses of a naval war" (another striking example of the way people thought about war in those days). "To meet the attack of ironclads, ironclads are indispensable. . . . The country needs a Navy that will exempt it from war, but the only navy that will accomplish this is a navy that can wage war." The Secretary dramatically concluded that the "necessities of our vulnerable position" demanded the prompt creation of a fleet of twenty battleships— eight for the Pacific and twelve for the Atlantic and Gulf Coasts— twenty heavy coast defense monitors and a doubled force of cruisers. Nor was there any time to waste. In an argument which was to find far grimmer echo in later years, Mr. Tracy held that it would be a "fatal" mistake to imagine that one could wait until war actually threatened.

> Naval wars in the future [he said] will be short and sharp. It is morally certain that they will be fought out to the end with the force available at the beginning. The nation that is ready to strike the first blow will gain an advantage which its antagonist can never offset, and inflict an injury from which [since the antagonist's shipyards would all be destroyed] he can never recover.

Secretary Tracy asked for an immediate start on eight battleships, representing his estimate of available shipyard capacity, as well as a continuation of the cruiser building and a beginning on five torpedo boats. This program lost none of its startling character when in January 1890 the Naval Policy Board, which had been established to design a long-range naval program rather as the Endicott Board had done for the coastal defenses, backed up the Secretary's demand for some forty battleships and monitors and added some more detailed elaborations. It believed that ultimately we should also have no less than forty modern cruisers, as well as 117 large and small torpedo craft and eleven rams.[15] All this seemed megalomania even to some friends of the Navy; while peace societies and Friends' meetings deluged the Congress with protests against this new face of navalism. Representative Herbert of Alabama (a pro-Navy Democrat who was to become Secretary in Cleveland's second Cabinet) was "certain" that Congress "never will, unless in prospect of some more immediate danger of war than now confronts us, vote for any such establishment as that." It seemed that Secretary Tracy was (in the words of his next Republican successor) "far in advance of the country." The Congressional committees promptly cut his program down to size. But what emerged in the 1890 Appropriations Act was, nevertheless, an authorization for three "sea-going coastal battleships." It was a modest program; it clearly met none of the arguments with which Mr. Tracy had advanced his proposals and was actually an evasion of the underlying policy issue. Yet, as so often happens with our political and legislative evasions, it really decided that issue; it was this first "battleship bill" which set the nation upon the alluring, the somewhat metaphysical and hitherto untrodden paths of "sea power," which were to invite us to assert an aggressive force upon world affairs.

Through the winter and spring of 1890 there was another full-dress debate in Congress and the press over naval policy. Tracy and Mahan may have been striking boldly for a new strategic concept; the Quakers and their allies may have sensed that this was the real implication of the bill. If so, the issue was as confused as always. The elder Henry Cabot Lodge of Massachusetts (young then and still a Representative)

---

[15] The "ram" was a low-lying, cigar-shaped craft armed only with its massive pointed prow, which it was supposed to drive into an enemy's side. The Navy built one, U.S.S. *Katahdin*; she was never imitated here nor, it is believed, anywhere else.

gave a graceful speech to show that the three-ship bill was no more than a "continuance" of the policies of Cleveland and Arthur and, indeed, of policies which had remained unchanged since 1812. However artful the demonstration, in a sense it was true. Like the steel cruisers of the early '80's, the new battleships were less a bid for "sea power" than a response to the remorseless advance of technology. The coast-defense monitors, even in their highly modernized form, would no longer suffice; their speed, range and sea-keeping characteristics were deficient in face of the new European battleship types. But even the Navy was unprepared to abandon coast defense altogether and stake everything on Mahan's concept of a united and mobile high seas fleet—as is indicated by the fact that both Tracy and the Policy Board recommended a score of monitors. With the report of the Endicott Board only four years before, it was not easy to accept the idea that coastal defense was unnecessary. Commander W. T. Sampson, a very able officer who was later to wear the (disputed) laurels of Santiago, had been the naval member of the Endicott Board and had put his name to recommendations for "floating batteries," torpedo-boat flotillas and mines as well as for sea-coast artillery. He was also a member of the Policy Board which recommended the monitor fleet.

Few of those who voted the battleships seem to have realized that a new policy was being adopted; nor was it, perhaps, in fact. The term applied to the vessels—"sea-going coastal battleships"—may seem today to have been merely a semantic triumph over the political and strategic controversies surrounding their inception; yet it describes quite accurately what the ships were intended to be.

When it became plain that the Harrison administration would back an expanded naval building program, the naval architects and strategists had to face the problem of what to build. They came up with two answers: One was a battleship of force equal to the best abroad, capable of operating anywhere in the world. This worked out to a ship of about 10,000 tons, with cruising radius of 13,000 miles, heavily armed but able to carry only a rather dangerously light armor belt (5 inches) and too deep of draft even so for many of our harbors. The other idea was a design of about 8,500 tons, better protected, with a main battery of 13-inch guns (heavier than any mounted in the European navies) and drawing only twenty-four feet, but with a cruising radius of no more than 5,000 miles. The second was the recommended solution and was adopted by the Naval Affairs Committee. When enough of them were available, such vessels, operating as a united battle fleet, could command the coast from Panama to Nova Scotia, but would be unable to undertake transoceanic operations; in that sense, they were "coastal" ships.

In the debate great emphasis was laid upon their purely defensive and restricted function. Representative Boutelle of Maine, chairman of Naval Affairs, explained that their purpose was "to assume the actual defense of our coast, to break the blockade of any of our great maritime ports . . . to drive off foreign aggression from our shores and to seize and hold those bases of supply in the immediate vicinity of the American coast which . . . would be absolutely essential to the maintenance of the safety of our coastline." This did not differ significantly from the concept behind the monitors then building; indeed, Mr. Boutelle explained that the new ships would depart from the monitor principle only in having a somewhat higher freeboard, enabling them to "steam and fight" in the open sea.

An opponent pressed the question: "To fight where? What is the need for them? If we become involved in war with any foreign nation, where will the fight be? . . . We will not go out upon the ocean to give battle. Will not go to a foreign shore. . . . We are not thinking of foreign conquest." Dolliver of Iowa supplied an answer: "We have not undertaken to build foreign sea-going ships, . . . [only] three warships that will be available for coast protection, . . . limited by their coal capacity to the coast of the United States. . . . We must have ships, not to make war on anybody, but to keep other people from disturbing either our prestige or our rights."

Although the first three battleships were finally to come out at over 10,000 tons instead of 8,500, they retained the 24-foot draft and comparatively limited cruising radius. In the minds of those who voted for them they were, apparently, little more than up-to-date versions of the monitors; and they might not have been voted had it seemed that they were intended to be anything else. Mr. Tracy was "far in advance of the country." But in the general interest in naval policy attendant upon the Republicans' return to power, Captain Mahan had found what for some time he had been looking for—a publisher. In May 1890 Little, Brown & Co. of Boston presented to the public the first edition of *The Influence of Sea Power on History, 1660-1783.*

Unquestionably, this was a remarkable book, alike in its conception, its content and its extraordinary later fame. Mahan had been detailed to prepare a lecture course on naval history and tactics, and the bulk of the work is a dutiful record of naval wars and battle actions from the Anglo-Dutch conflicts of the seventeenth century down to the general peace which, among other things, concluded the American Revolution. But Mahan framed this somewhat technical narrative in an opening and a closing chapter which generalized his deductions from the facts into the famous theory of "sea power," which was to exert so vast an influence in the world.

It is difficult to resist the impression that Mahan's major impulse was simply to produce an argument for more naval building. His emphasis on the importance of naval power in war was compelling; but it was not easy to drive home in a time of profound peace. As the naval debate showed, neither Congress nor the country would accept huge programs of aggressive naval expansion at a time when the European powers were sufficiently occupied with each other and there seemed no possible threat from any other quarter. However valuable a navy might be in war, something else was needed to start a major navalist effort amid the still tranquil horizons of 1890. Captain Mahan supplied it. He produced, not only a sound rationale of sea power in time of war, but a rationale of sea power in time of peace, much less sound but much better adapted to the thirsting needs of all the new forces—the rising nationalists, the armament manufacturers, the ship and engine builders, military men hoping to enlarge their careers, bankers looking for foreign investment, merchants interested in colonial markets, investors in the "banana republics"—who might find a big program of naval building and an aggressive foreign policy to their advantage.

The Mahan thesis can be divided (not without some difficulty) into two parts. One concerns the strategic employment of naval vessels in war; it is the best part of Mahan's work and its principles stand today. It was not, perhaps, too original; Mahan himself deprecated claims of originality for his ideas, and they may be found elsewhere in the earlier literature of the period. But if Mahan, in Philip Guedalla's phrase, "discovered nothing in particular, he discovered it very well." It has always been difficult for people who spend their lives ashore to understand what a few war vessels, operating in the illimitable ocean reaches, really do, or how they contribute to the mass struggle of men against men which war is assumed to be. Mahan stressed the significance of the sea as logistical highway and avenue of enemy approach; he emphasized the power with which "due use and control" of sea communications would endow any belligerent, and argued that this "due use and control" had been and was attainable by powerful battle fleets organized and operating as units. The principle that one should never "divide the fleet" became almost an obsession with him. He was scornful of commerce raiding, an activity which might injure an enemy but which could not be decisive, could not attain "command of the sea" nor seriously challenge it if held by another. "Sea power" was vital to success in war, and the only means of attaining it was the dominant "fleet in being."

Mahan could have had no prevision of the commerce-raiding submarines which in two world wars were to slip out beneath the control of the battle fleets and come close to negating their domination. Under the technology of his time, his analysis of the strategic problem was entirely valid. It is only as one approaches the second part of his demonstration—the application of this strategic analysis to peacetime policy—that the questions begin to arise. And it is only here that one finds the source of his tremendous influence after the turn of the century. To dominate the oceanic highways, the battle fleet must have the power to range the globe. That was simple for the "storm-beaten" and almost wholly self-contained sail-powered ships of Nelson's day; it was impossible for the steam-driven men-of-war without widely available coaling stations and repair bases. But coaling stations and repair bases meant colonies where they might be established and defended. Moreover, it would be of little use to "command" the sea in wartime unless one had a flourishing merchant marine to travel the highways thus secured, and to provide the reserves of ships, of trained seamen and of ship and engine building capacity which naval or overseas army operations would require. But the colonies necessary for coaling and repair bases would provide the trade to nourish such a merchant marine; in peace the Navy would "protect" it (against what was never very clear) and in war it would be there to sustain the Navy. The whole wrapped up amazingly into one glorious package of power, protection and profits. A big Navy would "pay," even in peace.

This demonstration was Mahan's decisive achievement; it was this which was to give him his enormous fame abroad, which later washed back to the United States to make his works the bible and himself the prophet of American navalism. It was for this that he was devoured by British admirals and naval commentators, that he was read by the Kaiser and von Tirpitz, by Theodore Roosevelt and Henry Cabot Lodge. It is hardly necessary to point out that there were flaws in the argument, nor is it particularly relevant. It was not that what he said was profound, but that he had the luck to say it at a moment in history when countless prosperous and influential persons were looking for precisely this justification for courses which they wished for their own reasons to pursue. Mahan taught that sea power, in and of itself, was a good in peace or war; and in so doing he tossed an apple of discord into the affairs of nations for which there was to be no lack of ambitious contenders.

It is perhaps easier today than it was at the time to detect the note of competitive aggressiveness on the world stage that sounded in Mahan. President Harrison, in his inaugural address of 1889, had warned that our interests were not "so exclusively American that our entire inattention to any events that may transpire elsewhere can be taken for granted." We would protect our foreign trade and our far-flung merchants "in their personal and commercial rights." The "necessities of our Navy" required "convenient" coaling and repair bases; these, the President somewhat piously added, would be obtained only by non-coercive means, "however feeble the government from which we ask such concessions." But they would be obtained.

In 1891 young Mr. Rudyard Kipling announced in his *American Notes* that:

> The big, fat Republic that is afraid of nothing because nothing up to the present date has happened to make her afraid, is as unprotected as a jellyfish. . . . There is ransom and loot past the counting of man on her seaboard alone—plunder that would enrich a nation—and she has neither a navy nor half-a-dozen first-class forts to guard the whole.

This did not unduly alarm the "jellyfish," nor did it mute a new touch of bumptiousness in its policy. Harrison, in his annual message at the end of the same year, called for more battleships:

> The world needs no assurances of the peaceful purposes of the United States, but we shall probably be in the future more largely a competitor in the commerce of the world, and it is essential to the dignity of this nation and to that peaceful influence which it should exercise on this hemisphere that its Navy should be adequate both upon the shores of the Atlantic and of the Pacific.

"Adequate" was a word of Protean meaning in military and naval debates which was to come in for much hard usage. At the time, the standards of "adequacy" were quite modest. Harrison secured only one more battleship, U.S.S. *Iowa.* Together with the first three (*Massachusetts, Indiana* and *Oregon*) and the obsolescent *Texas,* she completed the entire battleship fleet with which we were to fight the Spanish-American War. But increasingly we were finding our cruising ships safeguarding property and protecting American lives in revolutionary and other disturbances all over the hemisphere. In the last six months of 1893, naval vessels were sent to no less than six Latin-American countries and to Honolulu because of insurrectionary troubles; the strain was so great that it was necessary to use a lowly vessel of the Fish Commission for patrol in the Bering Sea.

Amid such excitements, the ebullient '90's were in fact to see a considerable improvement in the military posture. Harrison got the first four battleships under construction. When Cleveland returned to the White House in March 1893, he found that the engineers and designers, after much study and experiment, were ready to get seriously to work upon the 1886 recommendations of the Endicott Board; and the seacoast fortifications were to be pressed forward with energy. Cleveland also found that the experts had achieved agreement on a replacement for the obsolete 1873 black powder Springfield shoulder rifle. They had adopted the Danish Krag-Jorgensen magazine rifle, firing smokeless powder, and by 1897 the whole of the small regular Army was equipped with it—though not, unhappily, the National Guard. At the time of its adoption none could have guessed that it would leave its name in a line of popular verse, announcing the resolve to "civilize 'em with a Krag."

Cleveland was the opposite of an imperialist; but he believed in naval power for the defense of American waters and he would doubtless have continued the Harrison battleship program had times been propitious. But he was to find himself overwhelmed in his first summer by the disastrous Panic of 1893. When the time came to present the estimates in December, the President felt that the lamentably "depleted state of the Treasury," together with the fact that the shipyards were still crowded with the unfinished orders from the Harrison administration, forbade the undertaking of any new hulls. But in the following year a suggestive new factor appeared in the equation; more impressively, perhaps, because of the disorders attendant upon the great Pullman strike of 1894. Cleveland had felt obliged to order out Federal troops to "protect the mails"; again there was more than a hint of social revolution in the air, and the suggestion that if it was not (in Cleveland's celebrated phrase) the function of government "to support the people" it might be its function to see that they had the means of supporting themselves. The four-battleship program was now approaching fulfillment. As the President observed in his annual message of 1894:

> The manufacture of armor requires expensive plants and the aggregation of many skilled workmen. All the armor necessary to complete the vessels now building will be delivered before the 1st of June next. If no new contracts are given out, contractors must disband their workmen and their plants must lie idle.

It was an argument for new naval contracts which had apparently occurred forcibly to the contractors; it had occurred to the workmen as well. In creating an industry to build the complex new armaments, we had inevitably created new pressures to expand the armaments in order to sustain the industry. It is hardly deniable that this factor was repeatedly to affect armament programs thereafter, both in the United States and abroad. To assess its real importance in military history is, however, very difficult. The picture which, in the 1930's, the Nye investigation into the "merchants of death" sought to establish, was certainly exaggerated. Even where economic rather than military considerations seem to have generated the pressures for arms building, the motives were not necessarily questionable. If private owners might wish to keep the arms plants going for the sake of profits, high-minded statesmen often wished to do the same for the sake of combating unemployment. Labor was often just as much involved as capital in these pressures. As the scale of both industry and government expanded, and as each became more inextricably intertwined with the other, reality tended to fade out of the old methods of cost-accounting our affairs. It may be said that in any social activity as vast as the production of modern armaments, private greed and interest are bound to become entangled with public policy; but no study of which the present writer is aware has been sufficiently sensitive to distinguish the relative roles of the two.

At all events, Congress, for whatever reason, resumed the battle-ship building program in 1894 and also authorized an expansion of torpedo-boat building. When Cleveland left office in March 1897 he could claim for his administration a significant advance in military affairs. Modern guns were going into the seacoast emplacements; the regular Army had been rearmed; the officer schools were improving and expanding; the competence of the National Guard was greater and its instruction was better; while there were now no less than nine first-class battleships built or building. The gun-forging and armor-plate industries had become a significant, if scarcely dominant, element in the industrial complex. The inspiration, however, was all still defensive and isolationist. The Army was still very small, an esoteric service quite lost amid the gigantic domestic battles of the industrial titans, the political parties, the agrarian Populists and labor unions, which filled the air. The Navy was more formidable than before, but its resurgence had not progressed greatly. In 1897 the truest symbol of American military policy was still the heavy, immovable and purely defensive sea-coast gun.

Yet the adventurous impulses were rising. More people were reading Mahan. More people were taking pride in the magnificent "White Squadron" and in military and naval matters in general. Since the now remote Samoan crisis of 1889, there had been a succession of more and more exciting (if undangerous) "incidents" upon far horizons. In 1895 there had come the Venezuelan incident, when Cleveland's Secretary of State, Richard Olney, calmly informed an astonished Downing Street that "the United States is practically sovereign on this continent and its fiat is law." It was more or less a fact, in the first place, and, in the second place, Americans enthusiastically accepted it as such. The strenuous and romantic Mr. Theodore Roosevelt was quite willing to let war come; he did not care "whether our seacoast cities are bombarded or not; we would take Canada." It was an attitude toward war which, since the appearance of the nuclear bombs, has become altogether impossible to any rational mind. But in the '90's nuclear weapons still were in the unimaginable future. The atmosphere of the time was heady. More and more people were reading Mr. Kipling's works. And more and more were taking an interest in the dramatically reported insurrection which had been under way in Cuba—Spain's last great possession in the Western Hemisphere—since 1895. Captain Mahan alone could never have converted the United States to an aggressive navalism. But on February 15, 1898 U.S.S. *Maine* blew up in Havana harbor with the loss of 260 men and officers. The Spanish-American War was to change everything.

4.

The farther that "splendid little war" recedes in time, the more decisive a turning point in our history does it seem. For the American (if not for the unhappy Spanish) forces the serious combat action was confined almost entirely to a single day, July 1, 1898, at El Caney and

San Juan. Yet the diplomatic, political and psychological consequences were enormous. Young Mr. Roosevelt, as Acting Secretary of the Navy on his chief's day off, had seized the opportunity to send Commodore Dewey the battle orders which were to ensure that in freeing Cuba we would also gather in the Philippines. That was to make us a colonial power. It was also to make us a Far Eastern power, entangled thereby in the rivalries of the European states in China. That, in turn, inevitably involved us, without our quite knowing it, in the European power complex.

"Responsibilities" upon the world stage which would have seemed quite fantastic to most Americans in 1897 had by 1899 come to appear patently "inescapable"; and we hardly needed Mr. Kipling's exhortation to "take up the white man's burden" after a much higher Authority, in direct response to prayer, had shown President McKinley the path of duty. The election of 1900 was to turn upon the issue of "imperialism"—hardly imaginable only four years before amid the impassioned metaphysics of bimetallism—and if the debate was as confused as usual, the decision was clear. It confirmed our entry into the new role of a politically and militarily positive, basically aggressive, force upon the world stage; and thereby cast a die which all subsequent disputations over "isolationism" as opposed to "internationalism" were never to recall.

Military policy was to undergo a corresponding transformation. After the long and dreadful agony of the sectional conflict we had returned by the late '60's to military and naval institutions hardly distinguishable from those of the '50's. After the brief and by comparison almost bloodless excursion into tropical conquest in 1898, we rebuilt our whole naval and military system, recast the structure of ideas and attitudes on which our military institutions had rested and, however unconsciously and haltingly, began to gird ourselves for the major and fundamentally aggressive interventions upon the world stage that were to involve us in the global conflicts which followed. It would be absurd to suggest that the transformations in our military policy after 1898 were the "cause" of our entanglement in the European power complex; but it is not so absurd to say that they provided the means without which we could not have become so deeply engaged. It may even be erroneous to ascribe the profound diplomatic, political and military changes after 1898 to the war; the war unquestionably forced new solutions in all these fields, but may have been itself less a cause than a consequence of new pressures which would have produced similar results even without the misfortunes of the Cubans which triggered them off.

That these pressures were building up is now apparent. Mahan was by no means their only prophet. In June 1897 the new President's new and unpredictable Assistant Secretary of the Navy had journeyed to the War College at Newport to inform the Navy and the nation that "those who wish to see this country at peace . . . will be wise if they place reliance upon a first-class fleet of first-class battleships, rather than upon any arbitration treaty the wit of man can devise. . . . Diplomacy is utterly useless," Mr. Roosevelt had added, in what today seems a rather startling reversal of Clausewitz, "where there is no force behind it; the diplomat is the servant, not the master, of the soldier." [16] In the fall of 1897 Mr. Roosevelt was hoping for a war in Cuba, "on the ground both of humanity and self-interest." Humanity would, of course, be served by freeing the Cubans. Self-interest would be served by the opportunity for "trying both the Army and the Navy in actual practise," and the Assistant Secretary was anxious only that there should really be "some fighting to do" so that the test would be as instructive as possible. This proposal to use the Spaniards (to say nothing of our own troops and the Cubans) as guinea pigs on whom to test the instruments of war, just as the Spaniards were to be used in 1936 by the Nazis and the Communists, was not so much callous as naïve. It reflects the vast naïveté with which the generation of Kipling, of the young TR and of the young Winston Churchill (who was a correspondent in Cuba for a time) regarded the war institution.

Roosevelt was abetted by other, perhaps shrewder, nationalists, like his friend Cabot Lodge, the "scholar in politics," now elevated to the Senate. But these younger romantics were far from representative of their times. McKinley was a pacific politician, who took office in the expectation that he could avoid a war over Cuba. The program which

[16] Henry Pringle, *Theodore Roosevelt* (New York, Harcourt, Brace, 1931), p. 172.

he presented to the Congress in December 1897 made no provision whatever for fighting a war; indeed, it would have cut in half the Cleveland naval building programs. Even after the destruction of the *Maine,* when Congress resoundingly appropriated $50 million "for defense," the War Department remained under the unfortunate impression that the act meant what it said and that "no part of this sum was available for offensive purposes." So most of the Army's share was solemnly allotted to the coastal fortifications, and only after the passage of the war resolution did the Army feel free to prepare for hostilities.

On April 20, 1898, when the President signed the war resolution, the United States Army consisted of a little over 28,000 men and officers, scattered in company or battalion size detachments all over the country. There were supposed to be about 100,000 effective Spanish troops, most of them regulars, in Cuba. As the War Department began frantically to assemble the Army and fill out its skeletonized units, the President issued his first call for 125,000 volunteers. The primary source for these were the organized formations of the National Guard, then considerably below its authorized strength, but consisting of about 114,000 presumed effectives. The Guard units were expected to volunteer *en bloc* and most of them did so. But thousands of untrained recruits had to be taken in to fill the regular and Guard organizations, to form the Federal volunteer regiments (of which Mr. Roosevelt's Rough Riders was the most celebrated) which Congress enthusiastically voted, and to meet the second call for an additional 75,000 men issued toward the end of May. In all, about 225,000 men were brought into the Federal service. Very few were to see action, and two-thirds of them never left the United States; but the problems of receiving, housing, feeding and equipping this host were soon to compound into what may fairly be called the major military disaster of the war.

The Navy also underwent expansion. It bought up what cruisers were available in the European arms markets, acquired merchant auxiliaries in large numbers, converted the more eminent craft of the New York Yacht Club fleet into gunboats, and even brought out the totally useless Civil War monitors, the ones which had not been rebuilt and still carried their original 15-inch smooth-bores and wrought-iron armor, for a completely unnecessary harbor defense. The Navy, with its four good battleships and now numerous lesser types, was more than a match for anything in the half-obsolete and half-unfinished Spanish Military Marine. This did not, however, dampen the Congressional ardor; and amid the spate of measures to prepare for the war there was thrown in an authorization for three more battleships, which could not possibly be completed until long after the war was over.

When the next naval appropriation bill came up in the spring of 1899, the war with Spain was over. There were already a dozen battleships built, building or authorized; but now we were contemplating a new overseas empire stretching from the rim of the Antilles into the farthest reaches of the western Pacific. That its responsibilities must demand a greatly enlarged naval establishment seemed too obvious to require demonstration, and without much thought Congress tossed three more battleships and three big armored cruisers into the busy hoppers of naval construction. There is little to suggest that any serious strategic analysis lay behind this program. Despite the seeming geographic enlargement, the new responsibilities were virtually the same as the old—except in one important respect. We had for long been committed to the defense of the China trade, of the integrity of the Monroe Doctrine and of our own coastal waters against European machinations. In only one way had this commitment been enlarged; we were now obligated to a defense of the Philippines against Japan. But there is little indication that this new commitment had much influence over the naval and military programs adopted at the turn of the century.

In 1900 another pair of battleships and three more armored cruisers were authorized. Most of these ships were not actually laid down until much later. But the remarkable and unanticipated result was that when the McKinley administration went to the polls it could show on paper a sea-going battleship and heavy cruiser fleet of formidable proportions by comparison with all other navies save that of Great Britain. At that point, the martial impulse began to run out; no new heavy ships were authorized in 1901 and it is curious to speculate upon what our naval history might have been had McKinley lived. But he was struck down; and when, by one of the stranger accidents of history, the militaristic Theodore Roosevelt came to office in the fall of 1901, he was to find ready to his hand a mighty foundation of actual and projected naval strength on which he was mightily to build.[17]

The new Navy was thus begun almost by accident and in absent-mindedness. It provided the dramatic and obvious symbols of the new

[17] A recapitulation of the battleship building programs may be useful. From the redevelopment of an efficient battleship type around 1890 down to the eve of the Second World War the size of the battle fleet was the generally accepted standard of relative naval power. It was not a very good standard; much experience was to show that other types were also important in the naval calculation. But the battleship remained through some forty years the great symbol of naval strength. Here is the record of our battleship building during the earlier period:

Cleveland's first administration:

1 *Maine*	4 10-inch			Destroyed, Feb. 1898
1 *Texas*	2 10-inch			In action, Sp.-Am. War

Harrison's administration:

3 *Oregons*	4 13-inch	8 8-inch		In action, Sp.-Am. War
1 *Iowa*	4 13-inch	8 8-inch		In action, Sp.-Am. War

Cleveland's second administration:

2 *Kearsarges*	4 13-inch	4 8-inch	18 5-inch	Completed, 1900
3 *Alabamas*	4 13-inch		14 6-inch	Completed, 1900-1

McKinley's administration:

3 *Ohios*	4 12-inch		16 6-inch	Completed, 1902-04
5 *Georgias*	4 12-inch	8 8-inch	12 6-inch	Completed, 1906-07

In addition to the obsolete *Texas,* Theodore Roosevelt thus inherited seventeen battleships, though only nine were complete when he took office, and the last five (the *Georgias,* peculiar ships, with two of their 8-inch turrets superposed on the 12-inch gunhouses) had not even been laid down. He also inherited the five coast-defense monitors and four more modern ships of this type launched in 1900 and 1901; as well as six fine armored cruisers which were laid down in 1901 and 1902. Roosevelt brought all these to completion; he secured authorization for four still more powerful armored cruisers and added to the battleship fleet:

Roosevelt's administration:

6 *Connecticuts*	4 12-inch	8 8-inch	12 7-inch	Completed, 1906-08
2 *Idahos*	4 12-inch	8 8-inch	8 7-inch	Completed, 1908
2 *Michigans*	8 12-inch		22 3-inch	Completed, 1909

All but the last two were complete when Roosevelt left office; thus, whereas we fought the Spanish-American War with five battleships and two armored cruisers, we ended the Roosevelt era with twenty-five battleships and ten heavy cruisers in commission. Ironically enough, all of them were by that time obsolete, retired by the all-big-gun "dreadnought" battleships and battle cruisers. Data from *Jane's Fighting Ships,* 1914 ed.

militarism that ruled after 1898. The slender, tall-funneled ships of the new programs, beautiful in their highly unmilitary white and buff paint, were well calculated to make the patriotic heart swell with pride; but the fact that they were of no visible use under the actual international contexts of the times diminished their practical significance. Costly as they were, they had no more than a peripheral effect upon the main streams of American life and American foreign policy.

With the new Army, matters were rather different. It was "a condition and not a theory" which confronted Mr. Elihu Root when, in July 1899, he accepted President McKinley's unexpected offer of the War Department. Russell A. Alger, the harmless Michigan politician and Civil War veteran who had the misfortune to be Secretary of War in 1898, had been swept from office under the storm of unmitigated, and largely unmerited, abuse that had descended upon the Army's "mismanagement" of a war with which it had never been organized or equipped to deal. Root was a wholly unmilitary New York corporation lawyer, not given to blood-and-thunder speeches. When the White House summoned him to the telephone from his Long Island country house, he protested that he knew nothing about war or the Army. McKinley answered that he didn't want anyone familiar with war or the Army; he wanted a competent lawyer who could administer the new conquests—the Philippines, Cuba and Puerto Rico—which had perforce fallen to the War Department as the occupying authority. Root accepted and was to prove his ability as a colonial administrator. But the Army was his major administrative tool. Inevitably, if ironically, he found that he would first have to meet the problems of the Army and of military policy before he could address those of colonial governance. It was, after all, in the field of Army reform that he was to meet his greatest challenge and to make his greatest fame.

In the late summer of 1899 one could argue about the amount of naval power that might be needed four or five years in the future (the earliest date at which it could be completed) to "support" the new empire; but there was no argument at all about the immediate need of infantrymen to make good the conquest of that empire in the jungles of Luzon and Mindanao. Most of the volunteers of '98 had been mustered out by the end of that year. In March 1899 McKinley had secured from Congress an act temporarily raising the regular establishment to 65,000 men and authorizing an additional 35,000 United States volunteers. These troops, bypassing all the troublesome problems of state authority and patronage, were in the process of being raised and officered when Root took office.

Put to the test the year before, the National Guard had on the whole proved a grievous disappointment. Though most of the units had volunteered, as expected, the "crack" 7th Regiment of New York, the most famous and probably the best of all the National Guard outfits of that day, had proudly refused to merge its identity in a Federal army run by "West Point martinets." Many of its members had, of course, volunteered individually to see what service there was; it was unit pride and not cowardice which had dictated the vote. But the regiment earned a black mark for which it was not wholly forgiven, while its action had come as a rather shocking indication of the weakness in the dual military system. Considerably more shocking, if in a different way, was the condition of the Guard units which did appear. They were untrained, ill-equipped, sometimes without proper clothing and even without shoes; none had modern weapons and they were wretchedly deficient in the simplest skills of military life, such as hygiene, cooking, shelter and supply. Their officers were seldom competent. Fortunately, only two National Guard regiments were to get into the single hard fight (July 1, 1898); and one of these, the 71st New York, was to have an unhappy experience which left it unjustly under a cloud. It was obvious that it would have taken a long time to make an effective force out of the National Guard units which turned out in 1898; it was even more obvious that the whole Army system called for reform.

There was more time to organize and train the Federal volunteers of 1899, but here Root ran into another kind of trouble. The officers were to be chosen on merit—since the complications of the state political patronage had been overpassed—but when Root asked the regular Army bureaucracy for names, all that he got was a plan for "seconding" regular officers into the new volunteer regiments on a strict seniority basis. It was one of Root's first indications that something would have to be done about the old Army bureaucracy. In the end, the volunteer regiments were well officered by men who had demonstrated their abilities in the war, and they made good records. But the establishment of which they were a part was only temporary. As the law stood, the country would revert in July 1901 to the regular force of about 25,000 men. The Philippines were still far from pacified; permanent legislation more suitable to the immediate problem was inescapable.

Speaking in Chicago in October 1899, only two months after his appointment, Root boldly declared that "the American soldier today is part of a great machine which we call military organization. . . . The machine today is defective; it needs improvement; it ought to be improved." It was apparent to his hearers that the Army needed improvement. But the idea that the American soldier was simply a cog in a "great machine" was by no means as acceptable in 1899 as it has become today. For many, war was still a matter of young men "springing to arms" and fighting the issue out with bullet, butt and bayonet in a deadly personal encounter. The thought of maintaining in peace a military "machine" which would be promptly mobilizable, which would be scientifically managed and deployed, which could be efficiently dispatched overseas if necessary and would thus daily exert its potential power upon the great stage of world politics, had scarcely occurred to most Americans. All of its implications can hardly have been apparent to Root. But in his first annual report (December 1899), the lawyer who a few months before had protested that he knew nothing about war, was outlining a comprehensive plan of Army reorganization which may well have been of greater historical significance than all the Navy's big shipbuilding programs put together.

The immediate problem was obviously the Philippines. But in his first report Root took in a larger area; we should, he began, "settle upon the true principle which should govern the use to be made of the Army." Here "two propositions" struck him as "fundamental." "First, the real object of having an army is to provide for war. Second, that the regular establishment of the United States will probably never be by itself the whole machine with which any war is fought." Some increase in the permanent regular Army was essential in order to take care of the new colonial commitments and to garrison the more extensive sea-coast fortifications which were coming to completion. But measures of this kind, necessary to meet peacetime requirements, would never suffice to "prepare for war." For that, Root felt that four things were necessary: a staff organization capable of studying the larger problems of military science and making a systematic preparation of war plans; a similar agency capable of evaluating new weapons systems, materials and military inventions and of recommending on their adoption; an adequate process for selecting officers for appointment and promotion, and an exercise and training system that would drill officers and men in "the movements of large bodies of troops." In addition, something would have to be done to insure a supply of trained men to reinforce the regular establishment in time of need—in short, to establish a reserve system.

With these recommendations, Root was proposing to bring the managerial revolution in warfare to the United States. They patently went far beyond the immediate problem of providing sufficient police forces for the Philippines. It was a large concept, bound to challenge hoary institutions and vested interests at many points. The proposed general staff would destroy the entrenched power of the existing staff corps and perhaps weaken the tradition of "civilian control." An effective reserve would mean the subordination if not the elimination of the National Guard. Root himself did not see that at the end of his plan for a professional, scientifically directed and organized system of war preparedness, there stood the inevitable corollary of universal conscription. But he knew that he faced a long, hard campaign of education and persuasion; and his initial proposals were modest, going little beyond the recommendation for an increase in the permanent establishment and for an Army War College to perform at least some of the functions which he envisaged for his general staff. He was, however, careful to give his report as wide circulation and as much publicity as he could.

It was not for another year that he secured even the enlargement of the permanent establishment. In February 1901, with the deadline for the temporary forces in the Philippines rapidly running out, Congress at last fixed the regular Army at thirty regiments of infantry, fifteen regiments of cavalry, three battalions of engineers and a "corps" of artillery embracing both field batteries and fortress companies, the aggregate strength to be varied between 60,000 and 100,000 men at the President's discretion. The Philippine Scouts and the Puerto Rican Regiment of Infantry were established as regular United States troops; the anomaly of the old artillery regiments was ended.[18] In November 1901 the War College was formally instituted by Executive Order.

Roosevelt was now President; his heart was in the Navy, but he lent vigorous support to his methodical Secretary of War. Yet the going was still hard and, as the fighting died away in the Philippines and the brief excitement of the Peking Legations passed, popular interest in Army organization sank to the vanishing point. The general staff bill was introduced early in 1902, but the opposition of the bureaus and of the Commanding General (the somewhat pompous but politically powerful General Nelson A. Miles) was too strong. In the meanwhile it had become evident, as Root put it, that the National Guard lobby would be able "to defeat any measure" for a reserve system "which did not commend itself to them"; so the Secretary had to abandon his ideas for incorporating the Guard into a Federally controlled reserve. At a meeting with the National Guard Association in January 1902 a compromise was reached; it fell considerably short of what Root had wanted, but it was still a step forward.

The general staff bill was withdrawn and rewritten during the summer in simplified form. Finally, in January and February 1903 the Dick Act, embodying the National Guard compromise, and the Reorganization Act, creating the general staff, were adopted. The Root program, though in an attenuated form, was complete. It was to take years of controversy to work out all its implications; but Root and the brilliant younger officers who had worked with him and advised him had provided the nation with the rudiments of a machine capable of waging both large-scale and transoceanic war.

---

[18] In 1907 the coast and field artillery were finally divided. The former retained its company organization, with 170 separate companies. The latter was given a regimental organization of its own, there being six regiments each of six four-gun batteries. Three were of light (field) artillery proper, two of mountain or pack artillery and one of horse artillery.

The regular Army, if still small by European standards, was nevertheless fixed at about four times the strength it had enjoyed in 1897. It was beginning to receive modern weapons. The Model 1903 Springfield, which replaced the Krag, was to be considered for a generation the best military shoulder rifle in the world; it remained the basic weapon of the American foot soldier throughout one world war and down to the eve of a second. The artillery, which had gone to Cuba with obsolete pieces fixed on the carriages and firing black powder, received the Model 1902 and later 3-inch field guns, using smokeless powder to fire efficient shrapnel and high-explosive shell and mounted on carriages with complete recoil and training devices and equipped with optical sights. The weapon was approximately the equal of the field guns which would be used by all the armies in the First World War. It was not quite as good as the French 75 (developed at about the same time), but the fact that the American artillery adopted the latter in 1917-18 was due more to its availability than to its margin of superiority. In other respects, particularly in the development of a satisfactory machine gun, the Army was more laggard; but it was at least aware of the contemporary world and its probable requirements.

The Army now had the rudiments of a general staff, which could exercise some foresight in planning. It had gone far toward solving a command problem which had plagued American military administration for a century. The office of Commanding General had been abolished. It had long been an anomaly. In peace the Commanding General had nothing to command; in war he had little means of exercising command (and often little competence to do so) over the field generals who led the fighting armies. Administration in peacetime was in the hands of the staff bureaus—Engineer, Ordnance, Quartermaster, Commissary and the powerful Adjutant General—which operated directly under the authority of the civilian Secretary of War; these were under chiefs holding permanent tenure and were staffed by officers who made their whole careers within their respective corps. Their objects in peacetime were economy and bureaucratic efficiency, not preparation for the huge wastes of war; but in dealing with the requirements of possible war, the Commanding General was hamstrung between the bureaus and the over-all responsibility of the civilian President. Root saw that there was no place for a Commanding General between the constitutional Commander-in-Chief—the President—and the staff bureaus which were responsible, through the Civilian Secretary, to the political administration. The essence of his reform was the replacement of the Commanding General with a Chief of Staff as the highest uniformed officer of the Army.

The new title more accurately indicated the true relationship of the uniformed head of the Army, in peacetime, to the civilian authority. On the one hand, it made the head of the military hierarchy the senior military advisor to the constitutional Commander-in-Chief, and to his civilian deputy, the Secretary of War. On the other hand, it gave him responsibility for and control over the staff bureaus; it thus gave him authority over both planning and administration, the two principal functions of high command in peacetime. If war should ever come again, field generals could direct the strategy and tactics within the framework of plan, training, weapons systems and logistics which had been worked out by the Chief of Staff, acting directly as agent for the civilian authority embodied in the President and the Secretary. It was a more logical system than the old one; it also made possible the selection of the ablest minds for the highest military post. Typically, the Commanding General had been the most senior and respected officer on the Army list who, once appointed, held office throughout the remainder of his military career. The Chief of Staff, however, was to be appointed for a limited term only; there was to be no permanent appointment to the new General Staff Corps which would serve him, but its officers would be rotated from line to staff and back again in order to keep planning, weapons design and administrative policy in constant touch with the "using arms."

Here were the elements of a genuine machine for the large-scale conduct of mass warfare. It would still have to be provided with the flesh and blood to do the fighting; it would require a mobilizable reserve. The famous Militia Act of 1792 was finally repealed by the Dick Act, and with it there went all but the ghost of the universal military obligation. The wholly volunteer National Guard was recognized as the "organized militia" and the first-line military reserve. It was to be organized, trained and equipped uniformly with the regular

Army; the Federal government assumed responsibility for providing weapons and equipment as well as regular Army officers as instructors. Minimum standards of weekly drill and the annual encampment time were imposed. But the Guard refused to surrender its state-supported independence. The Federal government could call it into service only for the constitutional purposes of keeping internal order or repelling invasion. For overseas operations or major foreign wars, the national authority could only ask it to volunteer. Washington was able to establish some control over the competence of the state officers by reserving the right to qualify them for equivalent commissions in any volunteer force that might be raised. The presumption was that in "emergency" the Guard would volunteer in units, and would thus arrive upon the scene of action well-equipped and well-officered. But in theory the National Guard remained simply a training school for soldiers who in another war would be raised *de novo* in Federal volunteer regiments; it was the essence of the Dick Act, as Root said, to "recognize the fact" that the Guard was "the great school of the volunteer soldier." It was not an entirely satisfactory solution. But Root labored under what was to prove the mistaken belief that "with our 80 millions of people there never will be the slightest difficulty in raising an army of any size which it is possible to put into the field. Our trouble never will be in raising soldiers; our trouble will always be the limit of possibility in transporting, clothing, arming, feeding and caring for our soldiers, and that requires organization."

In his effort to meet that requirement, Root brought the military managerial revolution to the United States. The German Great General Staff was admittedly his model; even if Root did not see it, the conscript mass army, available for aggressive action upon a world stage, was the logical end.[19] Years afterward, his Democratic succes-

---

[19] Rudyard Kipling's curious military fantasy, *An Army of a Dream*, published in 1904, supplies a grim hint of the direction in which the military-imperial romanticism of the Roosevelt years was leading even the democracies. Kipling envisaged a system of universal military training starting at the age of 8, in which boys over 10 would know "their company drill better than they knew the King's English," and everyone on reaching the age of 18 would be a highly trained soldier. Males from 18 to 35 would be required to "volunteer" for some form of regular or part-time reserve service, on pain of losing their vote

sor, Newton D. Baker, was to declare that Root's creation of the General Staff was "the outstanding contribution made by any Secretary of War from the beginning of history. Without that contribution from him, the participation of the United States in the [First] World War would necessarily have been a confused, ineffective and discreditable episode." [20] The thought lingers that without that contribution the participation might never have taken place at all. But Root, like all large figures, was only a reflection of his times. There were many other architects of the great disaster of militarism which was to supervene in 1914-18.

5.

In November 1904 Theodore Roosevelt was elected President "in his own right," and the "imperial years" of American military and foreign policy were to begin. But that fall was to witness other events of possibly even greater historic importance. The newspapers which reported the Presidential campaign were also full of the Russo-Japanese War, of the dramatic naval battle of August 10 in the Gulf of Chihli, of the great Battle of Liao-Yang on September 10 and the developing siege of Port Arthur—actions in which the Japanese deployed fleets and armies that in size, in the modernity of their equipment and tactics and in the skill of their leadership reduced our own effort of 1898 to the tragicomic. This sobering spectacle of a supposedly second-class Oriental power using the latest Occidental military techniques to crush back the Russian colossus, thereby altering all the balances of Asian and world politics, made an impression.

Americans were unaware, however, of another bit of military history in these days which was also to be of considerable significance. It

---

—and their access to poor relief! The story depicts the entire British population joyously absorbed in military training, military maneuvers and war games to the exclusion, it would seem, of every other interest. This oddity is worth re-examination: it reads like a cheerful forecast of the Nazi and Communist system of training children to war from the cradle, a kind of Orwell *1984* in reverse, since the author seems completely approving of the total militarization and regimentation which he describes.

[20] Philip C. Jessup, *Elihu Root* (New York, Dodd, Mead, 1938), Vol. I, p. 240.

was in October 1904 that the picturesque, forceful and highly intelligent "Jackie" Fisher became First Sea Lord of the Royal Navy. The result was to be a "technological breakthrough" in naval war of shattering effect. Fisher had realized that the standard sea-going battleship of the time—the type with which our shipyards were crammed in 1904 and which Roosevelt, like naval authorities elsewhere, was continuing to lay down—was already obsolete. Typically, these were ships like the American *Connecticut* class, of 16,000 tons, designed for 18 knots, mounting a main battery of four 12-inch and eight 8-inch guns, only half of the latter being available on either broadside. This combination of calibers had made sense only because the 12-inch rifles were so inaccurate at their longer range, and the 8-inch so much more rapid in service at their shorter range, that the two might be expected to do a rough equality of damage at practicable combat distances. But the revelation in the Battle of Santiago of the inaccuracy of all varieties of fire had given rise to much thought about gunnery. As early as 1898 the British had begun seriously to experiment in improving the long-range practice of their heaviest weapons, and the results had by 1904 convinced Fisher that the smaller weapons had been rendered useless. The 12-inch gun was now capable of deciding an action before the 8-inch guns would come within range. The obvious answer was an all-big-gun ship, carrying nothing in its main armament save the heaviest weapons available, and nothing else larger than what might be required for close-in defense against torpedo attack.

Fisher also reviewed the armored cruiser, a hybrid type which had proliferated in all the navies without too sound a reason. It had been intended primarily as a destroyer of commerce-raiding "protected" or unarmored cruising ships; but the armor and firepower it was given for this purpose would also permit it to reinforce any battle line in which 8-inch guns were still a part of the main battery. The retirement of the medium calibers from the battleships would end this function of the armored cruiser, unless she were given the heaviest guns as well. When Fisher took over as First Sea Lord in the autumn of 1904 he had already caused to be prepared preliminary designs for two all-big-gun ships. The first was to become H.M.S. *Dreadnought* and gave her name to the whole subsequent race of heavy battleships in the world's navies; the second was to become H.M.S. *Invincible,* the world's first "battle cruiser."

Fisher understood clearly that these new types would at a stroke render obsolete not only every battleship and armored cruiser in other navies but every one in Britain's own huge fleet as well. While he was about it, therefore, he stepped up the speed as well as the gunpower and range. The speeds of naval vessels tended to remain static, for the simple reason that they were designed to fight in squadrons, where the speed of the slowest ship would control; it was pointless to notch up the speeds of the newer ships unless one could contemplate a complete replacement. But this was precisely what Fisher intended. *Dreadnought* was given ten 12-inch rifles (and nothing else beyond antitorpedo armament) and designed for a speed of 21 knots. *Invincible* was more lightly armored and mounted only eight 12-inch guns, but she was designed for 25 knots (as against the armored cruiser's 22 knots or so) and made over 28 knots on her trials. These were ships of crushing power, speed and protection by comparison with the types they were intended to replace; once they appeared and their implications were understood, no more of the old types were to be laid down anywhere.[21]

Fisher's reason for instigating this revolution was a familiar one: if he did not, someone else would. Since a revolution was inevitable, Britain should be the first to profit by it, even at the cost of outmoding her whole existing fleet. In this case, the reasoning was justified. The all-big-gun ship had for some time been a lively subject of discussion in naval circles. The first two American vessels of the kind (U.S.S. *Michigan* and *South Carolina*) were actually authorized in March 1905, some weeks before Fisher secured his authorization for *Dreadnought* and *Invincible.* But when the American ships were voted, the all-big-gun design had not been finally decided on; Fisher, on the other hand, knew exactly what he wanted and proceeded with the utmost energy to build it. When the *Michigans,* which were at best only transition ships, were at last completed at the end of 1909,

[21] R. H. Bacon, *The Life of Lord Fisher* (London, 1929), *passim.*

Dreadnought had some three years of sea service behind her. Thus, Fisher was clearly ahead, but the naval revolution would have come in any event.

The *Dreadnought* battleship type was already on the way before the lessons of the Russo-Japanese War began to come in. As they did so, they were generally to lend powerful confirmation to the new military and naval trends; initially, however, they seem to have done little to lessen the uncertainty and confusion detectable in American naval policy on the morrow of TR's electoral victory. In his annual report of December 1904 Secretary Morton could deduce from the earlier naval actions the comforting reassurance that despite all the new weapons, such as mines and torpedo craft, "the day of the battleship is not over and the sphere of the lighter vessels, while important, is auxiliary only." This was just as well, as the big battleship programs we had voted just after the Spanish-American War had been slow in getting under way and were now piling up with cumulative effect. Although "never before," according to the Secretary, "were so many warships launched by this or any other nation in one year" as we had sent down the ways in fiscal '04, the yards were still jammed with uncompleted vessels. And yet the Navy wanted a new appropriation of over $100 million, "the largest ever proposed," and authorizations for three more battleships and numerous lesser types. This gave pause to many statesmen in both parties.

The House Naval Affairs Committee cut the recommendation to two more battleships and nothing else; even so, it was readily calculated that when all this construction had been completed we would emerge with a navy second only to that of Great Britain in effective combat strength. At a moment when, as all sides agreed, "the skies are clear" and there was no visible danger of war anywhere upon the horizon, this seemed somewhat excessive. In the naval race we had passed, or were about to pass, even France. "The cry can almost now be heard," exclaimed Mr. Rixey of Virginia in the House debate; "the buglers have announced it, having passed France, 'Let us have the greatest Navy in the world.' I believe the dangers attendant upon the greatest navy in the world are far greater than upon a navy of reasonable proportions."

The trouble was that there was no way by which Mr. Rixley or anyone else could know what might constitute "reasonable" proportions. The competitive standards, about which Mr. Rixley was so sarcastic, might be inescapable for a nation like Britain, facing the German building yards across the narrow breadth of the North Sea, but were really not applicable to the United States. The new military and naval managers were learning how to organize, train and deploy great forces; but they had not learned the most important lesson of all, which was how to devise and scale general policies of preparedness which would actually serve the "reasonable" ends of the state. It was scarcely deniable that there were, as Mr. Rixley suggested, very real dangers attendant upon an aggressive policy aiming at the "greatest navy in the world"; it was undeniable that there were dangers attendant upon a policy of naval neglect. Unfortunately, it was impossible to balance the one against the other or to draw a "reasonable" line between the extremes.

The introduction of scientific management into war had not overcome the fact that armies and navies were not and had never been technical, engineering answers to technical problems of defense. They were rather organic growths developing, as do most great social institutions, out of complex soils of vested interests, political and economic ambitions, unanalyzed fears and untested assumptions about historical causation. There were no clear standards by which to determine the point at which the operation of these intricate forces would carry American military preparation beyond the bounds of the "reasonable" into those of unreason.

Not a few had their doubts. Mr. Littlefield of Maine averaged the expenditures for the three years immediately before the Spanish-American War and for the three years immediately following. It seemed striking to him that whereas non-military expenditure had gone up by only 22 per cent, military expenditure had risen by 341 per cent. Of course, there were the new overseas "commitments." But did they really commit us to all that? With the Russo-Japanese War not yet decided, few grasped the fact that the emergence of Japan as a major military power would put a quite specific value upon our commitment to defend the Philippines. Here was a concrete problem

that might, it would seem, have reduced naval policy to certain concrete staff solutions. Yet it was to be reflected neither in the naval
debate of early 1905 nor in the reports, recommendations and arguments for many years thereafter. While many gestures were to be
made in the direction of defense against the Japanese, it is questionable whether any naval building program down to the eve of the
Second World War was clearly and consciously designed with the
defense of the Philippines primarily in mind.

The all-big-gun ship was on the horizon; it might have given rise
to a serious debate over the necessity for replacing the battleship fleet
which we were still expensively constructing. But the existence of
Fisher's designs was unknown in the United States in early 1905. The
Naval Affairs Committee had compromised, not only by cutting the
requested three ships to two, but by requiring that while they should
carry "the heaviest armor and most powerful armament for ships of
their class" and have "the highest practicable speed," they should do it
on the 16,000 tons displacement of the standard pre-dreadnought
battleship. This, of course, made it inevitable that the resultant ships
(the *Michigans*), while very fine battleships, should be inferior to the
big design which Fisher had boldly adopted.

There were still other doubts. It seemed strange to find evidence
that the newly formed Steel Trust was charging the United States Navy
half again as much for ship steels as it was asking from European
ship and armor builders. Was it necessary for the government, having
built up the United States Steel Corporation with tariff protection and
contracts, now to "turn the other cheek" and vote "two more un-
needed battleships" in order to afford to the corporation "a further
benefaction and an increased monopoly"? Since no one, unfortunately,
could really know whether the ships were "needed" or not, it was a
more or less unanswerable question. The administration put on the
pressure and the two ships were voted.

It was two months later, on May 27, 1905, that the naval Battle of
Tsu-Shima wrote its final bloody period to the Russo-Japanese War.
It also provided the one real combat test to which the pre-dreadnought
navies—which between 1890 and 1910 absorbed billions of dollars,
produced hundreds of costly ships and helped shape the whole frame-

work of international policy and diplomacy—were ever to be subjected. Lissa had come too early; Santiago, Manila Bay and a few
other actions were too minor and confused. On sea as on land the
Russo-Japanese War was the one large-scale, full-dress conflict between 1871 and 1914 to test out all the theories which had been
confided in innumerable papers to the service magazines of half a
dozen countries, expounded in books or argued over the mess and
wardroom tables. The land fighting in Manchuria might, perhaps, have
been studied somewhat more carefully. It quite clearly revealed the
battlefield predominance of the machine gun, the impossibility of the
frontal charge, the decisive significance of entrenchment and position
warfare. The great size of both the armies and their casualty lists were
sobering. On land, this was a new kind of warfare. At sea, it appeared
to be only the familiar kind, raised to new speeds and ranges by the
introduction of the steam-driven battleship. One new weapon, the
submarine, was not used at all. Torpedo and mine warfare, on the
other hand, assumed great prominence. For the first time, the automobile "fish" torpedo demonstrated its power. This was the first naval
war fought with the aid of wireless communications. But it still cen-
tered upon Mahan's battleship "fleet in being." Rozhdestvenski's remarkable voyage from the Baltic around the Cape of Good Hope to
the Sea of Japan provided the first important test of the fueling and
logistic problems involved in the distant operation of the steam-driven
battle fleet; and it was to reach its terrible climax at Tsu-Shima in a
full dress "fleet action" between battle lines of the kind of which
Mahan had dreamed.

For the first time naval experts and laymen alike were given some
concrete idea of what happened to men and ships when they were
smothered by 12-inch high explosive shell (the relative durability of
the ships and the terrible vulnerability of the men even behind their
armor was something of a surprise); for the first time there were some
positive data upon the effectiveness of all the complicated new tools
of naval war which had been developing mainly on theory throughout
the preceding fifteeen years. The results were not always too clear,
and even the great Mahan committed himself in the summer of 1906
to the view that the small battleship with a dual armament of 12-inch

and 8-inch guns had justified itself. But he was demolished in rebuttal by a younger naval theorist, a Lieutenant Commander W. S. Sims, not then known to history. There was nothing, however, in the naval war to dispute either the basic Mahanite concepts of sea power or the tactical calculations at which Admiral Sir John Fisher had already arrived.

Having rendered the Royal Navy as obsolete as all the others, Fisher threw all his tremendous energy into insuring that Britain would be first with the new battle fleets that would now have to be built. Authorized just before Tsu-Shima, in the spring of 1905, *Dreadnought's* keel was laid in early October, and she went to sea just one year later, October 3, 1906. Her trials had barely been run before Fisher, in late 1906 and early 1907, was laying down three consorts of the same type; and by the time the Germans rose to the challenge (their first all-big-gun ships were not begun until 1907) Britain was laying down dreadnoughts in batches of three and four or more at a time.

This was a development which neither the United States nor its ebullient President had anticipated. In his annual message of December 1905 the President, contemplating our splendid line of some twenty-five battleships and ten armored cruisers built, building or provided for, had suggested that this was enough. This represented an "adequate" Navy, and all that would now be required would be to replace old ships, perhaps at a rate of no more than one a year. Unfortunately, "replacement," both then and thereafter, was an elastic if not somewhat disingenuous concept. If we were going to "replace," it seemed logical to the General Board and the Navy Department to begin at least with the five battleships and two armored cruisers surviving from the Spanish War era, as well as with the ten coast-defense monitors still carried on the list. The Secretary of the Navy, Charles J. Bonaparte (a descendant of Napoleon's brother Jerome), felt that five new battleships would represent a fair exchange for the monitors; this left a "replacement" program of no less than ten battleships which the Secretary thought should be laid down over the next six years or so. For the coming year he asked not for one, as the President suggested, but for two.

In early 1906 Congress was more restive than it had been in 1905, and in the end it voted only one battleship. There was much confusion over the design problem. By that time news of Fisher's *Dreadnought* was circulating and the Bureau of Construction and Repair was working frantically upon the problem of a proper "answer." As a result, the ship voted in the spring of 1906 was to come out as U.S.S. *Delaware*—our first true dreadnought—of 20,000 tons, designed for 21 knots and with a main battery of ten 12-inch rifles. Plainly, this put an altogether new face upon the problem of "replacement." In his report in the fall of 1906, Secretary Bonaparte tacitly admitted that he might have been overhasty in declaring the year before that "the aggregate of our [heavy combat ships] built, building or authorized would seem . . . sufficient to provide for any contingencies within the limits of probability." Since then, "circumstances" had caused him to revise this view and to recommend "a moderate increase in the effective fighting strength of our Navy." By that time, *Dreadnought* was readying to go to sea. In addition to a number of lighter vessels, the Secretary asked for two more battleships, requesting immediate authorization for one of them so that she could be laid down as a consort for *Delaware*. On its face, this program did not differ from what had been asked the year before under the "replacement" concept, and the Secretary was vague as to the "circumstances" which had caused him to enlarge his estimate of future naval needs. But they may be guessed.

One, no doubt, was the Japanese victories in the Far East. Roosevelt had won the Nobel Peace Prize for presiding over the Russo-Japanese peace negotiations, which took place at Portsmouth, N. H. And almost immediately thereafter he had begun to worry about war. In October 1906, he was telling the chairman of the Senate Naval Affairs Committee that a war with Japan was "not improbable." Who knows what he really thought? Was the danger of a Japanese descent upon the Philippines (which was not in fact to materialize for another thirty years) his reason for urging more naval building, or was his desire for more naval building his reason for raising a hypothetical danger of war? Some gestures were to be made with the new Japanese menace clearly in mind. It was at this time that we began the refortification of Manila Bay, clearing the jungles on Corregidor for the heavy gun emplacements, magazines and tunnels which, while never used for the repulse of a hostile fleet, did serve MacArthur as base and final refuge in 1942. But neither then nor for long thereafter were the naval programs explicitly directed against Japan, nor were they technically well suited to the requirements of naval war in the far western Pacific. There is much reason to conclude that the principal "circumstance" which influenced Bonaparte was Fisher's technical revolution.

In his annual message at the end of 1906 Roosevelt, despite his Secretary's greater frankness, clung to the somewhat disingenuous position of the year before: "I do not ask that we continue to increase our Navy. I ask merely that it be maintained at its present strength." But the beauties of "replacement" were now more apparent; just to maintain "present strength" would require the construction every year of "at least" one first-class battleship, carrying "as large a number as possible of very heavy guns of one caliber," with "heavy armor, turbine engines and in short every modern device." "Of course," it would also require large numbers of cruisers, destroyers, and auxiliaries as well. But the real problem was certainly never made clear to the confused Congressmen. The real problem was how to maintain the naval power invested in those twenty-five splendid but now obsolete battleships in face of a technical development which would require the replacement, not simply of the more aging sisters, but of the entire lot. This Congress did not understand; possibly the naval experts and advisors did not too clearly understand it themselves. Congress ended by voting the one repeat *Delaware* for which Bonaparte had asked, but it did not advance the authorization and it refused the second ship. In the winter and spring of 1907 TR had many other things to think about, and he made no great fight over the matter. But as the end of the imperium dawned above the horizons of 1908 it was not absent from his mind.

As a militarist, Roosevelt was rather like the German Emperor, Wilhelm II, whom in many ways he curiously resembled. He loved military pomp and power, not because he had any particular idea of using it for great political ends, but simply because it was power— as well as discipline, patriotism, regimentation—in the abstract. Like the Kaiser, Roosevelt never really wanted to fight a war, but he wanted to leave a powerful and impressive Army and Navy behind him. But every great and "strong" military or naval establishment requires a menace on which to grow. For the eighty-five years between 1815 and 1900 our military institutions had in general languished because of the absence of any such menace (except those which we created from time to time by our own aggressive policies or internal divisions), and this lack was one of the continuing weaknesses beneath the military revival after 1898. Amid the stirring drumbeats of the Rooseveltian age there was always some backwoods Congressman to arise and ask, embarrassingly, what it was all about. TR seldom lacked for answers. In the dawn of our imperial expansion it was usually the Germans who provided the peril. They had, after all, been rude in the Samoan affair in 1889; their Admiral von Diederichs had been worse than tactless at Manila Bay in 1898; they were overbearing in the Venezuela crisis of 1902. Fantasies of German battle fleets convoying spike-helmeted divisions to aggressive landings in Latin America were to remain powerful incitations to American "preparedness" down to our own entry into the First World War. Yet in view of the growing European tensions, rendering adventure in the Western Hemisphere by any European power increasingly less likely, none of this was too convincing. It was at this juncture that a new menace appeared. Japan, which had commanded overwhelming American sympathy in her struggle against Czarist despotism, was overnight the new peril. For all those interested, for many varied motives of prestige or profit or political ambition, in naval expansion and navalism, she was a very useful one.

In the summer of 1907 there was real trouble in California over the Japanese land and immigration questions. There were numerous friends in more than one foreign diplomatic service to warn the President, for their own reasons, that war was "inevitable." Roosevelt was writing to Root that "I am more concerned over the Japanese situation than almost any other. Thank heavens, we have the Navy in good shape." There really was something of a war scare in 1907. Homer Lea produced his curious prophecy, *The Valor of Ignorance* (published in 1911), and popular magazines ran accounts of the forthcoming American-Japanese war, in which the destruction of the American war vessels was impressively depicted by photographs of the Russian wrecks of 1904-05. And it was out of such febrile imaginings that there arose the extraordinary, and still not wholly intelligible, plan for sending the United States battle fleet into the Pacific and around the world.

In retrospect this exploit can only be regarded as one of the more peculiar aberrations of Rooseveltian naval romanticism inflated with Mahanite gospel. In June 1907 Roosevelt had directed the Joint Board of the War and Navy Departments to formulate a strategic plan in case of war with the Japanese. One recommendation was, not unnaturally, that the battle fleet should be dispatched into the western Pacific. There was no obvious need for it anywhere else; and if we were preparing actual war it would seem plain that we should have the ships in the theater at the beginning rather than waiting, as had the Russians, to send them out at the end. But war was clearly not contemplated in the planning for the Navy's world cruise. Three motives are usually assigned for it: to overawe Japan by demonstrating that we could at will throw into the Pacific a force greater and more efficient than that which the Russians had sent out; to provide the Navy with the training patently essential if it was to be capable of such distant exertions of power; and to make propaganda for the big naval program which Roosevelt was planning to submit in December, as well as to emphasize the necessity for the Isthmian Canal which Roosevelt was driving toward completion. No doubt there was much to be said for the move under all three heads. But while the cruise was to be magnificent, it was certainly not war.

The announced destination, when they sailed from Hampton Roads in December 1907, was San Francisco only, even though rumors of greater things were rife. Some foreign commentators observed that the move must indicate the President's profound belief that no war was imminent, since it was in effect immobilizing virtually the whole combat strength of the American Navy in a voyage around South America which must take months to complete. At the time, the British were rearranging all their naval dispositions, cutting their distant stations to the bone and calling home everything of fighting value in prevision of the one real war which then already impended. Mr. Roosevelt, discharging sixteen American battleships into the blue (still wearing their peacetime white and buff paint, totally devoid of destroyer or cruiser screens, with their train, such as it was, sent ahead of them to the friendly harbors which would sustain their voyage and with no fortified bases of their own from which to operate should it come to hostilities), was plainly not making a warlike gesture. This was sufficiently apparent to the Japanese, who promptly issued the most cordial invitations and in fact received the fleet, when it arrived in their waters in the fall of 1908, with the utmost politeness and good will. If the voyage had any effect upon Japanese policy at all, it can only have been to stoke the fires of their own naval revival. They had humbled Russia; and they began to devote themselves the more earnestly to the naval building which would one day enable them to humble the United States as well—especially a United States which could imagine that this kind of empty naval parade represented a serious move in the grim game of war. "Ever since 1909," as a recent Japanese naval writer [22] has observed, "the Japanese Navy had made the United States Navy its sole imaginary enemy."

If the cruise was less than successful in overawing the Japanese, it did do much to improve naval training and especially the Navy's understanding of logistics in long overseas operations. But one cannot resist the feeling that its third purpose, to make propaganda for the Roosevelt program submitted in December 1907, was the most significant. The Congressional session of 1907-08 was to bring the climactic battle of the Roosevelt years. It was TR's last good chance to impose his will and his personality on national affairs; a successor would be elected in November 1908 and the ensuing short session would be only an interregnum. The annual message of December 3, 1907 was inordinately long; military and naval policy were reached only near the end after discussion of many other matters which in those days seemed of greater import. But the paragraphs made it clear that the ex-colonel of the Rough Riders wished to leave a martial legacy behind him. He praised the efficiency of the regular Army but

---

[22] Shigera Fukudome, USNIP, Vol. 81 (Dec. 1955), p. 1317.

announced that "it is too small." There were not enough officers and
it was impossible to recruit even the modest authorized enlisted
strength. "We should maintain in peace a fairly complete skeleton of
a large army. . . . It is essential that we should possess a number of
extra officers trained in peace to perform efficiently the duties urgently
required" in war. It was the strongest hint so far of a mass army
mobilization plan.

But with Roosevelt it was the Navy which really counted. The
"replacement" theory of 1905 was now openly abandoned. After the
recent failure of the Second Hague Conference to make even a beginning on naval arms limitation it would, the President declared, "be
most unwise for us to stop the upbuilding of our Navy." Constructing
one battleship a year, even of the most modern type, would "barely
keep our fleet up to its present force. This is not enough. In my
judgment we should this year provide four battleships" as well as
"plenty of torpedo boats and destroyers" together with men, training
facilities, docks, coaling stations, supply ships and "fortifications of
the best type" for all our harbors on both coasts. This was a fairly
plain bid to enter the United States as a third runner in the Anglo-
German dreadnought building race.

The message was dated December 3, 1907. On the 15th the President boarded his official yacht, *Mayflower,* to arrive in Hampton
Roads next morning. A splendid pageant ensued. Under the command
of Rear Admiral Robley D. Evans (the most durable reputation surviving from the Spanish-American War) "sixteen hard-hitting, steel-
belted American battleships . . . sparkling white in their immaculate
dressings of peace, sailed away today under the dazzling sun of a
cloudless winter sky on their . . . sea expedition of 14,000 miles . . . to
the West Coast of the United States." It was most certainly not war
even though the bands had played "Auld Lang Syne" and "The Girl
I Left Behind Me"; even though there were scores of disconsolate
ladies on the porch of the Old Point Comfort Hotel to watch them go;
and even though there were all kinds of rumors as to the possibility
that the fleet would have to fight the Japanese before its return. After
taking the review, *Mayflower* weighed and returned to Washington.

The only war which this operation was to involve was to be fought in the committee rooms and on the floor of Congress.

Roosevelt knew that he would have a fight on his hands to get the four new battleships for which he had so dramatically asked. On February 21 he was telling "Uncle Joe" Cannon, the powerful and canny Speaker, that the "present military and naval needs" were great. A few days later he was writing again that he could not "with wisdom . . . put all on paper that I feel . . . I am acting with a view to emergencies that . . . may arise within the next decade or two." [23] The idea of preparing against emergencies which might not emerge for another twenty years seems a little odd. But the emergency which Roosevelt seems really to have had in mind had already occurred; it was the arrival of the new technology which had outmoded his great and costly battle fleet, even then on its futile and final journey around the world. For two years both Roosevelt and the Navy Department had been flirting with the edges of the problem. In a special message to Congress on April 14, 1908 he at last came out with it.

The failure of the Hague Conference (in which neither Roosevelt nor anyone else had entertained the slightest confidence from the beginning) was again the pretext. It was now plain, the President said, that there was no chance of limiting naval construction by agreement. But "coincidentally with this discovery" (in itself a quaint word) there had occurred "a radical change in the building of battleships among the great military nations—a change . . . which doubles or more probably trebles their effectiveness. Every other great naval nation has or is building a number of ships of this kind; we have provided for but two, and therefore the balance of power is declining against us. Under these conditions, to provide for but one or two battleships a year is to provide that this Nation, instead of advancing, shall go backward in naval rank and relative power. . . . There is imposed on me a solemn responsibility. . . . I earnestly advise that the Congress now provide four battleships of the most advanced type."

The standard, interestingly enough, had nothing to do with any specific problems of national policy or national defense; it was the

[23] Henry Pringle, *op. cit., passim.*

purely comparative standard of "naval *rank* and *relative* power." In
short, the great effort and many millions of dollars wrapped up in
Evans' sixteen battleships had come to nothing; a new naval race had
begun and if we were to retain our proud claims to "sea power" it
would all have to be done over again. But Congress refused. The
demand for four battleships "precipitated one of the bitterest legislative struggles in American naval history." [24] The interests involved
were as complex, the arguments on both sides as uninformed and
unrealistic, as usual, and the decision, again as usual, was in the
nature of a compromise. But it was clear enough nevertheless. Roosevelt got only two, not four, new ships.

As the dust settled he wrote Henry White that "I knew I would not
get two . . . unless I made a violent fight for four." But Roosevelt had
a liking for such impish statements, especially if they served to cover
a defeat. And this was a defeat. It is difficult to believe that the President made the original solemn demand for four ships with the levity
of which this remark would seem to convict him. If the United States
was to play the same role in the new naval race as we had, almost
unwittingly, fulfilled in that now closing, four ships a year would be
about the minimum. But Congress and the country would not rise to
an effort for which there seemed, at best, but little strategic necessity.
Congress compromised upon a continuance of the now established
two ships a year policy; Roosevelt was unable to commit his successor
to anything more; and in the result the Anglo-German naval race
swept past us—fortunately, as events were to prove.

Naval statistics are peculiarly tricky, but two tables may fairly illustrate the outcome. In 1906 a writer in the *Proceedings* of the U. S.
Naval Institute projected the figures for the pre-dreadnought fleets
then built or building to show what would be complete by 1908.
Excluding the antiquities of the Spanish War era, this gave the following result:

First-line battleships to be complete by 1908:

US	UK	Germany	Japan	France
19	32	13	9	8

[24] Sprouts, *op. cit.*, p. 264.

From *Jane's Fighting Ships, 1914* one derives the following for dread-nought battleships and battle cruisers completed by the end of 1914:

US	UK	Germany	Japan	France
8	34	21	4	4

Between the end of the Roosevelt era and the beginning of the First World War, the United States thus dropped from second to third place, whereas Britain had more than replaced her huge pre-dread-nought fleet (in numbers of units) with the new-type vessels, and the Germans had replaced theirs by one and a half times, the United States had replaced less than half of her pre-dreadnought fleet with the new monsters. The United States had fallen even farther "behind" because of her niggardliness in regard to light cruisers and destroyers, which were becoming indispensable supports to the operations of the heavy ships.

On February 22, 1909, in the last days of the Roosevelt Presidency, the sixteen battleships of the round-the-world fleet passed in through the Virginia Capes. (Two of the original fleet had been detached and replaced by the two battleships just completed on the West Coast.) Once more they were reviewed by the President. "Not until some American fleet returns victorious from a great sea battle," he told the admirals and captains assembled in *Mayflower*'s cabin, "will there be another such home-coming; another such sight as this. I drink to the American Navy." The salutes resounded, the bands played, the flags fluttered and the ladies welcomed their returning sailors. But it was the end of an era all the same. There were to be numerous American naval victories thereafter, but never one great "home-coming" from one great battle of the kind Roosevelt envisaged. The new ships of the Atlantic Fleet which welcomed the returning argosy were already wearing "battleship gray," and shortly after its arrival the battleship fleet itself was repainted to the same grim, businesslike color. The traditional and most unmilitary white topsides and buff upper works, which had characterized our steam and steel Navy since its rebirth in the '80's, disappeared for good. It was a symbolic touch. Things were getting serious. They were getting too serious for the military histrionics of the Roosevelt era or for the amateurs of war and diplomacy who had guided our military and foreign policy since the late '90's.

6.

In July 1910 Leonard Wood—the onetime Army surgeon who had become the first colonel of the Rough Riders, who had risen to be the military governor of Cuba and later the Commanding General in the Philippines—became Chief of Staff of the United States Army. A man of driving ambition, outstanding abilities and a keen political sense, with many enemies in the Army and many friends among the high-ranking Republican politicians, Wood assumed the post resolved to establish its power and to modernize the still creaking institution of which he was now the highest uniformed head.

The Army of 1910 had come a long way from that of 1897. It had been roughly quadrupled in size; it had been re-equipped; many of its officers now had behind them the combat experience of Cuba or the Philippines while many had command and staff school training; their horizons had been broadened by their work as colonial administrators, diplomats, engineers or police officers in far corners of the earth. The Army had a General Staff; it even had some, quite rudimentary, war plans. But essentially it was still the "old Army," a small, isolated, inbred and professionalized service. Its core of career officers and long-service NCO's and enlisted men was filled out by what riffraff the recruiting offices could entice out of the then somewhat depressed civilian economy. The term of enlistment was only three years but many, aspiring to stripes or liking the life, re-enlisted for several "hitches," thus providing the cadre of experienced men who were to serve the civilian armies so well when they were called to the colors in 1917. The Army was still widely scattered in the small posts which local politics had insisted on preserving, long after their military utility had passed. It was still operated on a rigid caste system, in which the enlisted man still addressed the officer in the third person. It had failed to establish a satisfactory relationship with the National Guard and was still looked upon with profound suspicion (whenever they remembered it at all) by the labor unions, the liberals, the paci-fists and other forces of social change.

The Root reforms had taken only partial effect. The bureaus were still powerful; the War College and the General Staff still weak; the reserve system based upon the National Guard still virtually nonexistent. There had been great improvements in weapons, tactics and training, but there was still no mobilizable force for major war on a scale like that of the Russo-Japanese conflict. Like even the best of military reformers, Root had tended to design his system to refight the war just over rather than to meet the possible problems of the war to come. He had produced a system reasonably effective for making another descent on Cuba (indeed, it did so with economy and dispatch in 1906) or exercising police powers anywhere in the Western Hemisphere. But by 1910, with the Russo-Japanese example before us, that sort of thing was no longer "war."

To a military professional of Wood's energy, intelligence and intense ambition the situation was intolerable. Well before he achieved the top command, Wood was writing Roosevelt (August 1908): "We are not ready. We have not got the necessary artillery, engineer trains, etc., etc. Forty per cent of our colonels and 30 per cent of our field officers would be a detriment to the troops." He wrote to another in May 1909: "We shall drift on, I suppose, in a fool's paradise until some day we find ourselves up against a really respectable adversary." [25] That was the trouble; there was no "respectable adversary" reasonably within sight, and there was still none when Wood became Chief of Staff. The European Great Powers were sinking more and more obviously into the power deadlock which made it impossible for any of them seriously to threaten the Western Hemisphere. Japan might one day become a threat to the Philippines, but the Taft administration, though inclined to a firm diplomatic stand in the Far East, was too much involved in internecine political conflict and recession budgets to make serious preparation for a war in the western Pacific. It had resigned the Rooseveltian trident of "sea power" in the abstract. It continued to build some ships, some forts and bases, but it certainly had no intention—since it saw no need for it—of converting the United States into a garrison state on the European model.

[25] Hermann Hagedorn, *Leonard Wood* (New York, Harper's 1931), Vol. II, pp. 87 f.

Wood knew no more than anyone else when, where or how another "great war" might confront the United States. But he had grasped the central fact of the new militarism. The "little," professional outpost wars of the colonial era had gone by; no important war could be anything save a clash of mass armies embracing something approaching the total power of the state, and to be ready for that meant regimenting the whole population. Wood had achieved a concept of "readiness" not unlike Mahan's and Roosevelt's concept of "sea power." It was a concept of military strength in the abstract, designed not to meet any specific or visible military problem but to master any unforeseeable contingency which might arise. He wanted an army scaled to the size and efficiency of the great hosts of continental Europe. The fact that these hosts were drilling to destroy each other, not the United States, was more or less irrelevant.

Wood saw, with an admirable shrewdness, that the key to his problem lay not in military planning but in public opinion. A big Navy was more a matter of dollars than anything else, since its personnel would be relatively small; but a mass army was a matter primarily of public relations. Unless the psychology of "defense" and "preparedness" could be instilled into the nation as a whole, one was unlikely to draw from it in peacetime a great military organization capable of mobilizing for major land war. Wood became a military evangelist. His name is associated with few contributions to military strategy or technology, but is imperishably linked with the great campaign for preparedness which was to convert the American people from their free-born, insouciant ways to acceptance of the conscript army and the rudiments of the garrison state.

The first requisite was to establish the authority of the central military directorate—the Chief of Staff. Wood's titanic struggle with the Adjutant General, Ainsworth, ending in the latter's utter rout, was to make history and the headlines. But the power struggle between the two men was more than merely personal. It was a battle between the old-line, professional and easily manageable army of tradition and the new cadre or "reserve" army of illimitable potentialities and perhaps uncontrollable impact upon the society. One of the chief issues between the two officers was over the term of enlistment. Wood wanted to reduce it two years in order more rapidly to pass young men into a trained reserve. Ainsworth's partisans insisted upon raising it to five, mainly, no doubt, in order to spite Wood, but with the argument that this would conduce to economy and efficiency. (It is always cheaper to retain trained men for long periods than to be constantly training fresh batches of recruits for replacement.) "The Army's worst enemies," Wood exploded in 1911, "are within itself. The stupid fools who argue for perpetual re-enlistment!" The reserve was, as always, the really critical question. The cadre army, relying upon trained reservists to fill its ranks swiftly to colossal wartime proportions, was the great military invention of continental Europe. But its foundation was universal conscription, which no American officer in 1910 could have dared even to hint at. Wood had to establish his cadre army first; the conscription would follow (as in fact it did) almost inevitably. Even for a volunteer cadre army, however, an effective reserve was a first requisite.

Wood's initial proposal was quite modest. Of course retaining the volunteer principle, he recommended the reduction of the term of enlistment from three years to two but with the addition of an obligation to serve for seven or eight years more in the reserve. He would have organized the reservists thus provided into regimental units and required a few brief periods of refresher training. Within a few years this would have yielded, over and above the regular establishment, a trained and organized reserve army of 280,000 men—nearly three hundred infantry regiments—without having to bother with the National Guard at all. That this would also have put a forbiddingly inequitable military obligation on those who enlisted in the first place apparently did not greatly concern the Chief of Staff; nor did the problem of providing the weapons and equipment, the divisional "slice" and corps troops and staff, without which the three hundred infantry regiments would not have been good for much. But such details did not matter nearly as much as the spreading of the word of American "unreadiness" and of the vital necessity to "prepare." Long before the outbreak of war in Europe, Wood was making propaganda for "preparedness" in speeches, testimony before Congressional committees, letters to his influential friends and by every other means at his command. It was a wonderfully useful concept, because it left so conveniently blank the question of what it was against which we were to prepare. In this it resembled Mahan's sea power; and it was to have an almost equally spectacular future.

It made no great progress, however, in the chilly and pacific climate of the Taft administration. In December 1910, at the height of a row over the deficiencies of the Army, Taft pointedly rebuked both his Secretary of War, Dickinson, and his Chief of Staff by announcing (at a dinner of the American Society for the Judicial Settlement of International Disputes) that the defense system was entirely sufficient since "there is not the slightest prospect of a war in any part of the world in which the United States could conceivably have a part." Nor was there, in 1910. Taft was quite right in thus summarily disposing both of Roosevelt's "yellow peril" and the fantasies of German divisions landing on Latin American beaches. And if the United States was ultimately to find a part in the great European War, already shaping upon the horizons, it was in some degree due to Wood's proselytizing for the means which were to enable the country to assume it.

Wood was able to do a good deal for the existing regular Army, especially in the latter part of the Taft administration, when he had the backing of Henry L. Stimson, who succeeded Dickinson as Secretary of War. At least a paper brigade and divisional organization was worked out to embrace both regulars and National Guard. With the outbreak of revolution in Mexico in 1911, Wood mobilized a whole division of regulars on the border. It is interesting to compare the operation with Polk's mobilization of Taylor's little "army" at Corpus Christi in 1845; nothing so vividly reveals the differences wrought in all popular attitudes toward war and military policy by the passage of no more than sixty-five years. In 1911 it took a distressingly long time to gather the regulars in from their still scattered little posts, and weeks more to fill them to even approximate combat strength. Yet the result was still a maneuver division—the first ever seen in the United States in peacetime—and like the Navy's cruise around the world, it was to provide valuable training for the grim age that was to come. "It was this operation," in Ganoe's view, "more than any other that

marked the decided change between the old Army and the new."
Wood himself was not impressed: "While everybody clapped and said
'How beautiful!'... the real expression should have been 'How
little!'" This one division was a long way from the sixty army corps,
more or less, which Germany was preparing to fling into the first days
of a European struggle.

In February 1909 Roosevelt, in the sunset of his Presidency, had
welcomed the returning fleet. In February 1913, in the sunset of Taft's,
there were sudden disturbances in Mexico City and a two o'clock in
the morning conference at the White House between the President,
the Secretary of War and the Chief of Staff. If we had to intervene,
how long would it take? Proudly the Secretary of War could announce
that a single telegram would suffice; and next morning he in fact sent
a telegram to the commander of the Department of the East alerting
the New England Brigade, which consisted of the 3rd, 5th and 29th
Infantry. But it proved unnecessary to send an "action" order after
it. Probably this was just as well.[26]

In March Wilson and the unwarlike Democrats (most of them were
unwarlike, anyway, and if Wilson was no pacifist he was at least a
hard-bitten anti-militarist) came into power. Wood was to survive as
Chief of Staff until his term expired a year later. When he went from
Washington in April 1914 back to the command at Governor's Island
—within easy reach of all the best publicity media in the United States
—the American people still remained to be converted to the gospel
of preparedness. But Wood was tireless and he was mightily to continue the preachment.

7.

So 1914 dawned—the year which was to bring the great catastrophe
of militarism, the cataclysm which had been preparing, step by step,
for over a century and which when finally it burst was to decimate a
generation and destroy a whole age. It had been heralded by the
Balkan Wars. In December 1912 Sir Cecil Spring Rice, then British

[26] Hagedorn, *op. cit.*, Vol. II, p. 127.

Minister at Stockholm, was dashing off one of his chatty letters to
Henry Adams and the Washington circle:

> Isn't it curious that we are all supposing ourselves to be stand-
> ing on the edge of the most terrific disaster (for Europe) which
> has ever taken place? Even the hardened dip. looks a little solemn
> when the subject is alluded to at dinner. The appearance of the
> *Red Man* in a particularly realistic manner, in the middle of the
> cocked hats and laced coats, has had a rather calming effect.[27]

It was so curious that even the "hardened diplomats" of Europe
could not really grasp what was happening, much less the innocents in
Washington, the now aging survivors of the great years of Rooseveltian
"high policy." But the ominous rumblings continued. In 1912 the
Haldane Mission, intended to arrest the insane Anglo-German naval
rivalry (one of Admiral Mahan's gifts to history), ended in failure.
Mahan himself, who had for some time considered that a navy second
only to Great Britain's represented the minimum American requirement, reached the extraordinary conclusion that nothing less than a
"preponderant" fleet, second to none, would now serve, since the
British Fleet was "pinned down by Germany" and the United States
could no longer "depend on it."

The British continued furiously to lay down "two keels for one,"
at £2,000,000 a keel. In 1913 there came the German and French
army laws, stepping up both forces and imposing a three-year term of
active service on the Frenchmen. In 1913 also the Wilson administration took office in Washington, more innocent, but perhaps not much
more innocent, in these great and grim matters than its Republican
predecessors. When Colonel House reached Europe in the spring of
1914 as Wilson's emissary of peace and reason, he was shocked. "The
situation is extraordinary," he wrote his principal. "It is militarism run
stark mad. Unless you or someone acting for you can bring about a
different understanding, there is some day to be an awful cataclysm." [28]

[27] Stephen Gwynn, *The Letters and Friendships of Sir Cecil Spring Rice*
(Boston, Houghton Mifflin, 1929), Vol. II, p. 181.

[28] Charles Seymour, ed., *The Intimate Papers of Colonel House* (Boston,
Houghton Mifflin, 1926), Vol. I, p. 249.

The Colonel was naïve in supposing that either Wilson or even the Colonel "acting for him" had the power or the understanding to alter the frightful situation which had developed. He was right in his diagnosis of the impending disaster as a disaster of hypertrophied militarism more than anything else. The international world of 1914 would have seemed both insane and incredible to the eighteenth century American statesmen who had insisted upon an armed populace as the one means of controlling the tyranny of "standing armies" and guaranteeing the "liberties of the people" against government. It had never occurred to them that "the people" might themselves generate standing armies more massive, more oppressive and more deadly to the best interests of the state than anything which kings could produce from a few "royal hirelings." They had not foreseen that the armed yokels of 1775 would lead to the *levée en masse* of 1793; that this would in turn lead to the Prussian conscript army of the "War of Liberation"; that this would give rise to the huge peacetime conscription and mobilization systems of the Continent after 1870. No one saw it clearly during the long middle years of the nineteenth century. While the Continental armies all adopted the principle of mass conscription giving rise to a trained reserve, most of the actual wars were minor and were fought by professionals. The French allowed exemptions and substitutions which destroyed most of the system's meaning. The British, isolated behind their Channel moat and their fleet, had none of it. The Americans, lying behind far wider oceanic moats and unthreatened by any danger, scarcely understood what it implied. But after the enormous success of the Germans in 1870-71, the mass conscript army began to be taken seriously everywhere else on the Continent. The Russians, the Austrians, the Italians tightened up their military structure, and in 1899 the French enacted a stringent universal service law.

By 1914 war had become something totally different from what it had seemed to be in 1775. The democratic revolution had, paradoxically, brought with it the universal military obligation. The industrial revolution had made it possible to weapon, equip and transport the enormous forces which a universal obligation would yield. The managerial revolution had now made it possible almost instantly to assemble and hurl these forces upon an opponent. It was the devoted labor of the general staffs which had ensured that they would all have the latest weapons in adequate quantity; that had worked out the mobilization tables and the logistic requirements; that had drawn up the war plans—Plan XVII or the Schlieffen Plan or their counterparts—ready for use in any emergency.

War was now in the hands, not simply of professionals, but of highly trained, technically expert professionals who could in crisis levy upon every industrial and manpower resource of the now highly integrated modern state. The French Army law of 1913 required three years' active duty in uniform of all young Frenchmen, plus eleven years in the reserve and fourteen more in the "territorial" formations —a total obligation of twenty-eight years, or most of a man's active life. With a larger population, the Germans retained their active service period at two years, but they enlarged the number and size of their mobilizable formations. Both countries kept some 800,000 men, more or less, in uniform in peacetime, but the precise figures are not significant as these represented simply the framework on which the wartime hosts would be filled out from the trained reserve. Both countries had built up large cadres of reserve officers; in both the active forces spent their time training the drafts of two-year or three-year conscripts, to pass them into the reserve formations, where they would be immediately available in emergency. On mobilization, some of these would go to filling the regular forces to war strength; most would go into reserve divisions, already provided with officers, weapons and equipment and capable of prompt activation as combat troops. The Germans were said to be able to put into the field about 1,750,000 first-line troops in this way; the French about 1,500,000. Similar masses were immediately mobilizable everywhere else on the Continent, while all the countries had provided for calling out of their reserves large additional numbers of rear-echelon, garrison and replacement troops as necessity might demand.

Thus the machinery had been set up for calling millions of armed and usually well-trained men to the colors at the drop of the "Red Man's" hat. They could be assembled, equipped, sheltered, fed and deployed over the rail nets to the battlefield. Just what they were to do when they got there had not, perhaps, been so well worked out.

War in 1914 was still basically a business of using the infantry mass to destroy the enemy and capture ground. This was what war had always been. If the process could be facilitated by surrounding and eliminating the enemy's armed forces, so much the better, but the underlying aim was to march armed men into enemy territory, to seize his land and resources and, if possible, the levers of police and political power through which he expressed his "will."

The techniques, of course, had changed since 1865 or 1871. All the armies were now equipped with field artillery firing both shrapnel and high explosive at an optimum range of 3,000 yards (a mile and a half). The rifle battalions bore magazine repeating weapons with an optimum range of 500 to 800 yards, say a quarter of a mile. All had machine guns of the same range as the rifles but with a volume of fire more deadly than most soldiers had realized. The scientific Germans had more of them than anyone else, but even they had not fully grasped their power at the opening of the war.

All the armies maintained large numbers of cavalry, but it was recognized that their functions would be confined to those of reconnaissance, screening and pursuit. The infantry still carried bayonets and were everywhere trained in bayonet fighting, but it was apparent that the old type of bayonet charge in more or less dressed ranks was no longer practicable. After the Russo-Japanese War it was reasonably clear that the central fact of battle would lie in the balance between artillery and infantry. To win, the infantry still had to get forward, to come to grips with the enemy infantry and drive it from the field; to enable it to do so, its own artillery could now fire a heavy and continuous barrage over its head, but the enemy artillery could tear its advancing ranks to pieces. The attacking infantry had to scatter, to advance in small detachments and "by rushes," one little group trying to work forward while others maintained "fire support," and with the enemy machine guns coming to dominate the whole lethal operation, against the best efforts of one's own supporting artillery.

As a result, the battle was to be greatly opened out in both space and time. The concept of the one great, decisive clash was to be replaced by the concept of "pressure," rising here or falling away there as reserves were fed in or were exhausted, and spreading in its dread-

ful and fluid way over weeks of time and whole countrysides of wreck
and desolation. And the end, after 1914, was to be another disappearance into the ground, like that which characterized the final year
of the Civil War, the later stages of the Russo-Japanese War, some
phases of the Second World War and the later period of the war in
Korea. Technically, as well as politically, war by 1914 no longer
resembled the popular ideas entertained of it. But this was not fully
apparent to the war offices; it was certainly not apparent to the
patriotic crowds who poured out in all the capitals, shouting their "On
to Berlin" or "Nach Paris," leaving their unforgettable tribute to the
meaning of "popular" war.

Technology had altered the conditions of war at sea as well. The
complicated mastodons of the dreadnought era could not, like Nelson's
three-deckers, be called leisurely forth from ordinary whenever occasion might demand. H.M.S. *Victory* represented naval power in general; she could cruise anywhere in the world and bring her hundred
guns to bear anywhere that power might be useful or desirable. The
dreadnoughts had to be designed from the beginning for more specific naval tasks; fuel capacity, gun power and protection had to be
calculated against very definite contingencies. It took a long time to
train crews to operate them, so they had to be kept constantly at near
war complements; they also had to be surrounded by an expensive
apparatus of lesser vessels—fast scout cruisers to observe and screen
for them, large torpedo flotillas for protection against enemy torpedo
craft and for close action at night. The Mahanite concept of the battle
fleet united and "in being," which would establish "command of the
sea" if not by its existence alone, then by one great fleet action on the
model of Trafalgar, reigned supreme. Such a fleet, like the armies
which it was to support, had to be ready on the word. It lent a further
rigidity and tension to any impending war crisis. In 1913 Mr. Walter
Hines Page, arriving in Britain as Wilson's Ambassador, was surprised
to learn that the Admiralty was on a twenty-four-hour war watch and
that Jellicoe, the First Sea Lord, was never out of telephone reach.

Such was the achievement of the scientific soldiers and sailors, the
highly trained, studious and devoted men who had taken over the
management of arms from the earlier entrepreneurs, swashbucklers

and uneducated aristocratic triflers. In taking every military precaution, in ensuring that their nations would be ready for anything, they had managed to create a situation in which their nations were actually ready for nothing save a universal catastrophe. Unintentionally, they had rendered it impossible for the major European powers to fight any war with each other except a war of all-out effort and destruction. The nineteenth century "wars of convenience" had been excluded by the managerial revolution. It was now all or nothing. The German civilian diplomats could no longer consider a war against Russia alone, for they were the prisoners of a mobilization plan which, designed to meet the exigency of a two-front war, had to start with a two-front war if it started at all. The British could no longer remain on the side lines of a Continental conflict, as they had done forty years before, for they had been obliged to commit themselves, more completely than their cabinet realized, to the French war plan. This was the horrible complex which had been created in Europe. The prospect it offered was so horrible that it successfully kept peace upon the Continent for forty years after 1871. But it had kept the peace only at the frightful price of ensuring that once the system cracked and broke, it would break in total disaster for all concerned.

The rather naïve American statesmen, still inflated on Rooseveltian oratory, neither knew nor understood anything of all this. House could exclaim at "militarism run stark mad," as if psychotherapy would meet the peril. Walter Hines Page, rather more than half seriously, suggested that the cure might lie in putting all these huge armies cooperatively at work on civilizing and "sanitating" the backward areas of the earth. Mahan was deciding that we needed a "preponderant" Navy, and Wood was carrying the torch of "preparedness," not as a means of meeting any recognizable peril but in imitation of the huge European armies, already too completely pinned down by each other to present any conceivable military threat to the Western Hemisphere. In the summer of 1914 the Wilson administration was not greatly interested in any of them. It was still absorbed in its great domestic reforms. The main preoccupation of its Secretary of State, William Jennings Bryan, was in the negotiation of treaties of peace and arbitration. And then, suddenly for all, the great storm broke. In the first days of August 1914 the elaborate house of cards which the diplomats had for years been carefully balancing and propping was blown away upon the great winds of war; the general staffs took command; the troop trains started to roll; the millions moved into their pre-planned positions; and the great tragedy which all the scientific and expert managers of war had so thoroughly prepared began to develop in all its unanticipated and unimagined horror. This was something for which nobody was really ready and of which no one in the United States—not Root nor Roosevelt nor Wood nor Mahan—had the slightest prevision. This was the great catastrophe of militarism which had been building up for over a hundred years.

CHAPTER IV

The Mechanization of War

1.

AMERICAN policy, like the American people, reacted to the cataclysm in a state of uncomprehending shock. It took days merely to grasp what had happened, weeks to sense something of what it implied, months to realize the true scale of the disaster; while the whole two and a half years of the neutrality period were insufficient to rescue our policy from the initial bewilderment and re-establish it on a firm basis of military and diplomatic plan. Many of the inconsistencies and seeming absurdities of the Wilsonian neutrality period may be put down to the suddenness of the surprise and to the violence with which it tore up most of the accepted concepts of the past three or four decades of international history.

It was impossible to extricate the requirements of the frightful present from the entanglements of the peaceful past. Wilson, compelled to deal with the problem of the German submarine, seems never to have understood it or its true military implications. The legal principles developed in the days of the wood-and-sail navies to govern sea warfare were simply inapplicable to the complex new conditions. In land warfare, in diplomacy, in finance, much the same thing was true. The old guides in almost every field of national policy were far less serviceable than anyone realized; the discovery of this fact was bound to be confused and painful and the effort to develop new guiding principles was bound to give rise to inconsistency and error—which remained for easy exploitation by subsequent critics.

Europe was taken almost as badly by surprise as were the Americans, although the Europeans had to pay in blood where the Americans paid initially only in bewilderment. The scientific soldiers had carefully and methodically designed the disaster, but in general had no prevision of how disastrous it would be. The staffs had planned the war on the model of 1870—a massive mobilization, a quick, steampowered deployment, and the prompt crushing of the enemy under the weight of one's own hordes before his hordes could be fielded. The million armed and trained men whom the Germans flung through Belgium onto the borders of France were expected to wind up the whole business in the West in the space of a few weeks. But so were the million Frenchmen deployed under Plan XVII. Britain was to contribute her command of the sea and her six expeditionary divisions; these highly trained regulars were not, however, much more than a token force for a war expected to be short and decisive. But nothing turned out as had been expected. The French Plan XVII broke down; so, in the moment of near victory, did the Germans' modified Schlieffen Plan. The British Expeditionary Force was decimated in the terrible retreat from Mons; and the "island" strategy, inherited from the Napoleonic era and calling for only secondary interventions in the land wars of the Continental masses, was left in ruins as the British found that they, too, had been committed to an all-out struggle for national survival.

The mass armies ran down into a bloody stalemate. As the "race to the sea" in the later weeks of 1914 ended with a solid line of trenches and barbed wire running impregnably from Switzerland to the Belgian coast, the bankruptcy of a generation of military thought and planning began to become apparent. By September 1914 it was demonstrated, as Foch later put it, that "the new means of action furnished by automatic weapons and long-range guns enabled the defense to hold up any attempt at breaking through long enough for a counter-attack to be launched with saving effect." [1] By early 1915 all the belligerents found themselves in what the British called the "shell crisis." Not even the German General Staff had foreseen the enormous artillery am-

[1] David Lloyd George, *War Memoirs* (Boston, Little, Brown, 1933), Vol. I, p. 80.

munition requirements of this kind of war; and there was something of a pause while all turned to develop the huge new industrial capacity necessary to feed the insatiable guns. The British started to organize their "new armies"—mass, popular armies—on a scale adequate to meet the suddenly revealed manpower requirements of an all-out Continental war. They were to cling to the volunteer principle until early 1916; in Britain as in Civil War America, the first great outpouring of volunteer enthusiasm carried a long way. But it was growing increasingly evident that in the long run only compulsion could fill the demands of slaughter on these new levels.

In early 1915, also, the belligerents sought by ingenuity to escape the dreadful *contretemps* to which their staff planners had brought them. The British summoned up the troop strengths of the Dominions and, with the help of the Australian-New Zealand Army Corps (the "Anzacs"), attempted Mr. Churchill's famous "end run" through Gallipoli. Responding to similar pressures the Germans introduced poison gas (thus adding immeasurably to the miseries of the combat troops without greatly affecting the course of the struggle) and tried their own "end run" around the citadels of British sea power with their first experiments in submarine warfare against commerce. It was this tentative effort which, with the sinking of *Lusitania* in April 1915, was to bring the United States fairly into the complex.

As *Lusitania's* tall funnels settled under the placid surface of the Irish Sea, leaving hundreds of drowned and drowning people behind them amid the debris, it should have been apparent that this was a new kind of war, calling for drastically new approaches to the problems it presented. But Woodrow Wilson's United States was unable to rise to the difficult challenge; it did not understand its own power in the circumstances or how to apply it with effect. It did not understand the new warfare sufficiently to develop an applicable military policy of its own. In early 1915 Colonel House was again sent abroad to "mediate" the struggle. But by that time mediation, certainly in House's mind and probably in practical politics as well, had become no more than a thin disguise for a policy of ensuring that whatever happened the Germans would not win and the Allies would not lose. This sharply limited its effectiveness in practical diplomacy and rendered it useless as a means of bringing the war to an end. From none of their leaders in either party did the American people receive a workable diplomatic or military policy which might have controlled events. Instead, it received from all the loudest, the shrillest and the most respected voices in the land, the great cry for preparedness. That was something else.

The preparedness campaign of 1915-16 must surely stand as one of the more remarkable episodes in our long and generally aberrant military history. That it had strong roots in partisan politics was apparent well before the outbreak of the European War. Wood ended his term as Chief of Staff in April 1914. In the following month one of the younger Engineer officers, then with the occupation forces at Vera Cruz and already possessing a well-developed sense of partisan and service politics, was writing him:

> General Funston is handling things very well . . . but I miss the inspiration, my dear General, of your own clean-cut, decisive methods. I hope sincerely that affairs will shape themselves so that you will shortly take the field for the campaign which, if death does not call you, can have but one ending—the White House.[2]

It was signed by Captain Douglas MacArthur. In the campaign on which Wood was actually embarking there was no great peril of death; but that its objective was the White House—if not for the General, at all events for the Republicans—was to become more obvious with each month that passed.

As early as October 1914 Representative Augustus F. Gardiner, Republican of Massachusetts and son-in-law of the elder Cabot Lodge, was launching a frontal attack upon the Democrats' supine attitude toward preparedness. It alarmed Colonel House, who in November was lunching with Wood at the latter's Governor's Island headquarters and loading himself with "memoranda and data" for the President. But Wilson was not unduly impressed. No matter how the Great War turned out, no one—not even the Germans if they were victorious— would be in any position to menace the United States for "years to

[2] Hermann Hagedorn, *Leonard Wood* (New York, Harper's, 1931), Vol. II, p. 147.

come." House "combatted this idea," but without much success. In the December annual message Wilson took a calm view:

> It is said in some quarters that we are not prepared for war. What is meant by being prepared? Is it meant that we are not ready upon brief notice to put a nation in the field, a nation of men trained to arms? Of course we are not ready to do that; and we shall never be in time of peace so long as we retain our present political principles and institutions. . . . To defend ourselves against attack? We have always found means to do that, and shall find them whenever it is necessary, without calling our people away from their necessary tasks to render compulsory military service in time of peace.

The President went on to observe that we were "at peace with all the nations of the world"; that no issue with any of the belligerents reasonably threatened a "breach," and that the "gravest threats against our national peace and safety have been uttered within our own borders." Under these circumstances, he concluded:

> We must depend in every time of national peril not upon a standing army nor yet upon a reserve army, but upon a citizenry trained and accustomed to arms, . . . a system by which every citizen who will volunteer for the training may be made familiar with the use of modern arms.

It seemed an intellectually respectable position; doubtless Mr. Wilson himself did not realize the extent to which it was an evasion of the fundamental issue. The cold fact, which then and later lay like a lump of lead at the bottom of vast seas of bad argument, was that a 1914-type Continental mass army could not be created on the volunteer principle. Peacetime conscription was the inescapable prerequisite to preparing this type of force. The focal question was whether the United States should or should not create such a force. Whether it was demanded as a means of intervening in the European struggle then in progress, or only as a means of defending us against whomever might prove the victor was not, perhaps, very relevant.

Wilson was correct in declaring that we could not create "a nation of men trained to arms" without doing grave violence to "our present political principles and institutions." If he had argued firmly that there was no need, in the existing international complex, for a "nation trained to arms" he would have been on sound ground. But he destroyed his own position by implying that the equivalent could be produced by asking men in peacetime to "volunteer for the training." This was impractical. Our statesmen and soldiers have rarely been willing frankly to face up to it; but the fact is that the vision of a "small regular Army supported by a great reserve of citizens trained to arms" is a vision only, requiring universal peacetime conscription to infuse it with reality. Even the famous frontiersmen, trained to their skills with the rifle and in woodsmanship, had generally turned out to be rather indifferent soldiers when the country called. Basically, what Wilson's opponents in 1915 wanted was, precisely, a nation trained and regimented in arms, regardless of political principles and the Constitution. The President's position was bound to be weak so long as he argued that this goal could be achieved by half-measures and volunteering.

A fortnight after the President's annual message, General Wood "ostentatiously appeared before the Merchants' Association in New York with 1,500 people acclaiming him" to repudiate (by rather delicate implication) Wilson's disinterest in preparedness. Wilson's Secretary of War, Lindley M. Garrison, a lawyer and jurist from New Jersey, was irritated by Wood's campaign but infected by it all the same, as House apparently had been. Even the pacifistic (and politically-minded) Secretary of the Navy, Josephus Daniels, was showing himself responsive to the grandiose plans being elaborated by the admirals on the General Board. He cut back their recommendations for four new battleships to two, but showed himself not illiberal with lesser types.

Through 1915 Garrison tried to work out a rational Army program while Wood and his cohorts, with Theodore Roosevelt prominent among them, were beating ever more loudly the war drums of preparedness. A curious situation began to develop. After the *Lusitania,* Wilson was primarily interested in avoiding physical entanglement in a war the outcome of which he had more and more come to believe was critical to the American national interest. His opponents were primarily interested in preparing for a war—always envisaged as coming only after the European struggle should be decided—which few of them really believed would ever happen. It was an issue which could never be decided because it could not fairly be joined. There was much partisan hypocrisy on both sides. The Republicans chanted for preparedness while never explaining what it was for which they wished to prepare; the Democrats were to chant with an equal emotionalism that "he kept us out of war" without ever explaining what practical sacrifices they would make to maintain the peace.

This was the irrational atmosphere in which the military programs —matters of concrete dollars and cents—had to be ground out. To begin with, Garrison found his soldiers a bit slow, or perhaps only dazed by the idea that the politicians were at last prepared to spend some money on the Army. Their first proposals hardly went beyond filling the regular Army to the authorized standards dating from 1901. That would never do, either for the possible requirements of a war with a European great power or the imminent requirements of the 1916 Presidential election. Garrison spurred the War College Division of the General Staff to higher things, while Daniels set the General Board to work on an enlarged strategic vision. These labors proceeded through the nightmare summer of 1915, in which such names as Przemysl, Ypres, Festubert, the Dogger Bank and the Dardanelles were making their unfamiliar appearance on American front pages. The results, as they appeared in the Wilson defense program submitted in December 1915, were remarkable.

The one overwhelming military fact at the end of 1915 was the European War. To this, the Army and Navy programs bore no relation. The General Staff had submitted in September a report on "The Proper Military Policy for the United States." It was based upon a calculation as to the rapidity with which a European army, assumed to be free from any European threat to its flank or rear, could be landed in the Western Hemisphere; and it called for a trained, mobilizable force of 1,500,000 men. This would include an active regular Army of 281,000 with trained reserves available to expand it immediately to 500,000 in emergency; a "Continental Army" of part-time trainees (in effect, a Federal National Guard) to provide another 500,000 to be ready for combat within ninety days; and a third increment of 500,000 "bodies" to replace casualties. The National Guard itself was written off as being too far beyond Federal control to be worth troubling with.

The immediate result of this last proposal was, naturally, to bring all the high-ranking, politically influential officers of the National Guard down upon Washington "with blood in their eye." Garrison cut the program to what he thought the traffic would bear: a regular Army of 142,000; a Continental Army of 400,000, to be raised in three annual increments of 133,000 each; and a sop to the National Guard in the form of increased Federal recognition and support. This represented the most, he felt, which was practicable without conscription. Wilson accepted it and backed it in his message of December 1915. He also accepted the massive building program which the Navy had been generating for Secretary Daniels, calling for the construction over the next five years of no less than sixteen dreadnought battleships and battle cruisers and large numbers of lesser types.

The respective time periods of three and five years appeared to ensure that these programs could not be brought to completion before the European War would be over—when, of course, the entire military and diplomatic equation would be transformed, whoever won. In the minds of their designers, the principal rationale for these programs seems to have been as insurance against a German victory, which would be followed—as it was widely imagined—by an immediate thrust for "world domination" against the Western Hemisphere. No one dared so much as to hint that the programs might be intended to facilitate an American intervention in the war then in progress in order to prevent such a victory; nor were they, in fact, well designed for such a purpose. When in early 1916 Senator William J. Stone of Missouri, the powerful chairman of the Foreign Relations Committee, got wind of Colonel House's secret negotiations looking toward an American intervention, he could write the President: "I have heard some talk to the effect . . . that after all, it may be possible that the program of preparedness, so called, has some relation to such a situation [the submarine controversy with Germany] as we are now called upon to meet." The Senator was alarmed by the idea that we might actually be preparing for the military contingencies then most immediately before us. When Frederick Palmer, the war correspondent, returned from Europe at the end of 1915 to lecture on his experiences, the preparedness campaign struck him as preposterous. He wanted to tell his audiences that this was the historic hour; that the United States should raise an army to intervene now in the European struggle, when the intervention might be of effect, and that all the fantastic propaganda about German divisions landing in South America or about saving New Jersey farm girls from ravishment by the invader was nonsense. He was hastily shushed by his advisers. Intervention was not the idea at all. With Hudson Maxim's *Defenceless America* flooding the bookstores and the mails; with the gory motion picture, "The Battle Cry of Peace," showing in hundreds of movie houses across the land, one could not decry the perils to which our defenseless state exposed the New Jersey farm girls.

And, indeed, the great power of the preparedness campaign lay in the mixture of motives behind it. Many who fanned the hysteria plainly did so with the conscious intention of promoting an American intervention against Germany. Others felt it desirable, considering the dangerous state of the submarine controversy, to get some greater military strength in hand in case we should become entangled. Even Wilson—whose emissary, House, was at the moment conditionally negotiating a possible American entry—must have felt that preparedness might "after all" have some relevance to the war then in progress. Though he may not have believed that the new trainees and new ships would ever actually be deployed, he apparently thought that the show of strength and military resolution would influence the Germans to submit to our demands and so permit us to maintain our precarious neutrality.

This was, of course, a miscalculation. Wilson, in developing his policies, was always curiously blind to the military factors on which ultimately they had to rest. By 1916 the Germans were beyond influencing by mere military gestures. But very few in the United States really understood the military situation at that time. Few imagined that, even if we did break with Germany, our intervention would be much more than a "token" affair. There was little realization of the desperate state of the Allied cause. It was rather generally assumed that Germany would be defeated in another year at most and that even if we entered the war, it would be as unnecessary, as it then would have seemed impossible, for us to ship 2,000,000 men to Europe to bring it to a close.

To many, perhaps most, of its evangelists preparedness really was for the future, not the grim present. It was a means of making America powerful in the unpredictable post-war era—Mahan's sea power in the abstract or Wood's armed might for any purpose. Admiral Austin M. Knight, the president of the Naval War College, succinctly explained the reasoning of the General Board:

> First, what do we want and when do we want it? We want a Navy equal to the largest maintained by any nation in the world and we want it now. . . . The other side of the shield is, When can we get it? . . . We are limited this year [by shipyard capacity]. . . . Build all we can this year with what we know now. Build all we can next year with what we know next year.

Clearly this was not planning for war in any given international context; it was planning for power, in what was certain to be the wrecked and chaotic post-war world. There were still other motives woven into the preparedness campaign. Undoubtedly, it appealed to the steel, shipbuilding and munitions industries as a cushion against the end of the war in Europe. Some soldiers may have supported it as a means of building a great mass military system that would enhance their own power and prestige. There was in it the thirst for "promotions, profits and politics" as Representative Oscar Callaway, the Texas Democrat who was the shrewdest and most hard-headed critic of the preparedness mania, put it. But a mass military system, necessarily resting on conscription, had attractions for others than soldiers.

A dozen years before Elihu Root had confidently declared that "our trouble will never be in raising soldiers," but only in organizing, equipping and training them. Now the technical and managerial revolutions had demonstrated solutions for these latter problems, but had put a new face on that of manpower. By 1916 Root was writing that "the vast change in the way of carrying on war has created a situation in which it is perfectly plain that no country can be ready to defend her independence . . . except by universal military training." A dozen years before he had declared the Militia Act of 1792, with its theoretically universal obligation, to be "obsolete." Now it was the volunteer system which had become obsolete and Root believed it necessary to return to "the principles and requirements" of the Militia Act of 1792. It was scarcely arguable that this was essential if we were to prepare to fight a war of the kind then leaving its ghastly mark on Europe. But then, as later, there were many to embrace universal military training for reasons other than strictly military. It would be a means of "disciplining" the young and improving their physique. It would teach them "patriotism." To draft a man to risk death on the battlefield is to give him (if he survives) rights and claims against the state of a kind which the ruling groups of 1915 (like those of 1783) might be unwilling to meet; but to draft him for "healthy" peacetime military training would only regiment him into a military structure that would teach him to be cooperative, obedient and docile to those who profit most from the operations of the state and have the largest voice in forming its policies.

Preparedness was an inspired idea. There was something in it for everyone. It provided all the excitement and glamour of war, while promising to keep the country out of combat. To the elders it was an assurance of security and social stability. To the youngsters it was a chance for patriotic service; it was also a practical training which held out some hope for survival should they ever find themselves on the battlefield. All could and did respond to it—the patriot and the profit-maker, the young and dedicated, the old and crafty, the men who might have to fight and the women who hoped that this would avert the necessity. During the summer of 1916 the monster "preparedness parades" were to fill the streets of American cities from dawn to dusk; the propaganda filled the air and absorbed the mind during those frenetic months when the National Guard was on the Mexican border, while two dreadful names stood above all—Verdun and the Somme. Preparedness laid the whole groundwork of ideas and conditioned the attitudes which were to make possible the American intervention upon those terrible fields. Only one thing it did not do. It did not prepare the nation or its military structure for that intervention—which was so soon to come.

Garrison's program for the Army was the first to run into trouble. Initially it had been accepted, not only by the President but by the powerful chairman of the House Military Affairs Committee, Representative James Hay of Virginia. But as the new session got under way, Mr. Hay began to manifest doubts, and soon told Garrison that the committee would write its own bill. Mr. Hay was a more experienced politician than the Secretary or the General Staff officers; and the Continental Army seemed to him neither practical politics nor, perhaps, practical military policy. The National Guard was in violent protest against its own proposed emasculation; and in those days the "militia interest" was much more powerful in Washington than is now the case. It also represented one of the remaining vestiges of state sovereignty, now being so rapidly swept away upon the tides of a massive centralization. Mr. Hay was unwilling to accept the supersession of the National Guard. Nor did he believe that in peacetime 133,000 men a year could be induced to volunteer for a wholly Federal reserve training system; while behind the whole plan there stood the shadow of conscription and of the great, Federally commanded standing army which the nation had traditionally feared and rejected. Both Garrison and his Chief of Staff, Hugh Scott, believed that compulsory universal military training was the only real solution; and they did not help their cause with the Congressmen when, in reply to the objection that the volunteer trainees could not be obtained, they argued that in that case it would be proved to the country that there was no alternative to compulsion.

Hay insisted that there was an alternative and that the National Guard could provide it. Instead of superseding the state Guards with a Federal reserve of similar character, he proposed to convert the state forces themselves into a Federal reserve. Under the Hay Bill, which was to remain until 1955 the foundation stone in all our reserve planning, the Federal government would assume full responsibility not only for equipping and training the state troops but also for providing their drill pay. (National Guardsmen are paid for the time they spend in drills, summer encampments and more extended active duty, pro rata with the pay scales for the regulars.) In return, the states would undertake to maintain Federally established standards of efficiency; while on entering the Guard the individual officers and men would take an oath to respond *en bloc* to a Federal call to service. This would end such prideful mutinies as that of New York's 7th Regiment in 1898, and by rendering the Guardsmen instantly convertible into Federal troops would circumvent the constitutional restriction of the militia to "the repulse of invasion." Called into Federal service, they would be liable like any other volunteers to whatever duty might be required. The Federal government, by reserving the right to qualify the state officers for equivalent commissions on being called to Federal duty, could curb the evil of the governors' political and patronage appointments.

The Hay plan would quench the fury of the "militia interest," thus considerably improving the prospects with Congress; it would at the same time use the Federal "power of the purse" to cure most of the defects of the dual system; while if there was any chance of securing a 400,000 man volunteer reserve, it would be made brighter by relying on the National Guard, with its long tradition and strong elements of local support, than by creating a huge new structure of centrally commanded and wholly Federal units. The Hay plan was far more consonant than the Continental Army plan with the genius of the Constitution and the American political tradition. When at a conference on January 11, 1916 Mr. Hay discussed it with the President, the latter was evidently not disposed to reject it out of hand; and its outlines were made public.

Secretary Garrison thereupon exploded with a violence which seems curious. On January 12 he wrote the President to draw a fundamental issue of principle between himself and the chairman of the Military Affairs Committee:

> There can be no honest or worthy solution which does not result in national forces under the exclusive control and authority of the national government. . . . The very first line of cleavage . . . is between reliance upon a system of state troops, forever subject to constitutional limitations, . . . or reliance upon national forces, raised, officered, trained and controlled by national authority. . . .

> The difficulty ... does not arise out of the government being
> unable to take over these [state] troops in time of war, but arises
> out of its inability, under the Constitution, to have the essential
> unity of responsibility, authority and control in the raising, officer-
> ing, training and governing of its military forces.

It seems less a military than a political and moral issue. The Secretary said nothing about the concrete tactical, logistical and command
problems of fighting another war. This was a question of the locus of
power, of authority, within the constitutional framework. The Secretary made it plain by inference that he wanted to amend the military
clauses of the Constitution, but why he wished to do so remained
obscure. "Those who are conscientiously convinced that nothing but
national forces can properly be the basis of a policy of national defense cannot possibly accept a policy based upon state forces." This
was the voice of "principle," not of practicality.

Wilson was about to depart on the "preparedness" speaking tour,
which was to reach its climax at St. Louis on February 3 where—after
declaring in the afternoon that "we must keep our resources and our
strength untouched by that flame [of European war] in order that we
may be in a condition to serve the restoration of the world, the healing processes"—he rashly committed himself the same evening to
"incomparably the greatest navy in the world." His contemporaries,
even among the Democrats, generally assumed that his motives were
those of partisan politics; the Republicans, seeing their leading issue
for 1916 being thus basely appropriated, were sure of it. As Theodore
Roosevelt bitterly concluded:

> Wilson, with his adroit, unscrupulous cunning, his readiness
> to about-face, his timidity about any manly assertion of our
> rights, his pandering to the feelings of those who love ease and
> the chance of material profit, and his lack of all convictions and
> willingness to follow every gust of popular opinion, will be sup-
> ported by the mass of our fellow citizens.[3]

[3] Selections from the Correspondence of Theodore Roosevelt and Henry
Cabot Lodge (New York, Scribner, 1925), Vol. II, p. 478.

The prediction was to prove accurate; it seemed that those who loved ease and profits were, as they usually are, a majority. But the election was still months away. In the course of the tour, Wilson had continued to advocate Garrison's Continental Army plan. On his return in early February, however, he called a conference of Congressional leaders, from which intimations soon emerged that the President was no longer committed to the Garrison program. The Secretary asked for a showdown. Wilson's position was that the Hay plan offered simply another way of accomplishing virtually the same result as that promised by the Continental Army, and that Garrison was unduly stubborn in clinging to his own proposals. Either Wilson failed to see the fundamental issue of principle on which Garrison was insisting or, possibly, he did see it and saw that it ran much deeper into the political and social structure of the nation than Garrison realized. The Secretary felt that the President had welched on a commitment and forthwith resigned, together with his Assistant Secretary, Henry Breckinridge. The applause from the preparedness advocates and from Wilson's enemies was loud. Hay's motives were set down as those of petty National Guard politics and "pork" (an allusion to the proposal to furnish Federal drill pay to the states); but the chairman plodded ahead with his bill, and in June it emerged as the core of the National Defense Act of 1916.

The act of June 3, 1916 decreed that our land forces should consist of four "components": the regular Army, to be brought up over a five-year period to an authorized peace strength of 175,000; the new, Federally obligated National Guard, with an authorized strength of 475,000; a reserve, including officers (to be supplied mainly by reserve officers' training units in the colleges) and enlisted men, derived from those finishing their active-duty enlistment with the regulars; and finally a "Volunteer Army," a completely nebulous force, to be raised only in time of war. The act also established an Advisory Council of National Defense, as a rudimentary beginning upon the problems of industrial procurement and mobilization. On the other hand, echoing old fears and jealousies, it cut the General Staff corps to fifty-five officers, only half of whom were permitted to serve in the Washington area. Hugh Scott, the Chief of Staff, had few enough officers as it was to manage the appalling problems of the Mexican border mobilization, now under way; but as the wisdom of some serious preparation for actual war in Europe became more and more apparent, he was cut down to only eleven men to plan for it.

The Navy's General Board fared better than the Army's General Staff, though all was not smooth sailing even for the Navy. Its program, rooted in the simple concept of building a navy "second to none" as soon as possible, called for the construction within the next five years of ten dreadnought battleships, six battle cruisers, ten "scout" or light cruisers, fifty destroyers, fifteen sea-going submarines and eighty-five of a smaller coastal type, four gunboats and some further supply ships for the "train." The Navy asked for a start in the first year on two battleships, two battle cruisers and varying numbers of the smaller craft. Secretary Daniels and the President were strong in their support; but to a small group of determined "little navy men," mostly Democrats, in the House it seemed far too much. For weeks they were able to block the bill in the Naval Affairs Committee, despite the preparedness hysteria rising through the nation.

At the end of May they finally forced out a compromise bill, described in the Republican minority report as a "compromise between those who wanted nothing in the way of additional naval protection and those who wanted but little." As a compromise it was at least curious; the two requested battleships were disallowed, but five instead of two of the more expensive and almost equally powerful battle cruisers were accepted. The reasoning of the little navy men is obscure. Perhaps they had so often heard the battleship described as "the backbone of the fleet" as to consider it peculiarly the symbol of aggressive navalism. Moreover, we already had some seventeen dreadnought battleships built or building, but none of the big cruisers, as we had not imitated the British and Germans in developing that class. Now the war had given it a sudden prominence. Two British battle cruisers had swiftly annihilated von Spee's squadron off the Falkland Islands in December 1914, and the battle cruisers of both sides had been active in minor raiding operations across the North Sea. Our own naval experts were full of enthusiasm for this latest naval fashion and a procession of admirals testified before the House committee to the urgent "need" for such ships. The little navy men apparently concluded that if big cruisers were what was "needed" they would vote big cruisers and could thus cancel further battleship building, where they believed the danger of navalism to lie.

Since the Senate was standing ready to repair any derelictions by the House in its duty to "naval protection," this would not have mattered much except for its rather ironic result. The compromise bill passed the House on June 2. Just two days before, in a thundering, flame-shot murk over the North Sea, the Battle of Jutland had been fought to its inconclusive end. Like Trafalgar for the wooden walls, this was the last and greatest (indeed, very nearly the only) full-dress fleet action of the steel-and-steam surface navies. The mastodons we were then planning to refight just this kind of encounter would never see anything even closely comparable to it. But there was a more immediate irony. The House was on the point of voting battle cruisers. Unfortunately, of the nine British battle cruisers engaged, three had blown up and vanished almost at the first salvo. Of the five German ships of the type, one sank on her way home and another barely made port, whereas none of the huge fleets of modern battleships present was seriously injured. The result was not actually as damning as it seemed; it was mainly due to accident and to the fact that the battle cruisers had been in the van on both sides and so had taken the main brunt of the action. But the question of whether, after all, we really needed a fleet of these thin-skinned, over-engined leviathans became abruptly somewhat embarrassing.

When the House bill reached the Senate in July, however, there were no hesitations, except among a handful of anti-navalists. The Democratic President had spoken for "incomparably the greatest Navy in the world" (textual revision had reduced it by this time to "incomparably the most adequate," but the sense remained the same); Senator Claude A. Swanson of Virginia, chairman of Naval Affairs, was devoted to the cause of navalism, while the elder Cabot Lodge, the Republican expert in the naval mysteries, had already privately explained his policy: "I shall try to get everything I possibly can for the Navy, and of course shall move all the increases I can think of over

what the Secretary recommends." [4] If there was much more of politics
than war planning in all this, it produced results. The Senate not only
restored the full program of sixteen battleships and battle cruisers, as
well as the lesser types, but compressed its completion from five years
to within three, directing that no less than eight of the capital ships
should be laid down in the first year.

In the debate on the conference report, Representative Warren W.
Bailey, a little navy Democrat from Pennsylvania, could protest this
"smashing raid on the Treasury" in behalf of a program prepared, as
he not inaccurately put it, "exclusively with reference to remote contingencies . . . about as likely to materialize as a volcanic eruption in
the Mississippi Valley." His voice was drowned in the overwhelming
votes which adopted the naval act of August 29, 1916. On sea as on
land we had defined—virtually for the first time in our history—a
comprehensive, continuing structure of military plan and policy, intended to provide against all the accidents of the problematic future.
Unfortunately, there remained the rather more urgent issues of the
dangerous and distressful present.

2.

Unexpectedly, they first appeared not from Europe but from Mexico. The newspapers reporting Secretary Garrison's developing breach
with the President were also full of a new Mexican outrage, in which
Pancho Villa's bandits had held up a railway train and eighteen Americans had perished in the ensuing massacre. Garrison resigned on
February 10 and it was not until early March that Wilson found a
successor—in the slight, rather prim figure of Newton D. Baker,
lawyer and former Mayor of Cleveland, of liberal and, it was understood, pacifistic views. Mr. Baker was on his way to the War Department on March 9 to take the oath of office when the news arrived of
Villa's murderous raid on the town of Columbus, New Mexico. It
had happened earlier that morning; the place had been wrecked and
seventeen American citizens killed. Instantly, the President snatched

[4] *Correspondence, op. cit.,* Vol. II, p. 476.

up the military weapon and Baker's first official act was to endorse the orders for the "punitive expedition" into Mexico, under the command of Brigadier General John J. Pershing.

The outcome was to be the mobilization of 1916, that remarkable, fortuitous but extremely valuable dress rehearsal for the real war in Europe which was to come a year later. It not only provided training for commanders, staffs and logistical services without which the 1917 mobilization would have been extremely difficult; it not only provided training for large numbers of those who as junior or noncommissioned officers would help form the core of the World War I armies; it not only provided a test of the military structure as a whole and of the principles on which Congress was then proposing to reorganize it with the 1916 Defense Act; it also conditioned the American public to those sweeping measures of military action and regimentation which in 1917 were found to be necessary.

Virtually all the field forces of the small regular Army had long been deployed along the Mexican border; it took little time to throw together and launch Pershing's punitive column of about 5,000 regulars. But what remained? Congress decreed the immediate recruitment of the regulars to their full authorized strength of 123,000 men; but the response was "not good." With Pershing now deep in Mexico, the defense of the border itself against possible reprisals seemed somewhat scanty. On May 9 Mr. Baker called out the National Guard of Texas, New Mexico and Arizona to reinforce the frontier. These men were called as "militia" under the constitutional provision for the "repulse of invasion." But the situation had become more ominous. The pursuit of Villa had been undertaken on the theory that he was a mere bandit against whom the recognized Carranza government would be glad to have our assistance. Unhappily, the Carranzistas grew only more threatening and more insistent that our troops be removed from their country. The possibility of a fairly full-scale war with Mexico began to loom.

The new National Defense Act had been signed on June 3. Within a fortnight, on June 18, virtually the entire National Guard of the United States was called out under its provisions, neither as volunteers nor as three-months militiamen summoned to repel invasion, but as

men obligated by their oaths of enlistment to accept service under the
Federal government whenever it should be demanded of them. Despite
confusions arising from the fact that the guardsmen had not even had
time to take the new oaths, the Guard responded almost to a man.
There were a few units, mostly in the Coast Artillery, which were not
called; those that were had an authorized strength of about 140,000.
Recruiting was able to bring this up to a peak strength of 158,664 in
Federal service, but even this total was still some 100,000 short of the
full prescribed war strength of the units involved. The experience rather
strongly suggested the superiority of Mr. Hay's plan for relying upon
the Guard as a volunteer reserve over Mr. Garrison's and the General
Staff's proposal for a Federal volunteer reserve of similar character.
But the marked sluggishness of recruiting both for the regulars and
the Guard, even under these dramatic conditions, implied that no
volunteer reserve system could meet the demands of peacetime preparation for major war, or was likely to suffice even in the face of war
itself.

Mexico rather plainly announced that the outpouring of volunteers
for major war—on which both sides in the Civil War had primarily
relied and on which the British in the First World War relied up to
1916—was outdated. Volunteering had ceased to be a practical way
of allotting the burdens of modern war or efficiently utilizing a national
manpower which now had to perform many other military tasks besides pulling a trigger. Along the hot and dusty Texas border in 1916,
this was an argument which impressed itself forcibly upon numerous
more solid citizens—usually described as persons of "family and business responsibilities"—who had perhaps too rashly joined the National
Guard when its only obligations seemed to be those of weekly drill
nights and nearby summer encampments. In the extreme heat and
monotony of the border, many of them realized that "a relatively
small number of citizens were making a real sacrifice to serve their
country while the majority made none." The Guardsmen saw their
civilian jobs and opportunities for promotion going to those who had
stayed home, while they were languishing in a routine garrison duty
(it was all that the border ever actually offered) "of a type which

should be done by regular soldiers, men whose lives and interests are in the Army and not far away in a civilian community." [5] It seemed plain that the answer was a regular Army large enough to take care of such disagreeable situations, with "selective service" (capable of course of selecting out all those with family and business responsibilities) as the only fair method of meeting the major crises of full-scale war. The border made powerful propaganda for the selective service system of conscription which was, to nearly everyone's surprise, to be adopted so easily in the following year.

The 1916 mobilization rather clearly indicated that the basic manpower problem had not been adequately solved. It revealed deficiencies of other kinds in our military posture. In the spring of 1916, when Britain's Royal Flying Corps alone was putting seventy combat air squadrons into the skies over France, the Pershing punitive expedition set out with six already obsolete airplanes, all of which had crashed within a month. In that dreadful summer when the machine gun was slaughtering its countless thousands at Verdun and along the Somme, the American TO&E (Tables of Organization and Equipment) still allotted but four machine guns to an infantry regiment and the weapons were themselves of unsatisfactory design. Artillery and artillery ammunition were in short supply even for the Mexican operation, at a time when in Europe the guns were being lined up hub to hub to fire artillery barrages of unparalleled intensity and duration. Transport was lacking. The railroads were swamped by the strange problem of getting some 150,000 men to the border. The Pershing column, which had been ordered for political reasons not to use the Mexican railways, suffered extreme difficulty in maintaining its supply line by truck and mule wagon.

Congress made some gestures toward remedying such deficiencies. It voted $12 million for the development of machine guns and raised the funds for the Army's Aviation Section from $300,000 to $800,000 (it was to give it $700 million a year later). But if the Army was left without men or real means for waging a major war, it had learned in

[5] Henry J. O'Reilly in Frank Tompkins' *Chasing Villa* (Harrisburg, Military Service Publishing Co., 1934), p. 229.

Mexico what men and means would be required. Hugh Scott's annual report as Chief of Staff, dated September 30, 1916, was brutally frank:

> The difficulty that is now being experienced in obtaining recruits for the Regular Army and for the National Guard . . . raises sharply the question of whether we will be able to recruit the troops authorized by Congress in the National Defense Act. . . .
>
> Recruiting is found so difficult that many of the [Guard] units have not yet, over three months after the call, been raised to even minimum peace strength and likewise the units of the Regular Army have not been recruited to the minimum peace strength. . . .
>
> The failure should make the whole people to realize that the volunteer system does not and probably will not give us either the men we need for training in peace or for service in war. In my judgment the country will never be prepared for defense until we do as other great nations do that have large interests to guard, like Germany, Japan and France, where everybody is ready and does perform military service in time of peace as he would pay any other tax. . . . Universal military service has been the cornerstone upon which has been built every Republic in the history of the world.

Scott, of course, was no "Prussian militarist"; like most other American officers of the time he was a sincere patriot devoted to the accepted liberal democratic ideals. Yet here was the full outline of the great peacetime conscript army and the regimented state which it implied—things which we so much abhorred in the Germans, if not quite so much in the French and the Japanese. In the final sentence there was even a realization—although perhaps a dim one—that the question was as much political as military; the popular democratic mass state implied a popular mass army, just as a conscripted mass was necessary to defend the popular state. Here, at all events, were the outlines of the conscript mass system which in the following year we were in fact to apply to the solution of the problems posed by the European War, problems which objectively considered might seem to have permitted rather less drastic answers.

With all the complications of the Mexican problem, little progress could be made in setting up the military structure contemplated by the 1916 act. By the end of the year, the regular Army had not reached 122,000 effectives; while the National Guard, which was supposed to triple its numbers, had tended rather to diminish after the ardors of the border. It had been impossible to effect the reorganization of both Guard and regulars into the proposed divisional structure. Scott had convinced Secretary Baker of the necessity for peacetime conscription and in December the War College Division of the General Staff was set to work on the planning. Both Congress and the country were doubtless convinced by that time that conscription would be unavoidable if we got into a major war; but it seems unlikely that peacetime conscription, as a measure simply of preparedness for unforeseen contingencies, would have been acceptable. Yet there had been a great change in the whole climate of ideas. In August, General Wood was writing about the "tragic failure" of a mobilization which had shown that "not more than 20 per cent of the forces were even reasonably efficient." In the larger sense, "failure" was not, perhaps, the word. It was the Mexican mobilization which laid the foundations upon which all the concepts for which Wood had been ceaselessly propagandizing through the past half-dozen years were to arise in triumph. It was the mobilization which committed us to the mass army; and in a way it was the mass army which committed us to the totalistic intervention in a European issue of a kind with which a John Adams or a Jefferson would have dealt in a different, and much more economical, way.

Toward the end of 1916 not many, beyond a few of the very best informed, could have believed that a large-scale American intervention in the European War was at all probable. In his annual message, President Wilson made no mention of war, preparedness or military planning. When the decisive break with Germany came on February 3, 1917 Wilson still "refused to believe" that the Germans would force him into belligerency. As late as February 26, when he asked authority to arm American merchant ships, he could declare: "It is devoutly to be hoped that it will not be necessary to put armed forces anywhere into action. . . . I am not now preparing or contemplating war or any step that need lead to it." That he was doing nothing to "prepare" war, even then, is quite clear. But the staffs were at work. When, five weeks later, he read his War Message to the Congress, it included a complete plan for the massive mobilization of the nation for total war. What he demanded was no mere defense against the submarine, the ostensible cause of the break, but that the nation should "exert all its power and employ all its resources to bring the Government of the German Empire to terms and end the war"—the whole great war in Europe, that is, and all the complex issues of international relations which hung upon its outcome.

His summary recommendations had the hard ring of staff planning: full cooperation with the Allies; full supply to them of credit, food and war production; mobilization of the industrial resources of the country; immediate equipment of the Navy to deal with the submarine; immediate raising of existing regular and National Guard forces to the ultimate war strengths contemplated under the 1916 act; the prompt raising by "universal liability to service" of 500,000 men in addition, these to be followed by further similar increments as rapidly as reception and training facilities would permit. Ten days after the declaration of war he elaborated in an address to the nation: "We are about to create and equip a great army"; we would have to build merchant ships "by the hundreds" to get supplies to Europe; industry "must be made more prolific and more efficient." He more fully outlined the principles of selective service, under which the national manpower would be drafted to combat. This was the total organization of the state to apply, as he later put it, "force without stint or limit."

This dramatic conversion of what was at best a somewhat secondary issue over the conduct of sea warfare into a crusade for remaking the entire structure of international relations was a reflection, of course, of many "causes." It may be said that Wilson, trapped into a belligerency which he did not desire, had to expand his war aims to accord with the enormous human costs which he knew war would involve. It may be said that, once committed to the European struggle, Allied victory had become essential to the United States, and no costs were too great to secure it. But among many other factors which might be cited, one may also notice the fact that the managerial revolution in warfare, the preparedness agitation, the Mexican mobilization, the dreadful example in Europe, had conditioned the country to the making of a total military effort which it might otherwise have refused, and had at the same time supplied Wilson with an enormous military potential for aggressive intervention upon the world stage which he could not fail to employ. It is an ironic consideration that without "preparedness," advocated by both parties as a means of keeping us out of war, it would have been psychologically as well as physically impossible for us to have gone in, when we did go in, as deeply as we did.

Modern war is a great socializer, and great consequences were to follow upon the decision of April 1917—conscription, the temporary nationalization of the railroads and shipping, state centralization on a scale never before acceptable in the United States, high income taxation, the Creel Committee on Public Information, the Espionage acts, the hysterias of the subsequent "Red raids," the subversion of many once-cherished rights and liberties in the name of the new religion of nationalism. There was to come a conscript uniformed force of over 4,000,000 men (large numbers, of course, volunteered, but the compulsions of the draft act lay upon them all), and we were to ship half of them to combat on the farther side of the Atlantic. These things came, it may be said, for two reasons: the scale of the new warfare by great popular armies made them the inevitable price of participation in any decisive way upon the stage of world affairs; and our people had been trained over the preceding dozen years or so both to insist upon the participation and to accept the price.

All these things came, but not very quickly. As the result both of the Mexican mobilization and the 1916 act there were in April 1917 about 200,000 men actually under arms in the United States. But "everything," as Spaulding puts it, "was fluid." It was very fluid. In effect, a whole new military establishment had to be rebuilt almost from the ground up. Perhaps the saddest casualty was the Navy's great 1916 building program, which in meeting the demands of preparedness had quite neglected to prepare against the German submarines. The first of the sixteen magnificent capital ships for which Senators Lodge and Swanson had so nobly fought was laid down in April. She got no farther; and all the rest were abruptly tossed back into the filing cabinets. As an ally of Britain and France, whose huge fleets of capital ships were already overwhelmingly superior to anything of the sort which the enemy could produce, we had no need for these types whatever. But we were soon to learn what a desperate need there was for destroyers to combat the U-boats and new merchant tonnage to replace the appalling losses they were inflicting. The 1916 program had provided for fifty new destroyers; we were to build about three hundred before the war was over as well as millions of tons of merchant shipping.

It was only after we had declared war, when the Allied military missions began to arrive, that our statesmen seem to have come to any realization of the appalling military situation into which we had entered. But the plans, large to begin with, were revised upward with promptness. Six weeks after the declaration of war Congress (on May 18) produced the act to "Increase Temporarily the Military Establishment." This scrapped the 1916 Defense Act in favor of a completely new military structure. It provided for a regular Army of 488,000 men, a National Guard of 470,000 and a "National Army," to begin with 500,000 men raised by selective service and to be augmented by further similar increments as rapidly as receiving and training facilities could be provided.

The draft act before which soldiers, to say nothing of politicians and editors, had quailed only a few months before, was adopted (and later was to be enforced) without difficulty. The regulars and, so far as possible, the National Guard, were to be recruited from volunteers; but compulsion would supply the National Army as well as any deficiencies in the others. Bounties, the bane of all previous volunteer systems, and substitutions, the bane of all earlier experiments with compulsion, were expressly forbidden. Here was the total claim of the state over the individual. "It is a new thing in our history," the President accurately observed, "and a landmark in our progress," adding, rather less accurately: "It is in no sense a conscription of the unwilling; it is, rather, selection from a nation which has volunteered in mass." The President was given full power in the appointment of all officers and in prescribing the number, size and character of units to be raised; pay and allowances were made uniform throughout the whole structure. A completely Federal army, Federally drafted, administered and commanded, was established for the first time in our history; while the

Congress itself abdicated to the President its control over detailed planning and organization. The National Guard regiments even lost their historic state designations, New York's celebrated 7th Regiment, for example, becoming simply the 107th Infantry in the Army of the United States.

Initial planning envisaged forty-two big divisions; by the end of the war some sixty had been wholly or partially formed. After the "token" despatch of the 1st Division to Europe, beginning in May 1917, many long months were to elapse before any further combat-ready troops were to become available. Yet the speed with which such huge forces were inducted, housed, fed and put under training must still seem remarkable. Weapons, even though much simpler in those days than they were later to become, could not be conjured up as easily as men. The TO&E were revised to provide large increases in the proportion of artillery and machine guns to riflemen; but there were no field pieces and no machine guns with which to fill the tables. Toward the end of the war American-made machine guns began to meet the demand; but the artillery problem was solved by frankly adopting the French 75 (as well as their 155 howitzer) because the French could provide them in numbers and because they simplified the matter of ammunition supply. A great effort was made to produce airplanes in quantity, at the expense of the then enormous sum of about a billion dollars. It was an almost complete failure; even with the primitive designs of the period, a volume aircraft industry simply could not be set up in the time available.

In spite of such shortcomings, the mobilization of 1917-18 must seem a creditable outpouring of American energy and genius. It recorded such impressive achievements as the merchant ship and destroyer building programs, as the creation of the North Sea mine barrage, as the organization of the "bridge to France"—a logistic triumph that would have seemed impossible a few years before, but which permitted the deployment of about 2,000,000 combat troops in Europe. And one fact remains: for all the delays and occasional fumblings, the mobilization did the job. It did avert French and British defeat; it did end the war as we wished it to end. It was an effective, and therefore successful, response to the specific military problem which Wilson posed in April 1917. It is a simple fact often overlooked by those who harp upon the wastes and delays, and argue that if only we had been "prepared" everything could have been done much more quickly and at less cost in life and money.

The preparedness agitations and programs of 1915-16 survive to remind us that one cannot beyond a certain very limited point prepare for unknown eventualities. A nation cannot in more than the most general way make itself ready for the distant future; it is the here and now of international relations, by which the future will be shaped, which really counts. After all, it is the French Marshal Leboeuf, who in 1870 was "ready to the last gaiter-button," who remains the melancholy monument to perfect preparedness; it is the German Great General Staff, which by 1914 had created a military machine capable of meeting every eventuality, that brought down upon their country the total disaster which they had failed to foresee.

3.

Whether well or badly organized, the American military effort succeeded. The Government of the German Empire was brought to terms; the great agony was ended. The hopes which President Wilson, like great numbers of the ablest of his fellow-countrymen of both parties, had pinned upon this outcome—hopes of a new world of peace, democracy, disarmament, reason and equal justice for all—proved impossible of realization. If the United States had ever had any chance to assist in the "healing processes," it had been dissipated by our own entanglement in the struggle. As we confronted the wracked and bitter world of 1919, the overpowering impulse was, as usual, to rush for home and civil life. Our own and the other armies were demobilized as rapidly as the ships and rails could carry them, and while Wilson and his colleagues of the Big Four were still trying desperately at Paris to rebuild the world of peace and reason, the military foundations of their power to do so were draining swiftly away beneath their feet.

It was as imperative to reconstruct a military policy to meet the new situation as it was to re-erect a political and diplomatic edifice of peace. But the times were unpropitious. Wilson, wholly engrossed in the political effort, seems to have given no thought whatever to the military problem. The Secretaries, Baker and Daniels, were men of sense and administrative ability but were not geniuses. The professionals of the General Staff and the General Board were something less than original thinkers. Yet in the spring of 1919 they had to grind out programs and budgets for fiscal '20.

The Army's solution tended toward a plan which would make possible a 1917 type mass mobilization, but conducted with somewhat greater speed and efficiency. The Navy's solution was even simpler and more remarkable. It was merely to withdraw the great 1916 building program from the filing cases into which it had been tossed when real war had intervened, and to proceed as though nothing had happened. Nearly every aspect of the international and naval scene had been transformed; but the program remained in all its original beauty —the sixteen dreadnought battleships and battle cruisers, the numerous lesser types, the concept of a "Navy second to none," the Congressional authorizations for the whole lot and even the first-year appropriations, which, unlike Army appropriations, carried no constitutional time limit.

Here was a whole mechanism of major naval building waiting only to be set in motion; and this was not difficult to do, as the steel, shipbuilding and armament industries found themselves badly in need of support against the drastic outbreak of peace. The Navy set it in motion and dutifully began laying the keels which Congress in 1916 had ordered under totally different circumstances. In some respects it bordered almost upon the absurd; the Navy, for example, discovered that it had never made a start on twelve of the fifty destroyers authorized in 1916 because it had been too busy turning out the three hundred odd authorized under the wartime programs. With destroyers, so to speak, running out of its ears, it solemnly went to work upon the twelve neglected ships of the 1916 program.

Only later was the post-war world to overtake the Navy. The Army encountered its difficulties rather sooner. When the Army was able to shake itself sufficiently free from the torrential ebbtide of demobilization to think about future policy, it not unnaturally began with the 1917 mobilization. This had come at approximately the mid-point of

a war which in its first half had applied (and exhausted) the accumulated military wisdom of the past, and only in its second half had
produced in at least rudimentary forms the major outlines of the
future. The impact of many new weapons and techniques was, of
course, reflected in the 1919 planning. The new TO&E bristled with
machine guns, which had so dreadfully dominated the 1916 battlefield;
and the normal allotment of four to a regiment before our entry into
the war had risen to 250 to the then much larger regiment by 1919.
But the three really decisive developments of World War I, none of
which had taken clear shape until the last two years, were too revolutionary to grasp or allow for. They were automotive transport beyond
the railhead, self-propelled, armored combat vehicles (the tank), and
the military airplane.

The new defense act, adopted in 1920, could hardly deal with these
portents. General Crozier, the wartime Chief of Ordnance, writing in
that year, could still declare that "the most important weapon with
which nations go to war is the infantryman's rifle." He foresaw that
all the various field guns of 1914-18 were "destined to disappear, together with their motive power, the horse, to be replaced by a mechanically driven carriage and a heavier gun." [6] But he did not even mention the tank. As the "Great War" ended, aviation had shown itself
formidable in promise, but had done little in performance; and as most
who lived through the ensuing controversies are aware, it was to take
some twenty years of embittered argument before the airplane was
even approximately "domesticated" within the military structure.
Though it had found no part in the war, horse cavalry was still considered a useful arm of reconnaissance and exploitation; and on the
eve of the Second World War our own cavalry was still trying to meet
the challenge of the internal combustion engine by "porteeing" its
animal mounts in motor trucks. At the end of the First War field
artillery was still horse-drawn; the tank, designed as an infantry support weapon, had a speed of only about four miles an hour—a walking pace—and while the infantry might pick up motor transport by
good luck, it normally maneuvered and always fought on its own feet.

[6] William Crozier, *Ordnance and the World War* (New York, Scribner, 1920),
pp. 56, 243.

The railroads, of course, were far more effective than they had been in 1861 or 1870 for delivering great masses of men to the combat area, for supplying them there and for shifting them in strategic maneuver. But beyond the railhead, war in 1918 still largely proceeded at the foot pace which had characterized it since the dawn of history. The ranges had opened out; firepower had put an ever heavier premium of entrenchment and protection, but it was still the old kind of war. And it was to enable us to refight this kind of war that the 1920 amendment to the 1916 Defense Act was devised.

The one most obvious lesson of the First World War was politically so impossible of acceptance that it was hardly worth bringing up. This was that a 1914-18 type mass army could not be prepared without peacetime conscription. Scott had said this in 1916, when he had observed that the volunteer system would not provide "the men we need for training in peace." His successor, Peyton C. March, was bravely to stand out for the principle amid the confusions of 1919. Rather overconfidently, General March felt it to be a golden moment, in which all the elements were present out of which to fashion a sound and continuing military policy of universal conscription. We had millions of war-trained men, some 150,000 war-trained officers, mountains of munitions, a war industry just coming into full production and a populace which had accepted without a murmur the universal service act.

He based his calculations upon the old assumption of an invasion arriving upon the coasts of the Western Hemisphere—an assumption to which our own invasion of Europe had lent, perhaps, a little greater color of reality. Against such a contingency, he concluded, the "minimum force" we should maintain would be "one field army of five corps [of regulars] skeletonized to about 50 per cent of its strength. . . . With such a force, and with a system of universal military training which will ensure an adequate reserve . . . no foreign country could . . . disregard our rights or our military power." It was a good try; it was also hopeless, in the atmosphere of 1920.

General March did not grasp the depth and intensity of the revulsion against war in any form. Some were pinning their hopes for peace upon the League of Nations; others were fleeing into the depths of isolation from any "foreign entanglement." A large and expensive combat-ready military structure was the last thing which either group would support. In February 1920 a Democratic caucus in the House defied a strong recommendation from Wilson himself to resolve that "no measure should be passed by Congress providing for universal compulsory military service or training." It was noted from the floor that since the Armistice there had been "2,452 resignations from the regular Army" and "11,083 desertions" by regular NCO's and enlisted men. West Point had about 50 per cent vacancies, the greatest in its history. There was, as one Representative no doubt rightly observed, a "feeling of the people generally that they want to get away from military matters." There was no chance for either peacetime conscription or the mobilizable mass army of the German 1914 type, for which conscription was the indispensable foundation. But one could at least prepare a framework under which something like such an army could be drafted in another emergency, rather more efficiently and quickly than had been the case in 1917.

Such was the Army envisaged by the 1920 act. It authorized a regular force of 288,000; it made provision for a large National Guard and an Organized Reserve. It set up a peacetime tactical as well as administrative organization. The nation was divided into nine "corps areas," each under a regular major general. Each was to contain one regular division, two or three National Guard Divisions and two divisions of the Organized Reserves—a total of theoretically mobilizable divisions about equivalent to the sixty divisions which in November 1918 we had fully or partially formed. Initially, there seemed to be no problem either as to officers or equipment. Reserve commissions were freely offered to the great host of temporary officers leaving service, while the surplus war stocks provided an enormous store of weapons and ammunition.

It was a plan adequate for promptly remobilizing the army of 1918. It made too few provisions, unfortunately, against the fact that the 1918 army was already obsolescent and was certain to grow old. The ROTC courses were continued in the colleges to replenish the great corps of reserve officers. On the other hand, the gun, ammunition and airplane plants which had just been getting into production as the war ended, were demobilized; leaving nothing with which to replenish the war stocks, as they likewise became obsolete, except paper plans for a new industrial mobilization. But the most obvious deficiency of the new system was in the fact that it had no men. Almost all of the 4,000,-000 or so who had served in the war army had been drafted for "the duration" and owed no further duty. For a few years they would remain, of course, as a trained corpus which could in need be re-drafted; but aside from the element of injustice in such a procedure, their military value would very rapidly diminish. The only sources for a trained enlisted reserve to replace them were the few volunteers for the National Guard and the dribble of time-expired men released from the regulars. During the '20's the United States was to boast an Organized Reserve of some 100,000 officers (about the size of the entire regular Army after 1898) and a handful of enlisted men—a military force of at best doubtful utility.

Once more, the Defense Act of 1920 had designed only an "army of a dream," impossible to fill with reality. Congress promptly shattered even the dream. The authorized regular force of 288,000 was cut down by the appropriation acts to 150,000 and, after 1927, to less than 119,000. The projected nine regular divisions largely evaporated into "inactivization." The National Guard divisions, dependent upon Federal drill pay, were seldom to achieve even half strength. Since there was no money with which to order all the Reserve officers to drilling duty, none could be required to perform it. Some volunteered for what training could be offered; some took correspondence courses in the military arts and thereby qualified for promotion in the Reserve, but many lost interest in what seemed a farcical proceeding and were inactivated or separated. Within two or three years the military structure had become almost useless even as a mobilization base; and for two decades after 1920 the Army and the National Guard together were quite incapable of waging war. About their only military value was as a laboratory and school of the military arts. The wonder is that when crisis again appeared so many products of the reserve officers' correspondence courses were to prove competent juniors and so many of the youngish professionals, who had spent the intervening years in the dullness of a skeletonized army, were to emerge as top-flight administrators and brilliant leaders of men in battle.

The Navy's experience was perhaps even more bitter. Amid the confusions of 1919 the Navy had been cheerfully at work filling its 1916 authorizations. The whole impact of this program was quite different from anything contemplated when it had been designed three years before. The German fleet, the principal target of the 1916 plan, had disappeared; the Russian had disintegrated; the French and Italian had been far outclassed. There were but two powers remaining against which this great effort of capital ship building could be of use. One was Japan, which had hardly been considered in 1916; the other was Great Britain, our closest wartime ally with whom no one seriously believed that we would ever fight a war again. Worse than that, the ships authorized in 1916 had been intended as no more than counterparts for the dreadnoughts of the time. But the Battle of Jutland and another "quantum jump" in battleship design had intervened. The 12-inch guns of the early dreadnought classes had now been outranged and outpowered by 15-inch and 16-inch rifles; with these and numerous other improvements, the "post-Jutland" ship was really a "super" dreadnought, as superior to the older classes as *Dreadnought* herself had been to the standard ships which had preceded her. The British had only a few of these post-Jutland vessels, and no resources with which to plunge into a new building race. The program which in 1916 had not even been aimed at equality with the mighty British battle line, promised on its revival in 1919 to place us almost automatically in a position of unchallengeable supremacy.

Secretary Daniels, who seems in this period to manifest a certain emotional division between his pride in the great panoply of war over which he presided and his loyalty to his pacifist principles and his chief's League of Nations, happily stated the position in his report of December 1919:

> The United States Navy emerged from the war incomparably stronger and more powerful than ever before—second only to that of Great Britain and far in advance of any other foreign navy. ... The organization of the fleet in two great divisions gives us ample defense in the Pacific as well as in the Atlantic. With battle-

ships in service equal to or superior to any now in commission, six huge battle cruisers and twelve battleships now under construction, a number of them larger than any now in commission, to be armed with 16-inch guns, more powerful than any now afloat, the Navy is pressing forward to greater things.

The "greater things" were not further defined; but that world naval supremacy was among them seems clear. Through the summer of 1920 the Navy General Board was laboring upon the problem of continuing policy, after the 1916 authorizations should run out. These were the fantastic months when Wilson lay paralyzed, when the battle for the League was finally lost in the Senate, when the 1920 Presidential election was taking shape and the high hopes of Versailles were crumbling everywhere. The General Board reported on September 24:

> The navy second to none recommended by the General Board in 1915 is still required today. But in addition, the Great War has shown the importance of unimpeded ocean transportation for commerce.... The General Board believes that the policy... should be such that ultimately the United States will possess a Navy equal to the most powerful maintained by any other nation of the world.
>
> In arguing... this... there is no thought of instituting international competitive building. No other nation can in reason take exception to such a position. In assuming it the United States threatens no other nation by the mere act of placing itself on an equality with the strongest.

Unfortunately, our British friends, at whom alone this could be aimed, did not appreciate the non-competitive nature of this proposal to build a fleet which would not only equal but in practice surpass their own. But the General Board was unmoved; it developed a new three-year program to include another battle cruiser, three more battleships, no less than thirty light cruisers and numbers of other lesser types which had been prominent in the war. In December 1920 when Daniels had to present it to Congress, the great wreck had taken place. The League had been defeated, the Democrats had been defeated, Wilson was a feeble old man in a shawl and the Republicans under

Warren G. Harding were waiting to take over, their pledge to enter "a" League but not "the" League already swept away on the tide of votes. Daniels did the best he could amid disaster:

> If the United States is not to enter into any agreement with the other powers . . . now bound together in the League of Nations, I feel compelled to approve the recommendations of the General Board that Congress authorize another three-year program. . . . If, however, provision is made by our government . . . for a concert of nations, with strength to prevent war, it will be neither necessary nor wise to authorize either a three-year program or a large one-year program. It would be necessary . . . to authorize only ships which are required to round out the present fleet.

The General Board's ideas even on "rounding out" the existing authorizations were somewhat extensive; while the logic of completing the 1916 program itself should an authority with strength to "prevent" war come into being is not apparent. The passage is chiefly of value as illustrating the complete confusion into which everyone—navalists and anti-navalists, pro-Leaguers and anti-Leaguers, internationalists and isolationists alike—had fallen. It was a confusion from which, fortunately, history and the Harding administration were to save them.

From the time he had taken office in 1913 Daniels had been insisting upon the necessity for naval disarmament. The 1916 program had carried a clause requesting the President to call a naval disarmament conference as soon as hostilities in Europe should be over, and authorizing the cancellation of any of the ships then being voted should that be required by a resultant agreement. In 1919 Wilson's negotiations for the League and for disarmament were considered as fulfilling the directive. But with the defeat of the League and the collapse of the Wilson administration, this clause assumed importance. The Navy had revived the 1916 building program. Led by Charles Evans Hughes, its astute and high-minded Secretary of State, the Harding administration revived the 1916 disarmament clause to summon the Washington Conference of 1921-22, and so bring to an end the nonsense of a new naval race on which the General Board had been embarking.

The 1916 program died in the Washington Conference, and died for good reason. For years the Navy was not to forgive the State Department for destroying those magnificent battleships and battle cruisers whose keels had already been laid and for which the armor plate had already begun to accumulate. Yet it was unquestionably the most rational of all the post-war settlements. Hughes saw clearly that a naval race between the United States and Great Britain was senseless in the new international context, and that it was the Far East which presented this country with its one significant naval problem. By linking a political settlement in the Far East (the Nine-Power Treaty) directly with the general structure of naval limitation, he solved the problem probably as well and as permanently as it could be solved—certainly far better than it could have been solved by amassing huge fleets of "sea power" in the abstract. In a sense, it was a denial of Mahan, for it was a demonstration that sea power in and of itself is meaningless. The one concrete naval requirement before us was to constrain Japanese expansionist navalism and this the Washington treaties, by establishing an alliance between the American and the Royal Navies, were for a time to do. Our own navalists did not see this, and they were to waste the next ten years in futile controversy with the British over the irrelevant symbols of naval supremacy. It is unnecessary to pursue the details, which were to drag us through the "Coolidge" Conference of 1927 and the London Conference of 1930, until the Japanese finally destroyed the system in 1935. But for a time it worked well—which is more than can be said for the solutions returned for any of the other complicated military, political and economic issues which were to arise between the nations in the twenty years after 1919.

Immediately, it rescued the Navy from its bemusement with the 1916 program. Of the sixteen great ships therein provided, three battleships—the 16-inch gun *Marylands*—were completed. Two only of the battle cruiser hulls were preserved for conversion into *Lexington* and *Saratoga,* our first combat aircraft carriers. The British agreed to scrap most of the huge battle fleet they had deployed at Jutland, and the United States and Japan threw in lesser numbers of similar craft, all of which were now obsolete. Much useless hardware was thus removed from the scene to the relief of the taxpayers, and all were left free to follow the new naval trends, which were toward aircraft carriers and cruisers, submarines and anti-submarine vessels, rather than the ponderous battleships.

At all events, the Washington treaties completed the structure of our own post-war military policy. With regard to the Army it was to maintain the merest skeleton of a system which in another great war emergency could be filled out into a 1917 type mass infantry army. With the Navy it was to maintain "parity" with Great Britain and a 5:3 ratio of "superiority" (to the extent which appropriations might allow) over Japan—an arithmetical standard of policy which might correspond only loosely, if at all, to the actual measure of effective naval strength for specific naval purposes. With both services we were committed to a defensive maintenance of the *status quo;* and we thought of this task primarily in terms of maintaining the bones of a World War I military establishment against some distant and unforeseeable future emergency. It was the traditional American attitude. The idea that it is impossible to lay up military power, like insurance, for only future withdrawal, that wars are not unpredictable "emergencies" but outgrowths of present trends and present uses of the existing military power relationships, had scarcely occurred to us in 1919.

4.

Nor was there any realization of the extent to which the introduction of the machine upon the battlefield had already outmoded the 1917 type of military and naval establishment. In defending his wartime machine gun designs, General Crozier made a suggestive remark. "It must be remembered," he said, "that these weapons are machines, operating with tremendous pressures and tremendous velocities of moving parts, the Benet-Mercié giving out about one horsepower for each pound of its weight, approximately double the output per pound of the Liberty [airplane] engine." In the automatic gun, it was mechanical power which had been harnessed to spewing out rifle bullets in previously impossible volumes. It was mechanical power which lugged men forward behind armor protection, which was already towing the heavier artillery into its emplacements; it was power output from engines which hoisted men into the air to perform the cavalry functions of screen and reconnaissance and many artillery functions more effectively than the horsemen or gunners could do. Prior to 1914 the machine had seemed chiefly important in transport and logistics; by 1918 the mechanization of combat itself was clearly adumbrated. But no one could clearly see the consequences.

Obviously, there was a great deal about the First World War to call in question the principles and techniques by which it had been conducted. The enormous ruin of life and resources, useless because it hád for so long failed to return the decision which is the one social justification for war, was the central fact of the vast tragedy. Some simply fled from it in abhorrence of the whole idea of war itself. Some bitterly criticized the stupidity of generals who had known no better than to immolate a generation of young Europeans upon these dreadful altars of military power. But there were many, at least among military men, to discern in the machine a possible solution. At many points, surely, mechanical power was capable of altering the whole equation, avoiding such another horrible stalemate as that of 1915-17 and restoring both fluidity and decision to war. There were students, like Fuller and Liddell-Hart in England or De Gaulle in France, to stress the significance of the new automotive ground mobility and to show what could be done, not only with fast tanks, but with truckborne infantry and mechanically towed artillery. Coupled with the fast-developing art of radio communications, these things promised tactics of speed, dispersion and hitting power which might displace the 1914 mass of foot-slogging rifle-and-bayonet carriers with a new kind of army of mechanical specialists. There was no branch of the military art which did not take an interest in the potentialities of the machine, and especially of the gasoline engine. Even the navies, badly shaken in their Mahanite dogma by the German U-boats, were receptive to new weapons, techniques and tactics resting upon the mechanical revolution.

But all these speculations and tentative departures were to be more or less swallowed up in the vast controversy which was to rage for some twenty years around the proper use and management of the military airplane. The airplane was a problem child from the begin ning. It had clearly demonstrated its remarkable potentialities. By 1918 it had been developed to such a point that Brigadier General William ("Billy") Mitchell, Pershing's leading combat air commander in France, was seriously proposing for 1919 an airborne division to be dropped by parachute behind enemy lines to attack from the rear, just as the airborne divisions of the Second World War were to attempt to do. It had opened even grander visions. Mitchell had visited with Major General Sir Hugh Trenchard, commanding the Royal Flying Corps, and had been impressed by his argument that the airplane was "an offensive and not a defensive weapon"; that its true mission was not to serve the older arms but to operate independently, far beyond the static battle lines, carrying "strategic" war direct to the core of the enemy's resistance.

It was more for administrative than for strategic or tactical reasons that the British, in June 1918, consolidated all their air activities under a single Air Ministry and established the Royal Air Force as an independent service, coequal with the British Army and the Royal Navy. The RAF was still responsible for the air needs of the surface forces. But one result of the reorganization was the appearance of an "Independent Force" under Trenchard, with the "strategic" mission of attacking, not the fighting armies, but the civilian industrial and human resources which sustained them.

In the Meuse-Argonne offensive Mitchell massed two hundred bombers, covered by 110 "pursuit" planes, for attack upon the enemy rear lines and reserves. This, of course, was still a strictly "tactical" intervention in the ground battle, but it gave rise to prophecy. An Associated Press dispatch described Mitchell's force as:

> The first definite American unit of major importance in the independent air forces which are being built up by the Entente powers. This navy of the air is to be expanded until no part of Germany is safe from the rain of bombs. It is a thing apart from the squadrons attached to the various army corps. The work of the independent air force is bombing munitions works, factories, cities and other important centers far beyond the German lines.[7]

[7] Wesley Frank Craven and James Lea Cate, eds., *The Army Air Forces in World War II* (Chicago, University of Chicago Press, 1948), Vol. I, pp. 12 f.

The bombing of cities was included. This was no longer war between the armies of embattled peoples, or even war confined to their military installations and supplies. It was war direct upon the peoples themselves, regardless of the slaughter of women, children and those regarded by earlier ages as noncombatants. But the apocalyptic vision was not realized. The Great War ended. Trenchard's Independent Force did not get beyond the planning stage. Mitchell's airborne division was never organized. The military aviators in all the nations were left in a state of frustration.

Conscious of immense possibilities before them, they had been cut off short with a record in which they had actually done very little. The Air Service of the AEF dropped only 138 tons of bombs and never penetrated more than 160 miles behind the ground battle front. While the airplane had showed itself spectacularly successful in reconnaissance, patrol and artillery observation, as a combat weapon it had exerted little effect upon the course of the ground war; its epic battles, mainly between "pursuit" pilots, had been fought with itself, and it had given no evidence to support its claims to independent power of control and decision in warfare.

It would have been difficult enough to fit this strange military vehicle into a pattern of land war. The problem was immensely complicated by the fact that it was the first military instrument in history to overpass what had always stood as a fixed division—the coastline. Until the appearance of aviation, warfare had been immutably compartmented between land and sea. Sailors could on occasion form landing parties, to be sure, and soldiers could (as in the times of the Romans and for long afterward) form the fighting complements of ships of war. It still remained as impossible to maneuver an army across the sea levels as to bring three-deckers ashore. From time immemorial military history, tradition, organization and tactics had been shaped by the fact of this impassable barrier. Now the airplane had overleaped it. The result was a poser, with which some of the best brains of a generation were to struggle to no very satisfactory conclusion.

The airmen's answer was exuberantly confident. Since they were masters of a new element, they should be constituted into a new serv-

ice, released from the obsolete traditions of the other two and set free
to develop "air power" while the old-fashioned generals and admirals
could continue to direct their "land power" and "sea power" in their
hide-bound ways. Logical as this seemed to many, it overlooked one
important fact. Whereas the coastline was an effective vertical barrier
which had separated land from sea power (in its absence, indeed, the
very concept of "sea power" would have been impossible), the horizontal division between surface and air was no barrier at all—"air
power," in fact, was completely meaningless except as it might operate
against the surface. All wars are about people; people can live permanently only on land, and all wars are really land wars. "Sea power"
itself is effective only as it controls events on land, and it was only
the physical barrier which gave the concept any validity.[8] To apply
it by analogy to a situation in which no such barrier existed was to
commit a solecism that was to mislead two generations of politicians,
editorialists and military commentators.

The immediate difficulty was a very practical one. Could "independent air power" in fact be trusted to win another war? It had shown
no ability to do so in 1914-18, and the demonstrations of the new
theorists were something less than convincing. But if one could not
confide the issue wholly to air power one would have to maintain the
conventional armies and navies as well. These, however, in order to
be able to operate at all, would now have to be provided with their
own panoply of air cover, air reconnaissance and air bombardment.
To put the whole apparatus of military aviation in the hands of a new
service, scornful of control by the two older services and committed
to its own independent dogmas, would be the best way of insuring
that the air needs of the older services would not be adequately met.

A further difficulty was not so apparent at the time; and it was one
which the airmen were inclined deliberately to suppress in their propaganda. "Independent" air power could operate only through the direct
attack upon, slaughter and starvation of the civil population. The civil
population and its means of subsistence were, in the final analysis,

[8] The armored battles in North Africa in the Second War closely resembled
sea fighting in tactics and strategy, but no one ever developed a theory of "desert
power" as an independent branch of warfare.

air power's only practicable targets, once it had turned its back upon the job of helping the surface military forces to advance. For all its cruelties, war had always been conducted in accordance with some rules and regulations; typically it had been a conflict between champions—a small warrior class of knights, a professional army, a comparatively small enrollment of expendable youths—acting as shield and agent for the great mass of the nation, for the woman and babies and old men, for the larger part of the economic producers, for the managers and the statesmen. Independent air war, as envisaged by the enthusiasts of the '20's, would put the women, babies and statesmen in the front lines, along with the factory hands and even many of the farmers, leaving the uniformed forces in the safer position.

Even after the Italian air general, Giulio Douhet, had fully expounded it, this aspect of air power was not too clearly seen. Douhet, "the Mahan of the air," in the early '20's pulled together the ideas of Mitchell, Trenchard and other World War I airmen, into a consistent body of doctrine, which was powerfully to influence the thought in cockpits and air headquarters thereafter. But if Douhet now reads like little more than a weak parody of Mahan, in a field to which the Mahan ideas were fundamentally inapplicable, one must admit that even in unconscious parody there may an uncomfortable revelation of truth. After all, Mahan's "sea power," with blockade—indiscriminately choking the whole civilian economy and starving women as well as soldiers—as its principal weapon, was not so different from Douhet's air war upon the helpless. It was not so different, for that matter, from Sherman's gutting of the civilian South in the march through Georgia in 1864. It was not the theorists who were changing; it was war itself, more and more terribly weaponed by the possibilities of modern science and technology.

Today it may seem that the answer to the challenges of the military airplane should have been obvious: set up an independent air force to develop the possibilities of "air power," meanwhile provide the Army and Navy with whatever they need in the way of aviation to perform their assigned missions. But such a solution was impossible. It would have involved the great sin of "duplication." The confusion between the airplane as a weapon (like a shoulder rifle or machine gun, equally useful to all services) and as a tactical unit (like a destroyer or infantry squad or tank company) with a specific role in the military drama, could never be overcome. Congress had no hesitation in supplying shoulder rifles impartially to Army, Navy, Marines and Coast Guard. It did not expect the Army's shoulder rifles to be handed over to the Marines, for example, when the latter might require them. But the airplane, which cost so much more than a shoulder rifle, was different. Since it was equally useful in land and naval missions, one airplane should suffice for both. Throughout the next two decades, the idea of supplying two or three different services with the airplanes which they might require to fulfill their military missions—to say nothing of the landing fields, shops, training facilities and all the rest of the necessary apparatus—would have seemed to the Congressmen to have been duplication in its most hideous and wastefully expensive form. The result was an internecine battle among the services for what little aviation money was available to any of them. It was a battle which only grew in bitterness, violence and disregard of the basic strategic factors as it progressed, and for which no resolution was possible. There was not enough money for the obvious solution; and there was not enough practical war experience with airplanes to settle the theoretical arguments over the allotment of what money there was.

As early as 1920 Senator Harry S. New of Indiana brought in a bill for an independent Department of the Air; it failed, but was a forerunner of innumerable others to similar effect. In the same year the House tacked a clause on the Army appropriations bill providing that the Army should "control all aerial operations from land bases and that naval aviation shall control all aerial operations attached to a fleet." Since the aircraft carrier was then in its infancy and there were virtually no aerial operations "attached" to the fleet, this would in effect have handed all aviation over to the Army. Secretary Daniels was severe concerning the "inaccurate and misleading statements" with which the clause had been supported and felt it "necessary" for the Navy Department to "protest vigorously." And it must be granted that inaccuracy and misrepresentation were to be salient features of the debate over the next twenty years. In this instance, the Senate obliged with an amendment which authorized the Navy to retain its shore bases and air stations; but the Senators were emphatic that this was no license for duplication.

These were preliminary skirmishes. It was when "Billy" Mitchell returned from Europe to plunge into the fray that the real war began. Unlike other leaders of the air faction, Mitchell was a West Pointer, who had started his military career stringing telegraph lines for the Signal Corps in Alaska, and through the Signal Corps had got into aviation in its primitive days. He was an unusually able, energetic and flamboyant personality; he combined a fanatic devotion to air power with a powerful flair for publicity. A rebel and maverick by nature, he was never permitted to rise higher than Assistant Chief of the Army Air Service; but he quickly became its spokesman, its idol and the center of the storms which were to rage around it.

Mitchell was the sleepless and extraordinarily vocal propagandist for air power. As Leonard Wood had apparently done before him, he early concluded that "changes in military systems come about only through the pressure of public opinion or disaster in war." Since there had been no disasters in war, Mitchell set himself to generate the pressures of public opinion. Quite like Wood in the pre-war era:

> He poured forth a steady stream of articles and newspaper stories and found time to write three books on air power. His published testimony before the [Congressional] committees alone constitutes a formidable corpus. He became an indefatigable lecturer and hardy after-dinner speaker; he courted interviews by the press. . . . He was capable of slanting an argument or of making claims for air power hardly justified by the performance of the aircraft then available.

This estimate, from the official history of the Air Force, illustrates the position. Mitchell's problem was not unlike that which had confronted Wood. Wood had wanted to build a powerful mass army at a time when the American people were uninterested in war and wished, above all, to escape the European entanglements. Mitchell wanted to build an independent air force—which by the airmen's own estimates could then have been of no value except in short-range operations from overseas air bases—at a time when the United States was even

less threatened by invasion and even more determined to shun transoceanic combat than had been the case in 1914. Like Wood, Mitchell's
only recourse was to defend the Atlantic beachheads. But where Wood
at least had the Germans to defend them from, Mitchell had nobody
except our close friends and allies, the Canadians and the British. The
menace of air attack delivered from "hostile bases" in the St. Lawrence
Valley (at that time about the only area from which such attacks could
be delivered) was less than impressive. But if Mitchell lacked suitable
foreign adversaries, there was one close at home—the Navy. Mitchell
set out to defend the Atlantic beaches against the sailors.

From the time in the summer of 1921 when Mitchell, in a famous
experiment, led his bombing squadrons against anchored ex-German
men-of-war off the Virginia Capes, in order to prove that "the airplane
could sink a battleship," this was the core of the controversy. The
sinkings were at best a somewhat unscientific military maneuver and
at worst a pure propaganda stunt. But Mitchell and his dedicated followers among the young pilots could thrive only on propaganda. What
he was trying to prove was not simply that the land-based airplane
might be a useful adjunct in repelling sea-borne invasion, but that it
could replace the Navy altogether with an equally efficient and much
cheaper substitute. (The argument from economy was to impress Congressmen and the public for many years; that it was fallacious is demonstrated by war and post-war Air Force budgets, but this experience
was not to come until much later.) The battle rose to ever more
violent heights since the issues were inherently unanswerable. Finally,
in 1925 Mitchell, in a vituperatively insubordinate press statement,
more or less deliberately challenged court-martial. It was accorded to
him; he was tried under the 96th Article of War ("conduct of a nature
to bring discredit upon the military service"), convicted and sen-
tenced to five years' suspension from active duty. He resigned shortly
thereafter.

Dramatic as this crisis was, it still did not answer the practical problem of how to bring the military airplane into the structure of basic
military policy and plan. In the two decades after 1919 there was
hardly a year in which some board or Congressional committee was
not sitting or reporting on the dilemma of air policy. None ever

reached a finding sufficiently persuasive to still the uproar, to which Mitchell after his resignation continued volubly to contribute. The Mitchell trial itself only added fuel to the flames. It has been described as less a trial of the general than "a trial of air power before the bar of public opinion"; it has also been endlessly repeated that "Billy Mitchell was right." Neither judgment can easily be accepted. Mitchell of course became the first martyr of the Army Air Service, and the affair doubtless served to embed his ideas more deeply in the canon and apocrypha of the Air Force faith. The great controversy committed the Army aviators to the Mitchell theories with a passionate emotionalism, and went far to make them the basis of our air policy and strategy in the Second War. Long afterward General H. H. ("Hap") Arnold, speaking of the USAAF's arrival in Europe, rather naïvely observed that "our program was still untested in combat, but we were sure that we were right." The event was to prove that in many respects they were not nearly so right as they thought they were; and there is much in the history to suggest that the Army Air Force may have sacrificed almost as many lives (its own and others') to its dogmatic faith in "independent air power" as to the conquest of the nation's enemies. Mitchell persuaded his colleagues and considerable sections of the public, but that does not prove that he was "right"; while the violence of his controversial methods perhaps did more to retard than to advance the development of the Air Force of which he dreamed.

The trial itself was all drama, emotion and propaganda; it was in no sense a reasoned analysis of the air power problem. Shortly before it began President Coolidge appointed a board under Dwight W. Morrow, the eminent New York banker; the motive may have been a desire to neutralize the political effects of the inevitable verdict, but the Morrow Board did make an earnest effort to reach a rational answer to the air policy problem. Its findings were not favorable to the colorful "General of the Hot Air Force," as his naval opponents delighted in describing him. While calling for some increase in Army aviation, it recommended basically the *status quo* so far as strategic doctrine and command arrangements went. Under the conditions and technology of 1925 it may have been the best possible answer. In the following year the recommendations were embodied in a new act, changing the name of the Army Air Service to the Army Air Corps, thus somewhat enhancing its prestige, and giving it an authorized strength of 1,800 planes with proportionate personnel. But the Air Corps still remained firmly under the control of the "longbowmen"— as Mitchell delighted in calling them—of the Army General Staff and chain of command; while Congress was seldom to find the money to fill its authorized strength.

The arguments were ceaselessly to continue. As the official history of the Air Force puts it, the three "paramount trends" in Army aviation between 1919 and 1939 were: "the effort to establish an independent air force; the development of a doctrine of strategic bombardment, and the search for a heavy bomber by which that doctrine could be applied." The order in which these aims are stated may seem curious, but is doubtless accurate. Independent power and authority came first; to attain the goal it was next necessary to develop a "doctrine" which would make it militarily valid; finally, with the doctrine established, it was necessary to invent a weapon which would justify the strategy. This was a reversal of what one might suppose to be the logical development of military policy but it is probable that military policies have always been made in this order, to a greater extent than is popularly recognized.

However generated, the Army aviators' "doctrine" was to be of historic influence. As Mahan had conditioned the American people to an aggressive navalism; as Wood had conditioned them to a mass conscript army capable of forceful intervention beyond the seas, so Mitchell and his devoted followers conditioned them to the concept of total war upon populations. In 1930 Mitchell was expounding the thesis that the "vital centers" of the enemy's will to resist were "the cities where the people live, areas where their food supplies are produced and the transport lines that carry these supplies from place to place." He continued:

> The hostile main army in the field is a false objective and the real objectives are the vital centers. The old theory that victory meant the destruction of the hostile main army is untenable.

Armies themselves can be disregarded by air power if a rapid strike is made against the opposing centers.[9]

The doctrine was, of course, defended as humane, on the ground that by taking war direct to the enemy people it would be made short and quickly decisive, with no such enormous bloodlettings as those of 1914-18. But implicit in it were such things as the destruction of Guernica, the dreadful "fire-storms" of Hamburg and Tokyo, the immolation of Hiroshima. A nation which had, at least ostensibly, gone into the European struggle in order to protect the laws of "civilized" war upon the sea, swallowed with little hesitation an air power doctrine which in effect repealed all the laws of war and reduced the political differences of modern states to a suicidal issue of utter, unbridled savagery. Like Wood, Mitchell did not convert the American people to his concept of war. But he prepared them to accept it, when war emergency next appeared, almost without question.

5.

In the later '20's and earlier '30's the clamant struggles of the Army aviators preoccupied what little attention anyone gave to military matters. Their strident claims for air power filled the headlines and the Sunday supplements; but they were by no means the only—perhaps they were not even the most significant—reflection of the advancing mechanical revolution in war. In the three-cornered, knock-down-and-drag-out battle between the Army aviators, the Navy and the General Staff, the fourth corner was occupied by the naval aviators. They were to have their own troubles with their "battleship admirals." But because they were not, like their Army counterparts, committed to a whole new theory of warfare, they were to make rather more practical progress. The Army aviators were aiming for an independence which would relegate both the ground army and the fleet to secondary roles; the Navy aviators, on the other hand, were aiming simply at a larger role within the accepted naval function. The Army flyers were strik-

---

[9] Craven and Cate: *op. cit.,* Vol. I, p. 41.

ing for a strategic revolution; the Navy flyers merely for a tactical one. They wished to rearm the fleet with air weapons which would improve its performance but would not alter its mission; and in the end they were to have considerably more success than their Army opposite numbers.

Sea-borne aviation had been in its infancy when the Great War ended. The British had experimented with various ideas, finally converting H.M.S. *Furious*—originally a battle cruiser, an ultimate expression of "Jackie" Fisher's obsession with speed and power, designed for 31 knots, with 18-inch guns and almost no armor—into the first true combat aircraft carrier. In 1921 the American Navy had converted a collier into an experimental ship and had gone earnestly to work upon the complex problems of flying wheeled aircraft on and off ships at sea. The prospects were so favorable that two of the battle cruiser hulls of 1916 were salvaged out of the Washington Conference for conversion to aircraft carriers (the Japanese saved two of their own for the same purpose) and in 1927 U.S.S. *Lexington* and *Saratoga* went to sea, at about the same time as the two Japanese ships. The Navy now had major combat ships with which to develop the theory and practice of naval air war; when they began, they were still flying biplanes off their decks, but progress in these strange techniques was to be rapid.

The Navy made other advances in mechanizing its operations. Rozhdestvenski's voyage in 1905 had served principally to demonstrate that the modern steam navy could not operate successfully at extreme distances from its bases, and the American world cruise of 1908 might have suggested that in war it could not operate over the ocean distances at all. But after 1918 our Navy applied itself seriously to the problem of distant operations; it developed techniques of underway refueling at sea, of carrying its supply and lighter repair facilities along with the fleet, of quickly setting up forward bases with floating drydocks and similar transportable equipment, techniques which, when developed, were to give it the remarkable range and mobility demonstrated in the Pacific War from 1942 onward.

A transoceanic advance would still require the seizure of forward bases, as well as bringing along the equipment which they would require. In 1923 an American Marine officer, Major Earl H. Ellis, died mysteriously in the Japanese mandate of Palau. Major Ellis had been investigating the problems of a possible Pacific war; his reports had already outlined the necessity for a step-by-step advance, the requirement this would impose for amphibious landings to capture defended island bases and the function of the Marine Corps in effecting the captures. At the time, the Marines were mainly engrossed in bush warfare in the Caribbean and were thinking of their probable role in another major conflict as like that which they had discharged in 1917-18, when they had provided simply a ready reinforcement for the Army's ground divisions. The Ellis reports helped to turn their attention to the more specific problem of an amphibious landing against opposition.[10]

It was soon realized that this was a special problem, no longer to be solved—in the face of hostile machine guns, artillery, barbed wire and prepared defenses—by the old practice of rowing ashore in Navy cutters, to leap overside with rifles at the ready. It demanded new weapons, new techniques, new vehicles. In 1933 the Fleet Marine Force was established at Quantico, Virginia; it was an official recognition that in another conflict the Marines' major job would be the seizure of fortified islands and beaches directly from the sea. The purely technical difficulties were intricate. A few experimental prototypes of the later landing craft had been developed, but a host of other problems concerning command arrangements, fire support, communications, had hardly been touched. Even by 1941 the answers were far from clear or complete; but by the early '30's the Marines were aware of the problem and were beginning to harness mechanical invention to its solution.

In November 1918 the United States had no less than 23,405 tanks on order. Only twenty-six were actually completed by the war's end. Using borrowed British and French vehicles, the AEF was able to deploy in the St. Mihiel and Meuse-Argonne offensives the 1st Tank

[10] Jeter A. Isely and Philip A. Crowl, *The U. S. Marines and Amphibious War* (Princeton, Princeton University Press, 1951), pp. 27 f.

Brigade, some 174 tanks under a youngish cavalry colonel, George S. Patton. Their performance, like that of the bombing airplane, was prophetic; but by November virtually all had been expended or destroyed without having contributed much. With the war's end, the vast orders were cancelled; the Tank Corps was abolished by the 1920 Defense Act and the whole subject of automotive combat was handed back to the infantry. It inherited a stock of about 1,100 completed vehicles—most of them copies of the light French Renault, the remainder copies of the lumbering British Mark VIII. For a decade or more this represented virtually the total stock of armor in the hands of the United States Army.

It was already obsolescent when the war ended. In 1924 the British produced their Mark I medium, hardly a satisfactory vehicle but—with its hull, track suspension, revolving turret and greatly increased speed—an authentic prototype of the standard tanks of the Second World War. For years there remained, however, a great uncertainty as to design and no money anywhere for intensive development. The American Ordnance Department experimented with armored cars, light tanks and weapons carriers of one sort or another, without definitive result. The cavalry began to take an interest in the gasoline engine and to ask for fast, light vehicles as weapons of reconnaissance and pursuit. But there were endless difficulties. The armored car was bound to the road; the light tank was weak and could not get across the trenches and other obstacles of position warfare. Even the new, faster tanks were still relatively blind, unhandy and exposed to traps and land mines. They needed infantry support to make up for these deficiencies when engaged at close quarters, as much as the infantry needed tank support in advancing on machine-gun nests or similar fixed defenses. Was the tank primarily a cavalry weapon of speed and shock, or an infantry weapon of protected fire support?

In 1927 the British organized an experimental "mechanized force" to help answer such questions. Dwight Davis, the American Secretary of War, happened to see it at a demonstration at Aldershot and immediately ordered the General Staff to go to work. The problem was handed to a cavalry officer then serving on the staff, Adna R. Chaffee, the son of the general of the same name who had been prominent as an Indian fighter and as a commander in the Spanish War era. Chaffee saw that the answer was neither an infantry nor a cavalry tank, but a new and independent arm. Built around the old cavalry concept of speed and shock power, it would include its own infantry and artillery, its own defensive as well as reconnaissance capabilities, the whole to be endowed with the mobility of the gasoline-powered and tracked vehicle. An experimental organization put together in 1928 out of the obsolete and quite unsuitable material then available proved of little value; but it enabled Chaffee to write a recommendation for a complete mechanized regiment. When Charles P. Summerall retired as Chief of Staff in 1930, one of his final directives was to "assemble that mechanized force now." [11]

In 1930 the United States, together with the rest of the world, was going over the brink into the Great Depression. While the ultimate result was to be a great revival of militarism and the Second World War, the immediate effect, especially in the United States, was adverse to further military development. Nine years later Chaffee's armored force had developed into no more than the "7th Cavalry Brigade (Mechanized)," an awkward and feeble conglomeration of light tanks, armored cars, infantry borne in undefended half-tracks and an artillery composed of 75-mm. mountain howitzers towed by trucks. During Douglas MacArthur's incumbency as Chief of Staff (1930-35) both the Army and the Army Air Corps were to be reduced to their nadir of efficiency. The Navy was allowed to fall far behind the treaty ratios. While it was precisely in these years that the full effects of the mechanical revolution—on the ground, in the air and at sea—were becoming apparent to the more thoughtful staff planners and commanders, there was little or no money with which to translate them into current military policy. A great deal of fairly solid theoretical work had been done, out of which the Second World War armies, navies and air forces were to arise with astonishing speed and effectiveness. But not until the totalitarian dictators—creatures, most of them,

[11] Mildred Harmon Gillie, *Forging the Thunderbolt* (Harrisburg, Military Service Publishing Co., 1947), p. 37 and *passim*.

of the Great Depression—had arisen to revive war and militarism as instruments of both international and domestic policy, did the democratic peoples begin to convert the new developments of the mechanical revolution in warfare into concrete military planning. And they were to be very slow about it, even so.

CHAPTER V

The Scientific Revolution

1.

AS LATE as the summer of 1933, when Laurence Stallings published his photographic history of *The First World War*, the title could still be considered a grisly witticism. Hitler (like Franklin Roosevelt) had been in power since the spring; Mussolini was making his bellicose speeches and gestures; two years before the Japanese, with their "Mukden incident" of 1931, had initiated their march to empire. Yet to announce that the Great War of 1914-18—that Armageddon of the peoples upon which we had hoped to erect a permanent rule of peace and disarmament—had been only the first of a series, and to suggest that a second was to be expected, still seemed shocking. Few were prepared to agree with the implications of Mr. Stallings' title; yet few could deny the accumulating evidences that another paroxysm of violence and bloodshed was approaching.

The American reaction to those evidences was initially a retreat into "neutrality." Much as in the "preparedness" hysteria of 1915-16, the strongest impulse was to isolate the nation from the possibly impending storms, rather than to exert our power on the world stage to prevent their breaking. In 1934, with the collapse of the naval limitation system already imminent, the Vinson-Trammell Act authorized the upbuilding of all segments of the fleet to full treaty ratios. But this was inspired as much by a desire to make work in the war against depression as by strategic considerations; Congress could never find the money to make good the authorizations, and though naval building was enlarged, it remained on a rather modest scale. It was also in 1934 that the Nye Committee began its investigation into the "merchants of death," with the object of proving that the great danger of war lay in the munitions makers' thirst for profits. The whole problem was conceived in the sterile terms of "staying out" of another great war, rather than in terms of meeting the political and power problems which such a war would be certain to present. The Neutrality Act of 1937 represented the high point of this mood, in which war was regarded rather as a disease, and the only question seemed to be how to immunize the United States against contagion in the event of another epidemic. Just as the generals have so often been accused of doing, the politicians and the publicists in 1937 were preparing, not to meet the issues of the future, but to refight those of twenty years before.

In a celebrated speech at Chicago in October 1937 President Roosevelt sought to turn the medical metaphor in the opposite direction. "The epidemic of world lawlessness," he said, "is spreading"; he suggested that it was the infected nations which should be placed "in quarantine," rather than that the United States should seek to quarantine itself against them. But this hint of forceful action received a "bad press," and Roosevelt more or less withdrew it a day or two later. In the late '30's the nation was more sophisticated than it had been in 1916; it was more conscious of its power, but also more aware of the terrible commitments to which the exercise of that power might lead. The basic policy issue was now explicit, as it had not been twenty years before. It was an issue between an active and unavoidably perilous intervention in a dire international situation in order to shape it to more tolerable ends, and a passive acceptance of that situation along with the frightful risk that it would lead to a world in which our national survival would become impossible. But because the issue was explicit, it was even less possible of resolution. The arguments on both sides were powerful, and they did not meet. The risks alike of intervention and of isolation were great, but there was no way of weighing the one set of risks against the other. And as long as this central issue remained undecided, it was as impossible as it had been in 1916 to construct an "adequate" military policy.

It was not until his annual message of January 1938 (three months after the "quarantine" speech) that Roosevelt was to issue a serious call for rearmament. The call was solemn enough: "In a world of high tension and disorder, in a world where stable civilization is actually threatened, it becomes the responsibility of each nation which strives for peace . . . to be strong." Japan had been pursuing her depredations in China for the past half-dozen years. The year 1935 alone had seen Mussolini's assault upon Ethiopia, the collapse of the naval limitation system and the announcement, which all were powerless to veto, of German rearmament. In 1936 Hitler, unopposed, re-occupied the Rhineland. By the beginning of 1938 there had been dreadful object lessons in the new warfare—as at Guernica in Spain and the shambles of the Chapei district in Shanghai. In a special message on January 28 the President was more explicit:

> Armaments increase today at an unprecedented and alarming rate. It is an ominous fact that at least one-fourth of the world's population is involved in merciless devastating conflict. . . . Armies are fighting in the Far East and in Europe; thousands of civilians are being driven from their homes and bombed from the air. . . . Our national defense is inadequate for purposes of national security and requires increase.

The warning was solemn, but the requested action was minuscule. The President asked for an increase of naval building authorizations by 20 per cent—this was asking for a "two-ocean Navy," as it was popularly called—but the total of additional appropriations for the ensuing fiscal year the President estimated at no more than some $28 million, and half of that would go into experimental development of light naval types. In addition, the President wanted a "small" appropriation to start work on two new battleships (they were the first to be built since 1921) and some $14 million to provide the Army with further anti-aircraft guns, with gauges and dies for some of the newer weapons and with a distant approach ($2 million worth) to an ammunition reserve. Later, Roosevelt was to describe this as "but the beginning of a vast program of rearmament." No doubt it marks the beginning, but the beginning was anything but "vast."

It did contain one other feature, a request for legislation "aimed at the prevention of profiteering in time of war and the equalization of burdens." At his press conference on January 28 he was asked whether this meant "drafting manpower, capital and manufacturers." "I don't quite like the word drafting," the President answered. A correspondent offered a substitute: "Mobilization?" "That's it," said the President, "mobilization."

Thus the shadow of the future was already plain; but there was nothing with which to give it substance. In January 1938 the American services, in relation to the probable actual demands of major war, were still the merest skeletons of effective military power. The Army Air Corps had made some progress. In the fall of 1933 still another board, this time under Major General Hugh A. Drum, had recommended a new solution for its perennial unrests—in effect, the detachment of the Army aviators from the ground divisional and corps commanders and their reconcentration into an air force reporting only to "general headquarters," and thus enjoying a more or less autonomous status. Before action could be taken, there ensued the tragic fiasco of the air mail. In the bitter winter of 1934, Roosevelt cancelled the domestic air mail subsidy contracts on the grounds that they had been obtained by collusion, and ordered the Air Corps to carry the mail. It responded to the best of its ability; but numerous fatal crashes were to show that it had neither the training, the instrumentation nor the equipment even to fly the United States commercial mail routes in the winter. The episode is still highly controversial; but the net result —that the Army Air Corps, for whatever reason, was quite incapable of fulfilling its claim to possess a world-ranging, all-weather, independent air power—was too conclusive to be denied.

The War Department summoned one more board, this time on the highest level and under the chairmanship of its former Secretary, Newton D. Baker. The Baker Board was severely critical of the whole theory of independent air power. It found that the Air Corps had "virtually been independent since its inception" and had very little to show as a result. "The time has arrived for the Air Corps to become in all respects a homogeneous part of the Army, under General Staff control." Like the Morrow Board ten years before, the Baker Board found that we were not threatened by air attack from any quarter, and that our best means of defense against any other form of assault was still the fleet, "the only entirely dependable force for operations at sea," and the Army which "with its own air forces remains the ultimately decisive factor in war." The history of the Second War was on the whole to justify this analysis. But perhaps it also justified the Baker Board's practical decision, which was to accept General Drum's recommendation for an autonomous "GHQ Air Force" with an authorized strength of 1,800 planes.

To the Army aviators this was, of course, much less than the independence and dominance of which they had dreamed; but it was much better than the old complete subjection to the ground generals and they were willing to settle for it. On March 1, 1935 the GHQ Air Force was brought into being; the ground army's corps areas were stripped of their aviation and the planes assembled at Langley Field (Virginia), Barksdale Field (Louisiana), and March Field (California). The commander was Major General Frank M. Andrews, reporting only to the Chief of Staff in peace and to the field commander in event of war. Autonomy had been achieved and was to be maintained about on this basis throughout the Second World War.

After 1935 the Army Air Corps was less concerned with changing "the basic organization of the national defense" than (as the official history rather oddly puts it) with finding "in the mission assigned to the GHQ Air Force the basis for an ambitious program of bomber development." Having achieved quasi-independence, in other words, the problem was to invent the weapon which would justify it. The celebrated Boeing B-17 (the first experimental model was flown in 1935) was the result. In the mid-'30's an "ambitious program of bomber development" could not be sustained on the theory that such weapons would be required for intervention in transoceanic wars in Europe or Asia. The only politically and propagandistically useful argument was that they would be required to defeat a sea-borne invasion of the Western Hemisphere—or, more crudely, to defeat the Navy, to which that function had been entrusted. The B-17 was designed for this purpose.

It was given great range, to seek out hostile squadrons far at sea; it had maximum ceiling, to evade ship-borne anti-aircraft; it was to carry the super-accurate Norden bombsight, to enable it to hit ship-size targets from great altitudes; it was equipped with what seemed powerful defensive gunnery, intended to protect it against hostile ship-borne fighters, since its great range precluded the possibility of sending defensive fighter cover along with it. That the B-17, like its companion Liberator, was a very fine and rugged airplane has never been denied. That it was also a failure in almost every function for which it was designed has seldom been admitted. But this would seem to be the lesson of the Second World War experience. In practice it was to turn out that the B-17 could not defend itself without accompanying fighter cover; it could not hit ships by its "pinpoint" bombing; it could not evade anti-aircraft. It was a good airplane, and many useful missions were to be found for it. But the theories behind its designing were not validated in practice; while the devotion which the Air Corps put into this development contributed to its neglect of the fighter and defensive airplane (our best fighter types were obsolescent when the war began) that was to cost us heavily after 1941.

In January 1938 the United States had several good prototype weapons; it had many good ideas in the minds of its Air Corps, Navy, Marine and ground Army officers; but it had nothing resembling an effective military structure and the President's call for another $30 million in military appropriations, mostly for naval surface ships, could do little to remedy the situation. It had done virtually nothing toward evoking the industrial base which a major war, certain to be mechanized beyond anything known in 1918, would plainly demand. Through 1938, for example, production for the Army Air Corps did not reach ninety airplanes a month; there was no volume production of tanks at all and little was done to create the huge capacities in artillery, ammunition, small arms, and instrumentation which would be required. Nor was there any agreed strategic concept on which an industrial base could have been designed, or popular acceptance of any given course of policy, indispensable as a foundation for a clear strategic concept.

Yet the external situation continued only to deteriorate. In September there came the Munich crisis, which shook the United States as deeply as the rest of the world. German armed power, rebuilt around the airplane and the armored column, was again a staggeringly effective fact. Everywhere the crisis was taken as a signal for intensified effort at armament; and Roosevelt responded to it. On November 14 the President summoned his principal military and civilian advisers to the White House and "on that occasion the effective rearming of the nation's ground and air forces took its start." [1] But how to rearm and what to rearm for were still unsettled questions. The President, who at the beginning of the year had been chiefly interested in naval building, now put all his emphasis upon a mighty program of land-based aircraft and anti-aircraft artillery. In this he was notably uninterested in the Air Corps' hopes for an independent "air force," with all the bases, trainers, communications and other apparatus that went with it; he wanted combat airplanes and nothing else. His purpose, apparently, was simply to overawe the Germans with the appearance, rather than the actuality, of power; one participant in the discussions even thought that the intention was to create a supply of planes for the French and British rather than for the USAAC. The President was even more uninterested in the really desperate needs of the ground Army for money, men and modern equipment. The staff planners withdrew to do the best they could toward balancing these directives into a rational program of military expansion.

Inevitably, since they were allowed no larger objective, they had to fall back on the old concept of Western Hemisphere defense. In the spring, the Air Corps had successfully dispatched six of its new long-range bombers on a ceremonial flight to Buenos Aires. It seemed a triumph of the distant exertion of air power; and it led the Air Corps to the discovery, revealed in a report of October, of "The Air Corps Mission Under the Monroe Doctrine." It would no longer confine itself to attacking hostile battle fleets approaching our shores; it would now attend to "taking out" any hostile air bases which might find lodgment anywhere in the Hemisphere. Since this task would patently call for many more than half a dozen bombers, it provided a sound strategic basis for vast Air Corps expansion without raising the specter of transoceanic intervention. The ground Army brought out its "Protective Mobilization Plan"—long languishing from acute anemia of

[1] Mark S. Watson, *Chief of Staff: Pre-War Plans and Preparations* (Washington, G.P.O., 1950), p. 126.

appropriations—in the hope of getting something with which to give it reality. "PMP" was theoretically based on the old calculation of the size and readiness of a ground army required to meet a sea-borne invasion; in fact, it was little more than a plan to mobilize all the regulars and the National Guard in sight. The Navy not only resumed the building of battleships; it also asked for more airplanes and was planning further additions to the carrier fleet, as well as building large additions to the submarine flotilla. But ostensibly, at least, it was still engaged, like the others, upon the defense of the Hemisphere; not in preparing for war either in the eastern Atlantic or the western Pacific.

Roosevelt in the end made considerable concessions to the practical needs of all three services—acute needs, if they were to be called upon to fight in a major war—but the first big rearmament program announced in January 1939 still put major emphasis on combat land-based airplanes. Before a public trained for twenty years in the propaganda of air power this was the showy course; whether it was militarily valid is another question. The program itself, at all events, was anything but excessive. The President thought that $500 million was the most he could get out of Congress for new weapons and equipment of any sort and the event was to prove it a lame answer to the actual military problems soon to confront us.

It was not, indeed, until May 1939 that the Army and Navy Joint Board pulled the planners of the General Staff and naval War Plans Division out of the hypothetical future, their normal habitat for so many years, back into the ominous and urgent present. They had been engaged upon studies of possible future wars with each of the great powers seriatim. Each was designated by a color (Japan, for example, was "Orange") and for a war with each there was a plan. Since there were almost no available forces with which to wage war with any and almost no likelihood that war would come in the form of an aggression by any single power, these studies were at best theoretical. But now the Joint Board initiated the series of "Rainbow" plans in which, as the name suggests, all the "color" plans were to be drawn together into a conspectus of the actual military probabilities as they existed. The five Rainbow plans considered as many possible situations, ranging from a simple defense of the Monroe Doctrine, the Hemisphere and outlying United States possessions (the isolationist requirement) down to the dispatch of decisive forces to Africa or Europe in order to defeat Germany or Italy or both in cooperation with Britain and France (the possible interventionist requirement). It was "Rainbow Five," dealing with the last contingency, which was actually to form the basis of American strategy in the Second World War. But while the isolationist-interventionist battle still raged it was politically impossible to admit that such a plan even existed, much less to make it the foundation of military and appropriation policies. With the Rainbow plans, military strategy had been reconnected with the actual world of international relations. It was still too early to reconnect national policy with military strategy. And it was politically impossible to fill any strategy with the content of trained men and expensive weaponry necessary to give it a chance of success.

Yet in the sultry summer of 1939 the most casual observer could almost feel the Second War approaching, with all the majestic tragedy of the inevitable. Everywhere in Europe the troops were drilling, the airplanes were formed on their fields, the tank columns were clanking through the streets, the bomb shelters were being dug in city parks, gas masks had been distributed (needlessly, as it turned out) to the civilians, and the speeches of demagogues and dictators were rising to new peaks of reckless violence. The tension was reaching a palpable breaking point; and in the crisis of late August and September it broke. Again most of Europe was at war. Incomprehensibly, the ghastly tragedy which had begun in August 1914—just a quarter of a century before—had been repeated. The lights went out across a continent and once more brute military power resumed the final authority in the affairs of men. Again, as in 1914, it was to turn out to be a very different war from that which had been anticipated; it was to be far worse in most respects, perhaps better in some, than had been prophesied; it was to disprove many calculations of the experts, reduce many plans to absurdity and impose new and terrible patterns of its own for which no one was really prepared. But whatever the outcome might be, the military factor was now central in the course of history.

2.

On September 8, 1939 President Roosevelt proclaimed a "limited national emergency." No one knew what that meant, constitutionally or practically, but the President used it to authorize immediate increases in the armed forces. Yet the scale was still tiny. The Army was authorized to add only 17,000 regulars, and the National Guard was to be raised by only 35,000 from its authorized 200,000 strength. This, as the President privately informed the Chief of Staff, was "all the public would be ready to accept without undue excitement." The Air Corps had already been authorized in April to raise its strength to 6,000 planes and 50,000 men and officers. But when the ground Army tried to work up its estimates for tanks, artillery, motor transport and all the rest of the needed panoply, it ran into a double problem: the reluctance of the Budget Bureau and the relapse of the European armies into the inactivity of the "phony war."

The power of the new mechanized warfare, for which the United States was so ill-equipped, was already sufficiently apparent. In the year before an important factor in the Munich settlement had been the 2,000 bombers which Goering reputedly had waiting on his airfields for the destruction of Britain. In the bloodless conquest of Czechoslovakia in the spring of 1939 Hitler had rolled powerful armored divisions down upon Prague. The swift and sudden evisceration of Poland on the outbreak of war, accomplished chiefly by the skillful use of the air-armor team, had plainly demonstrated what the new warfare would be like. But there were few among Western soldiers to read correctly the lessons of the Polish campaign; while the complete lull which followed bred dangerous misconceptions. The Roosevelt administration relapsed into a diplomacy of neutrality and a military policy which amounted to little more than taking out some slight preliminary insurance against the possibility of an Allied defeat, meanwhile lending all "moral" and available industrial support to France and Britain and endeavoring, with what feeble gestures were in its power, to "restrain" the Japanese.

Both the policy and the complacency which it reflected were to be swept suddenly away in the torrents of fire that burst over France and the Low Countries in May 1940. What the Germans had tried and catastrophically failed to do in 1914 they now achieved in a bare four weeks' campaign. The French Army, still widely considered the best and most competently led in the world, was fragmented and brought to abject defeat; the British Army was flung off the Continent, and while most of the men were brought off all of the generally excellent modern equipment had to be abandoned. Great Britain was left almost without ground defenses, while the occupation of nearly the whole Atlantic coast of Europe had opened innumerable unsealable gateways to the depredations of the U-boats. Suddenly, France was gone and Britain's survival in dire question. The shock to the United States was enormous; our entire concept of the international world had been shattered and a wave of anger, fear and dismay swept the nation.

On May 16 the President appeared before Congress to ask for 50,000 military airplanes and fresh defense appropriations of about $900 million. But if the European disaster suggested that airplanes were essential, it showed equally that they would not be enough. Two weeks later the President asked authority to call the National Guard into the Federal service; and in the following month, while both Roosevelt and the War Department still hesitated to call for conscription, a movement initiated by private citizens brought into Congress the Burke-Wadsworth bill for the reinstitution of selective service. The United States was finally making a beginning, at least, upon the creation of a new military structure, including a serious mobilization of industrial power and ground army forces as well as air and naval strength—a structure ultimately competent to fight upon the fields of global war.

Such proposals, however, could only intensify the struggle of the isolationists against the interventionist tendencies, while as it appeared that the British, under their great Prime Minister, might stand after all, the pressures of fear somewhat relaxed. It was not until the end of August that the President secured authority to call the National Guard; and not until September that the Selective Service Act was signed. It provided then for an Army of the United States of 1,400,000 —500,000 regulars, 270,000 National Guard and 630,000 drafted

men. Even this was only an interim goal; the General Staff had been
at work since the fall of France on production and manpower planning
for an ultimate ground army of 4,000,000 men and a military airplane
capacity of 36,000 planes a year.

As with the preparedness agitation of 1916 and the legislation which
emerged from it, the focus of the military planning in 1940 was almost
wholly on the defense of the Western Hemisphere, especially Latin
America, against a Germany victorious in Europe, rather than upon
American intervention in Europe to prevent the victory. This was
partly for the old reason that it was politically easier to get appropriations to create a defensive force than to build one which could aggressively intervene beyond the oceans. But in 1940 the peril, which in
1916 had lain principally in the overheated imaginations of the preparedness enthusiasts, was now certainly real. If Britain went down
her fleet might be lost or paralyzed, despite Churchill's promise to
preserve it; the airplane had reduced the gap between Dakar (French
territory in West Africa) and Brazil to a bridgeable one; the German
submarines could operate directly against our communications off the
coasts of the Americas and in the Caribbean. The danger of German
attack may have been exaggerated, but it was certainly not imaginary.
The President was serious when at the end of May he called upon the
Navy to plan for a movement in case of crisis of 10,000 men to
Brazil by air to be followed by 100,000 transported by sea; so were
the staffs when they wrestled with the problem of how far they dared
impair the available, trained units—all we had for the immediate protection of vital Western Hemisphere bases—in order to provide instructors for the new fleets and armies we were undertaking to create.

This time there was a real danger. But there was another reason
for the initial concentration on "hemisphere defense." It was all that
one could plan for in the existing state of our forces. It would take
many months to repair their deficiencies even for that purpose, considering the temper of the country; as it turned out, we were in effect
to shut down our whole military establishment "for alterations" during late 1940 and 1941. What was not clearly explained was the fact
that by the time the "alterations" to meet the hemisphere defense
problem had been completed—the troops raised and trained, the off-

shore bases secured, the war industry got going—we would have the framework of a military structure which could be expanded into one capable of a global exertion of American military power. The celebrated three hundred-mile neutral zone, popularly known as the "chastity belt," which Roosevelt drew around the American coasts may really have been intended in the beginning only as a means of "keeping war away from the Americas." But its actual military function, as the President can scarcely have failed to foresee, was to help make it possible for the United States to carry war to North Africa and Europe.

Franklin Roosevelt was bold enough to try to use all forms of power available to him—military power, industrial power, "moral" or propaganda power—to shape events as they developed, rather than waiting and planning against some future "emergency." He was astute enough to know that such powers could not be exercised except as the Congress and public opinion supported him in their use. Two reasons may explain the fact that he was less successful than he hoped to be in the management of the events of 1940-41. Wilson had possessed no understanding of military factors in society, or even much interest in them; Roosevelt, whose interest was keen enough, did not understand them as clearly as he thought. In the spring of 1940, just before the fall of France, he moved the United States Pacific Fleet out of the fleshpots of Los Angeles to base it in the more exposed and less comfortable surroundings of Pearl Harbor. The purpose was to "restrain" Japan; this was a practical use of current military power to secure concrete diplomatic (or political) results and Roosevelt refused to withdraw the fleet thereafter even in the face of serious technical, strategic arguments. He has been criticized for his refusal to listen to the technicians. The true criticism probably lies, not in the fact that he rejected the technicians, but in the fact that the movement of the fleet to Pearl Harbor had no discernible effect on Japanese policy. Roosevelt constantly overvalued the concrete results that could be achieved in any specific situation by a show of power. After May 1940 he no doubt believed that "all aid short of war" would probably pull the British through and that his policy really was one, therefore, of keeping the United States out of war. But the military calculation on which this belief rested was inadequate.

The second reason for Roosevelt's failure to control events lay in his inability to secure all-out popular support for any consistent line of policy. In retrospect it may seem plain that what he should have done in September 1939 was to call for a major national effort of industrial and military mobilization, capable of creating in the shortest possible time a military structure which could have dominated the world situation. He may be blamed today for the caution with which, even after the fall of France in 1940, he proceeded to revive an American military system. Certainly, it would have been better if he had announced at that point the 8,000,000 man army, the colossal fleets, the colossal air forces that we were in fact to create, and the vast machinery of war mobilization and rationalization in industry to which we were to come. But few who lived through those years will deny that it would also have been impossible. Since all of his specific requests in these years were accepted, and since the opinion polls were consistently with him, it is reasonable to conclude that Roosevelt's general view of the world problem was accepted by the majority. But in every effort to translate this view into concrete policy he was to meet an embittered opposition, which tended to hamstring the attempt and reduce every proposal to a minimum insufficient for the case in hand. Perhaps this is the essence of democratic politics. But one hesitates to accept the conclusion, for if true it would mean that democratic politics is no longer competent to direct the affairs of great nations in the military-political context of the modern world.

Through the fall and winter the American people watched with deepening horror and sympathy the progress of the Battle of Britain, including the first of the air war's great fire raids, used against London, and the then appalling destruction of most of Coventry. The American people learned also that the British were coming to the end of their financial resources, just as they had done in 1916, and that for us a policy of "cash-and-carry" neutrality was no longer sufficient to meet the very real problems with which the European War had presented us.

In his annual message on January 6, 1941 the President introduced his dramatic proposal to forego further commercial payment for our munitions exports, and instead to lease or lend the materials of war "to those nations which are now in actual war with aggressor nations." Here was a complete commitment, not to war, perhaps, but to the fortunes of the British in the war then under way, with its implied commitments to British (and French) interests throughout the world. It was bound to affect our relations, not only with Germany and Italy, but with Japan and the Soviet Union. It announced our part and partnership in a world complex of extraordinary difficulty and danger. On January 16, ten days after the delivery of the message, the President called in his Secretaries of State, War and Navy, the Chief of Naval Operations (Stark) and the Chief of Staff (Marshall) for a "lengthy conference."

According to Marshall's memorandum, the President "discussed the possibilities of sudden and simultaneous action on the part of Germany and Japan against the United States. He felt that there was one chance out of five of such an eventuality, and that it might culminate any day." The underlying problem was, very clearly, how to continue support for the British in Europe, how to "restrain" the Japanese and how to do both without too deeply impairing our own military build-up against the possibility that neither of these efforts would succeed. The meeting ended with a directive from the President in general terms but of striking interest:

> That we would stand on the defensive in the Pacific with the fleet based on Hawaii; that the Commander of the Asiatic Fleet would have discretionary authority as to how long he could remain based in the Philippines . . . ; that there would be no naval reinforcement of the Philippines; that the Navy should have under consideration the possibility of bombing attacks against Japanese cities.
>
> That the Navy should be prepared to convoy shipping in the Atlantic to England, and to maintain a patrol off-shore from Maine to the Virginia Capes.
>
> That the Army should not be committed to any aggressive action until it was fully prepared to undertake it; that our military course must be very conservative until our strength had de-

veloped; that it was assumed we could provide forces sufficiently trained to assist to a moderate degree in backing up friendly Latin-American government against Nazi-inspired fifth column movements.

That we should make every effort to go on the basis of continuing the supply of material to Great Britain, primarily in order to disappoint what he thought would be Hitler's principal objective in involving us in a war at this particular time, and also to buck up England.[2]

The basic strategy was plain: The underlying objective was to win the war in Europe. To this end we would endeavor to restrain the Japanese by whatever show of force was possible, but would accept the evacuation of the Philippines if that became unavoidable. The Army would plan to defend Latin America until it was "fully prepared" for larger things. The main point was to back Britain to success; all other interests, of local preparedness or even of Far Eastern war, would be subordinate to this goal.

It was a rational plan for the utilization of such military force as we then possessed or were likely soon to acquire. The lend-lease bill, which was its cornerstone, symbolically entitled "H.R. 1776," passed in March, after a debate in which the battle between the isolationists and interventionists sank to new lows of bitterness, passion and misrepresentation on both sides. Roosevelt's difficulty was that he would not or could not or dared not present the issue in its concrete terms. He felt it necessary to insist that a plan which accepted all the risks of war in the hope of thereby evading war and establishing a better foundation for world peace, was actually a plan for evading any kind of war whatever. There was certainly an element of insincerity behind his repeated declarations, in the Presidential campaign of 1940, that "your sons are not going to be sent into any foreign wars"; "there is no demand for sending an American expeditionary force outside our own borders. . . . You can nail any talk about sending armies to Europe as a deliberate untruth"; the British "do not need manpower. They do need billions worth of weapons for defense." Like the Demo-

2 Watson, *op. cit.*, p. 124.

cratic campaign of 1916 ("He kept us out of war") these passages represented at best but half-truths. But when the opposition descended to such levels as Senator Burton K. Wheeler's characterization of lend-lease as "the New Deal's 'Triple-A' foreign policy—to plow under every fourth American boy," the President's evasiveness is more understandable. Could the United States be brought, by fair means or foul, to face the truly critical international situation in which it was now involved? Neither side possessed a monopoly of intellectual integrity. But when the bill was passed in March by handsome majorities, the decision seemed clear. The United States was committed to securing British victory, or at least to averting British defeat, and was committed to placing its manpower and industrial capacity behind that objective.

In March 1941 Roosevelt could not have known what the Japanese were going to do. Apparently, he did already know that Hitler was planning the onslaught upon Russia and that knowledge would give a valid ground for the belief that "all aid short of war" might suffice. But there was no question but that the United States had become more deeply entangled in the complex. Committed, for reasons of our vital interest, to giving Britain "the tools" with which to "finish the job," we were also committed to seeing that they got to her through the increasingly stringent submarine blockade. The summer and fall of 1941 saw the bases and the large naval forces deployed in the Atlantic ostensibly for "hemisphere defense" inevitably converted into a defense of the sea lanes to Britain.

Hitler's invasion of Russia on June 22, 1941 instantly transformed the whole equation. The general staffs may have looked for another German victory within six weeks (and the Germans were in fact to come close to fulfilling such predictions) but to the world at large this development came as the first sign that the British and the Free French after all might have a chance for survival. We could now build up our economic support to Britain with greater confidence that it would pay out in the end. Discreetly and by gradual steps, our "chastity belt" in the Atlantic was transformed into the basis for a quasi-war at sea, directed toward getting the convoys safely into British ports. Roosevelt has often been condemned for his evasiveness in encouraging this war. But if his evasions were in part directed toward averting the savage opposition of the isolationists, there were other reasons as well. Roosevelt knew that Hitler, also, had read the history of 1917. The German dictator, who felt that he had matters very well under control, had no desire to invite a major American intervention in Europe. His submarines would of course shoot our convoy escorts out of water when opportunity served; and our ships would shoot back when attacked. But the danger of this resulting in a German declaration of war upon the United States was in fact not great. Hitler had long left behind him the old concepts of international law and he was never "at the mercy of an incident" except when he wanted to be. It was quite possible to defend our convoys in the Atlantic, even by shooting, without total involvement; and it is sometimes overlooked today that the quasi-war which ensued on the Atlantic sea lanes did not in fact lead to our total involvement. That was the work of the Japanese, and what would have happened had the Japanese bided their time remains today a rather curious speculation. The Japanese, however, did not bide their time and on December 7, 1941 they rashly thrust the United States into a full participation in a world war for which at the time we were emotionally at best only half prepared, to which our tactical and strategic ideas were only partly adjusted, and for which we yet had to build most of the industrial capacity, the trained manpower and the strategic doctrines by which victory was finally to be attained.

3.

By December 1941 it was clear that almost nothing in the new war had turned out as had been expected; it was much less clear what would be the ultimate shape of the struggle. Mechanization had left its mark upon every campaign; it had turned the dreadful deadlocks of the 1914 mass armies into a warfare of astonishing fluidity and speed, of deep penetrations and vast encirclements. Yet it had at the same time called up huge masses of foot soldiers. It had greatly enhanced the significance of industrial production, which now had to turn out enormous numbers of complicated airplanes, electronics devices, special weapons of many kinds, as well as the artillery, shells and small arms ammunition which were the staples of World War I. Yet probably more men (and now women as well) in proportion to the populations wore uniforms in the second struggle than in the first. The appearance of the bombing airplane put the civilians into the front lines to an extent previously unknown in modern times; yet the war was essentially concluded in the old way, by uniformed forces capturing ground. It was a war fought to a greater extent than before not simply by the men and the machines in the field, but by the embattled scientists at their drawing boards, waging a desperate and often critical struggle to outwit their opponents. Yet much of this effort, vital as it was, more or less cancelled out, leaving the ultimate decisions to the traditional factors of manpower, morale, and numbers of weapons.

The one great, determining factor which shaped the course of the Second War was not, as is so often said and so generally believed, independent air power. It was the mechanization of the ground battlefield with automotive transport, with the "tactical" airplane and above all with the tank. Air power in its independent form was, in sober fact, relatively ineffective. It was the teaming of the internal combustion engine in the air and on the surface, in order to take the traditional objectives of surface warfare which, together with the remarkable development of electronic communications, really determined the history of the Second World War.

The tactical airplane, with its tremendous mobility and firepower, was an essential element in this automotive team from beginning to end. So were the powered landing craft and amphibious vehicles of the Pacific War and the European invasion beaches. So were many other special applications of machinery to war. But the central weapon of World War II was the tank, the armored and mobile weapons carrier which dominated most campaigns and which more often than not found all other arms—the air and even the infantry, the traditional "queen of battles"—supporting it rather than being supported by it.

It was the fast-moving armored division, with the medium tank as its basic weapon, which opened up ground warfare and prevented the reappearance (except locally on some special fronts) of the trench stalemates of 1914-18. It was the tank column, slashing out far ahead of the infantry mass, which tore Poland to ribbons in 1939. It was Guderian's armored spearheads which paralyzed the French infantry army in 1940. Those who wretchedly watched the newspaper war maps in May and June of that year, with their long, black arrows striking remorselessly through all defenses to the sea, were actually watching armored columns—lines of hundreds of tanks, of hundreds more tracked and wheeled vehicles, usually strung out for scores of miles down the paved roads, stabbing far ahead of the main infantry army, with no flank protection and only the infantry and artillery support which they carried along with them, but already at large in rear areas where there was nothing much to oppose them. When a knot of resistance appeared they paused only long enough to deploy such of their force as seemed necessary to crush it, and then rolled on. If their own infantry divisions could not keep pace with them, neither could the bypassed enemy infantry fall back quickly enough to embay them. The German tank of 1940 was not, in fact, a particularly powerful vehicle; it was thin-skinned and weakly armed by later standards and was actually outnumbered in May 1940 by armored vehicles in British and French hands. Its triumph lay in the tactical skill and drive with which it was employed.

While others had been foreseeing a new war too completely in the apocalyptic terms of air power—the "strategic" war upon "vital centers," upon civilian populations, resources and communications— the Germans (and the Russians) had clung to the older, somewhat simpler concepts of territorial advance, of the paralysis or destruction of the enemy's shield of armed force and the occupation of his seats of power. The Germans clearly did not believe that the invention of the airplane had repealed von Clausewitz; and there was much of the nineteenth century in Hitler, for all his seeming novelty. His "blitzkrieg" was much less a new form of warfare than a necessary modernization of the traditional war of the armed mass, which by 1918 had grown so ponderous and so aimlessly destructive as to be inacceptable. What was needed was to restore to traditional warfare its speed, economy and power of decision (much as Napoleon had done a century before him); and Hitler, with his abler generals, like Guderian and Rommel, did it primarily by bringing the gasoline engine onto the battlefield. He added other new features in the way of political infiltration, propaganda and terrorism (even these seem not so new if one examines Napoleon's skill with such weapons), but in general it was the swift ground advance which was central to the Hitler strategy. When the Germans rebuilt an air force after 1933 it showed little reflection of the air power theories of Douhet, Mitchell or Trenchard. Its chief emphasis was on such ground cooperation types as the celebrated Stuka dive bomber. The Germans' tank tactics were the most advanced in the world. Their reward was Poland, and then France; it was, finally, the amazing sweeps through the huge Russian armies, the deep penetrations and encirclements which won them two-thirds of European Russia and carried them ultimately to the Caucasus and the Volga.

These great battles in Western Europe and in Russia were waged and won with a much greater economy of the soldiers' lives, especially German soldiers' lives, than in 1914-18. But meanwhile the "strategic" air war, of which civilians were the principal victims, had tended somewhat to redress the grim balance. For four years, from the evacuation of the Dunkerque beaches in June 1940 to the landing on those of Normandy in June 1944, Great Britain, later reinforced by the United States, waged independent air war with Germany in almost its pure form. Britain did not do so from choice but because so few other forms of warfare were available to her; and if the strategy had been more deliberately planned and supported it might, perhaps, have been more successful. Nevertheless, the four years of air battle across the Channel would seem to provide about as fair a test of military theory as history is ever likely to yield. The results were largely negative. Many tens of thousands of people were burned and blasted to death; some millions of homes were totally destroyed; holocausts, like that of the three-day "fire-storm" in Hamburg, rivaling the achievement of the atomic bomb at Hiroshima, were produced; factory capacity was at times brought down and cruel strains were imposed on the minds and hearts of the combatant populations. But the traceable military results were uniformly disappointing. One can hardly doubt that all this death and destruction helped to prepare the ultimate German collapse, yet the United States Strategic Bombing Survey reported after the war that German war production increased throughout to reach its peak in late 1944, well after the ground armies were ashore to make good the job at which the air fleets had been unsuccessful.

The weakness of the air power theories had been strikingly demonstrated in the summer of 1940, when Hitler's tank-air teams, having swept everything before them, arrived upon the Channel shore. The tanks were brought to a halt, leaving the Luftwaffe to fling itself alone upon the opposite coast. In accordance with the now classic doctrines of air power, Goering's squadrons proceeded against the southern England airfields in order to "take out" the defense and establish "command of the air." But the British, at least skeptical of the Douhet theory that air defense was impossible, had been specializing in defense. Their eight-gun Spitfire and Hurricane defensive fighters were the best in the world, while they had developed an early radar net which helped powerfully to save them. It proved impossible to "take out" the defense, and "command of the air" faded into illusion. Like Napoleon before him, Hitler had already begun to collect his landing craft in the Channel ports, but without air cover his navy dared not risk invasion on the broad front which the army believed to be essential. The three services fell into a dispute which came down to the fact that none had sufficient confidence in the other two or in the feasibility of the project to make it practicable; and Hitler, again like Napoleon, turned his face eastward. It was the first significant Western victory of the war; and the first lesson in the limitations of independent air power.

In the fall of 1941 the American statesmen and military men had little time to read such lessons correctly. A year after the Battle of Britain had reached its peak there was no appreciation at Pearl Harbor (and not much in Manila) of the vital importance of getting a radar warning net in operation. Our best fighter planes were obsolete. We were entertaining grossly exaggerated ideas of the power of the high-level bomber. A month before Pearl Harbor the force of thirty-five B-17's which the Army managed to get into the

Philippines looked very formidable to Washington; Stimson, the Secretary of War, thought that his colleagues would show a stiffer attitude toward Japan if they knew "what the Army is doing with the big bombers and how ready we are to pitch in." Half of them were to be destroyed on the ground on the first day of war and a month after Pearl Harbor the force had virtually ceased to exist, having made no significant contribution to the course of the conflict. But even if there had been a sounder appreciation in Washington of the true nature of the war which impended, it could hardly have made much difference. Before December 7 the staffs and production planners were too desperately busy trying to lay the foundations of some sort of military power to be able to do much in the way of planning its exact size and shape; after December 7 the sky suddenly became the limit for every form of military activity: Army, Navy and Army Air Force alike could revise their plans (none of which were even close to fulfillment at the time) on the largest scale which manpower, production and raw material facilities would permit.

And in the end it was all, or nearly all, useful and necessary. Undeniably, there were immense confusions in the resultant production effort and there were mistakes and misdirections of effort in the military planning. The Navy laid down too many super-dreadnought battleships and was too slow in developing anti-submarine craft for the Atlantic war. It may be argued that the Army Air Force put too much into its heavy strategic bombers and was too slow in developing either the fighter cover to go with them or the tactical ground cooperation air forces. The Army may have been slow in working out satisfactory armored tactics and in developing its armored forces, but at least there were no Army or Marine divisions which were not required in the ground warfare, and nearly all of those raised saw some kind of battle action before the end. With the Japanese attack, the three services set out to provide every form of military power in as large quantities as possible. It was perhaps less than a scientific approach to the problem of modern war, yet roughly it worked. In one sense, of course, all war is "waste." But in this colossal and somewhat helter-skelter effort the waste, in terms of the men, machines and effort required for victory, was certainly not great. By 1945, as by 1918, both the human and the material pipelines were, of course, becoming clogged with men and weapons which on the coming of peace were to become supernumerary. But most of the vast effort and the vast production was indispensable to securing the peace.

It may be said that it took the United States about two years, from September 1939 to December 1941, to lay the foundations of a military structure adequate to wage global war and at least to begin upon the productive capacity required to sustain it. It was to take another year of the most intensive effort, from Pearl Harbor to Guadalcanal (August 1942) and North Africa (November 1942), before this mobilization even began to exert positive effect upon the course of the vast struggle, and at least another year before the huge build-up of Army, Navy and Air forces began (with the fall of Italy in September 1943, the start of the Pacific counterattack at Lae in September and Tarawa in November, the appearance of the 8th Air Force heavy bombers over Germany in significant numbers in the summer and fall) to exert any decisive effect upon the hopes and calculations of the enemy.

It was a war which was always difficult to grasp, because the basic shape of this mechanical and scientific struggle was so different from the wars of experience. Those had always been fought in big, set battle pieces or campaigns in which victory had usually gone to the side with the most manpower on the field, the most rifles and artillery. This was a war in which strategy seemed constantly more important than tactics. While it put colossal numbers into uniform, somehow fewer of them than ever before seemed to get into severe combat action. Certainly, great numbers were killed and maimed, yet most of the critical actions seemed to involve relatively few combat men. Thus, the Marines and naval forces who took Tarawa, for example, suffered 17 per cent in casualties—but there were only 18,000 engaged, out of the 15,000,000 or so whom the United States was to put into uniform. And Tarawa was the decisive action which most clearly foretold the end of the Japanese island empire. Where former wars had represented great clashes of men on extended fronts, here great numbers of men always seemed to be waiting on the sidelines, in support or training or the enormously swollen logistic services, while results of the greatest strategic consequence were achieved by relative handfuls—the famous "few" fighter pilots who defended Britain in 1940, the few who actually flew in the strategic bombers, who waded ashore in invasions, who manned the tanks at the spearheads of the armored divisions. This was the curious result of the introduction of the machine, not simply into war, but into every phase of combat.

Once involved in the global struggle, the United States devoted itself to developing every mechanical and scientific aid to victory which seemed to offer any promise. It was not until the spring maneuvers in 1941 that George Patton was able to bring the 2nd Armored Division into the training field as a competent fighting force; before the war was over we had put twenty armored divisions into action of some kind. According to General Brereton there were in October 1941 only sixty-four Army Air Force first pilots qualified to fly four-engined bombers; there were some thousands by the time the war ended. At the time of Pearl Harbor the Navy had seven combat aircraft carriers in commission; by V-J Day it had completed or nearly completed twenty-seven more, besides eleven lighter carriers converted from cruiser hulls and well over one hundred anti-submarine "escort carriers," many converted from merchant ship hulls. The Army was to organize seventy-four infantry and airborne divisions in addition to the armored divisions; the Marine Corps rose from a strength equivalent to about one division to six ground divisions with corps, support and aviation troops in addition.

In the course of these huge expansions, combat experience, the limitations of resources and shifts in the strategic problem were, naturally, to bring many changes of plan and emphasis. The German U-boats, which through many dreadful months in 1942 illuminated New Jersey beach resorts with the glare of blazing tankers, forced the Navy into drastic upward revisions of its program for anti-submarine craft. Air Force doctrine was to undergo some forcible modification. When in the late summer of 1942 the USAAF finally got into the cross-channel air war, it found that the British had accepted night bombing—inaccurate and almost random as it often was—as the only practicable strategy. Their four-engine bombers, like the Lancasters, were enormous weight carriers but with ceilings too low and with too little defensive armament to be operable in daylight. The Americans, with their doctrine of pinpoint day bombing, with their supposedly safe ceilings and heavy armament, were "sure that they were right." For a year they tried to prove it; until, in the two great attacks on the Schweinfurt ball bearing factories in the autumn of 1943 they met what was in fact (though it was never so announced) one of the major defeats of the war.

Many theories had to be abandoned. Even with the Flying Fortress (the B-17) and the almost equally powerful B-24 Liberator the losses had proved prohibitive; and the daylight attack on Germany had to be suspended or confined to easier targets, until long-range fighter cover could be developed to support it. Even worse, perhaps, was the demonstration that "precision" bombing of a few selected "bottleneck" targets was far less effective than had been hoped. The Schweinfurt factories seemed to offer a perfect test. Ball bearings are of course absolutely essential to all forms of mechanical war; they are difficult to make, requiring the most precise tolerances and even controlled temperatures in the factories, and German production was heavily concentrated in the Schweinfurt area. But even when the plants were hit accurately, the damage to the machines was much less and much more easily reparable than seemed possible from the photographs; while the repairs were being made, there were other sources of supply available (in Germany and in Sweden) and in the grim conclusion of the U. S. Strategic Bombing Survey "there is no evidence that the attacks on the ball bearing industry had any measurable effect on essential war production."

By reviving a neglected design, the Republic P-47 Thunderbolt fighter, the Air Force secured "long-legged" fighter cover to convoy its battleplanes. It worked out a fairly effective combination of American precision day bombing with the British night or area bombing. Yet when the American Army Air Force at last came within range of Japan, it abandoned the daylight, precision dogma as completely as had the British. It adopted the indiscriminate area raid, the low-level attack with incendiaries, the fire-storms and all the general destruction and slaughter of night bombing attack, for much the same reasons that had led the British to such tactics in Europe. Night bombing cut the losses and increased the visible damage. It also probably reduced the actual military effect, but since that was incalculable anyway it did not matter much. The result was the piling up of the impressive photographs of damage and the great totals of bomb tonnages "dropped" that looked so well in the statistics—which could not record where, how or with what military effect the bombs had landed. That night bombing also piled up the "innocent" dead was hardly a consideration by 1945.

This dumping of enormous quantities of high explosive directly upon civilian homes, factories, power and communications facilities, and upon the cowering people who lived in or manned them, was perhaps the most striking feature of the Second War; it produced ruins more vast and somber than those of antiquity, of a kind which civilized man had never expected to see again. But if it was the machine's most gruesome and dramatic contribution to warfare, it was by no means militarily the most significant. The combination of the tank and the tactical airplane continued to dominate most theaters down to the end.

The armored division was of course no "absolute weapon." There were campaigns in which it was relatively ineffective because of terrain or climate. Its earlier and greatest successes flowed in part from the fact that the enemy was unprepared for it. The Germans' opponents soon learned to wage armored warfare themselves, as well as to develop a host of defensive weapons—tank traps, land mines, the "bazooka" rocket launcher firing a shaped charge which could penetrate heavy armor. The tank was at its best in break-through and deep exploitation, and when opposing tank armies appeared to produce frontal clashes of armor against armor, as in North Africa, the problem changed. Guderian's drive on Moscow at the end of 1941 failed partly because his vehicles were immobilized in the winter snows and ice, partly because the Russians surprised him by introducing their new T-34 tanks, more heavily gunned and armored than his own panzers. On the small islands and amid the constricting jungles of the

Pacific there was little opportunity for armored warfare as such and no full armored divisions were deployed in the Pacific theaters; but tank companies or battalions were everywhere present as support for the hard-fighting infantry. And the sweep of Patton's Third Army through France in 1944, and thence onward through the Palatinate and beyond the Rhine, was in conception and tactics a close copy of Guderian's sweep in the opposite direction in 1940.

The application of powered machinery to naval and amphibious war was hardly less striking; it had the same effect of restoring a mobility and power of decision which many believed to have been lost. Just as the World War I armies had apparently grown too ponderous to be practicable, so it seemed to many that naval battle lines like those at Tsu-Shima and Jutland had reached a stalemate. The failure at the Dardanelles in 1915 had reinforced the long-standing conviction that ships of war could not operate successfully against land defenses. The development of the submarine and the appearance of the bombing airplane seemed to make it even more impossible for naval power successfully to approach a distant coast, much less to land significant forces upon it. It was argued that, whatever the battleship "ratio," the United States Navy could not operate in the Western Pacific nor the Japanese Navy in our waters; the distant exertion of sea power was no longer practicable, and the sea war of the future would return to the *guerre de course* of commerce-raiding and convoy protection, so scorned by Mahan. The colossal sea-air-ground teams built up after 1942 to carry the American advance back across the world's greatest ocean were to disprove the argument. There was, it is true, no single great fleet action, on the Jutland pattern, to establish "command of the sea." But the squadrons of big carriers were able to put up a cover of offensive and defensive aviation capable of dealing with whatever Japan could exert from her land bases; the battleship artillery could smother the land fortifications; the Marines were equipped with an astonishing array of landing craft, including armored amphibious tanks, which could get them and their heaviest weapons ashore in quantity against the fiercest opposition. The problems of resupply, of evacuation of casualties, of repair of battle damage, of rapid construction of air and sea bases, had all been worked out, primarily through the use of the gasoline and diesel engine. In World War I the British had never felt able to employ even their tremendous naval superiority for a landing across the North Sea behind the deadlocked battle lines in France. In the Second War, sea power—in the Pacific and to a lesser extent in the Mediterranean, across the Channel into Normandy, in the Bay of Bengal—assumed offensive capabilities and endowed its possessors with powers of maneuver not before supposed possible.

Such were the triumphs of the mechanical revolution in warfare, the major outlines of which had already been clearly established by 1939. But the war itself was to engender still another revolution, the ultimate effects of which are anything but clear today. This may be called the scientific revolution. Wars always, of course, bring developments of military technology; but in the past they had not often had critical consequences for the struggles which produced them. Most of the arms laid down at Appomattox were very like those taken up at Sumter, despite the fact that many new tools of war, from balloons to breach-loading repeating rifles, had in the meanwhile received combat tests. Most of the weapons in the hands of the nations in 1918 had been developed before 1914, while the really new contributions—poison gas, the airplane and the tank—had not profoundly affected the course of events. The military inventions of one war have usually exerted their principal effects upon the next one. But in the Second World War, to a far greater extent than ever before, the scientist, the engineer and the technologist were harnessed directly to the conduct of the struggle; the "battle of the drawing boards" was no empty metaphor when a battle of blood and bullets only a few months later might turn upon its outcome, and never before could the fluctuations of fortune upon the battlefield be related so closely to the success or failure of the designers, researchers and inventors.

The examples are many. At the beginning, it was probably the advanced British development of radar which won the Battle of Britain, but the Germans subsequently were able to reduce the effectiveness of the British air counterattack by various radar jamming devices. The Pearl Harbor raid might well have been turned had the Americans had a keener interest in radar; later, the greatly superior development of radar by the American Navy contributed importantly to the defeat of the Japanese in the naval actions around Guadalcanal. The superiority of the Japanese torpedo design (and torpedo tactics) was largely responsible for their earlier successes; undetected defects in American torpedoes, not finally discovered and corrected until 1943, wasted much of the heroic efforts of our submarine crews in the Pacific in the earlier period.

The sea war in general was a constant struggle of ingenuity and counter-ingenuity. The Germans opened it with the "secret weapon" of the magnetic mine, planted on Britain's coastal approaches; the British answered with "de-Gaussing" gear on the ships, rendering it impotent; the Germans riposted with new kinds of sonic and delayed-action mines and the British replied with new mine-sweeping devices and techniques—all of this calling for the most intensive (and frequently hazardous) work by the men in the laboratories and at the drawing boards. The British met the onslaught of the submarines with World War I sonic detection devices which soon proved insufficient; the Germans on their side remained too long unaware of the power of the radar and later ultra-high-frequency radar brought against their craft; when they realized the danger they replied with the snorkel submarine and plans (never brought to service use) for a "true" submarine powered by hydrogen peroxide. The embattled Allied engineers found answers, not only in the "jeep" aircraft carriers to escort the convoys, but in such things as improved detection devices and weapons like the "hedgehog," which flung out the depth charges (themselves of improved design and sensitivity) ahead of the attacking ship rather than waiting to drop them, less accurately, astern.

The fierce, continuous competition in aircraft design, in destructiveness of bombs and in electronic detection and guidance systems is too familiar to be labored. By 1944 it had brought the Germans not only to the V-1 and the appalling V-2 rocket (against the latter there was no defense save in its own inaccuracy) but also to the jet-powered fighter plane. Many believe that had the Germans acquired these weapons only a little sooner and in larger quantities the outcome of the war would have been different. Another constant battle was waged in tank design. At the beginning, vehicles carrying one-inch armor and a 37-mm. or at most a "short" 75-mm. gun as main armament were considered sufficient; by the end tanks were carrying 88 or 90-mm. high velocity "long" guns behind armor up to three and four inches thick, with vastly improved fire-control and communications systems. It is a tribute to the military significance of the engineers that in the back-and-forth tank fighting in North Africa victory seemed to descend with striking regularity on the side possessing the latest model weapons.

The VT ("variable time") or proximity anti-aircraft fuse had been test-fired in the United States in the autumn of 1941. Rapidly developed after the Japanese attack, it was to become one of the most important single scientific achievements of the war. The gunners no longer had to make a direct hit upon a hostile airplane; the fuse would detonate a shell which passed no more than fairly close. The secret was considered so vital that for a long time the shells were not allowed to be used over land, lest the enemy learn of them through recovery of a dud. Without the VT-fuse the great naval advance might not have proved possible; it would certainly have been far more costly even than it was.

These are but a few examples of the innumerable ways in which the scientist, the engineer and the technical expert were mobilized for the war. Their contributions to military medicine were enormous. By producing training aids of amazing ingenuity and powerful teaching techniques they were able to turn out the armies of specialists— in almost every discipline and technical skill, from Oriental languages to cookery, from cryptography to electronic engineering—whose services the war was to demand. Perhaps some of this scientific mobilization, especially when the "behavioral scientists" were summoned up, represented unnecessary trimmings. Perhaps the public, the politicians and even the soldiers were misled into a belief that war could be converted into a less gruesome and more precise art than it is or is ever likely to be. But the waste motion was surely not great; while the deadliness of the embattled scientist and engineer was to be attested on a thousand battlefields.

It was probably fortunate on the whole that the greatest and deadliest of all scientific contributions did not reach combat until six days before the war's end. It was just before Pearl Harbor that the decision was taken in Washington to proceed with an all-out effort to develop a nuclear fission bomb. Four years later the scientists and engineers of the "Manhattan District" only barely won what they had thought was a race against the enemy physicists and was actually a race against time. No one can say what the frightful consequences might have been had the bomb come in 1943, say, rather than in 1945. As it was, this climactic achievement of the scientific revolution in warfare came not as a gift to the Second World War, which had engendered it, but as a gift to a future which it was itself profoundly to affect.

4.

The Second World War was thus, unexpectedly enough, both a fluid war of machines and experts and also a total war of the regimented mass. Those military writers of the inter-war years (the then Captain Charles de Gaulle was among them) who foresaw another conflict as one which would be fought to quick decision by small, highly trained "career" armies of air and tank specialists, were perhaps justified by the conquests of Poland and France; but their expectations were disappointed by the vast miseries which thereafter unrolled. In the Second War much greater total numbers were placed in uniform; total casualties (civilian and military) were doubtless vastly greater, even as the total volume of industrial war production mounted to colossally greater heights than in World War I. The destruction of physical capital values—homes, factory plant and equipment, communications and transport facilities—was on a correspondingly more enormous scale. These agonies and losses were, however, distributed more evenly than in the First War—as between the several nations involved, between the uniformed and the civilian populations, between the age and sex groups.

The United States, which mobilized three times as many men and women and suffered three times as many battle casualties as in the First War, bore a greater burden than before; the French bore a lesser one. The sufferings of the First War were concentrated rather heavily upon a single generation of French, British, German and Russian youths. In the Second War, the combat spearheads upon whom the hardest and most continuous fighting fell (and which frequently took very heavy casualties) were probably much smaller in relation to the aggregate in uniform; but one must also consider not only the civilian victims of the bombs and sinkings, but the much greater casual exposure of rear area and line-of-communications troops and noncombatant medical personnel who in previous wars had been relatively safe. The factors are too complex for useful statistical analysis. The fact remains that this was the most "total," mass war in history, fought very directly between whole peoples and decided in the end by great masses of ground soldiers advancing, capturing and occupying ground.

Out of this first war of both the mass and the machine, this first truly global conflict, one salient and shocking fact was to emerge: the almost unbelievable power of the modern centralized, managerial and nationalistic state to drain the whole physical, intellectual, economic, emotional and moral resources of its citizens to the single end of military victory. By the mid-'30's the Western world was acutely aware of the grim internal strength of the totalitarian regimes, ruling by dictatorial mass organization, by propaganda and by the secret police. What was less often appreciated was the extent to which, for the purposes of war, at least, these techniques were advancing in the British and American democracies. Triumphs of "monolithic" organization and direction which were quite out of the question in meeting the problems of the Great Depression were achieved overnight in meeting those of the Second War. Sacrifices, not only of life but of property, which Western governments in earlier wars would hardly have dreamed of asking, were imposed and accepted without question. Politics, which might be defined as the expression in society of individual difference, idiosyncrasy, variety and recalcitrance, were suspended everywhere for the "duration."

The competitive economic system was temporarily abolished under rigid wage, price and raw material controls; even in the democracies, severe limitations were placed upon the freedoms of thought, information and dissenting speech. It was not only in Russia and Germany but in Britain and the United States that war proved again the great forcing-bed of the unitary state. For the French, who failed to respond to its unifying pressures, the penalty was a division and defeat which leave even the survival of French democracy today in doubt.

A striking result of this developed power of the nationalistic state is seen in the fact that whereas the First War shook the fabric of Western social organization to its foundations, the Second War, vastly more destructive and entailing a far greater agony of death and mutilation, did not. The stress and strain of the First War left elements of social revolution everywhere; even in the United States the pre-war era of untaxed incomes and unregulated sweatshops, of the super-rich at Newport enjoying the fruits of the six-day week and ten- or twelve-hour day elsewhere, had disappeared. The Second War produced enormous changes in international relationships, but there were no internal upheavals at all comparable to those which were associated with the First. In its basic social and economic structure the world after 1945 resembled that of 1939 much more closely than the world of 1918 resembled that which had passed forever into the shadows with the pistol shot at Sarajevo.

The modern nation-state had learned not only how to mobilize the entire emotional and material resources of its inhabitants for success in war, but also how to insure itself and its institutions against what might seem to be the probable results of the sacrifices thus demanded. The sacrifices of 1939-45 were enormous, but so far from themselves producing revolutionary change, the most that can be said is that they were exploited by the revolutionary systems and states created in 1918 to secure advantage in struggles that long antedated 1939. Toward the end of the Napoleonic period, the Prussian Army reforms of Scharnhorst and Gneisenau were opposed by Prussian conservatives on the ground that to arm and train a whole people was to put a dangerous power in its hands. During the nineteenth century it was generally the liberals who were to be found on the side of the big, conscript mass army which, it was supposed, would keep military power in the control of the "people." In the preparedness agitation in the United States after 1914, the argument for universal conscription as the only "democratic" military system, and for military service itself as a democratic duty, was prominent. Liberals could be scornful of the "strutitudinous" excesses of Prussian militarism even while they were prepared to introduce its basic concepts into our own system. In the grimly ironic end, both liberals and conservatives alike were to be disappointed. The arming of the modern populace was to give it even less control than before over its destinies. Its regimentation, on the other hand, was to give the propertied classes no more power to limit the advance of the welfare and egalitarian state than they had previously enjoyed.

The popular mass armies have not been without their effect upon social and economic policy. By their demands for adequate pay, pensions and recognition of their services they have made a considerable contribution—much greater, probably, than the leaders of the American Legion realize—to the modern welfare state. The "homes for heroes" which Lloyd George promised the British veterans in 1918, the benefits and bonus acts exacted by the American Legion in the inter-war period, the GI Bill of Rights accorded the veterans of 1945 and 1953, were all highly "socialistic" if not communist measures, in that they recognized a communal responsibility for ardors and agonies suffered in the communal service of the state. That they encouraged the recognition of similar responsibilities to other large groups—the farmers, the unemployed wage workers, the "ill-housed," the Negro minority—who had also contributed to the national greatness, is obvious. Yet the mass army, as a political force, has been on the whole rather surprisingly neutralized in the modern community. Those who expected the Russian soldiers, returning from their contacts with the outer world, to cause trouble for the Kremlin were just as disappointed as was the Kremlin in its hopes of exporting Communist revolution with its soldiers. The Second World War was terrible in its spread of death and devastation, but it was singularly apolitical in its effects.

It was a revelation of the remarkable strength of the modern nationalistic state. While the Napoleonic wars were the first great manifestations of popular nationalism, they were still fought by armies in which the mercenary was common, in which men of all nations found themselves suffering by choice or accident under strange flags, and in which internal dissension and even mutiny were not uncommon. In the American Civil War, the Northern copperheads and Southern appeasers and recalcitrants were constant problems for both governments. A draft act could still produce bloody riots and resistance in the North; a Southern effort to combine the railways into a national military transport system could still go to pieces on the rocks of individual initiative among the railway companies. Late in the war the South, in its management of the vital blockade-running business, was still experiencing difficulty in disentangling the claims of private enterprise from those of national survival. Lincoln was never allowed to forget the foundations in party politics on which his administration, and with it the survival of the Union, rested; and in the conduct of the war he made concessions to partisan considerations which in a modern President would not seem allowable.

In the crisis of 1914 the world was somewhat surprised when the socialist parties in all the belligerent nations enthusiastically backed that capitalist, imperialist (but also nationalist) war against which they were supposed to be aligned. The tremendous centripetal power of nationalism was so little understood as late as 1917 that many seriously doubted in that year whether the United States could conscript its citizens for battle. The doubt was unfounded; but popular dissent still had a powerful leverage upon history, especially when expressed by men with guns in their hands. The peace movement at the end of 1916 evoked a popular response which seriously alarmed the leaders in all the belligerent powers. It was the mutiny of the Russian soldiers and people in 1917 which overthrew the Czardom and took Russia out of the war. The French Army mutinies in the same year for a time virtually paralyzed the state. In 1918 it was the war weariness of the German people, brought to a head by a mutiny in the German Navy, which shattered Ludendorff's nerve and so made plain the defeat to which the generals in fact had come.

There were no similar episodes in 1945; the modern state, whether democratic or totalitarian, had learned to insure against their recurrence.

Since the great mobilization of the First War, a quasi-religious nationalism had been sedulously cultivated in the United States. It had acquired its creed (the oath of allegiance), its icons (the Flag), its ritual observances (the elaborate ceremonial drill with which patriotic societies like the American Legion, to say nothing of the armed forces, surrounded the nationalist symbols). At the end of the nineteenth century the scarcely radical New York *Journal of Commerce* had deplored the "artificial patriotism" being worked up at the time and the "remarkable fashion of hanging the flag over every schoolhouse and of giving the boys military drill." A half century later a national commander of the American Legion could nostalgically recall the days when people saluted the flag not just because they "had to"; and, unaware that they frequently never saluted it at all, could advocate a compulsory, ritual patriotism to restore the "old" faith.

The First War and its aftermath had converted most Americans to this ritualistic attitude toward the state. Its symbols were of great power, beauty and emotional force. Only a rather cheap cynicism could remain unmoved as the flag is brought down at sunset in some distant foreign post; or could fail to "salute the quarter deck" of a naval vessel whose people (in the old naval phrase) had, perhaps, done bloody and agonizing things in defense of their community. To hold that such rituals are meaningless would be to deny much in our social heritage. But that they brought a powerful reinforcement to the monolithic and warlike state is hardly controvertible. By 1941 it was universally assumed that war would require the general conscription of manpower, heavy taxation distributed as equitably as possible among all, price controls, rationing and governmental allocation of raw materials, a massive governmental intervention directly into private industry with government-built armament plants and transportation facilities. The press bowed immediately to a voluntary censorship which was to be dutifully observed. No one doubted the necessity for a considerable secret police—the

FBI—to protect against spies and saboteurs. Few even questioned so brutal an invasion of individual rights as the concentration and removal from the West Coast of some 80,000 American citizens of Japanese ancestry. A degree of regimentation and centralization which was never possible during the Civil War, which was still at least strange and disquieting after 1917, had by 1941 become no more than a normal and patently necessary order of affairs.

The centralized modern state had developed into an incomparable instrument for waging war. Whether in its totalitarian or democratic form, it could now mobilize its entire people, command all their loyalties and energies, provide them with weapons of incredible intricacy and give them command and staff organizations capable of utilizing their resources and their sacrifices with efficiency. The state could guarantee something like a just wage to its combatants, with paternal care thereafter. It could not avoid condemning a certain number of its citizens to being blasted or burned or shot to death, to enduring tortures by fire or evisceration possibly worse than those of earlier wars. But it was at least as economical as possible of such sacrifices, while the enormous strides of modern medicine enabled it to mitigate the agonies to a significant extent. It could provide its troops with clothing, housing, food and comforts of previously impossible excellence. By these and many other methods it demonstrated its capacity to hold the loyalty of its citizens through strains unparalleled in earlier wars; it was armored within as well as without; it had sufficiently reconciled its own internal struggles of class and interest to enter with confidence any war which might threaten it.

Unfortunately, in making itself into a superb instrument of scientific war, it had not been able to prevent other great states from doing the same thing. It had failed to reduce the institution of war itself to a usable and practicable instrument of policy—a means, that is to say, of adjusting the relations of peoples and securing the necessary decisions between their clashing interests at a bearable cost in other human values. In the newly shattered world of late 1945, with the first atomic clouds drifting away like great question marks upon the sky, this fact stood starkly on the world's intellectual horizons.

For the Second World War, unlike any earlier struggle in its origins, its character and its development, was even more dramatically different in its end. The argument as to whether the Hiroshima and Nagasaki atomic bombs "caused" the Japanese surrender seems somewhat academic. There is much reason to believe that without them events would have proceeded much as they actually did; but whatever their influence upon the war just closing, their enormous significance was for the future. Here in the very last days of the great conflict the power of airborne demolition bombardment had been suddenly stepped up by a factor of 20,000. Nothing like this had ever happened before. The weapons and techniques developed in the course of earlier wars had usually carried important hints of coming change, but no one such revolutionary change as this had actually been demonstrated. This eleventh-hour triumph of the embattled scientists altered at a stroke almost every calculation and every formula on which statesmen, strategists and military technicians had been accustomed to rely. The general staffs of 1914—highly trained, thoroughly expert and devoted men of war—had compounded a disaster for which there seemed no answer. So the mobilized scientists of 1945—also highly trained, expert and devoted to the furtherance of the country's interest—had compounded a terrible problem for which no rational solution was apparent to themselves or to anyone else. Science—building upon the work of the patriot democrats of 1776, upon the creators of the Napoleonic mass army, the steam engineers and technologists of the mid-nineteenth century, the managerial skills of the general staffs and big industry and much more beside—had produced in the nuclear weapon something which at least looked like the negation of all war. This fact was so extraordinary in human experience that the ten years between the end of the Second War in 1945 and the Geneva Conference in mid-summer of 1955 were devoted to the attempt to assimilate and adjust to it. The attempt was to be at best only partially and precariously successful; but it remains the central theme of the last decade of international and military history.

CHAPTER VI

The Hypertrophy of War

1.

SUPERFICIALLY, the situation at the end of 1945 resembled that at the end of 1918 in many ways. As the Second World War was ending a thousand newspaper editorials and political utterances had announced that this time we would not repeat the 1918 mistake of disarming; yet the World War II hosts were to dissolve almost as rapidly as their predecessors. The combat divisions were "inactivated"; the huge fleets, including many fine and costly ships which had never seen service, went into "mothballs"; billions of dollars' worth of planes and equipment were left to rust in the pipelines or disintegrate on storage fields. The statesmen addressed themselves to setting up another world organization which would render another war impossible. The soldiers, sailors and airmen turned to re-establishing a peacetime military structure which would make it possible to refight another war like that of 1941-45. The scientists hoped to undo their terrible work and sought, with many others, to remove nuclear weapons as instruments of warfare, just as so many in 1918 had pinned all their hopes on disarmament. The flavor of 1918 was strong in all these efforts. Unfortunately, the time was not 1918; it was 1946.

President Roosevelt had learned just before his death that his final effort to establish, at Yalta, a practicable coexistence between the Soviet Empire and the West had probably ended in failure. President Truman was to face the grim fact in the first hours of his incumbency: it meant that unless the failure could somehow be repaired, the new world organization could not function as had been hoped. Without an effective United Nations the development of sound foreign and economic policy was bound to be difficult enough. But the development of sound military policy was to be almost impossible. The Truman administration was at least professedly committed to the view that in face of this dubious and dangerous situation the nation should remain militarily strong; but no one knew what measure of strength to apply nor, indeed, what constituted military strength under the complex new conditions.

We confronted a world which would be dominated by three major factors all quite foreign to our own experience and even to the experience of Western Europe. The first was the emergence of the United States into a position of power and responsibility beyond anything of which we had ever dreamed; the second was the rise of the Soviet Union, a rival and obviously hostile system, to a position of about equal power, leaving all the rest of the world more or less helplessly polarized between these two giant centers of strength; the third was the development of the new warfare, which had reduced all conventional military and diplomatic solutions to uncertainty. The first two factors created a power problem unique in modern history; the third introduced problems in the organization and application of power almost equally novel.

While the air-delivered atomic weapons were by far the most salient features in this third problem, they were by no means the only ones. Much else had invaded the once pure sanctuaries of the general staffs: "psychological warfare," propaganda, policy aims, infiltrative methods, espionage, terror, threat, "economic warfare," industrial base, and many other methods by which one nation might affect the fortunes and policies of another beside the simple detonation of high explosive. In 1914-18 it had been politically and psychologically possible to give a whole generation of young men into the hands of the military specialists to be slaughtered for no very apparent reason. In the inter-war period this had already come to seem impracticable to nearly everyone outside the totalitarian dictatorships. Yet in the Second War it was not merely the young men but whole populations who were exposed to death, agony and destruction. Upright and thoughtful soldiers like Eisenhower, Bradley, and Ridgway could still insist upon a rigid division between the "military" and "political" spheres in policy; yet this division (if it ever really existed) had been largely erased in fact. Unfortunately, there remained no clear and effective way of dealing with either sphere under the twin shadows of the new power complex and the new weapons.

Here the United States was more fortunate than other nations. The armed services had never been a political force of any consequence in themselves. We had never had to deal with a military caste or camarilla of the kind which had so often elsewhere pulled the strings of policy in its own institutional interest. We had the history of the Grand Army of the Republic, of the "militia interest" at the turn of the century, of the American Legion in the '20's, to remind us that soldiers and ex-soldiers could be organized into powerful pressure groups. A Wood, a Mitchell or a MacArthur might awake memories of a McClellan or a Butler from the Civil War era; but all these were essentially soldiers acting as civil politicians, not military politicians exercising the power of the bayonet in civil affairs. The "political general" of Europe was to us an almost unknown species. Yet the professional officer corps of the three services unavoidably constituted interest groups, each supported by powerful private industrial interests.

This last was particularly true of the air components. From the time of Eli Whitney down to the end of the First War the armament industry in the United States was never more than auxiliary to the great enterprises which found their main business in supplying a usually ravenous civilian market. The steel, shipbuilding and other powerful industries might promote military orders in times of recession or as profitable *lagniappe* (as was alleged against the shipbuilders at the time of the Coolidge naval conference) when an opportunity offered. Holders of armament patents might lobby fiercely to secure acceptance of their particular product as against rivals. Generally, however, it has overwhelmingly been government's demand (often government's ukase) which has evoked profitable armament enterprise in this country, rather than a thirst for profits which has instigated the government demand. This was more or less true of the development of the aircraft industry. But the multi-billion-dollar aviation industrial complex almost wholly dependent on government orders with which we emerged from the Second War provided something of a new phenomenon. With the end of the war, government buying was a much larger fraction of every industry's market than it had been before. The rival armed service interest groups, with such powerful forces as these behind them, did not simplify the problem of designing rational military policy in the murky atmosphere of late 1945 and 1946.

Each of the three services (and they were by this time three in fact, though not yet in the letter of the law) emerged from the conflict with its own plans for the future. No one of the plans was correlated to the other two. On none had the atomic bombs left any visible trace; it was hardly possible that they could do so since official policy was directed toward the abolition of the weapons and their future even on technical grounds was still completely obscure. The Navy contented itself with indicating the large number of ships and air groups which it felt to be indispensable to fulfilling its missions in routine peacetime operation. The Army was scarcely able, in the context of the times, to propose a fixed number of divisions to be permanently maintained (most of the divisions it had were draining away beneath it all too rapidly as it was) and it made its major plea for a return to the old idea of Universal Military Training.

UMT had been kicking about for the past thirty years. Its principal virtue (and reason for its longevity) would seem to be that it represented about the nearest that this country was ever likely to come in peacetime to the European conscript system. In theory, it would enable us to carry on with only a small, professional standing army by providing a trained male populace—something like the hardy frontiersmen of the distant past—from whom it would be possible promptly to fill whatever divisions another emergency might require. To many, including most of the Congressmen who then and thereafter were called upon to judge it, it looked like a bad compromise. Even the theory was questionable. The essence of the 1914 European universal conscription systems was not that they permitted a small standing army to substitute for a big one. On the contrary, their purpose was to make it possible to expand the largest practicable standing army into something much larger still. So far from allowing a reduction in the regular forces, they compelled an expansion of the standing army to the maximum economic limits, in order that it could receive and train a maximum of conscripts, to pass them then into a compulsory and genuinely mobilizable reserve, instantly available. The European systems of 1914 were in no sense substitutes for large standing armies; they were mechanisms for mobilizing on the first days of war trained, fully officered and weaponed forces on a scale much larger than could be maintained in time of peace. But to do it, the peacetime establishment had to be maintained not on the smallest but on the greatest possible scale of strength.

Forces comparable to the reserve divisions deployed in 1914 could not possibly be created out of a horde of unorganized civilians with a smattering of some basic training. Even the old frontier farmers, who possessed the essential military skills of the time—marksmanship, woodsmanship and knowledge of survival techniques—often made very indifferent soldiers. And a few months' "basic" for all would make little difference today in the supply of the complex technical skills required by modern warfare. UMT was no real alternative even for the 1914 type conscription system; and by 1945 that system was itself largely outmoded. Probably the only valid alternative to universal conscription is the "Swiss system," in which the regular army is reduced to the smallest possible professional cadre, all the rest being drafted for part-time training comparable to that in our National Guard. But the Swiss system was never suitable to a power of world-wide and frequently aggressive responsibilities; while it may be doubted whether it is technically adequate today, even for a people in the peculiar and protected situation of the Swiss. UMT always had an air of unreality about it that proved fatal to its acceptance. President Truman has explained his own support of the proposal on the grounds that:

> This was not a military training program in the conventional sense. The military phase was incidental to what I had in mind. While the training was to offer every qualified young man a

chance to perfect himself ... in some military capacity, I envisioned [sic] a program that would at the same time provide ample opportunity for self-improvement. Part of the training was calculated to develop skills that could be used in civilian life, to raise the physical standard of the nation's manpower, to lower the illiteracy rate, to develop citizenship responsibilities and to foster the moral and spiritual welfare of our young people.[1]

This was, indeed, one of the worst troubles about the whole proposal. Here was the ancient notion that military training is really only a school for the moral and civic virtues. It is a notion which at worst leads directly into the regimented state (the elders and the élite training the young in what is good for them) and at best into an exposure of the hollowness of most current military plan and thought. The young will readily accept military training if they think the state really may have need of their battle services. But once they are told that their government's principal interest is in their physical improvement and their "moral and spiritual welfare" they are likely to lose their enthusiasm.

Meanwhile, the Army Air Force had arrived, by a process never clearly explained to the public, at the somewhat mystic figure of seventy air groups as the fixed, irreducible minimum of regular air power. This figure should be achieved and thereafter firmly maintained through a future in which every factor which one might suppose would affect air policy promised to shift with the utmost fluidity and unpredictability. Since the actual land-based air requirements of the next few years were all but impossible even to estimate, it seems reasonable to infer that it was a figure resting more on a deduction as to what the taxpayer would stand for and the air industry could reasonably supply than on a calculation of the probable military requirements. The Army Air Force was in fact in a somewhat embarrassing position. So bitter had been the arguments over air power, going back to the times of "Billy" Mitchell, that the Roosevelt administration established, as the war drew toward its close, the United States Strategic Bombing Survey, to move in with the conquering armies, examine the ruins and the

[1] Harry S. Truman, *Memoirs* (Garden City, Doubleday, 1955), Vol. I, p. 511.

results and report upon the facts. The findings were embodied in over two hundred detailed reports, many of them subsequently published in pamphlet form. They varied in point of view and precision of analysis; but it would probably be fair to summarize the net conclusion as showing that strategic bombing, when armed only with TNT and incendiary weapons, had cost much more in over-all effort, had involved much greater casualties and had produced much smaller military results than had been expected. The evidence was fairly overwhelming that the TNT bomb, even in its later "blockbuster" sizes, had been a relatively ineffective weapon in terms of the life, money and manpower put into its manufacture and delivery.

What the results of this conclusion would have been without the appearance of the atomic bomb it is of course impossible to say. It is at least a question whether the heavy, strategic bomber might not, like the battleship, have passed from the scene as a primary weapon. The British had estimated during the mid-period of the conflict that to wage effective independent air war on Germany would call for an operating fleet of some 4,000 heavies, not counting reserves and replacements. In the spring of 1944, when the air war on Germany began to show some real results, there were about 5,000 British and American heavies committed to the effort. The Air Force seventy-group program called for only twenty-one groups of heavies, or an operating force of only 630 heavy bombers. In view of the wartime results, it seems fantastic to suppose that such a force, armed only with TNT, could have exerted any significant influence over international events, or over the course of a war should one break out. But the Air Force was no longer confined to TNT. In 1946 and 1947 no one could talk as if the atomic bombs formed a part of our military-diplomatic arsenal. We were committed to their neutralization or abolition; Air Force spokesmen rarely even mentioned their existence. Yet they were in existence; and it was this fact alone which lent any color of reality to the Air Force seventy-group program.

While the Truman administration maintained minimum Army and Marine occupation forces in the many troubled areas abroad, the basic military structure was liquidated in the tides of demobilization. The uncoordinated plans of the three services made little sense, and it was becoming more and more obvious that nothing could be done to meet the military problem until the whole system could be revised. Superficially, at least, it seemed in a completely anomalous state. In addition to its gunnery ships, the Navy had its own aviation, its own army (the Marines) and even its own peculiar kind of army aviation in the Marine air squadrons. The Army, on the other hand, while possessing a small naval transport and landing equipage, had no aviation of its own at all; for air support it was wholly dependent on the Army Air Force, which admitted only a distant responsibility to the General Staff and was primarily committed to its doctrine of independent air power. But while effective independent, strategic air power already rested almost wholly on the possibilities of the nuclear arsenal, the Air Force had no control over its development or even its custody, both of which were vested by the Atomic Energy Act of 1946 in a wholly civilian commission. Congress at the same time saw fit to wrap the entire subject of atomic energy in veils of "security" thicker than had ever been applied in any previous military legislation. As we were later to discover, the result was not to "preserve the secret," but to render it almost unmanageable by either military, political or public opinion. The reorganization of the military system had become imperative; it was to take some two years of argument before a new structure could be set up and put into operation, but until this was done American military power, as an effective instrument in the contemporary diplomatic context, was to remain largely in abeyance.

As the war ended, the idea of a complete unification which would abolish the services as such and put everyone into "one uniform" under a single head was popular with many top commanders. They had been through too many interservice as well as international jealousies, while they had found that in the field the system of integrating all forces under a single commander, regardless of whether he wore an Army, Navy or Air Force hat, had worked well. But even during the war, this kind of integration had never carried back to the high administrative levels in Washington; while as the prospect of unlimited appropriations for everybody began to dwindle with the war's end, the savagery of the inter-service competition for what might be left began proportionally to rise. "One uniform" would mean a single Chief of Staff; under the circumstances and attitudes of the time, he would almost certainly be an air general, committed to the air power theory of warfare. The ground army, which had no aviation of its own, was willing to accept this. The Navy, with its very large investment in air power, with visions of its airplanes being appropriated by the Air Force and its Marine divisions captured by the Army, was not.

The Navy made its resistance effective. Its Secretary, James Forrestal, deputed Ferdinand Eberstadt, an old associate in the New York investment banking field who had served on the War Production Board and in other high Washington posts, to make an enquiry into the whole subject; and the Eberstadt report was to become the basis of the act finally adopted. It recommended a "coordinated" rather than a "unified" structure. The core of the problem was, of course, the Army Air Force. Its wartime performance, its enormous growth and its own claims to independence made it impossible for it to continue as an even technically subordinate part of the ground army. The only practicable alternatives were one service or three; the Eberstadt report recommended three coequal services, these to be coordinated, however, under an over-all Secretary of Defense with a small administrative staff of his own, and under the Joint Chiefs of Staff as a corporate body with a statutory recognition which the Joint Chiefs had not enjoyed during the war.

In its effort to retain the virtues of both unity and diversity the Eberstadt report made other important recommendations. It was much concerned with the necessity for a higher integration which would relate military policy more directly to diplomatic and economic policy. It proposed the National Security Council, intended to institutionalize the relations between the political and military heads; it proposed the National Security Resources Board, intended to relate military plan to its bases in manpower, raw material and industrial resources. By placing the Central Intelligence Agency under the NSC it sought to bring order and efficiency not only into the collection but into the use of intelligence. These broad and bold objectives were to escape many commentators at the time. What was immediately visible was that out of all the pressure for "unification" in 1946 there emerged, with the 1947 act, three services instead of two, plus a fourth bureaucracy, the Department of Defense, to control the three and a number of new agencies to control or assist the Department of Defense. Yet experience seems only to have confirmed the conclusion that in 1947 neither the tactical nor strategic lessons of the Second War, still less the requirements of the future, had been worked out far enough to permit of a unitary solution. Had a monolithic military system been adopted in 1947, it would hardly have worked well in face of the complex and fluid crises which we were subsequently to confront.

Many Congressmen who supported the 1947 "unification" act did so under the impression that it was going to save money. But this was neither its primary purpose nor, markedly, its effect. Its aim was to provide the United States with a coherent and self-consistent system of military-political direction, fully informed by the best intelligence available, provided with sound industrial and resources planning and so organized that it might ensure that the broad international objectives of the American people would be realized as efficiently as possible. Of course, the aim was not achieved. The new structure could be (and unfortunately was) used to "save money," but it could not indicate whether the savings were safe or even advisable. Probably nothing, not even totalitarian dictatorship, could have created the mechanism of completely correlated and completely logical national policy formation which the Eberstadt report envisaged. It was impossible, for example, that the National Security Council, a board of appointed (not elected) officials, meeting in secret to adopt secret policy papers based on the secret intelligence supplied by the CIA, could shape the national policy of the American democracy. The Joint Chiefs of Staff, who had provided a magnificent instrument of centralized command under the unifying, simple and direct pressures of war, were less successful amid the less urgent but far more complicated divisions and distractions of peace. It turned out that the new Secretary of Defense was to have much more difficulty than had been anticipated in "coordinating" the fiercely jealous services over which he was appointed to preside; the result was to be a gradual but steady accumulation of centralized power in the hands of the civilian Defense

Secretary, which while doubtless unavoidable has seemed to many to carry with it certain of the dangers which the Eberstadt "coordinate" system was intended to avert.

The National Security Act of 1947 was a far more sophisticated piece of legislation than its predecessor, the National Defense Act of 1920. To a greater degree than the 1920 measure, it was oriented toward a fluid and unpredictable future rather than toward the immediate past. Where the 1920 measure sought in general to maintain a military machine for refighting the war just over, the 1947 act sought to create a policy-making system which could determine from time to time, in accordance with the changing realities of the international scene, what sort of military machine might be required. It was an effort at the higher organization and control of the enormous political, economic, psychological and military power generated by the modern state. It was an effort to harness these powers to civilian domination and make them into an effective instrument of policy within the framework of free, popular government. In this, it was at most only partially successful. Both military and diplomatic policy after 1947 were often as fumbling and confused as they had been before. It is difficult to regard the military policies which were in force on the eve of the first Russian nuclear explosion, on the eve of Korea, on the approach of the Indo-China crisis, in face of the growing threat in the Straits of Formosa, as models of clarity, firmness and adequacy. But until the passage of the 1947 act it had been virtually impossible to have any military policy at all.

2.

When James Forrestal took office as first Secretary of Defense in the late summer of 1947, the nation was facing a situation as grim as it had been, largely, unforeseen. Over a year before, in March 1946, Winston Churchill had journeyed to Fulton, Missouri, to issue his call for a "fraternal association of English speaking peoples" in opposition to Soviet encroachment. It had been received with considerable American skepticism. A year later the facts were incontrovertible. The Soviet Union had consolidated much of its satellite empire in Central Europe and was intensifying a remorseless pressure on territories beyond—on Czechoslovakia, Greece and Turkey. General Marshall's mission to China in 1946 had ended in failure; and it was clear that in Korea and North China the Soviet Union would permit no solution which did not establish its own power in those areas. The possibility that Italy would be taken by her own Communists was more and more ominous. There was now a full-scale civil war in Indo-China of the bitterest kind, the rebellion being led by the Moscow-trained Ho-Chi Minh. Palestine presented a seemingly ineradicable cancer. Western Europe was still prostrate, and something like a quarter of the French electorate was voting Communist. The United Nations which, it had been hoped, might deal with the problems of reconstruction, was virtually paralyzed by the Soviet-Western quarrel.

In early 1947 Britain had announced her inability to carry the burden in Greece any longer. It led to President Truman's announcement in March of the "Truman Doctrine," that "it must be the policy of the United States to support free peoples who are resisting attempted subjugation by armed minorities or by outside pressures," and to his demand upon Congress for $400 million to provide military and economic aid to Greece and Turkey. In June General Marshall, now Secretary of State, announced the "Marshall Plan" of massive economic aid to Western Europe. When the Soviet Union in effect ordered its Western satellites to have nothing to do with the proposal it seemed a plain declaration of the "cold war." Support for Greece and Turkey was (as it was to remain) economic and advisory only; but everywhere there was danger, everywhere our ultimate commitments had enlarged, and nowhere did we have any really ready and applicable force with which to meet them. At an NSC meeting early in 1948 Secretary Marshall summed up the situation: "He said that the trouble was that we are playing with fire while we have nothing with which to put it out." [2]

The National Security Act had looked toward the future; in one sense it had looked too exclusively toward the future. While Forrestal in late 1947 and early 1948 was still trying to put the new machinery

[2] James Forrestal, *The Forrestal Diaries* (New York, Viking, 1951), p. 373.

together and bring some real co-ordination to the warring services, the problem was still being conceived in future terms. The new mechanisms were designed to meet "another," presumably remote, emergency—such as a fire in a dwelling-house, which might or might never come. They had not been designed to provide present power to meet the actual and urgent crises which were growing before our eyes and which might be compared to a steady slipping of the foundations under the house in which we sat. Nor was it easy to see the developing international problem in these harsh terms of power politics. To many at the time the business of rooting out domestic spies, treasonable policy-makers and Communist conspirators seemed much more important (as it was also cheaper and easier) than the deployment of effective force against Communist expansion on the world stage. It was on the morrow of his announcement of the Truman Doctrine that the President formally established the system of testing all Federal employees for "loyalty"; while it was only a few days later that the extended Selective Service system was allowed to expire, thus continuing the skeletonization of the armed forces under the pressures for retrenchment.

We were "playing with fire with nothing to put it out." Nothing, that is, save one recourse—the atomic bomb monopoly. Before the United Nations we were still committed to the total abolition of atomic energy as a military instrument, but the new Atomic Energy Commission had by this time got the manufacture and development of these weapons back again to a high level and the nuclear arsenal began to play a larger and larger part in at least unofficial strategic plan and theory. The new Department of the Air hardly concealed its intense preoccupation with nuclear weapons; it was at the time fighting a bitter feud with the Navy for exclusive control of these devices. In January 1948 the Finletter Commission on Air Policy issued its report; this was framed wholly around the nuclear weapons of mass destruction, and its recommendations were based upon its predictions as to how soon Russia could be expected to penetrate "the secret." After the Finletter report, the public probably assumed that air-borne nuclear weapons were the only significant measures of military power.

To many conventional soldiers and sailors, however, such as Bradley, now Army Chief of Staff, and to many civilian administrators, such as Forrestal, the atomic monopoly seemed inapplicable to the actual military problems confronting us. How could one use atomic bombs to control the course of events in Greece? Or in Central Europe? Or in China or Korea or any other of the potentially dangerous situations confronting our policy? Whatever the future of the atomic weapons might be, Forrestal was acutely aware, as he put it, of "the limitations of our military power to deal" in the existing context "with the various potentially explosive areas over the world."

On February 18, 1948 Major General Alfred M. Gruenther, then director of the Joint Chiefs' joint staff, appeared to "brief" a White House gathering including the President, Marshall, Forrestal and others. His figures showed that the mighty wartime host of some 13,-000,000 uniformed men and women had sunk to an aggregate of only 1,374,000. Ground troops, Army and Marine, came to 631,000 effectives. Of these, 253,000 were on occupation duty in Europe and the Far East. After further substracting the huge overhead for administration and training—pledges against a possible all-out emergency—Gruenther could find only 2⅓ below-strength Army divisions and eleven Marine battalion landing teams as reserves currently available for putting out the fires with which General Marshall felt that we were playing. Gruenther mentioned Greece, Italy, Korea and Palestine as possible "explosive points," and observed that to employ more than one division in any of these areas would necessitate a "partial mobilization." [3]

Curiously enough, the quarter of a million armed men maintained on occupation duty in Germany and Japan were written off in this calculation; as late as the summer of 1948 they were regarded in the Pentagon as "political" forces unavailable for "military" planning. In the occupation forces combat training was allowed to sink to a low level; they were neither equipped, trained nor organized as more than a constabulary, and the divisions in the Far East were to pay heavily in life for this fact when, in July 1950, they were abruptly required for battle action. If General Gruenther had included the occupation

[3] Forrestal, *op. cit.*, pp. 374 f.

troops in his showing, he might have made it a little better; but considering their actual state of readiness it would not have been much better.

Just six days after the White House briefing the first "explosive point"—though not one listed by General Gruenther—blew up. On February 24 the Communists seized power in Czechoslovakia, and the last remaining Central European democracy passed behind the Iron Curtain.

To the Western world, the shock was profound. The subversion of whole nations, first by the Nazis and Fascists, later by the Communists, through the new methods of internal propaganda and conspiracy backed by external military force had become a commonplace. The victims, however, had typically been backward and disordered states with no strong democratic tradition to preserve them. Czechoslovakia was the first (as it is still the only) modern, liberal and prosperous capitalistic democracy to be overthrown by these techniques. It had been completely overrun and conquered by Hitler in 1939, but had still been able to rise from the ruin with its popular, capitalistic-democratic government intact. Now it had been swallowed, presumably forever, by Communist totalitarianism. This was a new form of warfare, in which rifles, artillery and high explosive offered no very certain recourse.

For Czechoslovakia there was no answer. It was a *fait accompli*. But if artillery and high explosive could not reverse the event, it still seemed essential for the Western democracies to get some artillery and high explosive at hand to prevent its recurrence. It was the Czechoslovak crisis in February 1948 which first seriously called in question the whole structure of American military planning since 1945. Alone, it would probably have led to some revision of our military as well as of our diplomatic policies. But it did not stand alone.

On March 5 there was a secret telegram of the most alarming import from General Lucius D. Clay, the American military governor in Berlin:

> For many months, based on logical analysis, I have felt and held that war was unlikely for at least ten years. Within the last few weeks I have felt a subtle change in Soviet attitude which I

cannot define but which now gives me a feeling that it may come with dramatic suddenness. . . .

General Clay explained that he had nothing specific on which to sustain this "feeling," but its effect on the White House and the Pentagon was cataclysmic. The CIA went furiously to work; not for eleven days was it to come up with an "appreciation," and the farthest this ventured to go was the conclusion that major war was not probable within sixty days.[4] On March 17 the President went before Congress to deliver in person a forceful message, identifying the Soviet Union as the "one nation" blocking all efforts to re-establish peace, as a "growing menace" pursuing a "ruthless course of action" with the "clear design to extend it to the remaining free nations of Europe." The Soviet Union was thus wholly responsible for "the critical situation in Europe today"; and the position of the United States "should be made unmistakably clear. . . There are times in world history when it is far wiser to act than to hesitate."

Unfortunately, the United States at that moment had neither a "clear" diplomatic position nor a military plan which would permit it to "act." The services were still deep in their quarrel over strategic concepts. Only the week before, Secretary Forrestal, by dint of dragging the Joint Chiefs away from their Washington desks and telephones to the seclusion of the Key West naval base, had just managed to get an agreement of sorts upon the "roles and missions" of the several services. The real argument, of course, was over possession of the atomic bomb, and the result was only another uneasy compromise. In return for recognizing the Air Force's sole right to maintain a "strategic air arm" and its paramount authority over the atomic bombs (whenever the President might release them), the Navy was "not to be denied the use of the A-bomb" against such specifically naval targets as submarine pens or air bases being used for coastal and maritime war. It was also to be allowed to continue with its projected giant aircraft carrier, designed for planes capable of carrying the atomic weapons; and it was allowed to retain its Marine Corps, provided that it did not again convert it into another "land army" like

[4] Forrestal, op. cit., pp. 387 f.

that which had been so successful and necessary in 1943-45. All that the Army got was support from the others for its much-desired UMT project, together with agreement that it should have a modest increase in its current troop strength. To provide this last, the Joint Chiefs would urge Congress to re-enact the expired Selective Service Act.

This compromise would no doubt have served well enough against war dangers not expected to materialize for another ten or twenty years. As an allotment of troop strengths and missions to meet the international issues then immediately before us it was very weak. It certainly provided no plan for action in the suddenly tense March of 1948. While the President's message on the 17th was forceful enough in tone, all that it actually asked for was adoption of the Marshall Plan, enactment of UMT and a "temporary" re-enactment of Selective Service "in order to maintain our armed forces at their authorized strength."

On the last day of the month another telegram from Clay brought the first hint of what was to become the Berlin Blockade; it was alarming, but the crisis appeared to pass. The Central Intelligence Agency had extended its forecast of peace. Meanwhile, there was obviously no possibility of getting any large rearmament program either through the Congress, which the Republicans had captured in the 1946 elections, or even through Mr. Truman's Budget Bureau. The regular budget, submitted at the beginning of the year, had asked $11 billion for defense. On March 25 Secretary Forrestal proposed a modest supplemental program. He first set UMT apart as a "long-term" proposal, thus exposing it to the defeat which was probably inevitable anyway; for the "short term" he asked an additional $775 million for airplane procurement and research, and for a re-enactment of the draft to add about 250,000 men to the Army and the Marines. The whole program would increase the budget by about $3 billion, and in the opinion of the Joint Chiefs would provide a rationally "balanced" expansion of the forces.

It ran into immediate trouble, for it provided for only fifty-five Air Force air groups instead of the mystic seventy which had for so long been the aviators' goal. The Air Force, though supposedly committed to the JCS recommendation through its own Chief of Staff, General Carl ("Touhey") Spaatz, lost no time in making it plain that whatever else was or was not done it would have to have the seventy groups. But Forrestal had no desire to see military policy distorted into a primarily air power concept and was chiefly interested in getting more ground forces for immediate use. He clung to the principle of "balance," and sought to escape the dilemma by demanding an estimate from the Joint Chiefs of the minimum costs of a military establishment "balanced" around seventy rather than fifty-five Air Force air groups.

This was hopeless. No one, really, had the slightest interest in a "balanced" force; the essence of the argument lay in the fact that there was no agreement upon any principles by which a balance could be struck. A common theory of war, broad enough to bring all the rival arms, services and weapons into a single context, did not exist. Confronted by Forrestal's demand for an estimate of the forces necessary to "balance" seventy air groups, the Joint Chiefs could really do little more than boost the Army and Navy estimates proportionately to those for the Air Force. At this task they labored, to arrive at the conclusion that a "balance" at the seventy-group level would require a $9 billion supplemental. This was so patently impossible of acceptance by either the Democratic administration or the Republican Congress as to be hardly worth submitting. But despite all the pressure Forrestal could bring, the Joint Chiefs refused to put their signatures to anything less.

By some skillful legerdemain, the Secretary finally got them to admit that while the $9 billion supplemental (which would bring the budget to $20 billion in all) represented the bottom limit of military "need," its actual appropriation and expenditure were matters of "phasing" which only Congress could decide. He even got them to accept a supplemental of only $3.5 billion as a reasonable first phase. At that point, the Budget Bureau intervened from one side to demand that this be cut to $2.5 billion; the Congress intervened from the other side to appropriate $800 million for new airplanes outside the budget. By this time the actual military implications of the world situation, in which the re-armament debate had begun, had almost disappeared from view. So had rearmament. In the end, the President put a flat $15 billion a year ceiling on military expenditure; UMT was defeated but Selective Service re-enacted; the Army got another 100,000 men or so and the other services some increments, and the "March crisis" receded into the past.

Soviet interferences with the communications of Berlin had been growing more irritating and more threatening. But when the military appropriations bills were passed it was the approaching Presidential election which was absorbing the minds of politicians and statesmen. In the latter part of June the Republican delegates assembled for the Philadelphia convention. And then, on June 24, the day Thomas E. Dewey of New York was placed in nomination, the Russians abruptly halted all ground communications with Berlin and left some 2,000,000 inhabitants of the city's Western sectors with nothing save air transport between them and starvation.

Again there was crisis. Again there was the familiar and brutal issue in an urgent local situation: Get out, temporize or fight. And again there was nothing to fight with. President Truman in the first days flatly told his advisers that we would not get out: "there was no discussion on that point, we were going to stay period." [5] The course adopted was to temporize; and it was to prove, with the remarkable development of the air lift, brilliantly successful. But in the first days this could not be foreseen. The possibility that we might have to "fight our way back" into the city was obvious; the almost instinctive reaction was to get some force into the theater if only as a precaution. But we had no disposable force—except the atomic bombs. It was in the summer of 1948 that the atomic arsenal first entered into the context of current military-political policy.

At that time the nuclear weapons were deliverable only by the big B-29 piston-engine bombers, slow, vulnerable and with ranges insufficient to enable them to reach significant Russian targets except from European bases. On June 27 the Pentagon not only asked Clay whether he wanted a reinforcement of B-29's in West Germany but also sounded out the British as to whether they would be willing to

[5] Forrestal, op. cit., p. 454.

receive two B-29 groups on the American Air Force fields in Britain. Somewhat to the Pentagon's surprise, the British promptly agreed. The American Ambassador (Lewis Douglas) was instructed to ask the British Foreign Minister whether he had "fully explored and considered the effect of the arrival of these two groups in Britain on British public opinion." Secretary Marshall was afraid that it might be "construed as a provocative action." Not until the middle of July was the decision finally taken to dispatch the B-29's. But when at last they roared off across the Atlantic, they were bringing the nuclear weapons for the first time directly into the system of diplomacy and violence by which the affairs of peoples, were thenceforth to be regulated.

Fortunately, the B-29's were to find no further role in the Berlin crisis. Oddly enough, it has never been made clear whether they actually carried atomic weapons in their bomb bays or not. "Custody" of the weapons had been vested in the Atomic Energy Commission. It was after the bombers had arrived in England that Forrestal suggested to the President that custody should be transferred to the using services. The President, who had once observed that he did not wish "to have some dashing lieutenant colonel decide when would be the proper time to drop one," decided to leave custody with the AEC. But this does not exclude the possibility that an AEC custodian may have ridden with the B-29's; and in effect, whether or not in fact, the nuclear arsenal had been brought to Europe. The Berlin crisis itself was successfully met by diplomacy, by the staunchness of the Berliners and by the skill, courage and occasional sacrifice of the Air Force, Navy and RAF air-lift crews who kept Berlin alive. These were all essentially nonmilitary means, and the fact that they succeeded may have contributed to the continued American inattention to the military foundations of the new world order which was developing. There was no real review of the military problem. The Truman $15 billion ceiling on defense expenditure was maintained; all the pressures were for economy and we were still to be vigorously economizing when in mid-1950 the Korean War broke out.

Thus it may be said that the whole excitement over rearmament in 1948 came to nothing. Yet in another sense, 1948 represents a major divide in American military thought. The atomic bombers had gone to Britain. Secretary Forrestal was much concerned, in mid-1948, as to whether public opinion would permit the "use" of what was then believed to be our atomic monopoly in the event of major emergency. In September he called a meeting of a score of prominent newspaper publishers and editors to brief them on the Berlin crisis and to ask their views. "There was unanimous agreement that in the event of war the American people would not only have no question as to the propriety of the use of the atomic bomb but would in fact expect it to be used." [6] Thus far had we come in the acceptance of a total and indiscriminate savagery as unavoidable (and acceptable) in the waging of war between modern peoples. The bombs exploded over Hiroshima and Nagasaki had represented a one-shot, last-ditch effort, so to speak, to bring to an end a war which already had taken its toll of millions; and the first impulse in the aftermath had been to insure that such things would never be used in war again. By 1948 the impulse had died; it was plain that the atomic arsenal had entered American thought as an appropriate instrument of policy for the future.

It was still a back-door, largely unacknowledged entrance. The supposed atomic monopoly lay somewhere behind nearly every policy decision in the military field, but outwardly things went on much as before. In the spring of 1949 Forrestal was succeeded as Secretary of Defense by Louis Johnson, former Assistant Secretary of War, a man of outstanding ability but also, many thought, of corrosive political ambition. All during the spring, summer and fall of 1949 the Chinese Communist armies were pressing southward, acquiring by defection the weapons we had been supplying to their Nationalist opponents, making one conquest after another until, as the year ran out, Generalissimo Chiang Kai-shek and his Nationalist remnants were expelled into Formosa. Communist China, its writ running from the Amur to the headwaters of the Mekong and the Irrawaddy, was an international fact. There is still the most virulent

[6] Forrestal, *op. cit.,* p. 487.

dispute over the question of whether this great debacle could have been averted had the Truman administration maintained and expanded its support for Chiang and the Nationalists; in the nature of things, this is a dispute over possibilities which can never be conclusively decided. The fact is that by the summer of 1949 the disaster had reached a point at which it was no longer reversible save by a massive American military intervention, certain to expend hundreds of thousands of American lives, unlikely to succeed in the end and of a kind which no section of American opinion would at that time have supported for a moment. Secretary Johnson devoted himself not to war but to economy, where the interests of the administration and his own political future appeared to lie.

He set out to "cut the fat" from the Defense Department; and one of his first decisions was to cancel the Navy's great supercarrier. This was a reckless destruction of the extremely delicate balances which his predecessor had been at such pains to establish. Secretary Johnson may have felt that he had logic on his side, but military growth and development are not logical processes. Soldiers, no less than lawyers, priests or doctors, are human; and the great institutions over which they all preside are organic rather than mechanical growths. Forrestal sensed this fact; Johnson scorned it and the immediate result was the envenomed "B-36 controversy" between the Navy and the Air Force, with the former retaliating for the loss of its supercarrier by assailing the latter's newest superbomber as a failure. It threatened for a time to wreck all rational military planning. But something more serious was in prospect. In September 1949 the Soviet Union fired its first atomic explosion, and the supposed American monopoly was at an end.

In the most dramatic possible way, the whole military problem had been transformed. The truly awful fact of a nuclear armaments race now stared us directly in the face; the scientific revolution in warfare was, as it were, complete. Unfortunately, this grim development did not greatly contribute to clarity of thought or policy. The major response by the United States was the decision, taken in the winter of 1949-50, to proceed with an all-out effort to develop the hydrogen or "thermonuclear" superbomb. This decision was doubtless inevitable and, in the light of our later knowledge of Soviet advances in the art, essential. Yet as men like Robert Oppenheimer and his colleagues on the AEC Advisory Commission saw with anguish, it was fundamentally both negative and tragic. It committed the nation to a nuclear armaments race which no one could win, which was very likely to render the whole problem of war in our society completely insoluble and to end, not in political victory for anyone, but in the total destruction of Western civilization. Necessary as it might be, this was no solution for the real problem, which by this time had passed far beyond mere questions of defense and had become the problem of war itself, of the whole meaning, effect and function of war as a central institution in civilized society. Since 1949 it has seemed no more than common sense to do our best to stay ahead of Soviet developments in the new warfare; but this has offered at most a bleak and uncertain prospect, while for the larger problem of war nothing like an adequate solution has as yet appeared.

In the autumn of 1949, however, these truly dire issues still seemed to lie in the future. It was hopefully argued that the Russians had, after all, produced only a nuclear "explosion" and might still be years away from a deliverable atomic bomb. Secretary Johnson continued to pursue the ends of economy. The North Atlantic Treaty, creating a defensive alliance for the protection of Western Europe, had been proclaimed in mid-1949, but it had yet to be filled with any effective military content. The American divisions in Germany were scattered in occupational and constabulary duties. It was also in mid-1949 that the last of the American occupation forces had been withdrawn from South Korea; while those maintained in Japan were in an even less effective combat state than those in Germany. The Soviet atomic explosion had made it, if anything, only more difficult than before to develop a sound military plan for meeting the increasingly acute issues of the existing cold war; and our military policy seemed to sink only more deeply into the fogs of uncertainty and confusion.

And then, abruptly and rudely, the fogs were dissipated. On June 24, 1950 the North Korean armies launched their invasion across the 38th Parallel. Action of some kind was suddenly imperative.

3.

President Truman responded in two ways: by committing the United Nations to the repulse of the attack (something which was possible only because of the fortuitous absence of the Russians) and by ordering available American air and naval forces to the support of the South Koreans under this international authorization. The diplomatic move was brilliantly successful and probably alone preserved the United Nations as an influence in international relations. It plainly broadened the position of the United States from one of a purely national and narrow opposition to Soviet imperial expansion into one of leadership in a great coalition of all non-Communist nations. Had the United States elected a unilateral defense (or none at all) in Korea, it is certainly doubtful whether the alliance system, which now includes a militarily effective NATO, SEATO, the Baghdad Pact, and other political combinations, could have been brought into being. Korea was to become the foundation of the international world as it actually existed in 1955.

But if the political solutions were brilliant, the immediate military response was inadequate and came close to disaster. The initial order to back the Korean ground army with American air and naval components reflected a generation of air power theory. It reflected, indeed, all the seas of words which had been poured out since Mahan himself to prove that wars could be won by ancillary and indirect weapons without putting one's men on the ground to fight out the issue in the old and bloody way. Within two or three days it turned out that air power was not going to be enough. What air power we had available in the theater was to prove helpless to control events, as air power had proved in nearly every other crisis in which it had been independently committed. It could not stem the tide of North Korean peasant manpower rolling down the Peninsula. The Republic of Korea troops were too few, too poorly trained and equipped, to withstand the deluge; and the American infantry divisions on occupation duty in Japan had to be flung into a breach which they, likewise, had been neither trained nor equipped to hold.

Caught in a situation for which they were unprepared either morally or materially, they were swept back almost as rapidly as their Korean colleagues. They had no medium tanks or even heavy mortars. The 24th Division lost its commanding general, Dean, who was to spend the rest of the war as a Communist prisoner. Only by the most desperate effort was a position finally reconstituted on the Pusan perimeter in the extreme southeastern corner of the Peninsula; and only by the most strenuous exertions was the Pentagon able to scrape together enough usable armed power out of the skeletonized bits and pieces of the World War II military system to restore the situation.

There followed the nation's third greatest foreign war. Battle casualties reached about one-third of those suffered in the First World War. The struggle was to last for nearly three years. Because of the time it lasted and because of the short "rotation" period adopted, the number of individuals who saw combat service was probably greater in proportion to the peak strengths deployed than in any previous struggle. Yet it was strangely unlike any foreign war we had previously experienced. Officially it was not a "war" at all, but a United Nations police operation. For the first time in our history we had been surprised by a military aggression which we ourselves had done nothing to invite and which we had not foreseen. The psychological consequences were curiously contrary to what one might expect. For some forty years the war problem had almost always been debated in the United States in terms of whether to "go into" or "stay out of" wars not directly of our own making. The decision between policies which might tend to "get us in" or "keep us out" seemed always one that we could control; as a result our major wars came, when they did come, as national crusades, things essentially of our own doing and in our own vital interest and demanding a full outpouring of the national energies to the one end of victory. Here was a fairly major war suddenly launched against us for reasons over which we had no control whatever and by mysterious men whose names, even, we hardly knew. To the American people it was a truly and completely unprovoked attack. The reaction was not (as it had been to Pearl Harbor) one of massive unity in defense and retaliation; it was one, rather, of bewilderment. Nothing quite like this had ever

happened to us before; we were uncertain, divided and often unen-
thusiastic in response to the obviously great perils which it presented.

Since the war was not even distantly of our own creation, there was
no impassioned nationalistic answer to its demands. The men in Korea
were often to complain that their sacrifices got no more than inside page
attention from the press. There was a fairly constant feeling that they
were not really being backed up by either the Truman administration
or the people. The troops did not always realize the extent to which
this was due to the administration's desire to limit the ardors being
demanded of them. In the two great crusades after 1917 and 1941
military service had been for "the duration"; and the unquestioned
mood was that expressed in the celebrated World War I ditty: "We
won't be back till it's over over there!" With Korea we returned to
principles of limited liability to service at least resembling those which
had ruled in 1812, in Mexico or in 1898. The fact was that while the
troops, the government and the people were all equally desirous of
keeping the new struggle within limits, our military system had not
been prepared for this kind of thing and no one knew the answers to
the innumerable problems which it raised.

Men had to be drafted again for the duty or called unwillingly
back from the reserve. Numbers of the reserve officers and National
Guardsmen, graduates of World War II, felt that this was a form of
double jeopardy, that they had done their duty and that new men,
who had escaped prior service, should now take over. But there were
no trained new men available. Many of the men called back to active
duty proved acutely interested in going home again, whether it was
"over over there" or not. A nine-month "rotation period" was established as a rough measure of justice in a war in which only a few at
a time could be used in combat service. It was reminiscent, at least,
of the three-month and six-month terms to which early militia duty
had been limited. Rotation did not make the Korean War safe or
easy for any caught in it. Many were killed before their nine months
were up, and the West Point class of 1950, which like that of '61
was graduated directly into the holocaust, was decimated as a result.
Rotation did, however, represent an attempt at least to grapple with
some of the issues which limited war presented to a technical age in

which the old solutions of small, long-service, professional and volunteer armies were no longer viable.

The war itself had to be fought with the fragments of the World War II military establishment. The 1st Marine Division was hurriedly reassembled and thrown into Pusan as the first reinforcement. When MacArthur, against the advice of more cautious minds, insisted upon the brilliantly successful "end run" landing at Inchon, the operation was made possible only because there were enough aging World War II landing craft present and enough World War II-trained officers available for the complicated staff work. Modern planes, tanks, recoilless rifles, mines, were slow in appearing—not because the nation failed to make huge new military exertions, but because these could not produce results in time.

There was also another reason. The primary object of the immense rearmament effort which finally began in the latter months of 1950 was not victory in Korea; it was defense against a third all-out world war. The Korean onslaught had produced something close to panic in all the Western governments. The overriding thought was not the specific outcome in Korea but whether or not the Russians were about to march. All the various competitive strategic theories, with their competitive appeals for appropriations, were brushed aside. What was wanted was military strength—every and any kind of military strength—and it was wanted immediately. In the winter of 1950-51 Congress quadrupled military appropriations, raising them from the $15 billion ceiling, which Mr. Truman and his budget bureau had considered the maximum which the economy could "stand," to about $60 billion. The North Atlantic Treaty Organization, which had been mainly a political and diplomatic alliance, was abruptly converted to a straight-out military system. General Eisenhower was drafted from the presidency of Columbia University and sent back to Europe as a Supreme Allied Commander who was soon projecting a European defense force of no less than one hundred active or immediately mobilizable ground divisions.

The American occupation troops in Germany were promptly reorganized into a combat force and increased to five combat divisions, plus three armored "cavalry" regimental combat teams which were equivalent to a sixth. A huge new tank production program was put under forced draft in the United States. The Air Force and the Navy, of course, profited as well. The "B-36 controversy" was forgotten as the Navy got funds to resume building its giant carrier and the Air Force was authorized not only to complete the B-36's but to proceed with the development of the jet bombers which would replace these already semi-obsolete piston-engine giants. Korea, which was to remain a singularly old-fashioned war throughout, got only a few leavings from the Gargantuan tables of the new preparedness. There the Army and the Marines were to do the hard work in the old, hard way, not because the country was not behind them, but because under the new conditions it was so difficult properly and effectively to focus military means to real military requirements.

In Korea, the reinforcements sufficed. The Pusan perimeter was held. The Inchon landing in September cut the North Korean communications and crumpled back their lines. The war was won. By October the UN troops had virtually destroyed the North Korean armies and were fanning out rapidly beyond the 38th Parallel. In mid-October the President flew to Wake Island to meet General MacArthur. The general assured him that the war in Korea had been won (as it had been) and that there was little danger of a Chinese or Soviet intervention to reverse the verdict. The general was unaware of the fact that in those very days the large-scale introduction of organized Red Chinese armies into Korea had begun. When the action at Unsan on October 26 revealed the presence of Chinese troops in force, the warning was disregarded or explained away.

In early November the general was demanding authority to bomb the Yalu bridges on the ground that Chinese reinforcements were "pouring" across them; but some three weeks later he mounted his November 24 offensive with the unofficial word that the campaign would be over by Christmas. The offensive had barely got under way before it was hit by a counterattack delivered by some 200,000 Red Chinese troops already in Korea and massed for the blow. The result was the second Korean debacle, the bloody and disastrous retreats of the 8th Army and the 10th Corps from their exposed and divided

positions, the evacuation from Hungnam, the final, desperate recon-
stitution of a line below Seoul, the re-establishment of a military
balance. MacArthur was correct in saying that a "new war" had been
opened by the Chinese. Whether he was correct in his prescription for
meeting it is more open to question.[7]

The one salient fact was that MacArthur had been taken by surprise and badly defeated in the moment of victory. And to MacArthur
this was intolerable. Some years before, General Stilwell in Burma
had had the courage to say that "we got the hell licked out of us"
and that the problem was to go on from there; the MacArthur
genius was not capable of such admissions. Since the disaster could
not be attributed to MacArthur it had to be the fault of the Truman
administration; and from this moment there dates the theory that
if only the general had been permitted to carry the war into China
and in particular to bomb the Chinese in their "sanctuary" bases
beyond the Yalu, victory would have been achieved. The military
soundness of this contention was and still is open to serious question; certainly the Chinese were to show themselves remarkably
adept at evading air interdiction, while it is difficult to see how the
other pressures available to us (such as blockade or "population"
bombing) could have broken the Communist will and ability to
resist. For its part, the administration was not primarily interested
in "victory." Its overriding concern was to avoid enlarging the struggle
into a possible third world war, as well as to retain the support of
our allies and, consequently, the international character of the operation. The administration may well have been unduly alarmed by
the possible results of carrying the war beyond the Yalu, just as
MacArthur may have been unduly confident; since the issue was
never put to the test, it was irresolvable then and later, and served
only to plunge the country deeper into the fogs of confusion, partisan
passion and sterile controversy.

It is not surprising that the public was uncertain, unhappy, divided and misled; that angry generals exploited differences of policy
into violent controversy; or that MacArthur, relieved for insubordi-

[7] S. L. A. Marshall: *The River and the Gauntlet* (New York, Morrow, 1953),
passim.

nation if not for deliberate sabotage of the civil administration's foreign policy, should have been deferentially received before a joint session of Congress. An elaborate "investigation" into his relief, prompted by the political opponents of the President, was conducted while the war was still under way. Such an episode, though familiar enough in Civil War history, would have been almost inconceivable in the First or Second World War. It could happen in the Korean War only because this was a limited struggle and because the underlying problems of waging limited war by democratic methods in the modern age had scarcely even been discerned, much less resolved.

The war was all the more bewildering because technically and tactically it fitted none of the accepted patterns. Years of propaganda and popular journalism had pretty well convinced Americans by 1950 that air power was the primary, if not almost the only, expression of modern military power. Yet this war was essentially an infantry fight on old, familiar lines. The battles of the Saberjets and MiG's over "bomb alley" along the Yalu were important in that they prevented the Communists from moving their air forces down to intervene in the ground war. The ability of the Air Force and the Navy to deploy unopposed tactical aviation in support of the ground war was important, in that it helped redress the great numerical superiority of the Communist infantry. But the air was at most a secondary factor. Korea was basically an affair of rifle platoons— now backed, of course, by a great apparatus of artillery, mortars, machine guns and many other weapons—fighting for ground.

Through the first six months it was a war of unusually rapid movement, not because of the tank (which played a relatively small part on account of the great difficulty of the terrain) but because it took time to fill up the area with an effective balance of force. From early 1951, when more or less continuous lines began to stabilize roughly along the 38th Parallel, the conflict sank into a position war of trenches, bunkers, patrols, strikingly reminiscent of the European trench stalemate of 1915-18, which had itself followed upon a six-month initial period of maneuver war. To come back after some thirty-five years of military history—which had seen the development of the military airplane, the tank, scores of new automatic weapons, motor-powered armies and electronic communications—to a pattern so closely resembling that of a war in which none of these things had been known in more than rudimentary form, was somewhat disconcerting.

It was particularly disconcerting because it seemed so sharply to devalue the gadgets on which the West, from even the earliest days of colonial warfare, had put such immense reliance, and to enhance the value of quite different devices of which the Communists appeared to be the masters. It was alarming when the Chinese Communists demonstrated, first, that by a sufficiently lavish expenditure of human life and labor they could match our superiority in weapons and mechanical equipment; and, second, that their political system, whatever its crimes and cruelties, was still capable of mobilizing, deploying and expending human beings in the quantities required. It was not only inexplicable to us that a Communist regime could command the loyalties and enforce the sacrifices which we witnessed; it was also frightening. The huge use of coolie labor; the Chinese soldier's capacity to live on little and expend his life recklessly against better-armed foes; the patience, ingenuity and toil that went into all kinds of expedients of camouflage and cover, overcame the mechanical superiority of the West and so produced a stalemate. The enormous ammunition expenditures of the West (several times the amount, per man, employed in the Second War), the unopposed tactical aviation, the superior weapons and communications, just balanced off in that difficult terrain against the Communist superiority in numbers, fanaticism, individual stamina and ruthlessness in command.

The old days of colonial warfare, when a few European troops armed with repeating rifles and breech-loading artillery had been able to defeat hordes of semi-barbarous warriors equipped with swords, spears and perhaps a few flintlocks, had obviously passed. After what the "westernized" Japanese had done in the Second War, this demonstration of what the "Communized" Chinese were capable of was not reassuring. One thought remained at the back of most minds— the atomic bomb. If the ground war in the mountains and bunkers was a stalemate unbreakable except at an inacceptable cost in life;

if air attack on the Chinese communications beyond the Yalu was too dangerous and too unlikely to produce reward; why could we not clear up the whole business by using our omnipotent weapon within Korea? The popular compunctions which had so concerned Forrestal in 1948 had largely evaporated. By 1951 American opinion, one regrets to say, would probably have had little hesitation in incinerating any number of Communist troops—or Communist women and babies—in the nuclear fires. Two atomic bombs had apparently ended the Pacific War in 1945; why were they not employed in Korea? The answers seem reasonably evident. Aside from the danger of Soviet atomic retaliation, with the consequent precipitation of a third global war, there were apparently too few of the weapons in existence at the time to warrant squandering them in a secondary theater, and too much risk that if they were used they would prove ineffective, thus dissipating the immense diplomatic and prestige values attaching to them.

Korea, after the stabilization of the lines in early 1951, offered about the worst imaginable theater for the employment of nuclear weapons. These horrible things were primarily instruments of mass destruction, not of field tactics. Even five years later, when much had been done to develop them as tactical arms, they were still probably of greatest efficiency when used against dense population centers, where human and industrial targets are huddled together for the slaughter and where there are great numbers of buildings to provide the fuel for the fires and glass and brick projectiles for the blast, which at Hiroshima and Nagasaki had done most of the damage. In Korea there were no such centers. In the field, the innumerable mountain ridges would have confined the blast effects; the Chinese troops were deeply bunkered and thus protected against anything save a hit in their immediate area, while the Americans at that time knew almost nothing about the exploitation of such a hit for a local break-through. Not until the Dienbienphu crisis in Indo-China in 1954 were American commanders in position even to consider the tactical use of atomic bombs in this kind of warfare, and the idea was then rejected.

"The object of war," as General MacArthur sententiously observed, "is victory." But here the American people faced for the first time (at least since 1814) a situation in which "victory" had become at once too expensive in life, too barren of any visible political result and too likely to invite much greater catastrophes, to be an acceptable goal. In the late spring of 1951 the Truman administration accepted the facts and, on the merest hint from the Communist side, asked for peace negotiations. It was an experience so novel in our history that many scarcely realized that it had happened or understood that since it was the United States which had asked for negotiation, a negotiated, compromise and unavoidably unsatisfactory settlement was the most that could now be attained.

Public attention at the time was absorbed by the hearings on General MacArthur's relief; the Congressmen were raking far back into the past history of our Far Eastern policy for evidences of weakness or betrayal, or advertising (without testing) the general's very vague prescription for victory. Senator McCarthy was bringing his campaign against what he was later to call "twenty years of treason" up to its full emotional pressure. Some soldiers, like General Van Fleet, by that time in command of the 8th Army, were to argue afterward that just as they were ready to press forward to success, they had been stopped by a pusillanimous Washington for unexplained but presumably disreputable reasons. But none offered a hard estimate of the many tens of thousands of lives which a renewed effort would have cost. Nobody seriously disputed Omar Bradley, Chairman of the Joint Chiefs, when he testified that to risk enlarging the war in China would be to risk "the wrong war, at the wrong time, in the wrong place." And when the Truman administration in effect sued for peace, no voice in the United States was raised in opposition. It was only much later, after the responsibility had been taken and the hard decision made, that criticism was to assume a freer rein.

Asking for peace was not the same thing as getting it and the war—now essentially a war of positions and patrols, though far from a picnic even so—was to drag on for another two years, until the new

Republican administration was able to complete the truce on the foundations laid down by its predecessors. It had been fought out as a limited ground war, to a partial and limited solution. It was to leave many recriminations in its wake, savage and embittered dispute and little sense of either triumph or accomplishment.

Because of its association with the larger world problem, it was also to leave behind it an enormously expanded military establishment, beyond anything we had ever contemplated in time of peace. It was an establishment absorbing the energies of about 3,500,000 uniformed men and women, making peacetime conscription unavoidable; it cost three or four times the budgets which had seemed sufficient in the late '40's; it had evoked a huge and apparently permanent armament industry, now wholly dependent, through large segments, on government and on government contracts and government controls. The Department of Defense had become without question the biggest industrial management operation in the world; the great private operations, like General Motors, du Pont, the leading airplane manufacturers, which the government had evoked to assist it, had assumed positions of monopoly power which, however unavoidable, at least seemed to raise new questions as to the legal and constitutional organization of the state. The Second War was a great crusade and therefore thought of as temporary and transitory in its effects. Korea, and its surrounding circumstances, was no crusade and by that very fact embedded its consequences deep in the permanent structure of our society.

One thing, however, it did not do. It produced the thermonuclear supergiant weapons; it poured out "families" of lesser atomic bombs; it developed guided missiles, the B-52 jet bomber, the Forrestal class of heavy carriers. It produced huge new fleets of tanks and new heavy weapons. It laid an eight-year "military obligation" on every young American male and left us with an apparently permanent system of peacetime conscription. What it failed to do was to combine these men and weapons into a practicable structure of military policy competent to meet the new political and military problems that now stood grimly before us. We were to face them in a large measure of bewilderment as to where the true paths of military policy might lead.

4.

Early in 1952 General of the Army Dwight D. Eisenhower abandoned the ardors of SHAPE (Supreme Headquarters Allied Powers in Europe, by that time established at Rocquencourt, in the western suburbs of Paris) for the more exciting business of running for the Presidency of the United States. The military structure which he left behind him had been hastily planned; it was at best not half-complete, uncertain in its direction and involved in political and strategic dilemmas not yet resolved. Eisenhower himself explained that he had assumed his responsibility thinking that a unified, supranational defense of the Atlantic community would be unattainable; he laid it down convinced that there was no alternative. But other men—Ridgway, Gruenther, Montgomery, Norstad, Juin, Carney and many more besides—were left to grapple with the hard problem of implementation.

The initial impulse had been to create a mobilizable NATO ground army of perhaps one hundred active and immediately available reserve divisions, a force comparable in character and size to the Soviet and satellite ground formations. By the time of the NATO meeting in Paris in the spring of 1953 it was apparent that such goals were unrealistic. They were politically and economically unattainable. All the powers, including the United States, were revising downward their estimates of what their taxpayers would stand in the interests of military defense against the Soviet Union. Many of the projected active divisions had not been brought into being and the reserve divisions, where they existed, were far from ready. The hoped-for twelve divisions from West Germany seemed only more nebulous than ever. Large potential reserves of formed manpower, like the British Territorials or the twenty-seven American National Guard divisions, had no place in the scheme at all. Ammunition supplies for even the available NATO divisions were gravely deficient. Combat airfields were too few in number and wrongly placed; oil pipelines to fuel a fighting front were lacking; the lines of communication for the American 7th Army in central and southern

Germany ran from Hamburg parallel to the front, an arrangement which while convenient in maintaining an occupation force would be catastrophic in war. It was felt that it would be better to concentrate upon remedying these defects of the "infrastructure," as it was called in the current diplomatic-military slang, than upon creating more paper combat units.

This was no doubt sound. But even rapid advance with the "infrastructure" could not overcome the fact that the essential problems of the superstructure remained unsolved. The greatest dilemma of the NATO planners, as of the nations which they served, lay in their ignorance of what kind of war they were preparing themselves to fight. It was beyond the capability of their taxpayers to match the huge conventional forces of the Red Army and its satellites; to rely on the "deterrent" and "retaliatory" capacity of the American Strategic Air Force was an uncertain recourse and one highly dangerous to the survival of Western European civilization, the most likely target (or hostage) in an atomic struggle. Inevitably, Western soldiers began to turn back to the idea of relatively small but highly trained, highly mechanized, highly mobile and professional tactical forces, teaming ground and air and equipped with the tactical atomic weapons which were just beginning to appear in quantity. From the military no less than the politicians' point of view, the solution seemed attractive. Yet it was also an uncertain expedient; it had proved inapplicable in Korea; if consistently adopted it was sure to be enormously expensive, while the problems of fitting the new weapons into a pattern of "conventional war" were very difficult.

Meanwhile, General Eisenhowever had become President and his administration was assiduously at work upon what was to be called the "New Look" at military policy. The "crash program" attributed to the Truman administration, in which the speed and scope of the rearmament effort had been at least theoretically based upon an assumed date of maximum danger, was to be revised into a permanent program (equally theoretical) supposed to meet military needs over a "long pull," taken as a ten- or twenty-year period. All this was largely euphemism for a simple reduction in both the pace and scale of rearmament in the interests of economy and budget relief. It scarcely represented any fundamental redesign of underlying military policy, as the inconsistencies of subsequent programs and the controversies which arose over them were to demonstrate. It was mainly another military "stretch-out," but one partly concealed by a renewed emphasis on both tactical and strategic nuclear weapons. The slogan was to "substitute machines for men"; the new weapons were to fill the gaps in the front lines to which we were unwilling to assign our manpower.

These were quite obviously slogans only. Beginning with the sudden appearance of excellent Soviet jet airplanes in quantity in Korea, we had received repeated evidence of the power of the Soviet military technology. It seemed in many ways equal to our own and in some, perhaps, superior. If the West could substitute new weapons for men, it was only reasonable to suppose that Russia could do the same, and that whatever military advantage we might gain in this way would be only temporary at most. Many students thought that in the end the new weapons would actually require more men rather than fewer; just how even tactical atomic bombs would operate in another ground war in Western Europe was a problem of great obscurity, while the enormous development of nearly every other kind of weapon since 1945—a development which ten years later had completely outmoded the planes, tanks, artillery, electronics systems, submarines and anti-submarine craft and even most of the surface ships employed in the Second War—left virtually every military issue in a cloud of uncertainty.

By 1953 the problem of war in international society was coming to seem insoluble. No one knew how any of the new weapons (including an intercontinental ballistic missile apparently already on the horizon) would actually affect any given war situation. Even if the specific military results could have been predicted, no one knew how to employ such frightful panoplies so as to achieve any given political or social end—presumably the only ends for which wars are ever fought. We and most of our allies, to say nothing of the enemy, had ourselves arrived at a situation like that which startled Colonel House in Germany in 1914: "It is militarism run stark mad." But we knew, no better than the Germans, what to do about it.

For the United States the whole problem was inordinately complicated by the fact that we could no longer plan only for another world war on the 1917 and 1941 patterns. The defense of Western Europe might be difficult enough; but solutions appropriate there were almost certainly inapplicable in the Far East, where the heavy outward pressure of the Communist empire was being most severely felt. We had barely reached the unhappy compromise truce in Korea before Indo-China was seen to be in a state of extreme and dangerous crisis. The popular revulsion against the Korean War was enough to veto another such intervention; and an administration in the process of bringing its ground troops home—"disengaging"— and trying to cut military costs could not have considered it. In January 1954 the Secretary of State, John Foster Dulles, made a resounding effort to "substitute machines for men" by announcing his policy of maintaining "a capacity for retaliation by means of our own choosing."

Unfortunately, this threat of the nuclear fires was largely beside the point. It was directed specifically toward preventing a large-scale Chinese intervention, like that in Korea, on behalf of the Viet Minh; but the actual situation had deteriorated far beyond the point at which such an intervention was necessary. The nuclear threat, in short, had been aimed at an unreal and irrelevant target. When the crisis at Dienbienphu presented a true target for military action, the atomic weapons were found to be either too dangerous internationally, or too likely to be ineffective in the local military context, to be usable. The Army Chief of Staff, Ridgway, pointed out that if we were to intervene usefully in Indo-China we would have to do it with not less than six or eight ground divisions, which were the kind of troops effective in that sort of war. There were few in the United States who would have supported that kind of action; the idea was dropped—the State Department pausing only long enough to blame the decision on the British—and in the summer of 1954 another compromise peace was accepted at Geneva.

The Formosa crisis came upon the heels of that in Indo-China. The Communist government of China began to work up a virulently threatening propaganda and to prepare troop bases and airfields opposite Formosa. The United States 7th Fleet and the Air Force, acting in support of the Chinese Nationalist armies in the island, could probably have defeated any attempt on Formosa itself. But the fortified coastal islands close under the mainland shore and still held by the Nationalists, were a more difficult problem. Like the fortress of Dienbienphu, they were not easily defensible by tactical atomic weapons employed locally. Secretary Dulles' threat of massive retaliation elsewhere may have stayed Peking's hand, it is impossible to say with confidence, but President Eisenhower in effect withdrew it. In a dramatic passage he asked and secured the unanimous assent of Congress to a defense of Formosa by any and all means, but ostentatiously left blank the question of what he would do in the event of attack upon the coastal islands. He forced Chiang Kai-shek to evacuate the most exposed, least defensible and strategically least important of the islands, but the two major groups of Quemoy and the Matsus were left hanging in uncertainty. Once again war, or the threat of war, had seemed too dangerous, unhandy and unpredictable an instrument to be used positively to control a serious issue of policy. The result seemed to be to create an extraordinarily perilous situation. By leaving uncertain what we would do in the case of an attack on the Matsus or Quemoy we seemed to invite the attack, but under circumstances in which we could scarcely allow it to succeed yet had neither the suitable weapons nor the resolve to repel it.

By the end of 1954 the world situation, alike in Europe and the Far East, had become so unstable, so dangerous and so pregnant of a total disaster for humanity as to demand a review. Joseph Stalin had died in March 1953. In the following month Winston Churchill (who in 1945 had been the first to sound the tocsin of the "cold war") had launched his proposal for an unpublicized, confidential conference "at the summit" to see whether the new men in Russia might not be willing and able to negotiate a truce. President Eisenhower, at that time under the full pressure of the anti-Communist campaign in the United States, was cool to the idea, and his answering address was more like a demand for a total Soviet surrender than an invitation to discussion. Two years later, however, both the perils and the incalculables of the world problem had reached a point at which this attitude was no longer viable.

The President was finally brought to accept a "summit" conference at Geneva in July 1955. While this gathering was very unlike the private, confidential and exploratory talks which Churchill had suggested two years before, while nothing was decided in terms, and while much of the bloom was removed by the subsequent Foreign Ministers' meeting in October, it may still stand as marking a turning point in modern history. For it appears at least tacitly to have recorded the decision that a major war between the United States and the Soviet Union is no longer acceptable as a possible or useful foundation for policy in either state.

The value of this decision is arguable. It did nothing to indicate how the many grave issues between the two great power systems were to be settled without a war, and it certainly did little or nothing to remove the issues themselves. It failed to show how far the "spirit of Geneva" might radiate from the Soviet representatives to their Chinese colleagues. No one knew whether the attitude of Bulganin and Khrushchev represented a long-term effort to avoid a great war or only a short-term maneuver to evade one in the current context. The Geneva Conference of July 1955 settled nothing. Yet its contribution may prove to be no less real. At least since 1948, the fundamental determinant of nearly all American foreign and military policy had been the vision of the Third World War; and this was doubtless as true of the Kremlin as of Washington. At Geneva this vision was at least temporarily laid aside as too dreadful any longer to contemplate. The possibility, at least, of nonmilitary solutions was revived; the basic effort on both sides appears to have been diverted away from total war and toward "coexistence," and at the Twentieth Communist Party Congress in February 1956 Khrushchev was calmly rewriting even Lenin himself to repeal the doctrine of inevitable war, at the same time that he was destroying the grim godhead of Stalin in favor of a possibly more reasonable "collective leadership."

Whatever there was of value in the "spirit of Geneva" may be swept away tomorrow by some new crisis, just as the "spirit of

Locarno," painfully achieved in Europe some thirty years ago, was engulfed in the Great Depression. It must still stand as a turning point in contemporary world history; for it marked a clear recognition, however fleeting, that the military elements in our great society have been swollen out of all proportion to the social ends which they exist to serve. The military policies being followed by our own and other governments are often self-contradictory; they are unclear in purpose and uncertain in effect. They are enormously burdensome, not only in a direct economic sense but in terms of individual liberty, political freedoms, the tolerances of a self-confident and democratic society. For perhaps a half the world's population they have extinguished such freedoms altogether; even in the United States they are pressing more heavily upon them than is generally realized. These policies, adopted everywhere in the name of "national security," have spread a corroding sense of insecurity through all the more advanced peoples of the earth, nor have they offered clear hope or promise to the poorer and more backward. And they have brought us within possible distance of the extinction of civilization, if not of humanity itself.

This extraordinary situation is the final gift of the democratic, the industrial, the managerial, the scientific and the political and propagandist revolutions in warfare which have marched through the modern world since the day on which the Massachusetts farmers pulled their triggers at Lexington and Concord. Successively they have converted war from a reasonable and on the whole acceptable "instrument of policy" in the adjustment of the relations of peoples and states, into a horror of potential slaughter and destruction intolerable to any rational and decent mind. This is the hypertrophy of war.

CHAPTER VII

The Future of War

1.

THIS commentary must end upon a question which is plainly unanswerable. Nowhere does there exist a clear and convincing concept of the future of war in our world society. The ablest students of the subject are either in complete contradiction or in a state of frank bewilderment. There is the widest disagreement on purely technical, strategic questions. There is no consensus as to the ends to which our military means should be applied, even if we understood their potentialities and could foresee the results of employing them. There is little grasp of the domestic social, legal and constitutional issues raised by the development of these immense, modern military institutions.

If today a group of men of the intellectual caliber of the Philadelphia Convention were summoned to prepare a new Constitution, they could hardly meet the problems of war and military organization with the freedom and simplicity employed by the statesmen of 1789. Many things which were left vague in the Constitution would now certainly have to be spelled out. More precise answers would have to be found as to the nature, the extent and the locus of the war-making power. Firmer definition would have to be given of the citizen's military obligation to the state, and of the state's reciprocal obligation to the citizen whom it drafts for military service and battle duty. The now quaint-seeming clause in the Bill of Rights which prohibits the billeting of troops in peacetime would have to be strengthened against many more modern military incursions upon the individual—upon his time, his education, his economic opportunities. It might be thought wise to put some limitation on the power of the administrative bureaucracy to shield its policies and operations behind the secrecy of military "security." It might be felt that the immense economic impact of modern military spending, with its pressures toward the supercombination of industry, toward super-government and supertaxation, called for closer regulation than now exists. Perhaps the old issue between "civilian" and "military" control would seem to have largely lost its meaning, since the danger of a standing army being used to subvert the liberties of the people has never appeared. But the control of the colossal modern military machinery, in which soldiers, industrialists and bureaucrats are combined in a military interest with a powerful influence over foreign, budgetary and manpower policies, might awake the attention of the new Constitution-makers.

Fortunately, no one is going to be called on to write a new Constitution. These domestic issues are real and some seem potentially serious; they may, however, be left to the Congress and the courts for resolution. The great military dilemmas created by the appearance of the nuclear arsenals and the polarization of the world society cannot be so resolved.

The central fact is, of course, the development of the nuclear arsenals. In this country and presumably in Russia there are in actual existence weapons in "deliverable" form, any one of which could "take out" New York or Moscow in a fraction of a second, piling up in the process some millions of innocent dead while leaving probably millions more to die of starvation, thirst, radiation or other disease in the ensuing chaos. Given a supply of atomic bombs as triggers, these so-called hydrogen bombs are neither very difficult nor very expensive to manufacture; and it would take only a few of them, accurately placed in the chief population centers, to reduce the United States to an unimaginable state of utter wreck and paralysis. Because of her larger area and simpler structure, Soviet Russia is less vulnerable to such attack than the United States, though it is doubtful whether the difference would be great enough to be significant in the calculations of her leaders. By 1955 it appeared to be physically possible, at least, to produce within the space of a few hours catastrophes of death, agony and destruction perhaps greater than those produced by all the wars of history.

A secondary fact is the obvious one that no political or social end of any modern state—not even that vaguely imagined end of "world domination"—could conceivably be furthered by actually producing such holocausts. The war of nuclear mass destruction is unusable for any positive end. It may be essential to maintain a nuclear arsenal as a deterrent against the use of such weapons by others; it might be employed as a last-ditch defense against a conventional attack threatening to overwhelm the state; it may even be maintained as a threat to deter conventional attack. But it is of no value to anyone as an instrument of positive policy. A large part of both our own and the Soviet total military effort continues to be devoted to the designing and preparation of these unimaginable horrors. Yet intercontinental nuclear warfare, waged with hydrogen bombs, can only put the world's two greatest power centers in the position, as Oppenheimer phrased it, of "two scorpions in a bottle," with simultaneous and mutual extinction as the only outcome of any difference between them which cannot be resolved by means short of a resort to total war.

That all-out nuclear warfare with the supergiant bombs was an impracticable concept seems to have been recognized in American policy for some time prior to 1955. It may have been recognized even earlier by the Soviet Union. It is possible that when Russia rejected the proffered atomic disarmament in 1946, thus retaining her freedom to develop a nuclear arsenal of her own, the motive was mainly to produce a deterrent or counterforce which would neutralize the one element of military strength in which the West was superior, rather than to produce for herself a greater nuclear power to be used against the West. The Soviet leaders, as George F. Kennan observed in 1954, believe that the bombs "may well be cancelled out by the prospect of retaliation. . . . They doubt that these weapons will ever be used." If so, the Kremlin's goal might seem to have been substantially achieved when the bombs failed to appear in Korea and when in January 1954 Secretary Dulles announced his policy of maintaining "a

capacity" for massive retaliation, rather than of retaliating massively
in fact. Since then, the aim of American, British and Soviet statesmen
alike has seemed to be to use only the threat of nuclear warfare, as an
instrument of policies in the furtherance of which nuclear warfare
itself can no longer be contemplated.

In this sense the "atomic stalemate" appears to be, for the present
at any rate, a reality. Yet the appalling dangers of a situation in which
one's principal diplomatic arm is the threat of a weapon which one
dares not employ; and the appalling difficulties of adjusting international power issues without recourse to the age-old arbitrament
of war, are apparent. The social utility of war, so often stressed
in this book, is the one factor which students of the subject usually
overlook. Writers like Sir Norman Angell, whose proof that "war
does not pay" appeared upon the eve of the greatest war which
history had then seen; or like Nicolai, who showed conclusively
that war was "unnatural" as he sat in the later stages of a war
in which millions of unquestionably "natural" and normal human
beings had been tearing themselves to shreds, were as much beside the
point as those of opposite tendency, like the German theoreticians or
even the youthful Theodore Roosevelt, who extolled war for its incul-
cation of the masculine and civic virtues. Whether war "paid" or was
"natural" or was virtuous, whether or not it supported the economic
or biological or moral values of society or was merely neutral in its
effect upon these values, it was still essential to the ordered conduct
of the relations of mankind. When, with the introduction of both the
giant weapons and the all-powerful state, it grew finally and palpably
to a point at which it became totally destructive to economic, biological and moral values alike, while at the same time losing its social
function and leaving behind it no substitute capable of discharging
that function, the result was the peculiar crisis in which the modern
world now stands.

2.

There seemed to be several possible avenues of escape from this
remarkable dilemma. One of the earliest was first prominently raised
by the scientists—the physicists, mathematicians and chemists who,

justifiably and honorably, felt pangs of conscience over the horrors they had evoked. It was Oppenheimer and his associates who first insisted upon exploring the possibilities of defense against the new weapons, and thus stepped into the midst of an old quarrel. Since the days of Douhet and "Billy" Mitchell it had been a more or less cardinal article of faith among airmen that there was no defense against air power. Douhet had not only brushed aside the possibility of anti-aircraft defense from the ground (which had proved feeble enough in World War I) but had demolished even air-borne defense as a futile waste of effort. The Second War was drastically to revise such concepts. Douhet had failed to foresee the power of defensive aviation; he had not foreseen radar, electronic computers and gun-directors, or such powerful AA weapons as the 90-mm. and 5-in. dual purpose gun with the proximity fuse. But experience is seldom a strong answer to dogma. With its firepower suddenly increased by a factor of 20,000 through the appearance of the atomic bomb, the post-war Air Force was as convinced of the invulnerability of the air offense as the pre-war Air Corps had been. The *offensive à outrance* reigned again. There was "no defense against the atomic bomb"; therefore the only practicable strategy was to create the most massive possible offensive and trigger it for instant use, so that one's own side would be sure of being the first to get in the one decisive and unparryable blow.

This doctrine of the irresistible weapon or tactical system has a long and almost uniformly unfortunate history in warfare. Nearly always the product of peacetime theory, it has nearly always turned out in war to be subject to correction. Paixhans in the 1820's had proposed to sweep Britain from the seas with his shell guns. In the late '80's Secretary Tracy was arguing for a big navy on the ground that "a nation that is ready to strike the first blow will gain an advantage which its antagonists can never offset." "Jackie" Fisher's superpowerful, superspeedy and thin-skinned cruisers reflected the same kind of reasoning. Even with the ponderous armies of 1914, the idea that quick victory would reward the side which first got its masses mobilized and deployed had a tragic effect in rendering the political crisis insoluble for "military" reasons. Despite Hitler's success in conventional war, even he seems, from his talk of "secret weapons," to have been unduly bemused by the idea of the irresistible strategy. The wars usually begin with the doctrine of the "irresistible" weapons and the all-out attack; they usually end with a more vivid appreciation of the powers of defense and a more practical balance between defensive and offensive means in warfare.

But when the scientists raised the question of defense against the nuclear weapons, the Air Force was not enthusiastic. In 1953 the Lincoln Laboratory at the Massachusetts Institute of Technology, which had played a major role in wartime electronic development, went to work on the problems of early interception of atomic bomb-carrying planes. The Summer Study Group sought seriously to analyze the problems of civil defense against atomic attack upon major population centers. The Army at the same time was developing its Nike homing AA missile. It was only too apparent that if early warning radar systems, anti-aircraft missiles, a fully ready radio and radar directed defensive fighter net and civil defense precautions on the ground could blunt a Soviet atomic attack on the United States, similar means and instruments in Soviet hands were just as likely to blunt the best efforts of the all-powerful Strategic Air Force against Russia. For SAC this was not a constructive thought.

This was at least in part the reason for a somewhat ironic and disagreeable episode: Oppenheimer (and by inference his fellow scientists) was immolated upon the altars of "security," but this was followed by the adoption of most of the policies upon which the scientists had been insisting. Oppenheimer was declared a "security risk"; but the SAC theory of irresistible offensive power, ending in mutual annihilation, was too barren to be acceptable. Indeed, it was too unfavorable to SAC itself to be maintained. Too many vocal laymen, accepting the argument at its face value, were asking why, if there was no defense against atomic weapons and if universal catastrophe was the only promise which the soldiers could offer, the whole military system should not be done away with. The Air Force responded to such criticisms and applied itself assiduously to the problems of air defense. Billions have gone into the all-weather interceptor fighters, the Distant Early Warning Line (DEW), the computers and communications systems as well as the Nike rockets and many other devices on which it seems that some defense might be raised. In our "air-atomic strategy," as Finletter has called it, defense now has a place second only to the offensive nuclear "strike."

This has restored a considerably better balance; unfortunately, no one yet knows how good either the defense or the offense in an airborne atomic war would be. The Air Force has made valiant efforts to reduce the problem to statistics; but the fact that it clung through years to the conclusion that "30 per cent of the attacking force would get through" seems to reflect the inapplicability of statistical analysis to this issue, rather than the accuracy of the result. The development of the techniques and strategy of defense has undoubtedly encouraged the "atomic stalemate." It has reduced the whole picture of an atomic war of mass destruction to an uncertainty that clearly militates strongly against its being tried by any general staff or political power center. This is an important gain. But it leaves the central problem unresolved.

If the Soviet statesmen calculated upon producing a nuclear stalemate under which the older processes of international war and diplomacy could proceed in more or less the old way, they were doomed to disappointment. So were the Western statesmen who may have had the same thought. After the insistence upon defense, the second leading solution for the nuclear dilemma was that adumbrated by NATO in the early '50's. This was the creation of a huge ground army which could more or less match the Red Army on its own terms, while the A-bombs would do no more than "hold the ring" and insure that the battle would be fought out by infantry and tanks on the World War II pattern. This solution soon collapsed. It foundered primarily on the rocks of economic and political limitations which made it quite impossible to raise a Western ground army capable of standing off the hordes of organized Soviet and satellite divisions; it was also embarrassed in the political shoals surrounding the matter of West German rearmament and among the strategic reefs represented by the rapid development of tactical nuclear weapons. By the spring of 1953 this second idea was virtually dead.

It has been replaced by a third idea. Since 1953 it has been apparent that the "age of atomic plenty"—a gruesome phrase if ever there was one—has arrived. It has been said that the two bombs fired against Japan in 1945 were the only two in existence at the time. By 1955 it was believed that the American stockpile was in four figures— if not in five—possibly 15,000 weapons. The Atomic Energy Commission has developed bombs that can be fired through cannon, carried by light airplanes, delivered by rockets and robot missiles. In addition to producing the fission-fusion supergiant weapons, it has brought atomic bombs themselves up to energy releases twenty-five times as great as those of the Hiroshima and Nagasaki bombs. It has brought new powers to air defense by developing atomic bombs as anti-aircraft weapons.

All this weaponry, together with the new high speed and rocket carriers, was available to the Western surface forces. If nuclear warfare had been ruled out of the strategic battle by the power of retaliation, it could now be brought back again into the tactical or conventional battle. Information concerning tactical atomic weapons was guardedly opened to the European NATO partners from 1953 onward; the British pressed forward with their own atomic energy development, while the American Army, Navy and Marine Corps threw themselves into intensive study of the use of atomic weapons by conventional forces operating in the conventional pattern, against the armed forces of an enemy rather than against his population. By 1954 Admiral Radford, the Chairman of the Joint Chiefs, was confidently announcing that atomic weapons had become practically conventional" in all the services. The substitution of atomic weapons for uniformed manpower in the ground battle was eagerly accepted on all sides. President Eisenhower spoke of their being employed against "military targets" only, and with "rifle-shot" accuracy. After the NATO meeting early in 1955, the Supreme Commander, General Alfred M. Gruenther, repeatedly emphasized his conviction that the conventional forces would have to be heavily armed with nuclear firepower, while Great Britain revised her whole military policy in accordance with the new strategic concept.

Yet this solution also raised difficulties. The most obvious has already been noted: that if the West introduced tactical atomic weapons the Russians must be expected to follow suit, thus restoring whatever advantage their superiority in numbers might give them. Russia's claimed reduction of her forces by 640,000 men and her announcement in May 1956 of a contemplated further reduction of 1,200,000 strongly suggested that this process had begun. A more ominous difficulty lay in the fact that it was very hard to fit atomic weapons into any kind of war which could be called "conventional" or to see how the war could remain conventional for long, once such weapons had been introduced into it.

When accepted military targets include airfields, port facilities, railway lines and yards, shipyards and munition factories, all of which are normally in or near large population centers, how could the bombs' effects be confined to military personnel? Atomic bombs are by their very nature weapons of "area" and "mass" destruction; formed troops deployed in the field are the best protected and therefore the least productive targets against which they can be used. It is unrealistic to imagine that once they had appeared upon the battlefield they could be confined to this least efficient form of employment. Attacks on airfields and lines of communication would merge rapidly into "strategic" attacks on war industries and cities (just as happened at Hiroshima); full-scale nuclear warfare, though exiled to the "tactical" battle, would surely return through these doors to the business of intercontinental mass destruction for which it was primarily designed.

It has, in fact, proved extraordinarily difficult to picture the course of a conventional war waged with atomic weapons on both sides. Commentators have been quick to point out that the first result would probably be a staggering dislocation of communications which would render the massing, transport and deployment of surface forces in large numbers, on the pattern of either the First or Second War, impossible. British military thought has tended to accept the consequences of such reasoning. The British are agreed that another major war in Western Europe will be of short duration, that it will have to be fought out to the end with no more than the forces available at the beginning, and that the available ground forces in Western Europe, even with the support of tactical atomic armaments, are probably incapable of sustaining an all-out Soviet onslaught. Consequently, the only real reliance is still upon the threat of thermonuclear retaliation to prevent the onslaught from being made. The British by 1956 were

either disbanding or frankly converting into Civil Defense disaster
relief forces all but two of their Territorial (reserve) divisions, on the
ground that two are the most which they could mobilize, fill up and
ship abroad in time to be of any use. The real function of the NATO
divisions on the Continent is to serve, in Sir John Slessor's phrase, as
a "trip-wire" force, powerful enough to prevent a surprise attack and
to ensure that any serious Soviet assault on the West would have to
be preceded by a build-up which would make the situation obvious and
permit of countermeasures.

American military policy had less clearly accepted these conclusions, which are so violently at variance with our traditional concepts.
Since our entry upon the world stage in 1898 (if not indeed from the
beginning) our military planning had been based on maintaining not
a posture of war, but a potential for war which could be roughly
scaled, both as to size and availability, by the fact of the oceanic bar-
riers. For defense, we need prepare to mobilize forces no greater than
those it would be possible to bring against us across the seas, and we
need do it no more rapidly than the enemy convoys could bring them.
After 1917, American power over world history was expressed, consciously or unconsciously, in terms of a military and industrial potential which could be mobilized and sent abroad in time to decide
issues which had originated among others and over which others had
been fighting and dying. The idea that even a conventional war in
Europe, if fought with atomic weapons, would be over in a few weeks
eviscerated this whole concept of the role of American military power.
But our ponderous mechanisms of military planning gave little sign
that they had accepted or adjusted to the fact.

Thus, the "New Look" at military policy, while arming our forward
echelons in Germany with atomic weapons, "disengaged" many of our
ground divisions from the exposed points in the Far East, to concentrate them in a "general reserve" in the United States from which the
speed of tactical atomic warfare and its probable destruction of communications might make it quite impossible for them to emerge again
in time. While the British were disbanding their reserve divisions,
the United States was adopting the National Reserve Act of 1955,
which contemplated (among other things) a force of no less than

thirty-seven National Guard and Reserve infantry and armored divisions—none, however, to be maintained at full strength or with full equipment, and the whole force requiring anywhere from three months to a year before it could be made combat-ready. If the tactical atomic weapons meant that a major war in Europe would be over long before it would be possible even to train or equip such forces and might in any event make their transport and supply impossible, then the reason for their existence seemed less than obvious. Yet in 1954 and 1955 American field exercises designed to test and develop tactical and organizational doctrines appropriate to the introduction of the new weapons were still postulating a clash between very large field armies composed of scores of divisions deployed and supplied more or less on the World War II pattern.

In the end, the idea of reinforcing the West's deficient ground manpower with nuclear weapons seemed to raise as many issues as it solved. So far as the military defense of Western Europe goes, perhaps it will serve; supported by the "umbrella" of thermonuclear strategic threat, it seems reasonable to anticipate that it will avert any war in Western Europe for years to come. If it does not, the resultant military problems will be of an appalling kind; if it does, it will still at best have met only half the problem.

If both the all-out intercontinental war of mutual mass extermination, waged directly between the two power centers of Russia and the United States, and also the major war for the capture of Western Europe may be excluded from the calculations of statesmanship, there remains the problem of the "periphery." Assuming that a substantial military equilibrium has been established on the major planes of grand strategy, this simply frees the Soviet Union to proceed in great areas of the world by those piecemeal tactics of disruption, subversion, propagandist and economic pressures backed by the existence of Soviet military power, which have actually been its weapons since 1945. Western capitalistic democracy, lacking both the unity and the ruthlessness of the totalitarian state, finds it difficult if not impossible to compete with such methods. In a few critical areas of the earth, a resort to force seems still to offer the only effective means to acceptable decision.

The American Army in particular has been much concerned with the problem of what are called, perhaps misleadingly, "brush-fire" wars. Korea was hardly a "brush-fire," by any standard. But the Army, and to some extent the Navy and Marines, have been devoting themselves assiduously to a concept of future war which, whether "big" or "brush-fire," could still be fought out between the uniformed forces without inviting in the mass and population bombers of all-out holocaust. General Ridgway, commander of 8th Army in Korea, NATO Supreme Commander and Army Chief of Staff, described this army of the future (after his retirement) in these words:

> The Army must be a streamlined, hard-hitting force armed with nuclear weapons in adequate numbers and with greatly improved nonnuclear weapons. Its basic combat units will probably be a grouping of small battle groups of all arms. . . . These units, and to a lesser degree the groups themselves, will be semi-independent, self-contained and capable of operating over great distances on a fluid battlefield for long periods with a minimum of control and support by higher headquarters. . . . All elements of these forces, except the heaviest armored units, should be transportable by air. . . . Stylized concepts of battle and formalized battle organizations as we have known them will no longer be employed. . . . It is obvious that the Army described above bears little resemblance to the massed, slow-moving armies of World War II.[1]

To some this may seem a rather curious commentary on Hitler's "blitzkrieg." The tactics of mobility, speed and striking power with which he had retired the massed, slow-moving armies of 1914, had become within ten years after the Second War, "stylized" concepts of "massed, slow-moving armies" to be abolished by the new mobility and firepower developed in the meanwhile. Just how the new concept is expected to work remains obscure to some observers. Many questions arise. What is one to do with completely air transportable forces who cannot bring with them the "heaviest armored units" comparable to those which they are certain to meet on the ground? More

---

[1] Matthew B. Ridgway: "My Battles in War and Peace," *Saturday Evening Post,* January 28, 1956; also *Soldier* (New York, Harper's, 1956), p. 298.

generally, how is air-borne mobility to match the numbers likely to be encountered on the ground? How are the "semi-independent" and "self-contained" units going to operate with a "minimum of control and support by higher headquarters"? The Second War was a battle of logistics more than of firepower. Almost as many lives, perhaps, went into the attack upon and defense of the supply systems (the air war against Germany, the Battle of the Atlantic, the supply of the Normandy invasion, getting the rations and ammunition up to a hundred Pacific battlefields) as went into the front-line contest for ground. When the air-borne armies go into action, what are the hostile AA and other defenses supposed to do? The German conquest of Crete in the Second War was probably the greatest exercise of air-borne ground warfare ever seen; it succeeded because the defense was inherently weak, but even so its success was achieved at a cost which made the tactics impracticable against more important targets. Nothing quite like the attack upon Crete was ever attempted by either side thereafter.

On the one hand, the vision of the ultramobile, air-borne, highly trained and professional "army of opportunity" seems to reduce to nonsense the whole concept of mass warfare still enshrined in American reserve and manpower planning. On the other hand, it does not seem capable in itself of resolving such "peripheral" issues as may arise with any certainty of success. Again, it has the look of another bad compromise; it seems only another variant of the idea that it is somehow possible to substitute gadgets for bloodshed in war. It has not been reduced to a practical application of military power to the military requirements of the modern world. In 1956 the United States was still struggling with the contradictory ideas of all-out nuclear war, tactical war waged with atomic weapons, mass armies expected to fight in the old pattern, and "brush-fire" troops maintained to fight peripheral or local or even colonial wars, but maintained mainly in the United States where they do the least good in contemporary diplomatic balances and run the greatest risk of being unusable in local crises.

Each of the four solutions for the military dilemma so far considered has its advantages; each may have contributed in one way or another to the uneasy military equilibrium which we seem actually to have achieved. But each carries great dangers within itself and all four together cannot be regarded as a satisfactory answer for the military dilemma in our society. The perils are still appalling; the practical utility of these vast military panoplies is not apparent. Civilization still remains, it would seem, at the mercy of a slip or miscalculation. If no one today either wants or expects a war, neither did more than a very few in 1914; yet we have set up a hair-trigger mechanism for universal catastrophe vastly more sensitive and more lethal than that created by the general staffs in the early years of the century.

It is a situation which has led many back to a fifth solution—in the old hope of universal disarmament. This was the conclusion at which a widely read book, published in 1954 by Thomas K. Finletter, former Secretary of the Air Force, finally arrived. Logic was on the side of Mr. Finletter and the many who agreed with him. The basic structure of human history and politics unfortunately was not. Through more than half a century, since the Czar of Russia in 1899 first seriously proposed disarmament as the answer to the modern military crisis, there has been no significant success in applying the idea. Disarmament conferences have been many—under the auspices of the Czar, the State Department, the League of Nations, the United Nations, supported by Presidents and Prime Ministers and Communist politicos—and all alike have ended in either total failure or (as in the case of the Washington Conference of 1921) in success of only the most partial and ephemeral kind.

Yet by 1955 the military crisis had become so obviously acute and so lethal that the United States again seriously took up this approach. It is probably fair to say that American policy had not been sincerely interested in disarmament since the Soviet rejection of the Acheson-Lilienthal-Baruch plan for atomic disarmament in 1946. The powerful initial impulse had been to remove these dreadful weapons from the world. But when the possibility of atomic disarmament disappeared, the debates in the United Nations committees (whether atomic or conventional weapons were under study) returned to the old and futile business of insuring that whatever measures were adopted must guarantee that the other side disarmed more fully than one's own.

For years, "disarmament" was certainly to the Russians and apparently to the State Department simply a diplomatic device for putting the other side in the wrong. The State Department would have been as astounded as the Kremlin had the other side offered to accept the proposals which were regularly and solemnly paraded for propaganda effect. By 1955, however, the military dilemma had become so dangerous as to suggest the need for a somewhat more serious attitude.

President Eisenhower appointed Harold Stassen as a special advisor to make a serious study of the whole problem, and at the Geneva conference in July 1955 the President produced his dramatic proposal for a system of aerial inspection and exchange of "blueprints." This was the first new idea introduced into the subject in many years. Instead of proposing disarmament, it suggested a neutralization of armaments by establishing a kind of early warning system capable of touching off the alarm bells if either great power should begin to mobilize for attack. That such a system would be of great value it is hard to doubt. It would at least remove from contemporary policy one fear which has done most, perhaps, to distort and bewilder it: the fear of all-out "sneak" attack. Unfortunately, the Eisenhower proposal remained nebulous. The technical difficulties which would be raised by any attempt to implement it were patently formidable; and since there was no effort, so far as the public was aware, either to explore or to expound them, an air of unreality clung to the proposal. The negotiations in London in the spring of 1956 indicated a more serious attitude on all sides, and suggested that some diminution in the level and terror of weapons might be achievable. Few believed, however, that they held out much hope of solution for the basic issues raised by the nuclear arsenals.

3.

Thus, by the middle of 1956 nothing was clear, nothing was final. The future of war was as uncertain as the future of the American military policies which might be adopted to meet its problems. Beginning with the farmers who swarmed to Lexington with their flintlocks, we had arrived at a point where we were spending around $40 billion a year (including the appropriations for atomic weapons and military stockpiling) on a peacetime military system. We were maintaining nearly 3,000,000 men in uniform at all times; to keep these ranks filled we were continuing an apparently permanent system of peacetime military conscription. We had laid an eight-year military "obligation" on all young American males and were trying to develop a reserve system large enough to ensure that none would escape its onerous duties.

In the name of military security we had done much more. We had expanded the Federal Bureau of Investigation into a secret political police of wide-ranging power, under tenuous control—something which would certainly have horrified even the most conservative authors of the Constitution. We had cloaked the operations of the Executive branch of government in veils of secrecy unknown to any previous epoch of our history. We had compartmented our science. We had created huge industrial complexes almost wholly dependent on government contract but beyond much effective government regulation. More than that, we had embedded a huge element of military production in our industrial system, so that the whole structure of American prosperity and economic productivity probably depended, to a degree previously unknown, upon military or military-associated orders.

We had come a long way from the days of the flintlock musket and the primitive "war steamer." The War Hawks of 1812 had been able to take up war as a practicable instrument of their political and economic policies as readily as a modern politician would appeal for votes. In the United States, indeed, there had always been—at least down to the earlier years of the twentieth century—an intimate relation between war and domestic politics which may represent a sounder sense of social organization than the attempts, as in Germany, to divorce completely these two aspects of social behavior. Polk, in the mid-'40's, could manipulate his war powers quite skillfully as a means of securing both political and national objectives which seemed important to him. It is certainly one source of Lincoln's greatness that for him war was always as much a political as a military operation; he not only remembered the requirements and limitations of domestic politics in the conduct of the war but also remembered that military violence, however necessary, was useful only as it could produce political results in the minds and in the relationships of men.

For McKinley in 1898 the avoidance of war as such loomed larger, perhaps, than it had done for Polk or even for Lincoln, and he was unquestionably sincere in his efforts to escape the resort to arms. He could still accept it, in the final crisis, both as a necessity of domestic politics and an expedient which at a probably small cost in either life or money would greatly advance the national interest. By Wilson's time, a bare sixteen years later, the problem had become immeasurably more difficult. War was now so terrible and desperate a recourse that it could no longer be used, as in the days of Madison or Polk or as Wilson himself had used it against Mexico in 1914 and 1916, to achieve limited national aims or make good narrow ends of foreign policy. If taken up at all, it could be taken up only for the grandest of total objectives—enshrined in such phrases as "a war to end war," a "world safe for democracy," a "lasting peace"—all implying a new world order which would revolutionize six thousand years of international history. Since these objectives were unattainable by military means, the result of the great crusade was to be disillusion and embittered frustration.

Within another twenty years, the problem confronting Franklin Roosevelt had become far more complex still. To Wilson and his contemporaries, the question of major war still presented itself in terms of a choice—"to go in or stay out"—the unspoken assumption being that either alternative was equally open. Twenty years later the issue was still to be debated by the Congressmen and the impassioned editors in these terms, but the terms had lost their meaning. The alternatives were no longer open. It was not a question of whether we would use our military and economic power, but how to use it, in a situation in which any course we might adopt was surrounded by enormous perils. It is no mere play with paradox to suggest that while the attitudes of the rather pacifistic Wilson administration were fundamentally egoistic and aggressive—"we" were sovereignly free to decide how we would use our strength and promote our interests—the attitudes of the much more martial Roosevelt administration were fundamentally defensive and even passive. "We" were surrounded by threats; any course, active or passive, might end, sooner or later, in a great war and a military catastrophe. Whether it did or not was something which we had no clear means of controlling; this was something which would be decided more by others than by ourselves, and to many it was a galling thought.

For most Americans, it was too galling to face. The "great debates" over foreign policy of 1940 and 1941 were of no practical help; they were little more than vast wastes of words revolving around unreal issues, producing only the hypocrisies and evasions of which both sides were guilty. Mortimer Adler has observed that there must be a certain minimum of agreement upon the nature of the problem under discussion in order to produce any useful disagreement and therefore any hope of rational solution. In 1940-41 there was no agreement upon the nature of the issues under discussion, and there was no useful result from the discussion. Roosevelt was in effect left to "play by ear" (a role not uncongenial to him) in a welter of polemics having little relation to the complicated perils which the outside world was forcing upon us.

Roosevelt resorted to his defensive expedients. His administration clearly revealed its "appeasement" tendencies in the tangled period of the Spanish Civil War and Munich. Its first response to the European struggle was "Hemisphere Defense"; and when it became convinced that defense of the American value systems would be impossible unless Great Britain were sustained and the Nazi aggression broken, its policy was still all aid "short" of war. Our commitment to one side in Europe helped to control our course in the Far East, but as the Japanese menace arose in that quarter, the guiding impulse of Roosevelt and Hull was one of temporization. The avoidance of a major war entanglement—but without loss of national positions which seemed vital—had become an overriding preoccupation; and even the total embargo against Japan of July 25, 1941, the act which now seems to have made the Pacific War inevitable, appears to have been inspired by a hope of averting the final resort to arms.

One after another, the expedients failed. "All aid short of war" could not control the gigantic events to which it was applied or maintain those great interests of the United States which seemed crucial to the President and to the majority of his countrymen. When the Japanese demonstrated this fact with their attack on December 7, the President was faced with the alternatives of either revising his whole concept of the world problem or else committing American manpower to a total struggle. With little difficulty he accepted the second, with the results which we have witnessed.

There are two recorded scenes which brilliantly illuminate the differences wrought by twenty-five years in the war problem. In April 1917 President Wilson, talking with F. I. Cobb in the early morning silences of the White House after his War Message had been written, spoke in terms of the contemplated action. He saw no alternative to what, by his own decision, was about to happen, but he was thinking of the larger consequences:

> "It would mean that we should lose our heads along with the rest, and stop weighing right and wrong." . . . There would be a dictated peace, a victorious peace. "It means," he said, "an attempt to reconstruct a peacetime civilization with war standards." . . . He had no illusions about the fashion in which we were likely to fight the war. . . . We couldn't fight Germany and maintain the ideals of government that all thinking men shared. . . . "Once lead this people into war," he said, "and they'll forget there ever was such a thing as tolerance. To fight you must be brutal and ruthless, and the spirit of ruthless brutality will enter into the very fibre of our national life." [2]

Nearly a quarter of a century later Franklin Roosevelt was talking with Harry Hopkins in that same White House. It was the evening of December 6, 1941; the Japanese were already known to be on the move and the message had just arrived which appeared to make war a certainty. Hopkins suggested that since war was undoubtedly coming, it was too bad that the United States could not get in the first blow. "No," said the President, "we can't do that. We are a democracy

---

[2] John L. Heaton, *Cobb of "The World,"* (New York, Dutton), p. 269.

and a peaceful people." Then he raised his voice: "But we have a good record." We would have to stand on it and await whatever the future might bring. In 1917 Wilson was "leading" a people into a war, foreseeing, and regretting, the inescapable consequences. In 1941 Roosevelt was accepting a war as unavoidable; he was waiting for a blow to strike; and it was the past "record" which was uppermost in his mind, not the future to which the war would lead.

Polk or McKinley could use war as an instrument of politics or policy. Wilson was constrained, as it were, to use policy as an instrument of war. With Roosevelt war had been magnified to a point at which it could neither serve a policy nor be justified by one; it had become a naked instrument of defense, of defense alone and of defense only in an extremity of crisis. The Second World War should, he suggested, be called "The War for Survival." As such, the war was a "success" from the American viewpoint. What it did not succeed in doing was to answer the problems of war itself as a social institution. If Wilson's problem was more complex than McKinley's, if Franklin Roosevelt's problem was more difficult than Wilson's, the problem confronted first by Truman and then by Eisenhower was far more baffling than what Roosevelt had been compelled to face. With Roosevelt, major war was at least a viable instrument for last-ditch defense of crucial positions on the world stage. After the introduction of the nuclear weapons, its utility even to this end was questionable, as even defense seemed more and more to imply total destruction.

By 1956 there appeared to be almost no way in which the deployment of military force—which means men armed with murderous weapons, whether Roman short swords or high-powered artillery or hydrogen bombs, for the slaughter of other men—could be brought rationally to bear upon the decision of any of the political, economic, emotional or philosophical issues by which men still remain divided. This is the great and unresolved dilemma of our age. One cannot doubt that a resolution of some kind will be found, for it is too difficult to accept a millennial view of history, a Twilight of the Gods, a prognosis of universal catastrophe and extinction. Presumably the human race will in the future, as it has done throughout the past, find means of getting along somehow, probably for the better rather than for the worse. But just how it will do so seems impossible to predict; while the old certainty of military action as the final answer to every problem—a certainty that has remained with us since the dawn of history —seems no longer available. It may be that for final sanctions in our human affairs we shall have to look toward other factors.

Note on Sources

What follows is intended as an acknowledgment of my principal debts, not as a guide to scholarship. The possibly relevant literature is so great that a bibliography, even a "selective" bibliography, would have little use or meaning. Direct quotations from other writers have been acknowledged in the text or notes—except in the case of quotations from official sources, such as the Congressional Record, the Messages of the Presidents, the reports of official boards and committees, where the source is reasonably obvious. But I owe facts, suggestions and ideas to a wide variety of works from which no direct quotations were drawn. I cannot list them all; but I mention here my principal guides and supports.

The useful literature falls into two categories: one, rather slim, which treats of American military policy as a whole or certain aspects of military policy over a considerable time period; and the other, as voluminous as one cares to make it, which deals with particular wars or special problems in weapons, organization or military issues of a particular time. While the categories are to some extent overlapping, I have divided this acknowledgment into two parts: first, a brief discussion of the general works; second, a listing of the principal sources used for each of my chapters.

1.

There are not many general surveys of this field. The foundation study of American military policy, but dealing with Army policy alone, is still Emory Upton's *The Military Policy of the United States from 1775* (Washington, Government Printing Office, 1904). Twenty years later this was supplemented and extended by William Addleman Ganoe's *The History of the United States Army* (New York, Appleton, 1924), in which the author observed that "no chronological record of the soldier's existence from 1775 to 1923 has ever been set down in any one place."

Colonel Ganoe is not always complete or discerning, but he did a lot of valuable spadework. Some years later Oliver Lyman Spaulding's *The United States Army in War and Peace* (New York, Putnam, 1937) added more.

Nothing really comparable on the naval side of our military policy appeared until the publication of Harold and Margaret Sprout's *The Rise of American Naval Power* (Princeton, Princeton University Press, 1939), supplemented by *Toward a New Order of Sea Power* (1940), an application of the professional historian's techniques to a field which social and historical scholarship had too largely neglected. Princeton became, under the leadership of Edward Mead Earle, our chief center of military-sociological studies. As late as 1952 the Princeton Military History Project found that there was "no single book or manageable group of books available for instruction" in the "general problems which democratic society faces in preparing for armed conflict and waging total war." As a result, the Project published *A History of Military Affairs in Western Society Since the Eighteenth Century* (Lithoprint, Ann Arbor, Edwards Bros., Inc., 1952)—a compilation of readings from works of authors "eminent in military affairs" edited by Gordon B. Tucker. While the selections are concerned with the war problem in the West as a whole, they are related primarily to issues in American policy.

A recent general history is that of C. Joseph Bernardo and Eugene H. Bacon, *American Military Policy: Its Development Since 1775* (Harrisburg, The Military Service Publishing Co., 1955), which covers both military and naval policy from the beginning, with close attention to both published and unpublished sources but also, perhaps, with a somewhat uncritical attitude toward the larger implications of the subject. A general study of a different kind is Alfred Vagts' *A History of Militarism* (New York, Norton, 1937), focused mainly on European and especially German developments but unusually stimulating and original in its analysis.

There are few other books that cover anything like the whole field, but I have used a number that follow some special segment of it down over a considerable time period. Frank M. Bennett's *The Steam Navy of the United States* (Pittsburgh, W. T. Nicholson, 1896) has been mined by everyone interested in the subject. So has William E. Birkhimer's *Historical Sketch of the Organization, Administration, Materiel and Tactics of the Artillery of the United States Army* (Washington, 1884). A much more recent work of similar scope is John K. Herr and Edward S. Wallace, *The Story of the United States Cavalry* (Boston, Little, 1953). Arcadi Gluckman's *United States Muskets, Rifles and Carbines* (Buffalo, Otto Ulbrich Co., Inc., 1948) provides a complete catalogue of American shoulder arms from the beginning. F. L. Robertson's *The Evolution of*

Naval Armament (London, Constable, 1921) is a useful study of the subject indicated by its title. In these more or less long-range works, one should not overlook Merle E. Curti's *The American Peace Crusade* (Durham, Duke University Press, 1929) or the recent book of Arthur E. Ekirch, Jr., *The Civilian and the Military,* described as "a history of the American anti-militarist tradition" (New York, Oxford, 1956).

In addition to the standard service magazines, I owe a good deal to *The Military Collector and Historian,* the journal of the military antiquarian society, the Company of Military Collectors and Historians, in which much curious information may be found.

2.

In addition to the books mentioned above, the more important sources relied on for the several chapters are as follows:

CHAPTER I

Bolton, Charles Knowles, *The Private Soldier Under Washington.* New York, Scribner, 1902.

Curtis, Edward Ely, *The Organization of the British Army in the American Revolution.* New Haven, Yale University Press, 1926.

Jacobs, James Ripley, *The Beginning of the U. S. Army, 1783–1812.* Princeton, Princeton University Press, 1947.

Jensen, Merrill, *The New Nation.* New York, Knopf, 1950.

Livermore, George, *An Historical Research.* Boston, 1862.

Mirsky, Jeanette, and Nevins, Allan, *The World of Eli Whitney.* New York, Macmillan, 1952.

Montross, Lynn, *The Reluctant Rebels: The Story of the Continental Congress, 1774–1789.* New York, Harper, 1950.

Palmer, John McAuley, *America in Arms.* New Haven, Yale University Press, 1941.

Sawyer, Charles Winthrop, *Firearms in American History.* Boston, 1910 and 1920.

Ward, Christopher, *The War of the Revolution.* New York, Macmillan, 1952.

CHAPTER II

Baxter, James Phinney, *The Introduction of the Ironclad Warship.* Cambridge, Harvard University Press, 1933.

Chapelle, Howard I., *The History of American Sailing Ships.* New York, Norton, 1935.

Dahlgren, J. A., *Shells and Shell Guns.* Philadelphia, 1856.

Durkin, Joseph T., *Stephen R. Mallory: Confederate Navy Chief*. Chapel Hill, University of North Carolina Press, 1954.

Eaton, Clement, *A History of the Southern Confederacy*. New York, Macmillan, 1954.

Grant, Ulysses S., *Personal Memoirs*. New York, C. L. Webster & Co., 1885–86.

James, Marquis, *Andrew Jackson*. Indianapolis, Bobbs, 1923.

Nevins, Allan, ed., *Polk: The Diary of a President, 1845–1849*. New York, Longmans, 1952.

Pratt, Julius W., *Expansionists of 1812*. New York, Macmillan, 1925.

Sherman, William T., *Memoirs*. New York, Appleton, 1875.

Smith, Justin H., *The War with Mexico*. New York, Macmillan, 1919.

Sumner, William H., *An Inquiry into the Importance of the Militia*. Boston, 1823.

Wiltse, Charles M., *John C. Calhoun, Nationalist, 1782–1828*. Indianapolis, Bobbs, 1944.

CHAPTER III

Alger, Russell A., *The Spanish-American War*. New York, Harper, 1901.

Bacon, R. H., *The Life of Lord Fisher*. London, Hodder and Stoughton, 1929.

Chadwick, French Ensor, *The Relations of the United States and Spain*. New York, Scribner, 1909 and 1911.

Custer, Elizabeth B., *Tenting on the Plains*. New York, Harper, 1889.

Hagedorn, Hermann, *Leonard Wood*. New York, Harper, 1911.

Hirsch, Mark D., *William C. Whitney*. New York, Dodd, 1948.

Jessup, Philip C., *Elihu Root*. New York, Dodd, 1938.

Lewis, Lloyd, *Sherman, Fighting Prophet*. New York, Harcourt, 1932.

Long, John D., *The New American Navy*. New York, Outlook, 1903.

Mahan, Alfred Thayer, *The Influence of Sea Power on History*. Boston, Little, 1890.

Nevins, Allan, ed., *Grover Cleveland: A Study in Courage*. New York, Dodd, 1932.

Pringle, Henry F., *Theodore Roosevelt*. New York, Harcourt, 1931.

Puleston, W. D., *Mahan: The Life and Work of Captain Alfred Thayer Mahan*. New Haven, Yale, 1939.

Root, Elihu, *The Military and Colonial Policy of the United States*. Cambridge, Harvard, 1916.

Selections from the Correspondence of Theodore Roosevelt and Henry Cabot Lodge, 1884–1918. New York, Scribner, 1925.

Semenoff, Vladimir, *The Battle of Tsu-Shima*. New York, Dutton, 1906.

Seymour, Charles, ed., *The Intimate Papers of Colonel House*. New York, Houghton, 1926.
Upton, Emory, *The Armies of Asia and Europe*. New York, Appleton, 1878.

CHAPTER IV

Craven, Wesley Frank and Cate, James Lea, *The Army Air Forces in World War II*. Harrisburg, The Military Service Publishing Co., 1934.
Crozier, William, *Ordnance and the World War*. New York, Scribner, 1920.
Gillie, Mildred Harmer, *Forging the Thunderbolt*. Harrisburg, The Military Service Publishing Co., 1947.
Icks, Robert J., *Tanks and Armored Vehicles*. New York, Duell, 1945.
Iseley, Jeter A. and Crowl, Philip A., *The U.S. Marines and Amphibious War*. Princeton, Princeton University Press, 1945.
Levine, Isaac Don, *Mitchell, Pioneer of Air Power*. New York, Duell, 1943.
Palmer, Frederick, *Newton D. Baker*. New York, Dodd, 1931.
Tompkins, Frank, *Chasing Villa*. Harrisburg, The Military Service Publishing Co., 1934.

CHAPTER V

Arnold, H. H., *Global Mission*. New York, Harper, 1949.
Baxter, James Phinney, *Scientists Against Time*. Boston, Atlantic-Little, 1946.
Guderian, Heinz, *Panzer Leader*. New York, Dutton, 1952.
Morison, Samuel E., *History of United States Naval Operations in World War II*. Boston, Atlantic-Little, 1947–56.
The War Reports, New York, Lippincott, 1947.
Watson, Mark S., *Chief of Staff: Pre-War Plans and Preparations*. Washington, GPO, 1950.

CHAPTER VI

Forrestal, James, *The Forrestal Diaries*. New York, Viking, 1951.
Marshall, S. L. A., *The River and the Gauntlet*. New York, Morrow, 1953.
Truman, Harry S., *Memoirs*. New York, Doubleday, 1955 and 1956.
Whitney, Courtney, *MacArthur*. New York, Knopf, 1956.

CHAPTER VII

Finletter, Thomas K., *Power and Policy*. New York, Harcourt, 1954.
Kaufman, William W., ed., *Military Policy and National Security*. Princeton, Princeton University Press, 1956.
Ridgway, Matthew B., *Soldier*. New York, Harper, 1956.

Index

References by name to *Battles, Forts, Ships* and military *Units* are grouped alphabetically under these headings. Merely passing or casual references are, for the most part, suppressed.